THE LITERARY
WITTGENSTEIN

Edited by
John Gibson and
Wolfgang Huemer

Routledge
Taylor & Francis Group

LONDON AND NEW YORK

First published 2004
by Routledge
29 West 35th Street, New York, NY 10001

Simultaneously published in the UK
by Routledge
11 New Fetter Lane, London EC4P 4EE

Routledge is an imprint of the Taylor & Francis Group

Typeset in Baskerville by
Taylor & Francis Books Ltd
Printed and bound in Great Britain by
TJ International, Padstow, Cornwall

British Library Cataloguing in Publication Data
A catalogue record for this book is available
from the British Library

Library of Congress Cataloging in Publication Data
Gibson, John, 1969–
The Literary Wittgenstein / John Gibson and Wolfgang Huemar.— 1st ed.
p. cm.
1. Criticism–History–20th century. 2. Literature–History and
criticism–Theory, etc. 3. Wittgenstein, Ludwig,
1889–1951–Contributions in criticism. I. Huemar, Wolfgang. 1968–
II. Title.
PN94.G53 2004
801'.95'092–dc22

2003021102

ISBN   0–415–28972–6 (hbk)
ISBN   0–415–28973–4 (pbk)

CONTENTS

CONTENTS

CONTENTS

CONTRIBUTORS

Alex Burri is Professor of Philosophy at the University of Erfurt. He is, together with Klaus Petrus, the founder and editor of *Facta Philosophica*, an international journal for contemporary philosophy.

Stanley Cavell officially retired six years ago after some four decades of teaching at Harvard. Two books from his hand are to appear next year, *Emerson's Transcendental Etudes* and *Cities of Words* (a presentation of a course offered in Harvard's Core Curriculum several times between 1987 and 1995).

Cora Diamond was Kenan Professor of Philosophy, University Professor and Professor of Law at the University of Virginia, where she is now Professor Emerita. She also taught at Princeton University, Aberdeen University and the University of Sussex. She is the author of *The Realistic Spirit: Wittgenstein, Philosophy, and the Mind* (MIT Press, 1991) and the editor of *Wittgenstein's Lectures on the Foundations of Mathematics, Cambridge 1939* (University of Chicago Press, 1976).

Richard Eldridge is the author of *An Introduction to the Philosophy of Art* (2003), *The Persistence of Romanticism* (2001), *Leading a Human Life: Wittgenstein, Intentionality, and Romanticism* (1997), and *On Moral Personhood* (1989). He edited *Stanley Cavell* (2003) and *Beyond Representation: Philosophy and Poetic Imagination.* (1996). He is a Professor of Philosophy at Swarthmore College.

John Gibson is currently Visiting Assistant Professor of Philosophy at Temple University. He works in the areas of philosophy of literature, aesthetics, and the philosophy of mind and language. He is currently completing a manuscript entitled *Fiction and the Weave of Life*.

Timothy Gould is the author of *Hearing Things: Voice and Method in the Writing of Stanley Cavell* and of articles on Kant's aesthetics and its romantic and modernist aftermaths. He is writing a manuscript entitled *Prophets of the Everyday*. He teaches at Metro State College in Denver.

James Guetti has been concerned since the early 1980s to show how Wittgenstein's work may illuminate and re-direct our accounts of certain experiences of reading. His *Wittgenstein and the Grammar of Literary Experience* appeared in 1993. He is retired and lives in Leverett, Massachusetts.

Garry L. Hagberg is the James H. Ottaway, Jr. Professor of Philosophy and Aesthetics at Bard College, where he is also director of the Program in Philosophy and the Arts. He is the author of *Art as Language: Wittgenstein, Meaning, and Aesthetic Theory* and *Meaning and Interpretation: Wittgenstein, Henry James, and Literary Knowledge*, as well as of numerous articles, essays, and reviews in aesthetics. He is presently at work on a book on philosophical issues of autobiographical knowledge, and is co-editor, with Denis Dutton, of *Philosophy and Literature*. Also a jazz guitarist for many years, he is co-author, with Howard Roberts, of the three-volume *Guitar Compendium: Technique, Improvisation, Musicianship, Theory*, and guest-edited a special issue of *The Journal of Aesthetics and Art Criticism* on Improvisation in the Arts.

Bernard Harrison is currently Emeritus E. E. Ericksen Professor of Philosophy in the University of Utah and Honorary Professor of Philosophy in the University of Sussex. His books include *Form and Content* (Blackwell, 1973), *Fielding's Tom Jones: The Novelist as Moral Philosopher* (Chatto/Sussex University Press, 1975), *Inconvenient Fictions: Literature and the Limits of Theory* (Yale University Press, 1991), and (with Patricia Hanna) *Word and World: Practice and the Foundations of Language* (Cambridge University Press, 2004).

Wolfgang Huemer teaches philosophy at the University of Erfurt. His research interests are – next to Wittgenstein and philosophy of literature – mainly in philosophy of mind, epistemology and early phenomenology (from Brentano to Husserl). He is co-editor (with Marc-Oliver Schuster) of *Writing the Austrian Traditions: Relations between Philosophy and Literature*, and is author of *The Constitution of Consciousness: A Study in Analytic Phenomenology* (Routledge, 2004).

Dale Jacquette is Professor of Philosophy at The Pennsylvania State University. He is the author of *Wittgenstein's Thought in Transition* (1998), editor of *American Philosophical Quarterly*, and is currently writing a monograph, tentatively titled *Early Wittgenstein on Identity*.

Joseph Margolis is Laura Carnell Professor at Temple University. He is Honorary President and Lifetime Member of the International Association of Aesthetics. Among his recent books are: *What, After All, is a Work of Art?: Lectures in the Philosophy of Art* (Pennsylvania University Press, 1999), *Selves and Other Texts: The Case for Cultural Realism* (Pennsylvania University Press, 2001), *Reinventing Pragmatism: American Philosophy at the End of the Twentieth Century* (Cornell University Press, 2002). He is currently completing the third volume in a trilogy of books on contemporary American philosophy.

Marjorie Perloff is Sadie D. Patek Professor Emerita of Humanities at Stanford University. Her most recent books are *Wittgenstein's Ladder* (Chicago, 1996), *Poetry On and Off the Page* (Northwestern, 1998), *21st Century Modernism* (Blackwell, 2002) and *The Vienna Paradox* (New Directions, 2003).

Rupert Read is Senior Lecturer in Philosophy at the University of East Anglia. He is a leading British advocate of the 'resolute' reading of Wittgenstein. See his *The New Wittgenstein* (Routledge, 2000), and his recent essays in *Philosophy, Philosophical Investigations* and *Philosophical Psychology*. His other books are *Kuhn* (Polity, 2002) and *The New Hume Debate* (Routledge, 2000). He is currently editing a volume entitled *Film as Philosophy* and working on the relationship between Buddhism and Wittgenstein.

David Schalkwyk is a Professor in the Department of English at the University of Cape Town. He has published articles on Shakespeare, Wittgenstein, Derrida and South African Prison Writing in the *Shakespeare Quarterly, English Literary Renaissance, Journal of Aesthetics and Art Criticism, Language Sciences, Pretexts* and *Journal of African Literatures*. Longer publications include *Speech and Performance in Shakespeare's Sonnets and Plays* (Cambridge: Cambridge University Press, 2002) and *Literature and the Touch of the Real* (London: Associated Presses and Newark: Delaware University Press, 2004), and a translation of Karel Schoeman's novel *'n Ander Land* as *Another Country*, published by Sinclair-Stephenson and Picador.

Joachim Schulte is a researcher, and teaches, at the Department of Philosophy of the University of Bielefeld. He is one of the Wittgenstein Trustees. He has written numerous articles and three books on Wittgenstein; two of these books are available in English (*Wittgenstein*, SUNY Press, 1992; *Experience and Expression*, Clarendon Press, 1993). He is a co-editor of the critical editions of Wittgenstein's *Tractatus* and *Philosophical Investigations*.

Sonia Sedivy is Associate Professor of Philosophy at the University of Toronto at Scarborough. Her research interests radiate from philosophy of mind and perception, epistemology and philosophy of art. To date, her work on Wittgenstein has focused primarily in philosophy of mind, "Wittgenstein's Diagnosis of Empiricism's third Dogma: why perception can't be an amalgam of sensation and conceptualization." But Wittgenstein's work also informs her *Beauty and the End of Art* (ms).

Martin Stone is Professor of Law at The Cardozo Law School of Yeshiva University, and Adjunct Professor at the Graduate Faculty of the The New School for Social Research, Department of Philosophy. His recent publications include "Wittgenstein on Deconstruction" in *The New Wittgenstein* (Routledge, 2000), "The Significance of Doing and Suffering" in *Philosophy and the Law of Torts* (Cambridge, 2001), and "Formalism" in *The Oxford Handbook of Jurisprudence and Philosophy of Law* (Oxford, 2002).

ACKNOWLEDGMENTS

We would like to offer thanks to all those who have helped us at various stages of this project. Alex Burri, Alice Crary, Richard Eldridge, and Garry Hagberg offered invaluable advice along the way. We are also indebted to Andrew Phoenix Jewell, Sharif McCray Roach, and Matthew Turner for their generous offer to help proofread and format the articles collected here. At Routledge, Tony Bruce and Tim Sydenham gave us the just right mixture of encouragement and criticism at the beginning of the project, and Zoe Drayson, Julia Rebaudo and Faye Kaliszczak often went beyond the call of duty in helping to bring it to completion. We are also very grateful to Luca Pocci, Simona Bertacco, and Melania Parisi for support and consistently perceptive counsel throughout.

Stanley Cavell, "The *Investigations'* Everyday Aesthetics of Itself" is reprinted from *The Cavell Reader*, © 1996 Blackwell Press. Reprinted with permission of Blackwell Press. Cora Diamond, "Having a Rough Story about What Moral Philosophy Is" is reprinted from *New Literary History* 15:1 (1983), 155–69. © *New Literary History*, University of Virginia. Reprinted with permission of The Johns Hopkins University Press. Bernard Harrison, "Imagined Worlds and the Real One: Plato, Wittgenstein, and Mimesis" is reprinted from *Philosophy and Literature* 17:1 (1993), 24–46. © The Johns Hopkins University Press. Reprinted with permission of The Johns Hopkins University Press.

INTRODUCTION: WITTGENSTEIN, LANGUAGE AND PHILOSOPHY OF LITERATURE

Wolfgang Huemer

The philosophy of Ludwig Wittgenstein is characterized by an extraordinary interest in language, with remarkable results. Wittgenstein developed a picture of language that radically broke with the tradition and revolutionized the way philosophers approached the topic in the twentieth century. While in his first book, the *Tractatus*,[1] Wittgenstein focused on the question of how words can depict the world, he later came to understand language not as an abstract system, but as a social practice. He counteracted a longstanding tendency among philosophers to reduce language to assertive statements and to focus exclusively on analyzing their logical form with the goal of creating an "ideal language." Wittgenstein's crucial move was to point out that understanding language requires us to focus on how it is used by members of the linguistic community, appreciating all the nuances and varieties of expression that characterize everyday communication. His analyses of "clear and simple language games" at the beginning of the *Investigations* "are not preparatory studies for a future regularization of language," but rather "*objects of comparison* which are meant to throw light on the facts of our language by way not only of similarities, but also of dissimilarities."[2] Wittgenstein, thus, privileges the richness and diversity of linguistic phenomena, which he explored with extraordinary sensitivity and insight, over the tendency to develop an ideal, rigorously regulated language, a tendency which sacrifices the variety of language games for unattainable exactness and universality.

For Wittgenstein language was not only one of the central problems of philosophy; it was also the key to their solution. Over and over he warned against our urge to misunderstand the workings of our language, pointing out the traps that are built into language and its powers to lead our philosophical paths into dark alleys, to "bewitch our minds."[3] Wittgenstein argued that to solve most philosophical problems we do not need better philosophical theories; we should not aim for *explanation*, but rather for a detailed *description* of the use of our words, providing a "perspicuous representation" (*PI* §122) by means of which we can gain a more profound understanding of language. Philosophical problems, Wittgenstein states, "are solved…by looking into the workings of our language, and that in such a way as to make us recognize those workings: *in despite of* an urge to misunderstand them" (*PI* §109). It is his contention that by making the risks that are inherent in our language manifest, by showing that "grammatical illusions" (*PI* §110) are the true source of most philosophical problems, we can solve these problems, like a therapist who cures his patients by showing them the source of their illness.[4]

Moreover, the importance of language for Wittgenstein is reflected not only by what he said, but also by how he said it: it has often been pointed out that the fascination of Wittgenstein's works lies to a considerable degree in their literary quality; like few other philosophers he succeeded in creating a harmony between the literary form and philosophical content of his texts. In the *Tractatus*, the importance of the structure of language is underlined by the strict form of the text – all statements are enumerated in a hierarchical system – and the aphoristic, yet concise style *shows* what Wittgenstein tries to express: "what can be said at all can be said clearly, and what we cannot talk about we must pass over in silence" (*TLP*, p. 3). The literary style is of central importance not only in Wittgenstein's first book, but also in his later writings, especially in the *Philosophical Investigations*. Once more, Wittgenstein did not adopt the stylistic conventions for philosophical texts at the time, but rather developed a new form of exposition – short *remarks* that are loosely connected to one another – which he thought more appropriate to express his ideas and in general to convey philosophical information. The harmony of style and content in both books that Wittgenstein published or prepared for publication in his lifetime comes not by accident; Wittgenstein struggled to develop a new form of presenting philosophical views,[5] which clearly expresses at a stylistic level his efforts to take new paths in philosophy, leaving the burden of tradition behind.

These three aspects explain why Wittgenstein had an enormous impact on writers and, more generally, on the artistic community. It is not by accident that Wittgenstein's centenary was celebrated in Vienna with a big exhibition, presenting works of art which, in one way or another, have been influenced by Wittgenstein's philosophy. Moreover, we find direct quotations from Wittgenstein's work in literary texts, his life was thematized in literary books as well as films, and there are poets who have even written theoretical texts on Wittgenstein's philosophy.[6] Terry Eagleton hit the nail on the head when he said:

> Frege is a philosopher's philosopher, Sartre the media's idea of an intellectual, and Bertrand Russell every shopkeeper's image of the sage....But Wittgenstein is the philosopher of poets and composers, playwrights and novelists, and snatches of his mighty *Tractatus* have even been set to music.[7]

Given this background it might surprise one that Wittgenstein said relatively little about literature. At some places he mentioned the names of authors he appreciated though without discussing the literary value of their work.[8] Moreover, there are only few theoretical remarks, and no developed theory on the role which language plays in literary contexts. Although Wittgenstein emphasizes that to understand language we need to take the diversity of linguistic phenomena into account, he hardly discusses questions that are central to the philosophical debates on literature, which might explain why his influence on philosophy of literature and literary theory is less dominant than that on, say, the philosophy of language or philosophy of mind.

The significance of Wittgenstein's philosophy for our theoretical understanding of literature is not so much based on his occasional remarks on aesthetics, however, but rather on his general philosophical position. With this volume we present a collection of essays from philosophers and literary theorists who develop Wittgensteinian accounts of literature, who use Wittgenstein's philosophical results to solve problems pertinent to the theory of literature, or show how topics that arise in our reflecting on literature can illuminate our understanding of Wittgenstein's philosophy. Before presenting the contributions to this volume in more detail, however, I want to offer a few considerations of how Wittgenstein's philosophy can be relevant for our theoretical understanding of literature. I will do so by sketching some of Wittgenstein's central moves and pointing out how a new understanding of language can solve problems that are discussed in philosophy of literature and literary theory. My goal is not to outline an uncontested common ground; I will not present basic assumptions that are shared by all contributors of the book – this would be impossible and unnecessary, for they approach the topic from very different perspectives and with different goals. I will rather sketch a rough picture in order to recall Wittgenstein's background and illustrate a few notable respects in which his philosophy can enrich our understanding of literature.

Wittgenstein's background: the referential picture of language

Wittgenstein developed his philosophy at a time when most philosophers, impressed by Russell's analysis of definite descriptions, tried to understand language on the basis of the notions of truth and reference. Both aspects of this referential picture of language, however, are not particularly apt to approach literature; unlike scientific ones, literary texts do not seem to deliver veridical descriptions of the world, but rather to describe fictional scenarios. Moreover, they typically do not refer to objects or events that exist in the actual world. Russell solved this tension in a radical way: he argued, as is well known, that statements containing definite descriptions or proper names are true only if there exists exactly one thing to which the name or description refers. Writing about *Hamlet* he states that "the propositions in the play are false because there was no such man."[9] The problems of this position seem obvious: if statements in literary texts are false, literature cannot be of cognitive value. This position seems to marginalize the value of literature in our society; it becomes mysterious why people are interested in spending their time with writing or reading literary texts in the first place.

Russell's treatment of literature was very influential on, but is not necessarily representative of, the role literature is assigned in the referential picture of language. Various philosophers have presented more subtle accounts which, like Russell's, are based on the concepts of truth and reference. Literature, it was argued, does not communicate truths, but is rather a game of make-believe; it consists of speech-acts similar to the ones we use in ordinary discourse, with some of the conventions that govern ordinary speech acts bracketed; some philosophers have argued that literary texts are taken to be true not of this, but of another possible world; and others that they refer not to ordinary, physical objects, but rather to a special kind of object, typically Meinongian objects, which do not exist, but subsist and, thus, can have properties and be referred to.[10]

All of these approaches struggle with the difficulties inherent to the referential picture: literary language cannot be adequately accounted for on the basis of the notions of truth and reference. As a consequence, it is often viewed as a border case, an aberrant use of language, in which the general rules of linguistic usage are bracketed. According to this view, writers only pretend to use words in the way they are used in ordinary language, but actually do not: they only act as if they made true statements, described the world, raised questions, gave orders, etc., as we do in ordinary language. Literature, however, misses the worldly engagement characteristic of our everyday use of language: descriptions in literary texts cannot be corrected, questions do not wait to be answered, and no one expects orders to be complied with – at least not by the reader. In consequence literature is not seen as part of our ordinary language, but rather as a niche, a language game isolated both from the world and from the rest of language, governed by its own rules. Thus, according to this position, literature can be disregarded in a general account of (ordinary) language.

This view of literature is highly problematic. The strict separation between literary and ordinary language presupposes that we can give criteria to distinguish the two. The argument that literary language works in radically different ways also raises the need to explain how we can understand literary texts in the first place, for that would presuppose that we need to learn this new language. Moreover, if one understands literature as an aberrant use of language one faces difficulties when explaining how we can refine our ordinary linguistic capacities by reading literary texts, and why the latter are often taken to be the paradigmatic cases of informed uses of language – proponents of this view cannot explain, for example, why the *Oxford English Dictionary* often quotes from literary texts to illustrate the use of a word.

A Wittgensteinian picture of literary language

Wittgensteinian accounts of literature can avoid these problems. There are various ways of adopting Wittgenstein's insights to address these and other problems related to literature – as the variety of positions elaborated in the contributions to this book show. Let me develop here one line of reasoning: Wittgenstein's later philosophy of language is characterized by a move from reference to use; "the meaning of a word," he famously states, "is its use in the language" (*PI* §43). By approaching language as a social practice, Wittgenstein does not put an emphasis on the relation between words and world; but rather focuses on detailed investigations of how words are used in diverse contexts of human practice. Moreover, he refuses the tendency prevalent in the referential picture to reduce all legitimate uses of language to assertive statements, or, more generally, to bearers of truth-value, but recognizes that language can be used in many different ways to pursue a variety of different goals. The aspects of truth and reference do not disappear from this picture, though. They do, however, play a less central role, for they are relevant only insofar as members of the linguistic community use language to refer to objects and events, and sometimes, but by far not always, assert declarative statements that have a truth-value.

Wittgenstein's move has immediate consequences for our understanding of literature. In this picture, literary language is no longer viewed as an aberrant border case, in which language does not work quite the way it does in ordinary discourse. It rather allows us to take literature seriously as one form of linguistic expression among others. Literature is not an isolated language game, the meaning of a word is not radically altered when it is used in a literary text, the general rules of language are not bracketed, and the expressions used do not refer to other kinds of object or other possible worlds; rather they are well grounded in our actual world.

This understanding of literature is not a mere side effect of the Wittgensteinian picture of language, rather it reveals that literary language plays a central role within that complex system of language. If we try to define what is particular about literary texts, we find that they put an emphasis not on *what* is said, but on *how* it is said; literary language makes itself manifest, it focuses more on the texture of expressions than on their content. "In its semantics," we might say with Lubomír Doležel, "literature (poetry) aims in the direction opposite to science: it is a communicative system for activating and putting to maximal use the resources of intensionality in language."[11] Accordingly we can state that at least to some extent in literary texts language itself becomes the topic. More than other texts, thus, literature displays the rules that govern the use of language. By showing what can be said and how it can be said it draws our attention to grammar – it shows in which contexts words can be used and how they can be combined with other words.[12]

The shift from content to form is a general characteristic of literary texts allowing, as it does, for degrees. All genres of literary texts can – in their respective ways – become relevant to our understanding of language. A Wittgensteinian approach to literature does not need to restrict itself to narrative texts like novels, short stories, or plays, but can also take other genres into account, especially poetry, which performs the shift from content to form in a most genuine way. This can open interesting perspectives, since most philosophers who discuss literature focus on questions concerning fictional texts and consequently restrict themselves mainly to texts that are primarily narrative. Poetry is hardly discussed, but rather treated like a negligible ornament. Richard Rorty, for example, explicitly states that his plea for literature does not extend to poetry. Rorty famously argues that literature – and not moral philosophy – is of central importance for the development of our moral sensitivity and understanding. If one looks at the actual effects that novels and the theories of moral philosophers had on people, Rorty argues, "you find yourself wishing that there had been more novels and fewer theories."[13] Rorty sees poetry in line not with the novelist's power to raise moral consciousness by describing unnecessary details, but rather with moral philosophy's damaging efforts to construct theories: "I have been suggesting," he states, "that we Westerners owe this consciousness and this sensitivity more to our novelists than to our philosophers or to our poets."[14]

Poetry cannot, of course, develop long-winded stories rich in unnecessary details. What Rorty does not appreciate, however, is that poetry can be valuable for our understanding of language precisely because it offers concise and well-wrought formulations. By concentrating on the necessary and finding new ways of saying what is difficult to express, poets take language to its extremes – and sometimes beyond. Even when violating the rules that govern ordinary language they draw our attention to these rules and open them up to critique. In short, they provide concise showcases of the workings of our language, and thus explore – and extend – its limits.[15]

What texts of all literary genres have in common, however, is that they do not only use language to express certain contents, but also direct the readers' attention to language itself. In doing so, literature can illuminate our understanding of the workings of our language; it can become a tool for grammatical investigation. Different genres fulfill this aspect in different ways: novels allow us to describe uncommon situations and to develop a new perspective on everyday situations. By telling stories they provide the context necessary for exploring not only the grammar of our language, but also the limits of our form of life.[16] In this way, literature can, as Rorty insisted, even contribute to raising our moral understanding, not by increasing our knowledge through the communication of information, but by describing situations that trigger our acknowledgment of the human condition.[17] Poets, on the other hand, provide short, carefully crafted texts that are particularly apt for minute and acute analyses and critique of single expressions and their roles in language. By developing new metaphors they shed light on the limitations of ordinary language to express certain situations or feelings; moreover, they denounce our unreflected, habitual perception of everyday situation by depicting them in an original way, thus developing new perspectives. In short, literature can provide important insights into the workings of our ordinary language – and, consequently, into our form of life and the reality we live in – something which it can do only because literary texts do not use language in some aberrant way; rather they use ordinary language towards which literature also draws our attention. Literature, thus, is not a niche-phenomenon; it must not be viewed as an unnecessary but entertaining orna-ment, but rather as a practice central to our language without which we might not even be able to master a language as complex as ours in the first place.

Wittgenstein's later picture of language has further important consequences for literary theory: his casting of language and meaning as primarily public, embedded in our social practices, entails a view of the relationship between a speaker's utterance and his intentions that can be illuminating for the way in which we approach literary texts. To understand what a person means with an utterance, according to this view, we do not need to read her mind to grasp the meaning she attaches to this utterance, but rather listen to what she says. Meanings are not in the head, they are in the words anchored in social practice and physical environment. This approach can shed an interesting light upon the question of whether knowing the author's intention is relevant for an under-standing of a literary text, as Colin Lyas has shown.[18] Following Wilmsatt and Beardsley's attack on the intentional fallacy – or, on the continental side, Barthes's and Foucault's point concerning the death of the author – many philosophers and literary theorists have argued that the author's intentions should not be relevant for the interpretation of a text. This argument presupposes that we can distin-guish between the text and the author's intentions, the latter being something over and above the text, something that can be located in the author's head. As soon as one allows for this distinction, the role of intentions for interpreting a text becomes dubious, for we can never know what the author really intended.

If we adopt a Wittgensteinian stance we can see that Wilmsatt and Beardsley have gone too far. We cannot completely dismiss the author's inten-tions for we would not be able to recognize something as a literary text if we did not assume that it was authored by a person to whom we ascribe certain intentions. If we want to know what the intentions of the author are, however, we have to read the text. Wilmsatt and Beardsley are right to point out that to understand a text we do not need to conjecture what the author could have meant. The author's intentions are relevant only insofar as they are manifest in the text – there is no other place to look for them but the text and the social practices that are connected to it.

The considerations developed in the last few paragraphs stem from a certain understanding of one aspect of Wittgenstein's philosophy: his move from the referential to a communitarian picture of language. They show, as I hope, that Wittgenstein's philosophy can prove extremely relevant for questions pertinent to literature. Moreover, they show that literature is not a niche-phenomenon, but a relevant part of our social practice. The urge to do philosophy comes from our urge to understand what is going on with and around us, or, as Wittgenstein once put it, to find our "way about" (*PI* §123). This involves an understanding of who we are and what is essential to our form of life. I have tried to show that a Wittgensteinian approach to literature can appreciate that in order to under-stand ourselves we need, among other things, to pay attention to the central role literature plays in our form of life.

The contributions to this book

This volume contains articles by philosophers and literary theorists who share the view that Wittgenstein's philosophy can provide stimulating insights for our theoretical understanding of literature. Rather than starting from one particular thesis as a common basis, however, each of them develops his or her own individual perspective, highlighting different aspects of Wittgenstein's philosophy, and discussing different problems of literary theory for which a Wittgensteinian solution is considered. The volume is subdivided into five parts, each of which collects contributions on similar topics or with similar approaches. In what follows I will give a short characterization of each of these parts.

It is a widespread opinion that we can draw a sharp line between philosophical and scientific texts on the one side and literary ones on the other. The former are often thought to concentrate exclusively on the truth value of their statements, while the latter seem to concentrate not on the content, but on the form of expression – rather than communicating truths they try to achieve beauty. The contributions to the first part of this volume challenge this view, showing that this distinction cannot always be sharply drawn. The arguments developed challenge the distinction from both directions: some focus on the literary quality of specific philosophical texts, namely Wittgenstein's own writing, and the philosophical significance of this aspect, while others raise the question of whether literature can inform us about reality.

In the opening article, Stanley Cavell describes how the *Philosophical Investigations* has become for him not simply an object, but also a means, of interpretation. He understands the *Investigations* as a work of modernity, since it perpetually questions its medium, which shows, amongst other things, that Wittgenstein's notion of "perspicuous representation" must also be applied to the style of the *Investigations* itself. Marjorie Perloff points out in her contribution that although Wittgenstein famously stated that "philosophy ought really to be written only as a *form of poetry*" (*CV* 24)[19], his texts do not suffer from translation like the poetry of, say, Rilke, where the translator faces the difficulty of doing justice to connotations, rhymes, rhythm and sound of the poem. Wittgenstein's remarks, Perloff argues, can be translated more easily, for they do not focus on one particular language, German, but on the workings of language in general. Perloff then goes on to show that a similar point can be made with regards to forms of experimental poetry and conceptual art that bring to light characteristics of language in general, rather than of any specific language. In the following article David Schalkwyk discusses Wittgenstein's contention that our misunderstanding of the workings of our language is a main source of philosophical problems. Exploring the spatial metaphors Wittgenstein uses he shows how his solution works: based on detailed grammatical investigations we are to develop a perspicuous representation of what lies open before our eyes. Schalkwyk shows not only that at least certain kinds of literature are already engaged in grammatical investigation, but also that literature is an indispensable tool in this enterprise. In the fourth contribution to the first part, Timothy Gould focuses on the therapeutic aspect – the search for a form of peace – of Wittgenstein's later philosophy. By offering a close reading of §§113–138 of the *Philosophical Investigations* he shows how Wittgenstein's literary style illustrates not only his struggles, but also the steps in his process of coming to peace.

The first part is rounded off with two articles that focus on the question of whether reading literary texts can inform us about reality. Bernard Harrison argues that the anti-humanist thesis, according to which works of art are not referential, has led to the view that literary works are self-referential systems of signs and, thus, cannot inform us about the world. Harrison demonstrates that the picture of language outlined in the *Philosophical Investigations* is at odds with a basic assumption that underlies these anti-humanist positions, according to which there are basic names, each of which refers to simples in the world. Following Wittgenstein's later philosophy of language, however, we cannot ask for the meaning of single words in isolation, rather we need to ask for their role in the web of our linguistic practices all of which, in some way or another, are closely connected to or embedded in reality. Based on this view, Harrison develops an argument that shows how literature can inform us about reality by bringing to light the workings of language itself. John Gibson in his contribution tries to reconcile two basic but apparently contradictory views about the nature of literature. One, traditionally linked to the mimetic view of art, treats literature as offering a window on our world. The other emphasizes the role of fiction in literature and invites a picture of literature as occupied with speaking about imaginary worlds rather than our world. Gibson argues that we can only reconcile these views if we develop a non-mimetic account of how literature can engage reality. He argues that the later Wittgenstein's writings on the nature of linguistic representation help us see how such an account might be developed.

The articles of the second part of the book demonstrate how Wittgenstein's contributions to the philosophy of language and mind can shed an interesting light on our practice of reading literary (and other) texts. Cora Diamond focuses on the relation of literature and the unsayable. Challenging Martha Nussbaum's claim that to understand the relation between moral philosophy and literature we must have a rough story about what moral philosophy is, she argues that literary texts can make points that are relevant to moral philosophy without, however, explicitly stating them. Based on Wittgenstein's distinction between saying and showing she argues that in literary texts – just like in the *Tractatus* – moral philosophy belongs to the unsayable; it is not explicitly stated, nor do we need an elaborated theory to understand it; rather it shows itself in the way the story is told. In her new introduction, Cora Diamond makes a connection between how things are shown in literature and how they are shown in the *Tractatus* – and also in Wittgenstein's later work – more explicitly. In the next article, Joachim Schulte argues that Wittgenstein's contrast between live and dead signs as well as his remarks on aspect seeing account for how we can grasp the content of a poem. Poetry is a language game governed by its own conventions; its goal is not (primarily) to convey information. Rather, it puts an emphasis on formal aspects, such as rhyme and rhythm, and thus foregrounds the musicality of language. Poets put the expressible in a way that adds new layers of signification to the established meanings of the signs – the signs become alive. These new aspects can be detected only by readers who are sensitive to this dimension of poetic language. Thus, not only writing, but also reading poetry requires special capacities; while the poet has to endow the signs with potential life, the reader has to be able to notice aspects and experience aspect changes. The following two articles in this part discuss one of the questions with which contemporary literary theory is most occupied: the nature of interpretation. It is often argued that all reading is interpretation, and that interpretation is itself inherently relative. The result is the idea that the meaning of a literary text, far from being internal to literary works, is actually generated by readers or interpretative communities in the act of reading. Sonia Sedivy and Martin Stone develop an argument that Wittgenstein offers us a way to reclaim the idea that literary texts and their meanings cannot be prised apart to the extent claimed by so much contemporary literary theory. Both show in their own particular ways how this permits us to counter the deconstructionist and "neo-pragmatist" versions of the radical relativity of interpretation currently in vogue.

The question of what it means to be human was at the center of Wittgenstein's philosophy throughout his life. The articles of Part III use literary texts as well as theoretical reflections from writers to shed light on this topic, discussing questions concerning personal identity, the nature of the self, the distinction between the inner and the outer, language as a practice shared by more than one person, the mind and its limits, as well as the status of psychopathology. Richard Eldridge points out that the interest of the *Investigations* goes far beyond their negative conclusions concerning rule-following and concept application. Turning around the "axis of investigation," Eldridge shows how Wittgenstein's remarks, a complex interplay of various voices, can be read as a narrative or parable of the disquietudes of the human. Based on Hölderlin's poetology, which was developed as an answer to Kant and Fichte, Eldridge demonstrates how the transitions and modulations of Wittgenstein's text offer a possibility for us to acknowledge the fundamental conditions of human life. Garry Hagberg outlines the development of Wittgenstein's notion of the self and inner life from his early writings, where he advocates a solipsistic position strongly influenced by Schopenhauer, to his later texts, where, in a therapeutic tone, he warns against misleading analogies and bewitching language. Words like "I" far too easily make us think that there must be an inner, metaphysically hidden ego to which this expression refers. Hagberg connects Wittgenstein's later views to a literary genre that promises us a glimpse into the inner life of another person: autobiographical writing. James Guetti demonstrates in his contribution that there are striking parallels between Wittgenstein's picture of language and the one underlying Joseph Conrad's novel *Heart of Darkness*. Refuting the skeptical aspects of Kripke's communitarian solution to the rule-following problem, Guetti points out that language can work only due to its dialogic nature; language is a game that could not be played if there was only one player. If one loses this insight one is capable only of solipsistic babbling – just like Kurtz at the end of the novel – and cannot be said to play a language game any longer: one is not really speaking any more. Rupert Read focuses on the question of whether we can understand persons who suffer from severe mental illnesses. He develops a Wittgensteinian approach to psychopathology, according to which severe mental illnesses cannot be understood, for utterings of the mentally ill are not even candidates for understanding, just like a statement uttered by a person who is sleeping and talking while dreaming is not a candidate for understanding. Read illustrates his point with Guetti's reading of Faulkner's *The Sound and the Fury*.

With his early work, the *Tractatus Logico-Philosophicus*, Wittgenstein aimed to solve all philosophical problems once and for all by proposing a rigorous ontology and a universal analysis of meaning. He did not, however, explicitly say anything about literary language, nor about the ontological status of fictional objects. The contributors to Part IV have taken up the challenge and show which role literature can or should play within a Tractarian framework. Alex Burri begins his article with a discussion concerning the ontological status of fictional objects. If we admit that fictional statements are not senseless, we face the question of what kind of entity they refer to. Considering various possible answers, Burri develops a Tractarian ontology of fiction. In the second part of his article he turns to the question of whether, viewed from a Tractarian perspective, literature can have cognitive value, i.e., whether we can gain genuine knowledge from literary texts. Dale Jacquette points out that Wittgenstein's ambitious program to develop a universal theory of meaning can be successful only if it allows for a logic of fiction. Jacquette states four minimal requirements for such a logic and discusses whether, to what extent, and how, Wittgenstein's early philosophy can meet them. Jacquette's discussion is instructive not only for the role of literature in a Tractarian framework, but also for gaining a better understanding of Wittgenstein's early views on psychology.

The last part of the book is reserved for a critical look at our project to adopt Wittgenstein's philosophy for literary theory. Joseph Margolis offers a critique of the very idea that Wittgenstein has anything like a "method" that might be of use to the theorist looking for a way to approach literature. He does so by looking at the work of two philosophers who have pioneered "Wittgensteinian" approaches to the arts, Garry Hagberg and Ben Tilghman. In criticizing their views, Margolis's contribution offers not only a critical stance the reader may apply to the essays in this volume, but just as importantly, it concludes the book by building a bridge from a discussion of Wittgenstein and literature to a way of approaching the theory of the arts in general through Wittgenstein.

This short overview of the book shows, as I hope, that although he did not explicitly develop a theory of literature, Wittgenstein's writings contain much that can improve our theoretical understanding of literature, but also, that questions that are discussed in contemporary literary theory and even the close reading of particular literary texts can deepen our understanding of Wittgenstein's philosophy.[20]

Notes

1 Ludwig Wittgenstein, *Tractatus Logico-Philosophicus*, trans. by D. F. Pears and B. F. McGuinness, London: Routledge & Kegan Paul, 1961. Cited in the text as *TLP*.

2 Ludwig Wittgenstein, *Philosophical Investigations*, trans. by G. E. M. Anscombe, Oxford: Basil Blackwell, 1953, §130. Cited in the text as *PI*.

3 Cf. *PI* §109: "Philosophy is a battle against the bewitchment of our intelligence by means of language."

4 For a collection of essays that put an emphasis on the therapeutic reading of Wittgenstein cf. Alice Crary and Rupert Read (eds.), *The New Wittgenstein*, London: Routledge, 2000.

5 In the preface to both *Tractatus* and *Philosophical Investigations*, Wittgenstein emphasizes the importance of style, as well as his fear that the result cannot live up to his expectations. In the preface to the *Tractatus* he notes: "If this work has any value, it consists in two things: the first is that thoughts are expressed in it, and on this score the better the thoughts are expressed – the more the nail has been hit on the head – the greater will be its value" (*TLP*, p. 4). In the preface to the *Investigations* he notes that he has given considerable thought to the form of the book. He lets us know that his ideas varied over the years, and that he finally understood that his views can be best expressed in the form of philosophical remarks: "my thoughts were soon crippled if I tried to force them on in any single direction against their natural inclination" (*PI*, p. v).

6 Umberto Eco, for example, quotes – without, of course, giving reference – Wittgenstein's ladder metaphor (*TLP* 6.54), translated into medieval German ("Er muoz gelîchesame die leiter abewerfen, sô er an ir ufgestigen"), in *The Name of the Rose*, trans. by William Weaver, New York: Harcourt Brace & Company, 1983, p. 492; Bruce Duffy presents a literary approach to Wittgenstein's life in *The World as I Found It*, New York: Ticknor & Fields, 1987; Derek Jarman and Terry Eagleton have made the film *Wittgenstein*; M. A. Numminen has set the *Tractatus* to music in his *Tractatus Suite*; and Ingeborg Bachmann presented her theoretical reflections in the article "Ludwig Wittgenstein. Zu einem Kapitel der jüngsten Philosophiegeschichte," *Frankfurter Hefte* 7 (1953), 540–5 (repr. in Ludwig Wittgenstein, *Schriften: Beiheft*, Frankfurt: Suhrkamp, 1960, pp. 7–15). The exhibition *Wittgenstein* took place at the *Wiener Secession* from September 13 to October 29, 1989.

7 Terry Eagleton, "My Wittgenstein," *Common Knowledge* 3 (1994), 152–7, pp. 153f.

8 A passage in a card to Ludwig von Ficker is very telling: Von Ficker was the editor of the literary journal *Der Brenner*, and whom Wittgenstein asked to distribute a considerable sum from his heritage among young writers. They decided to give the biggest donations to Rainer Maria Rilke and Georg Trakl. Wittgenstein writes in this card about Trakl's poems: "I do not understand them, but their *tone* makes me happy. It is the tone of a truly genial person. [*Ich verstehe sie nicht; aber ihr* Ton *beglückt mich. Es ist der Ton eines wahrhaft genialen Menschen.*]" (Ludwig Wittgenstein, *Briefe. Briefwechsel mit B. Russell, G. E. Moore, J. M. Keynes, F. P. Ramsey, W. Eccles, P. Engelmann und L. v. Ficker*. Brian McGuinness and Georg Henrik v. Wright (eds.), Frankfurt: Suhrkamp, 1980, p. 65.)

9 Bertrand Russell, *An Inquiry into Meaning and Truth*, London: Allen and Unwin, 1962, p. 277.

10 These short characterizations are, of course, very cursory and provide but caricatures of the positions in question. The point I want to stress is that if one accepts the basic insights of the referential picture of language, one faces difficulties to account for

literary language that should raise our doubts on whether this approach can do justice to the phenomenon of literary language, for it opens a gap between ordinary and literary language or between literature and the world.

11 Lubomír Doležel, *Heterocosmica. Fiction and Possible Worlds*, Baltimore: Johns Hopkins University Press, 1998, p. 138. In the preceding paragraph he explains his use of the notion of intensionality: "Literary texts thrive precisely on exploiting the semantic differences of expressions with the same informational content, revealing the vacuity of the notion of intensional equivalence (synonymy). They demonstrate that intension is necessarily linked to texture, to the form (structuring) of its expression; it is constituted by those meanings, which the verbal sign acquires through and in texture." Doležel's notion of intensionality seems to put less emphasis on preservation of truth, but rather on preservation of (literary) meaning.

12 David Schalkwyk has pointed at this aspect in his "Fiction as 'Grammatical' Investigation: A Wittgensteinian Account," *Journal of Aesthetics and Art Criticism* 53 (1995), 287–98. "Fiction," he states, "can make telling revelations: not by producing empirical discoveries, but by bringing into relief the surface connections – the conceptual relations of 'grammar' – that are always already 'there' in our practices" (296f).

13 Richard Rorty, "Heidegger, Kundera, and Dickens," *Essays on Heidegger and Others. Philosophical Papers, vol. 2*, Cambridge: Cambridge University Press, 1991, pp. 66–82, p. 80.

14 Ibid, p. 81.

15 Marjorie Perloff develops an argument along these lines in her *Wittgenstein's Ladder. Poetic Language and the Strangeness of the Ordinary*, Chicago: University of Chicago Press, 1996. Discussing Wittgenstein's famous statement that "philosophy ought really to be written only as a *form of poetry*" (*CV* 24) she states: "Presumably the converse would be equally valid: 'Poetry ought really to be written as a *form of philosophy*.' What this proposition implies is that poetry is not, as is commonly thought (and as Wittgenstein himself seems to have thought when he commented directly on specific poems), the *expression* or externalization of inner feeling; it is, more accurately, the critique of that expression" (184). Perloff slightly deviates from Winch's translation in: Ludwig Wittgenstein, *Culture and Value*, G.H.V. Wright (ed.), trans. by P. Winch, Chicago: Chicago University Press, 1980. Cited in the text as *CV*.

16 David Schalkwyk makes this point when he remarks that it "is because criteria are circumstance-dependent that longer genres of fiction (drama, the novel, or bodies of verse such as Shakespeare's sonnets) are especially suited for their extended exploration." ("Fiction as 'Grammatical' Investigation," op. cit., p. 296.)

17 The contrast between knowledge and acknowledgment was famously explored by Stanley Cavell in his "Knowing and Acknowledging," *Must We Mean What We Say?*, New York: Scribner, 1969, pp. 267–353. For the application of this distinction to the philosophy of literature, cf. John Gibson, "Between Truth and Triviality," *British Journal of Aesthetics* 43 (2003), 224–37.

18 Colin Lyas, "Wittgensteinian Intentions," Gary Iseminger (ed.) *Intention and Interpretation*, Philadelphia: Temple University Press, 1992, pp. 132–51.

19 Ludwig Wittgenstein, *Culture and Value* Blackwell, Oxford, 1980. Cited in the text as CV.

20 I want to thank Alex Burri, John Gibson, Daniel Müller Nielaba, Melania Parisi, and Luca Pocci, for illuminating discussions and for their helpful comments on earlier drafts of this text.

Part I

PHILOSOPHY AS A KIND OF LITERATURE/LITERATURE AS A KIND OF PHILOSOPHY

INTRODUCTORY NOTE TO "THE *INVESTIGATIONS*' EVERYDAY AESTHETICS OF ITSELF"

Stanley Cavell

More than any other single work, Wittgenstein's *Philosophical Investigations* has held out for me the promise of philosophy as a distinct, present activity to which I felt I had something to contribute. My encounter with it (which was at first fruitless – it took the intervention of the work of my teacher J. L. Austin, and a certain dissatisfaction with that intervention, in particular with Austin's dismissal of the significance of skepticism, to overcome my sense of the *Investigations* as a kind of unsystematic pragmatism) came at a time when many young readers of Wittgenstein's text believed Wittgenstein's apparent claim (more apparently unequivocal in the *Tractatus* than in the *Investigations*) that he had solved all the problems of philosophy that were open to solution, and accordingly abandoned the subject, sometimes intellectual life altogether. The effect upon me, when it came, was rather the opposite. The problems of philosophy – above all the problem of philosophy, philosophy as a problem – became live for me as if for the first time. Suppose it were true, as Wittgenstein early and late has been taken to assert, that the problems of philosophy arise from a misunderstanding of our language. What could be a more intimate study of human self-defeat – humanity distinguished, for many, from the rest of creation by its possession of language – than to seek to learn how, and why, for millennia mankind has engaged in tormenting itself in the creation of false systems of reason; how and why, as Kant puts the matter at the opening of *The Critique of Pure Reason*, human reason suffers the fate of asking itself questions that it can neither ignore nor answer?

Kant's answer to this question, and his attempt to create an intellectual structure to forestall this form of torment, stands as a great, for some the greatest, achievement of modern philosophy, although it has been under continuous attack since the decade of Kant's death. My first essay at getting something of my response to Wittgenstein into communicable form ("The Availability of Wittgenstein's Later Philosophy," the second piece in *Must We Mean What We Say?*, hence the second piece of published work that I still use) uncovers the connection with Kant and proposes explicitly, but with little characterization, the link between Wittgenstein's transfiguration of Kant's perception of the fate of human reason and the undisguised literary claims, let's call them, that

Wittgenstein's text continuously presses upon its reader's attention. I suppose I already sensed that the communication between reason's struggle with itself and the eruption of an expressive range of language generally associated with the work literature does, was part of a sense that, instead of Kant's attempt to confine or restrain the insatiability or perverseness of reason's ambition (which serves to increase its temptation to know all), philosophy's task should be rather to air the ambition.

In Wittgenstein's practice (in the work that goes into *Philosophical Investigations*), this means coming to think and write within persistent earshot of reason's dissatisfaction with itself, in the absence of any assurance that reason's limits can be penned along, or within, the totality of points at which it may find itself to stray (the points are as endless as the occasions of desire, as the promptings of speech), but only with the conviction that at each point it has the power to catch itself, draw even with its experience, for the moment. But then reason has to be refigured, not as something that as such must be limited, but as something still not discovered, as it were still outstanding, like a debt. Or like my self, which is always and never what I am.

Where Kant speaks of reason's laws as providing the conditions of a world of what we can know as objects, Wittgenstein speaks of returning to the world of the ordinary (returning from metaphysical intensities desiring to transgress our everyday requirements of exchange), a world in which each occupant has its conditions – this chair, this cow, this coin, this hand, this handle, this beetle, this rose, this aroma, this construction of stone or wood, this imaginary rubble, this mythical field of ice, this friction, this man in pain, this god, this ardor, this doubt, this equation, this drawing, this face. The liberation I felt getting into Wittgenstein's text, and for which I remain grateful, was its demonstration, or promise, that I can think philosophically about anything I want, or have, to think about, not merely what I am able to formulate in a particular way (which is what so much of philosophy as it was conveyed to me in school sought to impress me with – indispensably, but somehow, always, suspiciously). Now I could be impressed with anything my language is impressed by – if somehow, often, with suspicion; but then again, as often, with wonder. And now I have the sense of approaching from another direction what the *Tractatus* means in saying that the world is my world. I might accordingly learn how to say, with much of philosophy, that it is not mine, that, as Nietzsche puts the matter, the philosopher lives in opposition to today (Emerson having said, in aversion to conformity). Learn, I mean, how to be responsible for both gestures.

One way I have put such thoughts is to say that Wittgenstein's *Investigations* became for me not simply an object of interpretation but a means of interpretation. This formulation, however, is doubly insufficient. First, because the transition of object to means is apt to be true of any text to the degree that one takes it seriously. Second, because any text to whose understanding the *Investigations* (for example) contributes is one to whose interpretation it in some measure submits. But what confers the right to such intertextuality? And what shows it to be pertinent or perverse, trivial or deep, evasive or responsive? I have, for example, variously troubled over the years to emphasize the role of becoming lost, hence of finding oneself, or say one's footing, in the *Investigations*, and set it against the loss of way, or the question of finding one's way, at the opening of Emerson's essay "Experience," and of the Introduction to Nietzsche's *Genealogy of Morals*, and of the first Canto of *The Divine Comedy*. But this, as Wittgenstein roughly says about the act of naming, so far *says* nothing. (Cf. *Investigations*, §49: "Naming is so far not a move in the language-game – any more than putting a piece in its place on the board is a move in chess. We may say: *nothing* has so far been done, when a thing has been named.") Does my placing of these texts so much as mark specific places, within texts whose powers to inspire commentary can seem infinite, at which something of some interest is *to be* said? This at best remains to be seen.

But isn't the question *what* at best might be seen? What is the point of going over such knots of culture – for some tiresome, for others lurid? Well, for me, for example, expansiveness and illumination here would show that a work that represents, controversially, a contemporary site of philosophy (Wittgenstein) reaches back to a signal search for God (Dante), as well as to the assertion that the search has ended in trauma (Nietzsche), through a work willing to teach the suffering of America's perpetual discovery and loss of itself (Emerson). And because the philosophy in question is one whose originality is partly a function of its stress on the idea of the ordinary or everyday, especially its way of allowing philosophy's return to what it calls the everyday to show that what we accept as the order of the ordinary is a scene of obscurity, self-imposed as well as other-imposed, fraudulent, you might say metaphysical (the thing Emerson calls conformity and Nietzsche calls philistinism), it links its vision with aspects of the portraits Kierkegaard and Marx and Heidegger and Walter Benjamin make of what Mill calls our mutual intimidation, what Proust, we might say, shows to be our mutual incorporation.

Is this swirl of anachronism supposed to be a *benefit*, namely of inserting philosophy back from a profession of expertise into the mess of culture? But of course it is already inescapably inserted, whether professional philosophy is offended or not. And as for anachronism, culture is itself made of anachronistically buckled strata of past and present, as the self is. The philosophy I seek is not one that promises an always premature unity but one that allows me in principle to get from anywhere, any present desire, to anywhere else that I find matters to me.

I have from the first time I undertook to teach *Philosophical Investigations* sought to articulate my sense of it as a work of modernity, one that perpetually questions its medium and its sense of a break with the past. That I had turned to philosophy after a crisis in pursuing a life as a musician is no doubt in the background here. A chief contribution my text to follow here seeks to achieve, in presenting what I call the *Investigations*' aesthetics of itself, is to discover a contemporary form of Kant's portrayal of reason's self-torment that shows it, in

Wittgenstein's work, to elaborate into a portrait of the modern subject, which is to say, the reader for whom it understands itself as written.

If the *Investigations* occupies for me a privileged place among the texts I call means of interpretation, it is perhaps because as I go on learning to ask for further conditions of this text's existence – its form as fragments, its palette of terms of criticism, its sparseness of theoretical terms, as if every term of ordinary language can be shown to harbor the power of a theoretical term – I continue to find responses in its greatly compressed pages (Wittgenstein calls Part I "the precipitate" of sixteen years of philosophical work) that surprise me, that open spaces of understanding, and of further understanding, that are models of what I seek in finding my way in any text that elicits my interest, that is, in anything that is for me an object of interpretation. And nowhere more instructively than in its demonstration that an interpretation, however persistent it must at its best be, comes to an end somewhere – as though, precisely unlike the idea of a formal proof, philosophy's beginning and ending are matters of contestable judgment. And as though philosophical persistence is to an unavoidable extent a matter of awaiting the dawning of dissatisfaction with whatever end of invention one has so far arrived at. Emerson calls this patience.

1

THE *INVESTIGATIONS'* EVERYDAY AESTHETICS OF ITSELF

Stanley Cavell

We have all, I assume, heard it said that Wittgenstein is a writer of unusual powers. Perhaps that is worth saying just because the powers are so unusual, anyway in a philosopher, and of his time and place. But why is this worth repeating – I assume we have all heard it repeated – since as far as I know no one has denied it? Evidently the repetition expresses an uncertainty about whether Wittgenstein's writing is essential to his philosophizing; whether, or to what extent, the work of the one coincides with the work of the other. If you conceive the work of philosophy as, let's say, argumentation, then it will be as easy to admire as to dismiss the writing – to admire it, perhaps, as a kind of ornament of the contemporary, or near contemporary, scene of professional philosophy, hence as something that lodges no philosophical demand for an accounting. But if you cannot shake an intuition, or illusion, that more is at issue than ornamentation (not that that issue is itself clear), and you do not wish to deny argumentation, or something of the sort, as internal to philosophy, then a demand for some philosophical accounting of the writing is, awkwardly, hard to lose.

I describe what I am after as the *Investigations'* everyday aesthetics of itself to register at once that I know of no standing aesthetic theory that promises help in understanding the literariness of the *Investigations* – I mean the literary conditions of its philosophical aims – and to suggest the thought that no work will be powerful enough to yield this understanding of its philosophical aims aside from the *Investigations* itself. Does this mean that I seek an aesthetics within it? I take it to mean, rather, that I do not seek an aesthetic concern of the text that is separate from its central work. My idea here thus joins the idea of an essay of mine, "Declining Decline," which tracks the not unfamiliar sense of moral or religious fervor in the *Investigations* and finds that its moral work is not separate from its philosophical work, that something like the moral has become for it, or become again, pervasive for philosophy. (As Emerson words the idea in "Self-Reliance": "Character teaches above our wills [the will of the person and of the person's writing]. Men imagine that they communicate their virtue or vice only by overt actions, and do not see that virtue or vice emit a breath every moment.")

There is something more I want here out of the idea of an ordinary aesthetics. The *Investigations* describes its work, or the form its work takes, as that of perspicuous presentation (§122), evidently an articulation of a task of writing. And it declares the work of its writing as "lead[ing] words back from their metaphysical to their everyday use" (§116), a philosophically extraordinary commitment not only to judge philosophy by the dispensation of the ordinary, but to place philosophy's conviction in itself in the hands, or handling, of ordinary words. But we also know that Wittgenstein invokes, indeed harps on, the idea of the perspicuous as internal to the work of formal proofs. Then is his use of the idea, in this one section of the *Investigations* that explicitly invokes it, meant to signal an ideal of lucidity and conviction that he cannot literally expect in a work made of returns to ordinary words? Yet he goes on in the next paragraph to insist: "The concept of perspicuous presentation is of fundamental significance for us. It earmarks our form of presentation, how we look at things." So is the idea that the writing of the *Investigations* contains the equivalent, or some analogy or allegory, of proofs? Or that it is meant to project arguments of formal rigor, even though its surface form of presentation does not, to say the least, spell them out? How else could we account for the influence of this work, such as it is, in institutions of professional philosophy?

My somewhat different proposal is that Wittgenstein is claiming for the ordinary its own possibility of perspicuousness, as different from that of the mathematical as the experience of an interesting theorem is from the experience of an interesting sentence. But how can this be? Doesn't Wittgenstein's idea of the perspicuous just *mean*, as it were, the look of a formal proof? My proposal is rather to conceive that Wittgenstein once hit off an experience of the convincingness, perhaps of the unity, of a proof, with the concept of perspicuousness; and for some reason, later (or earlier), he hits off an experience of a unity, or a reordering, of ordinary words with the same concept, as if discovering a new manifestation of the concept in discovering something new about the ordinary. He had said, in the section in question: "A perspicuous presentation is a means to just that understanding which consists in 'seeing connections'." Understanding a proof surely requires seeing connections. So does understanding a unity among sentences. Is there an interesting connection to be seen between these?

I am encouraged to look for a specific manifestation of perspicuousness in the ordinary by the passage (§89) in which Wittgenstein asks: "In what sense is logic something sublime?" His answer, as I understand it, expresses one way of seeing his turn from the thoughts of the *Tractatus* to those of the *Investigations*. I almost never allow myself an opinion about the *Tractatus*, in which I do not know my way about. But I cannot avoid just this instance now. The *Investigations* answers: "For there seemed to pertain to logic a peculiar depth. Logic lay, it seemed, at the bottom of all the sciences." And then appears one of those dashes between sentences in this text, which often mark a moment at which a fantasy is allowed to spell itself out. It continues: "For logical investigation explores the essence of all things. It seems to see to the ground of things and is not meant to trouble itself over whether this or that actually happens." Is Wittgenstein fighting the fantasy or granting it? Then a larger dash, and following it: "[*Logic*] takes its rise, not from an interest in the facts of nature, nor from a need to grasp causal connections, but from a striving to understand the foundation, or essence, of everything empirical." But again, is this good or bad, illusory or practical? Then finally: "Not, however, as if to this end we had to hunt out new facts, it is much more essential for our investigation that we want to learn nothing *new* from it. We want to *understand* something that is already open to view. For *this* is what we seem in some sense not to understand." So something in this philosophical fantasizing turns out to be practical after all, and something that winds up sounding like a self-description of the *Investigations*.

More such self-descriptions are concentrated in the ensuing several dozen sections of the book (§§90–133). Logic, however, drops out – that is, as a formal ideal, not to say as the ultimate formal systematization of the unity of knowledge. But the *aim* of philosophy expressed by that fantasy of logic remains, if transformed, the mark of philosophy's intellectual seriousness. It demands an extraordinary understanding, but not of something new; it is not in competition with science. And the aim is still essence, the ground of everything empirical, but the means to this ground is as open to view, and as ungrasped, as what there is to be grasped essentially. The means is the ordinariness of our language. And there is no single or final order in which ordinariness and its articulation of essence is to be ordered, or presented, or formed – we might even say, reformed. The new route to the old aim Wittgenstein calls the grammatical investigation. What is its form, or order?

Wittgenstein says (§123): "A philosophical problem has the form: 'I cannot find mysel'" (as I might translate "Ich kenne mich nicht aus"). And I have said this is kin to the loss Dante suffers (loss of way) faced with the dark wood in the middle of life's journey, as he begins to narrate the journey. The implication of the connection is that Wittgenstein is here marking the beginning of something, to which it gives a certain form. Religion calls a similar beginning perdition. Such a moment marks the place from which Emerson, beginning "Experience," calls out, "Where do we find ourselves?" It is, accordingly, as the philosophical answer to this disorientation that Wittgenstein proposes the idea of perspicuousness – outside the realm of proof, and by means of a return to what he calls the ordinary, or "home" (I place the quotes to remind ourselves that we may never have been there). The section that names perspicuous presentation mentions "intermediate cases," hence suggests that the idea of understanding as "seeing connections" is one of supplying language games – as in the string of cases of "reading" (§156–178), or in comparing the grammar of the word "knows" to that of "can" or "in a position to" and also to "understands" (§150), or, more generally, in showing grammatical derivation, as of the grammar of "meaning" in part from "explaining the meaning," or in showing grammatical difference, as between "pointing to an object" and "pointing to the color of an object." Perspicuous representation is accordingly the end of a philosophical problem that has *this* form of beginning.

23

But the methods of language games, though perhaps the most famous form in which the *Investigations* is known, at least outside the precincts of professional philosophy, put no more literary pressure on language – they pose no greater problem for aesthetics – than Austin's appeal to what we should say when (not that his prose is easy to characterize – I have said something about that in taking up Derrida's treatment of *How To Do Things with Words*). I mean, it is not in this precinct of the perspicuous that the sense arises of accounting philosophically for the genius of this writing. What the provision of language games requires is apparently no more than the common mastery of a language. (It is a matter of asking for and providing, for example, the difference between doing something by accident and by mistake, or between seeing bread and seeing all the signs of bread, or between knowing the other from his or her behavior and knowing the other *only* from his or her behavior.) The genius would come in seeing how this mastery, and equally the loss of mastery, calls for philosophy. If writing of a certain character is essential to displaying what is thus seen, then this writing is essential to the philosophical work of the *Investigations*. And it, too, then would have to fall under the concept of perspicuous presentation.

Sometimes the movement from being lost to finding oneself happens at a stroke – of a pen, of genius – in any case without the means or intermediary methods of grammatical investigations. Here I adduce moments expressed in the words of such gestures as these: "What is your aim in philosophy?" "To show the fly the way out of the fly-bottle" (§309); "Why can't my right hand give my left hand money?" (§268); "We have got on to slippery ice where there is no friction and so in a certain sense the conditions are ideal, but also, just because of that, we are unable to walk" (§107); "If I have exhausted my grounds I have reached hard rock, and my spade is turned" (§217); "The human body is the best picture of the human soul" (p. 178); "If I am inclined to suppose that a mouse has come into being by spontaneous generation out of grey rags and dust, I shall do well to examine those rags very closely to see how a mouse may have hidden in them, how it may have got there and so on....But first we must learn to understand what it is that opposes such an examination of details in philosophy" (§52); "(Uttering a word is like striking a note on the keyboard of the imagination)" (§6); "But if you are *certain*, isn't it that you are shutting your eyes in front of doubt?" "They are shut" (p. 224). These are patently, all but ostentatiously, "literary" gestures of the *Investigations*, outstanding in the sense of that work as cultivating its literary grounds. How precisely?

I note that there is pleasure to be taken in them; and a shock of freedom to be experienced; and an anxiety of exposure (since they treacherously invite false steps of the reader: I have heard the observation about the keyboard of the imagination taken as Wittgenstein's own opinion about words, not as the spelling out of a fantasy); and they are at once plain and sudden, especially in context – let us say brilliant. But our question is whether they are essential to the work of the *Investigations*, which is before all to ask whether they represent work. So if we observe that the pleasure comes in being liberated from an unexpressed, apparently inexpressible, mood – call this being given expression – hence that it has required finding or inventing a specific order of words, then we have to ask whether providing expression is a form of work. The lines or gestures I just cited require a specific talent to compose, one perhaps dangerous to philosophy, or distracting; and they require a matching aesthetic effort to assess: for example, to see whether their pleasure and shock and anxiety are functions of their brilliance. Differences in the work philosophy does and the work that art does need not be slighted if it turns out that they cross paths, even to some extent share paths – for example, where they contest the ground on which the life of another is to be examined, call it the ground of therapy.

Let us approach the question of literary necessity in the *Investigations* by following out my suggestion just now that such lines are to be understood as further manifestations of what Wittgenstein calls perspicuousness and identifies as a distinguishing mark of his writing. To capture the pervasiveness and the specificity of the experience in question (the pleasure, liberation, anxiety), it will help to remember that texts' recurrence to scenes of pain, especially those of what I call inexpressiveness, from whose fixation the order of words in the ostentatiously literary gestures I cited offer freedom. I took this tack in a course I offered with Hilary Putnam in 1996, referred to earlier, prompted by my commitment to the class to go over, for the first time in such a setting, aspects of my own writing on the *Investigations* in Part One and Part Four of *The Claim of Reason*.

An air of pathos struck me – long before the description, near the opening of Part Four, of the fantasy of inexpressive privacy or suffocation – as gathering intensity at the close of both Chapters 4 and 5, which end Part One. There we find stifled screams in a Hemingway hospital ward; Keats's mourning for a dead poet; images of starving or abandoned children. My surprise was greeted with certain smiles of recognition from a number of the graduate students present, as though I was tardy in my literary self-observations. Naturally I attributed this pathos to the pathos of the *Investigations* itself, specifically to its portrait of – or its conviction that there is something to be seen as – the human condition, say the human as conditioned by the present stage of history.

Part of my sense of the *Investigations* as a modernist work is that its portrait of the human is recognizable as one of the modern self, or, as we are given to say, the modern subject. Since we are considering a work of philosophy, this portrait will not be unrelated to a classical portrait of the subject of philosophy, say that to be found in Plato's *Republic*, where a human soul finds itself chained in illusion, so estranged from itself and lost to reality that it attacks the one who comes to turn it around and free it by a way of speaking to it, and thus inciting it to seek the pleasures of the clear light of day. A difference of the modern self is that, no longer recognizing itself in Plato's environment, and subject to a thousand impertinent interventions, it no longer surmises its intelligibility or companionability. So the kind of work proposed in the text of the *Investigations* will at first seem to the one for whom it is addressed – the modern philosophical subject – obvious, uninteresting, remote. Then if for some reason it persists in considering the work, it may begin to divine its own voice there. Everything depends on the specificity with which its portrait is drawn.

I have begun specifying it in the philosophically recurrent sense – or the recurrence of philosophy in recognizing the sense – of lostness to oneself. This beginning of philosophy is related, I believe, to the feeling of philosophizing as an effort to achieve the indestructible (§55) but which perceives a Wittgensteinian experience of therapy initially as the destruction of everything great and important (§118), as if human self-destructiveness is at war with itself in philosophy. This is equally expressed in the sense that our ideal encloses us, suffocates us (§103). I have more than once noted the human sense of disappointment with the human, in the form of a disappointment with the language it is given ("A name ought really to signify a simple" (§39)); this pairs with human perverseness ("Why does it occur to one to want to make precisely this word into a name, when it evidently is *not* a name? –That is just the reason" (§39)). Then no wonder "The philosopher's treatment of a question is like the treatment of an illness" (§255), which Wittgenstein articulates as a sickness of the understanding (*Remarks on Mathematics*, p. 157) as well as a sickness of the will ("Why does it occur to us to *want* to make this word …?"; "[*Philosophical problems*] are solved … through an insight into the workings of language [*which takes place precisely*] despite a drive to misunderstand them" (§109)). Yet philosophy itself – the human creature in its grip – remains tormented, and must learn to give itself peace, which means to break itself off (§133). Add to these features the *Investigations'* beginning with (apart from an unnoticed child, and a curiously mechanical errand) a succession of primitive builders, and the strangeness of the human to itself is always before us – epitomized in its philosophizing and in the uncertainty of its grip on itself, or on the concept of itself (is it a *language* the builders have? is it *words* they use? if I do not know such things about them, how can I know them about myself?).

How shall we place the farther shore of perspicuousness, the literary? Let us say it is, alluding to Kant, a standpoint from which to see the methods of the *Investigations*, their leading words home, undoing the charms of metaphysics, a perspective apart from which there is no pressing issue of spiritual fervor, whether felt as religious, moral, or aesthetic. Standpoint implies an alternative, a competing standpoint, a near shore. For professional philosophers this shore is that of philosophical "problems" – in the Preface to *Philosophical Investigations* Wittgenstein lists them as "[*subjects such as*] the concepts of meaning, of understanding, of a proposition, of logic, the foundations of mathematics, states of consciousness, and other things." Without this shore, the *Investigations* would not press upon, and not belong in, an academic philosophical curriculum. Because of the farther shore, its belonging is, and should be, uneasy.

I wish I could make the two shores equally palpable, and sufficiently so to make questions as to which shore is the more important seem as foolish to us as it must seem to the river of philosophy that runs between. One without the other loses the pivot of the ordinary, the pressure of everyday life; one without the other thus loses, to my way of thinking, the signature of the *Investigations*.

There remains a question of priority. From each shore the other is almost ignorable, and each imagines itself to own the *seriousness* of the *Investigations'* work. When the farther ignores the rigors of the near, it consigns philosophy to the perennial, the perhaps customary eternal. When the near ignores the yearning for the farther, it merely conforms to the customary institutional demands of the university, hence risks consigning philosophy to present intellectual fashion. Each position has its advanced and its debased versions.

To count, as I do here, on a willingness to maintain a continuity between near and far, is to count on a certain way of following the continuities implied between the pleasures I claimed for certain literary gestures in the *Investigations* and the portrait of human pathos I sketched from it. The way of following requires a willingness to recognize in oneself the moments of strangeness, sickness, disappointment, self-destructiveness, perversity, suffocation, torment, lostness that are articulated in the language of the *Investigations*, and to recognize in its philosophizing that its pleasures (they will have to reach to instances of the ecstatic) will lie in the specific forms and moments of self-recovery it proposes – of familiarity (hence uncanniness, since the words of recovery were already familiar, too familiar), of soundness, of finitude, of the usefulness of friction, of acknowledgment, of peace.

But what kind of pleasure could be essential to philosophy, and worthy of it? I think it will help us find an answer if we pick up more concretely Wittgenstein's reiterated observation in the *Remarks on Mathematics* that "Proof must be perspicuous" (quoted in *This New Yet Unapproachable America*, p. 16), and look at a proof. Coming from me it had better be simple. I take an example remembered from Euclidean geometry, the earliest discourse in which I remember experiencing something like ecstasy in arriving at a conclusion. I assume it is to be proved that the sum of the inner angles of a triangle equals 180 degrees, the measure of a straight line. I draw a triangle and construct through its apex a line parallel to its base:

Proof: Assuming that we have proven that opposite interior angles of a transverse are equal, we know that the lower left angle is equal to the upper left angle

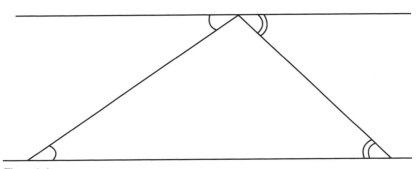

Figure 1.1

beneath the parallel, and that the lower right angle is equal to the upper right angle beneath the parallel. Now since the remaining angle at the vertex of the triangle is identical with the remaining angularity of the line, namely that between those upper left and right angles, the line's angularity is equal to the sum of the three angles of the triangle; which is to say, the sum is 180 degrees. QED. Look at it. The three angles precisely exhaust the line. This is perspicuous. It is a glimpse at the ground of everything empirical.

The obvious predicates of this experience remain, I find, pleasure of some kind, and a kind of liberation or relief, and, we might now specify, a sense of arrival, or completeness, as of relationship perfected, not finished but permanent. As well, therefore, as manifesting "the understanding which consists in 'seeing connections'," as in the section naming perspicuous representation (§122), the proof also manifests, it seems, what Wittgenstein calls, a few sections later, "the clarity that we aspire to," about which he says, "[it] is indeed *complete* clarity." Then he goes on to characterize this completeness in ways that no longer seem pertinent to such a proof as I have remembered from Euclidean geometry. "But this simply means that the philosophical problems" – that is, a certain sense of being at a loss – "should *completely* disappear....The real discovery is the one that makes me capable of breaking off philosophizing when I want to. The one that brings philosophy peace." We don't seem to require a background of philosophical torment to ask for such proofs and to receive their pleasure. This difference evidently goes with the fact that a proof is a structure that tells me something is over, a bottom reached, I do not have to consult my desire, there would be no intellectual pertinence in consulting it, to determine whether I may break off this thinking. The completed proof breaks it off. It affords me ecstasy not preceded by torment (but perhaps by the ups and downs of wonder). That is the beauty of it.

We seem to have rearrived at the question whether the concept of perspicuousness invited by the experience of certain formal proofs is further invited by a certain unity or reordering of ordinary words – supposing this to be something Wittgenstein means by his discovery of (non-formal) moments of complete clarity, ordinary words, that is, which are not meant to line up as premises to a conclusion. (Whatever structures of this kind are invited by the *Investigations*, and however welcome one may find them, they would raise no new problem about their source of clarity of the sort Wittgenstein describes himself as striving for.) Is there, perhaps, an ordering of words that is its own bottom line, sees to its own ground? Would we, I mean, be prepared to describe any such ordering in this way?

In answering affirmatively, I need a name for forms of ordinary words that I will claim partake of (satisfy the criteria of) completeness, pleasure, and the sense of breaking something off (the chief marks of perspicuous representation) – words that epitomize, separate a thought, with finish and permanence, from the general range of experience. To such a (non-formal) form of words I give the unsurprising name of the aphoristic. Having claimed that Wittgenstein's reconception of philosophy, or say of the form of a philosophical problem, required an extension of the discovery of formal perspicuousness to a discovery of non-formal perspicuousness, I extend this (or really just make explicit an extension within the insistence of Wittgenstein's writing) from the work of what Wittgenstein calls grammatical methods or treatments of language to the primitive fact of ordinary language, that it express desire, the point of language named by Augustine at the close of the citation with which Wittgenstein opens the *Investigations*.

So here's the surprising premise in my argument for taking Wittgenstein's writing as essential to his philosophizing, the manner to the method: The concept of the perspicuous, governed by the criteria of completeness, pleasure, and breaking off, is as surely invited by contexts of aphorism as it is by those of proof and of grammatical investigation.

Now this may seem, at best, to show only that the aphoristic belongs in *some* sense to the *Investigations*, not that it is essential to a manner of writing held to be essential to this philosophizing. I look at it somewhat differently. The power of grammatical investigations in *Philosophical Investigations* is a function of their leading a word back from its metaphysical capture by the appeal to its everyday use. The power of the aphoristic is a function of its granting the appeal, even in a sense the reality, of the metaphysical. It is a mode of reflecting the clarity brought by grammatical methods, one that in itself, as itself, exhibits this clarity, together with a satisfaction or acknowledgment of the obscurity from which clarity comes. To say that this exhibition is essential to the work of the *Investigations* is to say that appeals to the ordinary which fail this mode of reflection are not Wittgensteinian appeals, they do not take their bearing from the power to make philosophical problems completely disappear – hence appear. They do not, accordingly, express our interest in these problems, and so leave us subjected to them without understanding what kind of creatures we are, what our life form as talkers is, that we are thus fascinatable, that philosophy is seductive. (The philosophical sensibility here is radically different from Austin's.)

Since this claim for the aphoristic, say for its mode of expressiveness, rests upon experience, the claim's own perspicuousness depends upon attracting to itself sufficient pertinent experience. (The role of experience is critical. I am not supplying evidence for a hypothesis, but examples which call for a particular concept.) I will in the time left undertake to provide objects of this experience, noting that in the *Investigations* the aphoristic does not on the whole take the form of free-standing aphorisms (as in the cases of the fly and the fly-bottle or the body as the best picture of the soul), but is mostly directed, as I have indicated, to reflecting details of its methodicalness, its searching out criteria, articulating grammar, spelling out fantasies, calling attention to a fixated picture, presenting intermediate cases. To isolate the experience in independent aphorisms – to show that it is reliably housed in specific, recognizable linguistic structures – I will go outside *Philosophical Investigations* to Wittgenstein's aphorisms that find their way into Professor Von Wright's miscellany translated under the title *Culture and*

Value and select ten of them to pair with ten aphorisms composed between the last years of the eighteenth century and the end of the first half of the nineteenth. This is where Wittgenstein, early in the entries of *Culture and Value*, places his aspiration:

> I often wonder whether my cultural ideal is new, i.e. contemporary, or whether it comes from the time of Schumann. At least it strikes me as being a continuation of that idea, though of course not the continuation that actually happened. Thereby the second half of the nineteenth century is excluded.

(The excluded half-century includes Frege, *Tristan* and the future of music, Nietzsche, and, for example, Helmholtz.)

I present the ten pairs without beforehand identifying which member is Wittgenstein's.

I   (a) One age misunderstands another; and a *petty* age misunderstands all the others in its own nasty way.
(b) The age isn't ready for it, they always say. Is that a reason why it shouldn't happen?

II   (a) A mediocre writer must beware of too quickly replacing a crude, incorrect expression with a correct one. By doing so he kills his original idea, which was at least still a living seedling.
(b) How many authors are there among writers? Author means creator.

III   (a) Each of the sentences I write is trying to say the whole thing.
(b) In poetry too every whole can be a part and every part really a whole.

IV   (a) There is a pathos peculiar to the man who is happily in love as well as to the one who is unhappily in love.
(b) A so-called happy marriage is to love as a correct poem is to an improvised song.

V   (a) The idea is worn out by now and no longer usable....Like silver paper, which can never quite be smoothed out again once it has been crumpled.
(b) Isn't everything that is capable of becoming shopworn already twisted or trite to begin with?

VI   (a) If in life we are surrounded by death, so too in the health of our intellect we are surrounded by madness.
(b) Like animals, the spirit can only breathe in an atmosphere made up of life-giving oxygen mixed with nitrogen. To be unable to tolerate and under-

stand this fact is the essence of foolishness; to simply not want to do so is madness.

VII (a) Is this the sense of belief in the Devil: that not everything that comes to us as an inspiration comes from what is good?

(b) On my saying, "What have I to do with the sacredness of traditions, if I live wholly from within?" my friend suggested, – "But these impulses may be from below, not from above." I replied, "They do not seem to me to be such; but if I am the Devil's child, I will live then from the Devil."

VIII (a) My account will be hard to follow: because it says something new but still has egg-shells from the old view sticking to it.

(b) You're always demanding new ideas? Do something new, then something new might be said about it.

IX (a) One might say: Genius is *talent exercised with courage.*

(b) But one can never really have genius, only be one....Genius is actually a system of talents.

X (a) It may be that the essential thing with Shakespeare is his ease and authority and that you just have to accept him as he is if you are going to be able to admire him properly, in the way you accept nature.

(b) The simplest and most immediate questions, like Should we criticize Shakespeare's works as art or as nature?

In each case the first member of the pair is from Wittgenstein; the second is, with one exception, either from Friedrich or from August Wilhelm Schlegel (from either the *Critical* or the *Athenaeum Fragments*). That these figures take the preoccupations of Wittgenstein's sensibility deep into, or into the origin of, German Romanticism fits my sense of his continuing the Romantic's response to the psychic threat of skepticism. (The exception to the Schlegel brothers is Emerson's declaration of readiness to be, if need be, the Devil's child.)

Naturally I will not attempt to argue for the resemblance between the members of the pairs; nor even argue here that the pairs present aphorisms, as opposed to adages, or maxims of practical wisdom – beyond noting that they do not present standing, sociable responses to life's recurrences, but rather new, eccentric, personal responses, to some present crossroads of culture, characteristically marked by the recurrences of a word, as if the thought were turning on itself. ("One age misunderstands another; and a petty age misunderstands all the others in its own nasty way.") Nor shall I argue, on the basis of a score of examples, that aphorisms with this particular sense of breaking off complete fragments, so to speak, are apt to take on just these subjects – those of genius and talent, of life and death, of originality and banality, of human and animal, of madness, music, misunderstanding, religion. *Philosophical Investigations* touches on, and so continues, in its way, all of these topics – as, in its way, it continues to live on the sound of the fragment, the denial of system (while by no means the denial of the systematic).

But there is a coincidence of insight between a moment from *Culture and Value* and a moment from the *Investigations* which I find remarkable, and to bear so precisely on recent work of mine on Emersonian Perfectionism, that I will end by citing it along with a thought or two about it. It dates from 1949, four years after the Foreword to *Philosophical Investigations* was written, two years before Wittgenstein's death.

"Le style c'est l'homme," "Le style c'est l'homme même." The first expression has cheap epigrammatic brevity. The second, correct version opens up quite a different perspective. It says that a man's style is a *picture* of him.

The coincidence with the *Investigations* is – is it too obvious to mention, or too obscure to discuss? – with "The human body is the best picture of the human soul."

First let us venture a suggestion about what Wittgenstein finds cheap in the brief version – "Style is the man." Perhaps it is some resemblance to the saying "Clothes make the man," some unearned and cynical insight about the relation of social judgment to psychic reality, where the former is taken as open to view and the latter is taken to be of no interest even to the one in question. Or some resemblance to some such saying as "Life is the real work of art," which may at a stroke deny the seriousness and difficulty and beauty, such as they are, both of life and of art. How is the longer version different? – "Style is the man himself." Well, immediately it has the air of discovery in it, the winning through to an insight, both about what the man, in his way, has made out of something (a talent, a circumstance) and hence something about the character of the maker. This speaks to the image of the human body as a picture of the human soul. I do not think we need more out of the concept of the soul here than as a term for a subject's subjectivity, a thing possessed of mentality or mindedness or moodedness, one whose actions, as Heidegger roughly put it (making something of the German *Handlung* in his way), are ways of handling things (something Charlie Chaplin knew as well as Heidegger is not to happen on an assembly line). Do not need more, I mean, in order to note Wittgenstein's implied refusal of a metaphysical insistence that the body *is* the mind or the man. This insistence is ruled, in Wittgenstein's aphorism about the body as a picture, a kind of literary error, a case of poor reading. The insight of the aphorism is rather – along with an implied claim that an insight is necessary here – that every handling by the man (of an impulse or of a circumstance) is a signature, or a sketch that needs no signature for its attribution. I think this is something Nietzsche means, at the end of *The Genealogy of Morals*, when he speaks of man's being unable to empty himself of purpose and so finding a solution in taking emptiness as his purpose. The Hunger Artist conveys it somewhat differently, that being purely inexpressive is as exacting and unending a task as being purely expressive.

Allow me one further step. Prompted by Wittgenstein's reading of style as picturing the very man, I take his idea of the body's picturing to declare that his writing is (of) his body, that it is on the line, that his hand is in the manner of his text, in its melancholy accidents of reception (cf. *Walden*; I, 15) as well as in its successes with glad intentions. It is what you must expect of a perfectionist author, whose authority, such as it is, lies only in his example. Naturally, some find this attractive, others repellent; as some find it to be essential philosophy, others not.

2

"BUT ISN'T *THE SAME* AT LEAST THE SAME?"

Wittgenstein and the question of poetic translatability

Marjorie Perloff

The only way to do philosophy is to do everything twice.
(Ludwig Wittgenstein, *Lectures*)[1]

Poetry is a sort of inspired mathematics.
(Ezra Pound, *The Spirit of Romance*)[2]

We usually think of the "poetic" as that which cannot fully translate, that which is uniquely embedded in its particular language. The poetry of Rainer Marie Rilke is a case in point. The opening line of the *Duino Elegies* – *Wer, wenn ich schriee, hörte mich denn aus den Engel Ordnungen?* – has been translated into English literally dozens of times, but, as William Gass points out in his recent *Reading Rilke: Reflections on the Problems of Translation*, none of the translations seem satisfactory. Here are a few examples:

J. B. Leishman (1930) Who, if I cried, would hear me among the angelic orders?
A. J. Poulin (1977) And if I cried, who'd listen to me in those angelic orders?
Stephen Cohn (1989) Who, if I cried out, would hear me – among the ranked Angels?

Gass is very critical of these translations, but his own is, to my ear, no better: "Who if I cried, would hear me among the Dominions of Angels?"[3] The difficulty, as I have suggested elsewhere,[4] is that English syntax does not allow for the dramatic suspension of *Wer, wenn ich schriee...* and that the noun phrase *Engel Ordnungen*, which in German puts the stress, both phonically and semantically, on the angels themselves rather than their orders or hierarchies or dominions, defies effective translation. Moreover, Rilke's line contains the crucial and heavily stressed word *denn* (literally "then"), which here has the force of "Well, then" or, in contemporary idiom, "So," as in "So, who would hear me if I cried out...?" But "So" sounds too casual in the context of Rilke's urgent meditation, and translators have accordingly tended to elide the word *denn* completely, thus losing the immediacy of the question. And further: *denn* rhymes with *wenn* as well as with the first two syllables of *den En-gel*, the rhyme offsetting the intentionally contorted sound of the verb sequence *schriee, hörte* so as to create a dense sonic network which is inevitably lost in translation.

The same holds true when the German-into-English process is reversed. Here, for example, is the famous fifth stanza of Robert Lowell's "Skunk Hour":

> One dark night,
> my Tudor Ford climbed the hill's skull;
> I watched for love-cars. Lights turned down,
> they lay together, hull to hull,
> where the graveyard shelves on the town…
> My mind's not right.[5]

Manuel Pfister translates this as follows:

> In einer dunklen Nacht
> erklomm mein Tudor-Ford des Hügels Schädel;
> ich hielt Ausschau nach Liebesautos. Scheinwerfer ausgeschaltet,
> lagen sie beieinander, Rumpf bei Rumpf,
> wo der Friedhof sich zur Stadt neigt…
> Mein Geist ist wirr.[6]

This strikes me as a perfectly intelligent translation, without any of the obvious glitches we find in, say, William Gass's rendering of Rilke's *Ich verginge von seinem stärkeren Dasein* as "I would fade in the grip of that completer existence," or Stephen Cohn's, "I would die of the force of his being."[7] But what eludes Pfister is Lowell's particular tone. "One dark night," for starters, has a fairy-tale quality (as in "Once upon a time") that gives an ironic edge to the reference to St. John of the Cross's "Dark Night of the Soul" – a quality lost in the German *In einer dunklen Nacht*…. In line 2, the pun on "Tudor ("two-door") Ford disappears even though Pfister retains the absurdly pretentious brand name. And his rendition of the third line is at once too specific and too long-winded: Lowell's casual "I watched" becomes the emphatic *ich hielt Ausschau*, and *Scheinwerfer ausgeschaltet* ("headlights turned off") does not allow for the resonance of "lights" or of "turned down," which here connotes beds as well as the lights themselves. In the next line, the image of love-cars lying together *Rumpf bei Rumpf* is that of the trunks of two bodies or torsos locked together. But the punning "hull to hull" is more sinister, referring as it does to empty vessels as well as to empty plant husks. Love making, in this context, is itself a form of death. And the death motif is underscored in the next line, where the verb "shelves" suggests that the graveyard is emptying its contents (the dead) on the town itself. The force of "shelves" is dissipated in the German *neigt*, which means "inclines" or "bends." Finally, "My mind's not right" is not just the poet's *cri de Coeur* but an allusion to Satan's jealous response when he spies Adam and

Eve in *Paradise Lost*. Thus, although Pfister's translation – *Mein Geist ist wirr* – is accurate enough, the ironic self-deprecation of the poet–voyeur is absent. Then, too, Lowell's semantically charged rhyming lines – "One dark night" / "My mind's not right," or again, the rhyme "hill's skull"/ "hull to hull" – have no counterpart in Pfister's unrhymed version.

Translation, it seems, inevitably involves such slippage of meaning, especially in the case of poetry. Why is it, then, that the modernist philosopher perhaps most sensitive to such slippage, the philosopher who insisted that "*The limits of my language* mean the limits of my world" (*TLP* 5.6),[8] that indeed "Language is not *contiguous* to anything else" (*LEC 1* 112), is read around the world in dozens of different languages, without much concern as to the translatability of his propositions? I am speaking, of course, of Wittgenstein, whose writings on how words mean are not only judged to be reasonably translatable but were originally known – indeed largely continue to be known – not in the author's own German, but in the English of his Cambridge translators – G. H. von Wright, G. E. M. Anscombe, Alice Ambrose, Rush Rhees – years before his native Austria took him quite seriously. Then, too, most of these "writings" were not "writings" at all but transcriptions of Wittgenstein's Cambridge lectures as recorded by his students – lectures or, rather, "remarks" delivered in Wittgenstein's rather awkward, non-idiomatic English. Yet volumes of analysis have been based on such sentences as "A picture held us captive," where "picture" is not the only (or even necessarily the most adequate) translation of the German word *Bild*. Do the "limits of language," as Wittgenstein construed them, then have nothing to do with the actual language being used?

The answer is perhaps so obvious that we don't usually take it into account. In formulating his aphoristic propositions, Wittgenstein is not interested in connotation, nuance, or in word choice based on considerations of rhythm and sound, but in the uses of the *denotative* properties of words, phrases, and particular syntactic constructions. Hence, although, as in the case of any discourse, there are more and less adequate translations – translations that render as fully as possible the author's *intended* meaning – Wittgenstein's propositions are by no means *untranslatable* in the sense that Rilke's *Duino Elegies* or Lowell's "Skunk Hour" are untranslatable.

Consider the following from the facing pages (German–English) of *Philosophical Investigations*,[9] translated by G. E. M. Anscombe in 1958:

Warum kann ein Hund nicht Schmerzen heucheln? Ist er zu ehrlich? Könnte man einen Hund Schmerzen heucheln lehren?

Why can't a dog simulate pain? Is he too honest? Could one teach a dog to simulate pain?

(*PI* §250)

Or again:

Warum kann meine rechte Hand nicht meiner linken Geld schenken?—Meine rechte Hand kann es in meine linke geben. Meine rechte Hand kann eine Schenkungsurkunde schreiben und meine linke eine Quittung.—Aber die weitern praktischen Folgen wären nicht die einer Schenkung.

Why can't my right hand give my left hand money?—My right hand can put it into my left hand. My right hand can write a deed of gift and my left hand a receipt.—But the further practical consequences would not be those of a gift.

(*PI* §268)

And, for good measure, here is §268 in French, as translated by Jacques Bouveresse:

Pourquoi ma main droite ne peut-elle pas faire don d'une somme d'argent à ma main gauche?—Ma main droite peut rédiger un acte de donation et ma main gauche un reçu.—Mais les conséquences pratiques ultérieures ne seraient pas celles d'une donation.[10]

In such cases, the issue is neither the connotative power of synonymous words (the difference between "orders of angels," "hierarchies of angels," or "angel dominions"), nor syntactic suspension, as in Rilke's opening construction "*Wer, wenn ich schriee...*," nor punning as in Lowell's "they lay together, hull to hull." Rather, Wittgenstein is demonstrating the difficulties of pinning down the meanings of even the most ordinary, everyday words, such as *believe, hope, give, pain, right,* and *left.* If, as the central Wittgensteinian aphorism would have it, *Die Bedeutung eines Wortes ist sein Gebrauch in der Sprache* ("The meaning of a word is its use in the language," *PI* §43), then these words have no fixed denotative meaning, but depend largely on the context in which they appear. If my right hand puts money into your left hand I am *giving* you something. But if the left hand is my own, the act of putting money into it is maybe no more than a nervous habit, rather like playing with rubber bands. For both hands are mine and so the verb "to give" (*schenken, faire don*) does not seem applicable. Again, the word "pain" (*Schmerzen*) is one we all use regularly, but its simulation – perfectly understandable to a young child, who may well *simulate* pain so as to get attention or avoid having to do something – cannot be performed by a dog. And this is the case, whether the language in question is German, English, French, or Chinese.

The logical implication of the distinction I have been drawing is that *poetry* is that which deals with the connotative and tropical power of words and the rhythmic and sonic quality of phrases and sentences, whereas *philosophy* (literally "the love of wisdom") involves the conceptual and abstract language of making meaningful propositions. What, then – and this is my subject here – can Wittgenstein possibly have meant by the following entry (1933–34) in *Culture and Value?*[11]

Ich glaube meine Stellung zur Philosophie dadurch zusammengefaßt zu
haben, indem ich sagte: Philosophie dürfte man eigentlich nur dichten.
Daraus muß sich, scheint mir, ergeben, wie weit mein Denken der
Gegenwart, Zukunft, oder der Vergangenheit angehört. Denn ich habe
mich damit auch als einen bekannt, der nicht ganz kann, was er zu
können wünscht.

I think I summed up my position on philosophy when I said: One
should really only do philosophy as poetry. From this it seems to me it
must be clear to what extent my thought belongs to the present, to the
future, or to the past. For with this I have also revealed myself to be
someone who cannot quite do what he wishes he could do.

$(CV24)^{12}$

What does this enigmatic statement mean? If we note that the cognate noun
Dichtung also refers to *fictionality*, as in Goethe's title *Dichtung und Wahrheit*, where
Dichtung ("Fiction") is opposed to "Truth," why should philosophy, traditionally
the search for truth, be presented as poetic fiction? Given Wittgenstein's concern
for "meaningful" statement, aren't the two discourses antithetical? And why
should as rigorous a thinker as Wittgenstein declare that he himself is not quite
up to the task of formulating this new role for philosophy?

Wittgenstein's overt commentary on poetry sheds little light on this question.
His impatience with aesthetic theory is legendary: in the *Lectures on Aesthetics*, for
example, he declares "One might think Aesthetics is a science that tells us what's
beautiful – it's almost too ridiculous for words. I suppose this science would also
be able to tell us what sort of coffee tastes good."[13] And the notebook entries
collected in *Culture and Value* are given to statements like the following:

If I say A has beautiful eyes someone may ask me: what do you find
beautiful about his eyes, and perhaps I shall reply: the almond shape,
long eye-lashes, delicate lids. What do these eyes have in common with
a Gothic church that I find beautiful too? Should I say they make a
similar impression on me?

$(CV24)$

"The concept of 'the beautiful'," says Wittgenstein, "has caused a lot of
mischief" (CV 55). And again, "Am I to make the inane statement, 'It [*the musical
theme*] just sounds more beautiful when it is repeated'? (There you can see by the
way what a silly role the word 'beautiful' plays in aesthetics.) And yet there *is* just
no paradigm other than the theme itself" (CV 52).

At the same time, the Wittgenstein who refused to theorize about art was
quite ready, in his letters, journals, and conversations, to pronounce on a given
work with great conviction. The words *großartig* and *herrlich* appear again and
again with reference to a Mozart symphony, a Mörike poem, to Lessing's *Nathan*

the Wise, or Dostoevsky's *Brothers Karamazov*. Schubert's Quintet in C Sharp, op. 163 is *von phantastischer Großartigkeit* ("exhibits fantastic brilliance"), Mozart and Beethoven are called *die wahren Göttersöhne* ("the true sons of God"), the second movement of Beethoven's *Eroica* is *unglaublich* ("unbelievable," "fabulous"), Brahms's "Handel-variationen" *unheimlich* ("uncanny," "sublime").[14] Negative judgments are just as emphatic: Alfred Ehrenstein's poetry is *ein Hundedreck* ("dog shit"), Mahler's music is *nichts wert* ("worthless"), "the characters in the second part of 'Faust' *erregen unsere Teilnahme gar nicht* ("are ones with whom we can't identify at all").[15] The recitation of a fellow officer at Monte Cassino was so unbearable in its "false pathos," that it was like "receiving an electric shock."[16] And so on.

The almost comic vehemence of these extreme aesthetic judgments is a function of what we might call *le côté Viennoise* of Wittgenstein – the social code of his time whereby those who are *gebildet* (cultured, well educated) took it to be incumbent upon them to pronounce on the given art work or performance or concert as *großartig* or *schrecklich*, and so on. In this respect, as in his actual tastes for classical music and literature, Wittgenstein was very much of his time and place. To understand what he meant by the proposition that "One should only do philosophy as a form of *poetry*," we must, accordingly, look elsewhere – not at what Wittgenstein *said* about the poetic but at the example his own writing provides. In the Preface to what was, with the exception of the *Tractatus*, his one consciously designed book, the *Philosophical Investigations* (1953), he notes

> I have written down all these thoughts as *remarks [Bemerkungen]* short paragraphs, of which there is sometimes a fairly long chain about the same subject, while I sometimes make a sudden change, jumping from one topic to another...the essential thing was that the thoughts should proceed from one subject to another in a natural order and without breaks.
>
> After several unsuccessful attempts to weld my results together into such a whole, I realized that I should never succeed. The best that I could write would never be more *than philosophical remarks....* And this was, of course, connected with the very nature of the investigation. For this compels us to travel over a wide field of thought *criss-cross in every direction*...Thus this book is really only an album.
>
> (*PI* v, my emphasis)

Such commentary cleared the way for the publication of the many fragments found after Wittgenstein's death, some in notebooks, some on separate scraps of paper or *Zettel*, as a further assortment of Wittgenstein's remarks, this one left in a single box-file, is called. As G. H. von Wright, the editor of the *Vermischte Bemerkungen* ("Assorted Remarks," which came to be translated under the misleading title *Culture and Value*), explains:

In the manuscript material left by Wittgenstein there are numerous notes which do not belong directly with his philosophical works although they are scattered amongst the philosophical texts. Some of these notes are autobiographical, some are about the nature of philosophical activity, and some concern subjects of a general sort, such as questions about art or about religion. *It is not always possible to separate them sharply from the philosophical text...*

Some of these notes are ephemeral; others on the other hand – the majority – are of great interest. *Sometimes they are strikingly beautiful and profound.*

(Foreword, my emphasis)

Here Von Wright seems to be following Wittgenstein's own lead that "philosophy" shades into "poetry" and vice-versa. But how and why? Some early entries in *Culture and Value* (see *CV* 2–7) may be apropos:

Each morning you have to break through the dead rubble afresh so as to reach the living warm seed.

A new word is like a fresh seed sown on the ground of the discussion.

When we think of the world's future, we always mean the destination it will reach if it keeps going in the direction we can see it going in now; it does not occur to us that its path is not a straight line but a curve, constantly changing direction.

Each of the sentences I write is trying to say the whole thing, i.e. the same thing over and over again; it is as though they were all simply views of one object seen from different angles.

The thread that runs through these aphorisms and propositions is on the need for what Gertrude Stein had already called, in her "Composition as Explanation" (1926), *beginning again and again*. Truth is not something that can be uncovered; it can only be *rediscovered*, day after day. The value of breaking through the dead rubble each morning and in viewing each object from as many angles as possible is that one keeps one's mind *open*, that conclusions are always tentative, and that the process of discovery is always more important than any particular end result.

Not a straight line but a curve constantly changing direction. Theoretical formulation, generalization, moral injunction: these, for Wittgenstein, are dangerous. "Philosophy," we read in *Lectures 1930–32*, "is not a choice between different 'theories'. It is wrong to say that there is any one theory of truth, for truth is not a concept" (*LEC 1* 75). At the same time, the *process* of investigation is itself of value, provided one is able and willing to *revise* one's ideas and suppositions when

40

necessary. "I find it important in philosophizing," says Wittgenstein, "to keep changing my posture, not to stand for too long on *one* leg, so as not to get stiff. Like someone on a long up-hill climb who walks backwards for a while so as to refresh himself and stretch some different muscles" (*CV* 27). And further:

> If I am thinking just for myself, not with a view to writing a book, I jump all around the subject; this is the only natural way of thinking for me. With my thoughts forced into line, to think further is torture to me. Should I even try it?
>
> (*CV* 28)

This is, on the face of it, a very odd statement, for why should it be "torture" (*eine Qual*) simply to organize one's thoughts, to produce a coherent linear discourse? Isn't this precisely what we expect an "investigation," especially a philosophical investigation, to do?

Here we must come back to the 1933 statement about philosophy's link to poetry, in which Wittgenstein "reveals" himself as "someone who cannot quite do what he wishes he could do" (*CV* 25). If we read this mysterious paragraph biographically, it would seem that the student of Bertrand Russell, who had set out to become the mathematical logician that we find in the opening sections of the *Tractatus* (1922) – although even here the eccentricity of the numbering is a kind of poetic clinamen[17] – had discovered, by the early thirties, that his métier was a mode of writing that depended on constant revision, a casting off of the "egg-shells of the old, sticking to" his prior formulations (*CV* 43). Such writing inevitably takes the form of short fragmentary and often gnomic utterance. Not the "Tractatus" or linear discourse, not even the essay in the spirit of Montaigne or the Heideggerian meditation, but a sequence of "criss-cross" aphorisms, sometimes self-canceling or even self-contradictory. Indeed, it is discourse less designed to *say* than to be *seen as* showing something. And we think of the following aphorism in *Zettel*:

> Das Sprechen der Musik. Vergiß nicht, daß ein Gedicht, wenn auch in der Sprache der Mitteilung abgefaßt, nicht im Sprachspiel der Mitteilung verwendet wird.

> The way music speaks. Do not forget that a poem, even though it is composed in the language of information, is not used in the language-game of giving information.[18]

But, although this proposition allies poetry to philosophy (as Wittgenstein conceives it) in that neither is characterized by the information-giving function of the sciences or social sciences, our initial question remains: how can Wittgenstein's "philosophical remarks" be taken as *poetic* when they are so markedly stripped of the usual "poetic" trappings? And further: given that

41

Wittgenstein's propositions seem to have the same force whether we read them in the original German, or in English, French, or Japanese, what is the relation of "poetic" to "philosophical" meaning?

One possible answer – and this case is often made – is that what makes Wittgenstein's writing "poetic" is his use of homilies and proverbs animated by metaphors of charming and almost childlike simplicity: for example, "Talent is a spring from which fresh water is constantly flowing" (*CV* 10), "Ideas too sometimes fall from the tree before they are ripe" (*CV* 27), or the famous lines "What is your aim in philosophy?—To shew the fly the way out of the fly-bottle" in the *Investigations* (*PI* §309). But such figurative language may well have more to do with rhetorical strategy – the ethical argument that gives Wittgenstein credence as someone we can trust – than with the enigmatic nature of Wittgenstein's real questions, which, whatever homely metaphor is used for pedagogical purposes, ultimately revolve around the *literal* meaning of everyday words. "Why can't a dog simulate pain? Is he too honest?" (*PI* §250).

A better clue to Wittgenstein's concept of the poetic is provided by the distinction he repeatedly draws between *science* and *mathematics*. "Man," we read in a 1930 entry in *Culture and Value*, "perhaps populations in general – must awaken to wonder. Science is a way of putting him back to sleep" (*CV* 5). And again:

> People sometimes say they cannot make any judgment about this or that because they have not studied philosophy. This is irritating nonsense, because the assumption is that philosophy is some sort of science. And it is talked about almost as if it were the study of medicine.— But what one can say is that people who have never undertaken an investigation of a philosophical kind, as have, for example, most mathematicians, are not equipped with the right visual organs for this type of investigation or scrutiny.
>
> (*CV* 29)

Indeed, there is a "strange resemblance between a philosophical investigation (especially in mathematics) and an aesthetic one" (*CV* 25). And in 1946, when the first part of the *Philosophical Investigations* was finished, Wittgenstein noted in his journal, "My 'achievement' is very much like that of a mathematician who invents a calculus" (*CV* 50).

Invent is the key word here. Philosophy, as Wittgenstein sees it, is a form of continual re-invention with a view to making language more functional, the ideal being the precision of numbers. Language can never, of course, approximate that precision which is why the process of removing its false "signposts," its mistaken assumptions and usages, is so endlessly fascinating. And, as in mathematics, this is the case, regardless of time and place, regardless therefore of the specific language in question:

People say again and again that philosophy doesn't really progress, that we are still occupied with the same philosophical problems as were the Greeks. But the people who say this don't understand why it has to be so. It is because our language has remained the same and keeps seducing us into asking the same questions. As long as there continues to be a verb "to be" [*sein*] that looks as if it functions in the same way as "to eat" [*essen*] and "to drink" [*trinken*], as long as we still have the adjectives "identical" [*identisch*], "true" [*wahr*], "false" [*falsch*], "possible" [*möglich*], as long as we continue to talk of a river of time [*einem Fluß der Zeit*], of an expanse of space [*einer Ausdehnung des Raumes*], etc. etc., people will keep stumbling over the same puzzling difficulties and find themselves staring at something which no explanation seems capable of clearing up.

(*CV* 15)

I have put in some of the German terms here so as to show that indeed language, at the level Wittgenstein studies it, has "remained the same and keeps seducing us into asking the same questions." The *poetic*, as I remarked earlier, is not, for Wittgenstein, a question of heightening, of removing language from its everyday use by means of appropriate troping or rhetorical device. Rather, what makes philosophy poetic is its potential for invention, its status as what we now call *conceptual art* – the art that, in Sol LeWitt's words, "is made to engage the mind of the viewer rather than his eye" – or, more broadly speaking, his senses – the art, as it were, that tracks the process of *thinking* itself.[19]

In Wittgenstein's practice, conceptual art begins with the investigation of grammar, the description of the actual relations between words and phrases in the larger unit in which they are embedded. The surface word order, of course, will vary from language to language, according to the rules that language prescribes for the relationship between parts of speech. But the basic relationship of parts of speech – nouns, verbs, adjectives, prepositions – *to one another* will remain the same. Thus, if we take the earlier example "Why can't a dog simulate pain? Is he too honest?" the original German, *Warum kann ein Hund nicht Schmerzen heucheln? Ist er zu ehrlich?*, has a slightly different word order in English, where the noun "pain" follows the transitive verb whose object it is, and the negative ("can't") comes first in the sentence. But the basic syntax of the question and answer structure is perfectly clear, whichever the language. In fact, given the notion that "There are no gaps in grammar;— grammar is always complete" (*LEC 1* 16), the meanings of ordinary, everyday words become all the more tantalizing and a challenge to the philosopher as poet.

Take the following entry from *Culture and Value*:

Die Philosophen, welche sagen: "nach dem Tod wird ein zeitloser Zustand eintreten," oder, "mit dem Tod tritt ein zeitloser Zustand ein," und nicht merken, daß sie im zeitlichen Sinne "nach" und "mit" und "tritt ein" gesagt haben, und, daß die Zeitlichkeit in ihrer Grammatik liegt.

Philosophers who say: "after death a timeless state will begin," or "at death a timeless state begins," and do not notice that they have used the words "after" and "at" and "begins" in a temporal sense, and that temporality is embedded in their grammar.

(*CV* 22)

In its scrutiny of something as seemingly minor as a tense shift, a shift that in English, as in German, requires such words as "after" [*nach*] and "at" [*mit*], this little fragment – not even a complete sentence – embodies Wittgenstein's repeated insistence that "Language is not *contiguous* to anything else" (*LEC 1* 112). For it is only *inside* language that the basic paradox in question reveals itself – the paradox that the so-called "timeless state" [*zeitloser Zustand*] after death can be talked about only within the language of temporality which is ours, which is all that we have. Accordingly, as Wittgenstein had put it in the *Tractatus*, "Death is not an event in life. Death is not lived through." Indeed, "If by eternity is understood not endless temporal duration but timelessness, then he lives eternally who lives in the present" (*TLP* 6.4311).

To take another, very different consideration of temporality, consider the following analysis of the meaning of the word *interval* in *Lectures Cambridge 1932–35*:[20]

If we look at a river in which numbered logs are floating, we can describe events on land with reference to these, e.g., "*When* the 105th log passed, I ate dinner." Suppose the log makes a bang on passing me. We can say these bangs are separated by equal, or unequal, intervals. We could also say one set of bangs was twice as fast as another set. But the equality or inequality of intervals so measured is entirely different from that measured by a clock. The phrase "length of interval" has its sense in virtue of the way we determine it, and differs according to the method of measurement.

(*LEC 2* 13)

Here, Wittgenstein's investigation examines the curious shift in the meaning of a single word – *interval* – depending on the context in which it occurs. The "interval" measurable by the passage downstream of logs does not have the same status as the "interval" measured by a clock. But the mystery of the word has nothing to do with the specific language in question: in French, for example, we read, *Aussi les critères qui déterminent l'égalité des intervalles séparant le passage des rondins sont-ils différents de ceux qui déterminent l'égalité des intervalles mesurés par une horloge.*"[21] Whether *interval*, *intervalle*, or the German *Abstand*, the argument as to the possible meanings of "interval" remains intact.

"But isn't *the same* at least the same?" Wittgenstein's question in the *Investigations* (*PI* §215) elicits the "useless proposition" that, yes, "A thing is identical with itself." Useless, because, as Wittgenstein has already argued earlier in the book (*PI* §61), we still have not come to a "*general* agreement about the use of the expression 'to have the same meaning' or 'to achieve the same'. For it can be asked in what cases we say: 'These are merely two forms of the same game'." Or consider the following from the so-called "Big Typescript" of the late thirties: "The man who said that one cannot step into the same river twice said something wrong; one can step into the same river twice."[22] Literally this is the case: certainly, if Wittgenstein were walking along the banks of the Thames, he could easily step into the same river twice. But then Heraclitus, whose metaphorical aphorism Wittgenstein is calling into question, could respond that the second time round, it would not be quite the "same" river. Wittgenstein knows this but he also knows that the "same" in "same river" is not quite the same as the "same" of "I have the same pain you have." For how can I judge the intensity of your pain? How do I know, for that matter, that you're not just pretending to be in pain? What can "same" possibly mean in such verbal constructions? It is, as in the case of "interval," the inherent difference between one *same* and another that makes language so mysterious.

some thing black

An examination of Wittgenstein translations thus leads us to the understanding that, as David Antin has put it succinctly, Wittgenstein "is not a poet of the German language or the English language; he is a poet of thinking through language," "a poet of nearly pure cognition."[23] As such, the Wittgensteinian language game paves the way for some of the most interesting poetic experiments of our own moment. The French *Oulipo*, for example, seems to have exerted as powerful a force in translation as in the original, even though a lipogram like Georges Perec's *La Disparition* (1969), which excludes the most common of French letters, *e*, would seem to be entirely "untranslatable."[24] Interestingly, the English translation *A Void* (1995), rendered brilliantly by Gilbert Adair, has proved to be almost as popular as the original, the point being that the central motive and its working out are wholly translatable, whatever the surface details.

In *Oulipo*, the essential analogy, as was the case in Wittgenstein, is between literature and mathematics, specifically with respect to the concept of *configuration*. As Warren Motte puts it:

> One looks for a configuration each time one disposes of a finite number of objects, and one wishes to dispose them according to certain constraints postulated in advance; Latin squares and finite geometries are configurations, but so is the arrangement of packages of different sizes in a drawer that is too small, or the disposition of words or

sentences given in advance (on the condition that the given constraints be sufficiently "crafty" for the problem to be real)...

Another way of considering the Oulipian enterprise is as a sustained attack on the aleatory in literature, a crusade for the maximal motivation of the literary sign.[25]

Let us see how this works in practice. In 1986, the French *Oulipo* mathematician/poet/novelist Jacques Roubaud published a long poetic sequence, *Quelque chose noir*, prompted by the tragic death of his young wife, the photographer Alix Cléo Roubaud. The English translation, made by Rosmarie Waldrop, was published in 1990 as *some thing black*.[26] Formally, the sequence is based on the number nine: there are nine sections, each having nine poems, and each poem has nine strophes, ranging from a single line to a paragraph made of phrases and clauses, oddly punctuated by periods rather than commas and avoiding all initial capitals. The number scheme – 9 x 9 x 9 – gives us 729 sections, which, together with the final poem *Rien*, makes 730 or precisely 2 x 365 or two calendar years. *Rien* ("Nothing") is dated 1983 and marks the event of death itself, whereas the first poem of Part I is "Meditation of 5/12/85," evidently written two years later. The course of the painful two-year passage is noted throughout, thus fulfilling Roubaud's axiom that "A text written according to a constraint describes the constraint."[27]

But there is more. For *nine* is of course Beatrice's number in Dante's *Vita Nuova*. The first chapter opens with the sentences "Nine times the heaven of the light had revolved in its own movement since my birth and had almost returned to the same point when the woman whom my mind beholds in glory first appeared before my eyes. She was called Beatrice by many who did not know what it meant to call her this."[28] The poet first lays eyes on his *donna ideale* at the start of her ninth year and "almost at the end of his ninth." He finally meets her exactly nine years later, when he is eighteen, and she greets him for the first time on the ninth hour of that day. So it goes through a series of visions associated with #9 until we come to Chapter 29 and read:

> Now, according to the Arabic way of reckoning time, her most noble soul departed from us in the ninth hour of the ninth day of the month; according to the Syrian method, she died in the ninth month of the year (June), because the first month in that system is Tixryn the first, which we call October; and according to our way of reckoning, she departed this life in the year of our Christian era, that is of the years of Our Lord, in which the perfect number had been completed nine times in the century in which she had been placed in this world; for she was born a Christian of the thirteenth century. Why this number was so closely connected with her might be explained as follows. Since, according to Ptolemy and according to Christian truth, there are nine moving heavens, and according to common astrological opinion, these heavens affect the earth

below according to their conjunctions, this number was associated with her to show at her generation nine of the moving heavens were in perfect conjunction one with the other. This is one reason. But, thinking more deeply and guided by infallible truth, I say that she herself was this number nine; I mean this as an analogy, as I will explain. The number three is the root of nine, because, independent of any other number, multiplied by itself alone, it makes nine, as we see quite plainly when we say three threes are nine; therefore if three is the sole factor of nine, and the sole factor of miracles is three, that is, Father, Son and Holy Ghost, who are three and one, then this lady was accompanied by the number nine to convey that she was a nine, that is, a miracle, of which the root, that is, of the miracle, is nothing other than the miraculous Trinity itself. Perhaps a more subtle mind could find a still more subtle reason for it, but this is the one which I perceive and which pleases me the most.

Roubaud's 9 x 9 x 9 structure at once pays homage to and inverts the Dantean cosmos. Like the *Vita Nuova*, *Quelque chose noir* memorializes the beloved dead woman, but Roubaud's love is not an idealized image of female perfection but his actual wife, whose body he knows intimately and whose photographic representations, both her own and those of others, are all too "real." In Roubaud's secular cycle, there is no afterlife for "you," no vision beyond material death. Accordingly, the number nine shifts from referent to hidden formal principle, the two-year cycle moving to the near silence of the Coda *Rien* ("Nothing"), whose page is all but blank, its nineteen minimalist lines, justified at the right margin, representing a short-circuiting of speech itself:

Ce morceau de ciel
désormais
t'est dévolu

où la face aveugle
de l'église
s'incurve

compliquée
d'un marrionnier,

le soleil, là
hésite
laisse

du rouge
encore,
avant que la terre

émette

tant d'absence

que tes yeux
s'approchent
de

rien

Rosmarie Waldrop's translation follows the original closely, even as she can reproduce the page layout of the original to create a near match:

this patch of sky
henceforward
your inheritance

where the blind façade
of the church
curves inward

complicated
by a chestnut tree

here the sun
hesitates
leaves

some more
red
before the earth
emit

so much absence

that your eyes
approach

nothing

Lines like "tant d'absence / que tes yeux / s'approchent / de rien" can be trans-lated quite precisely: "so much absence / that your eyes / approach / nothing." But, as in Wittgenstein's riddling propositions, Roubaud's "simple" diction is nothing if not slippery. How does the earth "emit / so much absence"? How do the eyes of the dead approach "nothing"? Eyes, nails with blood caked under-neath them, arms, legs – these appear again and again in *Quelque chose noir* but remain elusive. In Antin's terms, Roubaud's is a poetry of cognition rather than of texture.

Or consider *Irresemblance* ("Unlikeness"), which is the fourth prose lyric of Part I.

L'irresemblance:

Le résultat de l'investigation était celui-ci: le précipité des ressemblances. la toile de la ressemblance. ses fils croisés et recroisés.

Parfois la ressemblance de partout. parfois la ressemblance là.

Ensuite que toi et ta mort n'avaient aucun air de famille.

Cela semble simple. alors: il n'y avait plus lieu d'une réquisition difficile. d'aucune interrogation rude. simplement le bavardage douloureux, inutile. superficiel et trivial.

"Un chien ne peut pas simuler la douleur. est-ce parce qu'il est trop honnête?"

Il faillait faire connaissance avec la description.

En quelque mots ce qui ne bougeait pas.

Car cela m'avait été renvoyé reconnu, alors que rien ne s'en déduisait de mon expérience.

Tu étais morte, et cela ne mentait pas.

(Q 17)

The result of the investigation: a deposit of likenesses. weave of likeness. threads crossed and recrossed.

Sometimes likeness from anywhere. sometimes this likeness *here*.

Then, that you and your death shared no family trait.

It seems simple. hence: no grounds for difficulties or demands for rude interrogation. just painful chatter. useless. superficial and trivial.

"Why can't a dog simulate pain? Is he too honest?"

I had to make friends with description.

In so many words, what did not move.

For this I recognized. though none of it derived from my experience.

You were dead. this was no lie.

(SB 15)

Here, Roubaud's "investigation" into the response of the living to death begins by probing *le précipité des ressemblances,* since any word or image, as Wittgenstein taught us, is part of a language game made up of family resemblances. If the body in question could only be like something familiar, it would not seem dead. But by the third sentence, the poet has recognized that *Ensuite que toi et ta mort n'avaient aucun air de famille.* There are no family resemblances between a person and a state of being or non-being – in this case, death. One recalls the aphorism in the *Tractatus*, "Death is not an event in life. Death is not lived through." "None of it," we read in the penultimate line, "derived from my experience" (*Rien ne s'en déduisait de mon expérience*"). And yet there is more than "painful chatter," for relationships between items do manifest themselves, even if they are negative ones. In the fifth strophe, Wittgenstein's "Why can't a dog simulate pain? Is he too honest?", which I cited earlier, is given an ironic twist. For since, in this case, the poet himself seems incapable of simulating feeling, for example, even the slightest pleasure, perhaps Wittgenstein's distinction between man and dog must be qualified, at least so far as human "honesty" is concerned. Given these circumstances, there can only be resignation – the recognition that *Il fallait faire connaissance avec la description* ("I had to make friends with description"). Philosophy, Wittgenstein was fond of saying, leaves everything as it is; it can only describe. The same, Roubaud suggests, may be said of poetry. And even then, the poet can only describe the physical facts – the *ce qui ne bougeait pas* or "what did not move." The ninth sentence is thus the flat recitation of fact: *Tu étais morte, et cela ne mentait pas* ("You were dead. this was no lie"). It is a statement that takes us back to the question of the dog's "honesty" above. Indeed, the beloved who has become a "black thing" is not, like Beatrice, "a nine, that is a miracle, of which the root, that is of the miracle, is solely the miraculous Trinity." She merely *is* or rather *was*.

Here is what we might call a conceptual poetry *à la lettre* – a set of strophes, largely written in denotative language, that modulate familiar abstract nouns, personal pronouns, and adverbs of time and place (*Parfois, là*). The network of likenesses and differences, so subtly articulated in the tension between numerical base and linguistic construction, creates what is a highly wrought poetic text that is nevertheless quite amenable to translation. Rosmarie Waldrop, herself an important poet who might well deviate from the original, were it desirable to do so, has here produced a remarkably literal translation. But then what were her alternatives? Take the line *Tu étais morte, et cela ne mentait pas*, which Waldrop renders as "You were dead. this was no lie." Grammatically, one can't say, following the French, "this did not lie." The construction "this was no lie" is thus the proper translation any textbook would use. *Cela*, of course, is normally translated as "that" rather than "this" (perhaps Waldrop chose "this" for intimacy), but otherwise the line offers no other translation possibilities. Or again, Waldrop's translation of *Il fallait faire connaissance avec la description*" as "I had to make friends with description" is not wholly literal (e.g., I had to get to know description), but "make friends" alludes slyly to Roubaud's own veiled reference to Gertrude Stein's important essay–poem "An Acquaintance with Description." There are, in other words, alternative possibilities available to the translator even in the case of Roubaud, but only within rather narrow perimeters.

And there, of course, is the rub. Precisely because Roubaud's poetry is, at one level, so *translatable*, it doesn't give the translator very much scope. And this is the case even for the *Oulipo* lipogram, where the translator must be extremely gifted so as to match the original. To translate texts like *Quelque chose noir* or *La Disparition* is to subordinate oneself to the original, even as Wittgenstein's translators devote them- selves to approximating the language of their master, so that there is surprisingly little talk, in Wittgenstein criticism, of the relative merits of translation A versus translation B or of the English translation of the *Tractatus* versus the French. The case of Rilke is the opposite. To speak of a translation of the *Duino Elegies* is to begin with the premise that X's version cannot be commensurate with the poem itself.

Wittgenstein himself would no doubt have preferred Rilke's poetry to Roubaud's, even as he preferred Brahms to Bruckner. But ironically, his own understanding of poetry as *invention*, as conceptual art, became an important paradigm for those writers and artists who came of age in the immediate wake of the *Philosophical Investigations*. Consider Samuel Beckett, whose great *Trilogy* (*Molloy*, *Malone Dies*, *The Unnamable*) was published, first in French, then in the author's own translation into English between 1951 and 1958. The relationship of the French to the English version of these short poetic novels raises interesting stylistic questions,[29] it is also the case that *Molloy*, say in the German translation made by Erich Franzen, is quite true to the spirit of the original. Here is the opening page of what was originally a French novel, first in English, then in German:

> I am in my mother's room. It's I who live there now. I don't know how I got there. Perhaps in an ambulance, certainly a vehicle of some kind. I was helped. I'd never have got there alone. Perhaps I got here thanks to him. He says not. He gives me money and takes away pages. So many pages, so much money. Yes, I work now, a little like I used to, except that I don't know how to work any more. That doesn't matter apparently. What I'd like now is to speak of the things that are left, say my good- byes, finish dying. They don't want that. Yes, there is more than one, apparently. But it's always the same one that comes.[30]

> Ich bin im Zimmer meiner Mutter. Ich wohne jetzt selbst darin. Wie ich hierhergekommen bin, weiß ich nicht. In einer Ambulanz vielleicht, bestimmt mit irgendeinem Gefährt. Man hat mir geholfen. Allein hätte ich es nicht geschafft. Vielleicht habe ich es diesem Mann, der jede Woche erscheint, zu verdanken, daß ich hier bin. Er streitet es ab. Er gibt mir etwas Geld und nimmt das Geschriebene mit sich. So viele Seiten, so viel Geld. Ja, ich arbeite jetzt, ein wenig wie früher, nur verstehe ich mich nicht mehr aufs Arbeiten. Das macht nichts, wie es scheint. Ich möchte jetzt gern von dem sprechen, was mir noch übrig bleibt, Abschied nehmen, aufhören zu sterben. Das wollen sie nicht. Ja, es sind mehrere, wie es scheint. Aber der eine, der herkommt, ist immer derselbe.[31]

Beckett's seemingly basic vocabulary, made up largely of personal and demonstrative pronouns, and ordinary verbs like "live," "know," "give," "take," and "work," applied to basic nouns like "mother," "money," "things," "pages," most of these organized into simple declarative sentences, translates neatly into German. And yet, like those propositions about "pain" or "colour" Wittgenstein lays out for us, Beckett's statements are highly elusive, indeterminate, and mysterious. The reference to the "ambulance" or "vehicle of some kind" in the fourth sentence suggests that it was at birth the narrator arrived in his mother's room and so he has been there ever since, but the reference to "It's I who live there now" (*Ich wohne jetzt selbst darin*) suggests that this hasn't always been the case. In Wittgenstein's terms, the meaning can only be established by studying each word group or sentence in the larger context in which it occurs. What does "now" (*jetzt*) mean in "It's I who live there *now*"?

In *Philosophical Investigations* §383, Wittgenstein writes:

> We are not analyzing a phenomenon (e.g. thought) but a concept (e.g. that of thinking), and therefore the use of a word. So it may look as if what we were doing were Nominalism. Nominalists make the mistake of interpreting all words as names, and so of not really describing their use, but only, so to speak, giving a paper draft on such a description.

Most modernist poets, we might note, are, in one form or another, nominalists: Ezra Pound, for example, builds his *Cantos* using collocations of proper names – a proliferation of restaurants, churches, frescoes, Provençal castles, Roman deities – so as to create a dense network of meanings. In more recent poetry, such nominalism has been practiced with beautiful irony by Frank O'Hara in poems like "Khrushchev is coming on the right day!"

But nominalism, as Wittgenstein understood so well, is a way of avoiding the concept, that is, the significance to linguistic understanding of "the use of a word." Unlike Pound, Beckett uses generic Irish names like Molloy, Malone, and Moran, and foregrounds everyday language – "Yes, I work now, a little like I used to," puncturing this matter-of-fact statement with the qualification, "except that I don't know how to work any more." No names, no data, only concept. What does it mean not to know how to work any more? Is it just an excuse? A loss of a particular ability? A consequence of old age?

Such language games will become increasingly prominent in an age of globalization where the availability of translation is taken for granted. Poets and fiction writers, I predict, will increasingly write in what we might call, keeping Wittgenstein's example in mind, a language of translatability. This does not mean that poetry will become "easier" and more "accessible"; quite the contrary. It simply means that the focus will be on *language* rather than on a *specific* language. As Wittgenstein reminds us, "You learned the *concept* 'pain' when you learned language" (*PI* §384).

Notes

1 Ludwig Wittgenstein, *Wittgenstein's Lectures, Cambridge 1930–32*. From the Notes of John King and Desmond Lee, Desmond Lee (ed.), Chicago: University of Chicago Press, 1989, p. 75. Cited in the text as *LEC 1*.
2 Ezra Pound, *The Spirit of Romance, 1910*, New York: New Directions, 1968, p. 14.
3 William H. Gass, *Reading Rilke: Reflections on the Problems of Translation*, New York: Alfred A. Knopf, 1999, pp. 57f.
4 Cf. Marjorie Perloff, "Reading Gass Reading Rilke," *Parnassus* 25 (2001), 486–507, pp. 491–3.
5 Eva Hesse and Heinz Ickstadt, *Amerikanische Dichtung von den Anfängen bis zur Gegenwart*, München: Beck, 2000, p. 374.
6 Ibid., p. 375.
7 Gass, op. cit., pp. 62f.
8 Ludwig Wittgenstein, *Tractatus Logico-Philosophicus*, 1922 [*German–English parallel text*], trans. C. K. Ogden, London: Routledge, 1991. Cited in the text as *TLP*. References are to numbered sections.
9 Ludwig Wittgenstein, *Philosophical Investigations*, 1953 [*German–English parallel text*], G. E. M. Anscombe and Rush Rhees (eds.), 2nd edn; Oxford: Blackwell, 1999. Cited in the text as *PI*. References [§] are to sections of Part I, and to pages of Part II.
10 Jacques Bouveresse, *Le Mythe de l'intériorité*, Paris: Editions de Minuit, 1987, p. 464.
11 Ludwig Wittgenstein, *Culture and Value*, 1980 [*German–English parallel text*], ed. G. H. von Wright, in collaboration with H. Nyman, trans. Peter Winch, Oxford: Blackwell, 1980. Cited in the text as *CV*.
12 There is no exact English equivalent of the German verb *Dichten*. The closest would be something like *poetize*, but this is not an actual English word. Peter Winch translates the sentence in question as "Philosophy ought really to be written only as a poetic composition." This seems to me to rationalize the German excessively, so I have used, for this passage, David Antin's idiomatic translation (David Antin, "Wittgenstein among the Poets," *Modernism, Modernity 5*, 1998, pp. 149–66, p. 161). The verb *Dichten* also means "to make thick or dense" and "to fictionalize." But these denotative meanings are all part of the same complex, the point being that Wittgenstein is saying he wants philosophy to be more like its seeming opposite – poetry or fiction – the thickening of language.
13 Ludwig Wittgenstein, *Lectures and Conversations on Aesthetics, Psychology and Religious Belief* [*1938–46*], Cyril Barrett (ed.), Berkeley: University of California Press, 1966, p. 11.
14 See Ludwig Wittgenstein, *Briefe*, Brian McGuinness and G. H. von Wright (eds.), Correspondence with B. Russell, G. E. Moore, J. M. Keynes, F. P. Ramsay, *et al.* In German, with original version of Wittgenstein's own letters (in English), in an Appendix; German translations J. Schulte, Frankfurt: Suhrkamp, 1980, pp. 222, 22, 47, and 78, respectively.
15 See ibid., p. 78; *CV,* p. 67, p. 41.
16 Franz Parak, "Wittgenstein in Monte Cassino," W. Baum (ed.), Ludwig Wittgenstein, *Geheime Tagebücher* [*1914–16*], Vienna: Turia & Kant, 1991, pp. 146–58, pp. 146, 152.
17 See Marjorie Perloff, *Wittgenstein's Ladder. Poetic Language and the Strangeness of the Ordinary*, Chicago: University of Chicago Press, 1996, pp. 42–3.
18 Ludwig Wittgenstein, *Zettel* [1945–48] [German–English parallel text], G. E. M. Anscombe and G. H. von Wright (eds.), trans. G. E. M. Anscombe, Berkeley: University of California Press, 1970, §160.
19 Sol LeWitt, "Paragraphs on Conceptual Art," *Artforum* 5 (1967), 79–83, p. 83. There are, of course, other important aspects of Conceptualism: see the excellent entries on "Conceptual Art" in Michael Kelly, *Encyclopedia of Aesthetics*, 4 vols., New York: Oxford University Press, vol. I, pp. 414–27. "The grand strategy," writes Yair Guttmann,

"was to resist the attempts to sever the art object from its context" (I, 422). The relation of Joseph Kosuth to Wittgenstein is discussed in I, 426–7.

20 Ludwig Wittgenstein, *Wittgenstein's Lectures, Cambridge 1932–35*, from the notes of Alice Ambrose and M. MacDonald, Alice Ambrose (ed.), Chicago: University of Chicago Press, 1982. Cited in the text as *LEC 2*.

21 *Les Cours de Cambridge 1932–1935*, Alice Ambrose (ed.), trans. from English by Elisabeth Rigal, Mauvezin: Trans-Europe Express, 1993, p. 26.

22 Ludwig Wittgenstein, *Philosophical Occasions 1912–1951* [German–English parallel texts where appropriate], James Klagge and Alfred Nordmann (eds.), Indianopolis: Hackett, 1993, p. 167.

23 David Antin, "Wittgenstein among Poets," op. cit., p. 163; cf. Marjorie Perloff, "Introduction," *David Antin Talking*, Chicago: Dalkey Archive, 2001, pp. i–viii, pp. iv–v.

24 The *Larousse* defines a lipogram as "a literary work in which one compels oneself strictly to exclude one or several letters of the alphabet." See Harry Matthews and Alastair Brotchie (eds.) *Oulipo Compendium*, London: Atlas, pp. 174f.

25 Warren F. Motte Jr. (ed. and trans.), *Oulipo: A Primer of Potential Literature*, Lincoln: University of Nebraska Press, 1986, pp. 16–7.

26 Rosmarie Waldrop, *some thing black*, Normal, IL: Dalkey Archive, 1990. Note that the space between "some" and "thing" (like "quelque" and "chose") suggests that the reference is not only to something black but to some black thing. Cited in the text as *SB*.

27 Jacques Roubaud, *Quelque chose noir*, Paris: Gallimard, 1986, p. 38. Cited in the text as *Q*.

28 Dante, *La Vita Nuova*, trans. Barbara Reynolds, New York: Penguin, 1969, p. 29.

29 See Ann Beer, "Beckett's Bilingualism," John Pilling (ed.), *The Cambridge Companion to Beckett*, Cambridge: Cambridge University Press, 1994, pp. 209–21.

30 Samuel Beckett, *Molloy*, 1955, New York: Grove Weidenfeld, 1989, p. 7.

31 Samuel Beckett, *Molloy*, 1955, trans. Erich Franzen, Frankfurt: Suhrkamp, 2001, p. 7.

3

WITTGENSTEIN'S "IMPERFECT GARDEN"

The ladders and labyrinths of philosophy as *Dichtung*

David Schalkwyk

> What is inexpressible (what I find mysterious and am not able to express) is the background against whatever I could express has its meaning.
>
> (Ludwig Wittgenstein, *Culture and Value*)[1]

Wittgenstein scholarship and criticism is always faced by a problem arising both from Wittgenstein's philosophical practice and the metaphors by which he tries to convey the modes and possibilities of that practice. Any attempt to offer a systematic account of his writings has to confront Wittgenstein's own declaration that such coherence escaped him in the very process of conducting his investigations, and, crucially, that this arose from the nature of the subject itself. We should take Wittgenstein at his word from the very beginning, when he confesses in the Preface to the *Philosophical Investigations*, "after several unsuccessful attempts to weld my results together into…a whole" (where "the thoughts should proceed from one subject to another in a natural order without breaks") "I realized that I should never succeed."[2]

One of the reasons for Wittgenstein's "failure" stems from his turning away, in his later work, from the search for an unsituated – we might say "philosophical" – perspective, to the insight that language can be defined only in terms of its situation or, better, of its multiplicity of situations. This turning towards the situatedness of language marks what is most distinctive about the later Wittgenstein. But it also arises from his peculiar conception of philosophy as the search for the "redeeming word" – the word that will put an end to intellectual restlessness: "In philosophy one comes to rest when the redeeming word is found."[3] I wish to focus on the complex relationship between this peculiarly Wittgensteinian sense of simultaneous situatedness and restlessness, and to show how it touches the degree to which fiction and imagination are central to his project of mapping the grammar of our language. A more "literary" reading of the *Investigations* than is traditionally offered, open to the philosophical force of metaphor and form, may thus see more of what Wittgenstein himself encountered on his philosophical journeyings than one which regards the literary and the metaphorical as tangential to proper philosophical investigation.[4]

At the time that he was writing the *Tractatus* Wittgenstein felt that to talk about ethics and aesthetics was merely "*schwefeln*" – "gassing." This view is confirmed in his correspondence with his friend Paul Englemann about a poem by Uhland that had made a deep impression on both of them: "if only you do not try to utter what is unutterable then *nothing* gets lost. But the unutterable will be – unutterably – *contained* in what is uttered!"[5] Whereas the unutterable is recognized as being central to the *Tractatus*, few commentators write about the inexpressible in the *Philosophical Investigations*. Even fewer have explored the sense in which Wittgenstein's later writings may attempt, or fail, to obey his repeated injunction that philosophy should be written *only* as one would write poetry. I shall relate these two concerns, with the inexpressible and the poetic – central to the *Tractatus* – by tracing the tortuous routes of metaphor in the later writing. I shall take Wittgenstein at his word when he claims: "What I invent are new *similes*" (*CV*, p. 19).

Dichten

The statement that philosophy should be written as poetry appears in *Culture and Value*: "Ich glaube meine Stellung zur Philosphie dadurch zusammengefaßt zu haben, indem ich sagte: Philosophie dürfte man eigentlich nur *dichten*" (*CV*, p. 24). Peter Winch translates this as: "I think I summed up my attitude to philosophy when I said: philosophy ought really to be written as a form of *poetic composition*."[6] But his formulation doesn't quite convey the sense of the original. This is not the translator's fault, because English has no equivalent for the word *dichten* – an intransitive verb meaning to write poetry. Wittgenstein is saying, somewhat more tersely and emphatically than the translation suggests, that the *activities* of writing philosophy and writing poetry are closely related: to philosophize is to poetize – one should write philosophy only ("*nur*") as one would write poetry; philosophy should be nothing other than the writing of poetry.

None of my reformulations conveys the exact sense of Wittgenstein's German, which itself highlights the nature of the poetic and its relation to discursive prose. Winch distances philosophy and poetry by introducing the qualifier, "as a form of poetic composition," thereby both separating the two activities more than is warranted by Wittgenstein's formulation and introducing a difference in kind between them. Philosophy should merely be a kind of poetic writing, not poetry itself, not "poetized" as Wittgenstein claims. Furthermore, Wittgenstein at least implicitly repeats the claim. The remark is an endorsement, an underlined repetition, of an earlier statement: "I think I summed up my attitude to philosophy *when I said…*" Here Wittgenstein is quoting himself, in order to re-emphasize a number of claims that may be traced in the *Nachlass*, which he now pronounces as a summation of what philosophy means to him.[7] But it is also an admission of defeat, or at least of a limitation. For he continues: "It must, it seems to me, be possible to gather from this how far my thinking belongs to the present, future or past. For I was thereby revealing myself as someone who cannot quite do what he would like to be able to do."

Is it because Wittgenstein was not a poet that he could not live up to his belief in the poetic nature of philosophical activity? Or was that belief so out of tune with the times that philosophy could not then be written as poetry? The first suggests a personal incapacity, the second a cultural or generic one. Wittgenstein feels both: "Just as I cannot write verse," he says at another point, "so too my ability to write prose extends *so far*, and no further. There is a quite definite limit to the prose I can write and I can no more overstep *that* than that I can write a poem" (*CV*, p. 59). But is writing *verse* the same as writing philosophy as poetry? I suspect not. And the difference lies precisely in the distinction that Winch's translation (unwittingly) obscures, between form ("verse," "a poem") and activity ("to poetize"). One can poetize in prose. In what sense, then, was Wittgenstein *already* writing philosophy as poetry? And in what sense is he right to acknowledge his incapacity to do so?

One of the almost insurmountable difficulties of answering these questions lies in the enigmatic nature of his understanding of *dichten* – to "poetize." The problem arises both from the lack of a sustained context for the remark and the absence of any systematic use of the notion of the poetic or the verb "*dichten*" in Wittgenstein's writing. The claims to which Wittgenstein alludes in the *Culture and Value* remark from 1933/4, that philosophy should be written only as poetry, may be found in the *Nachlass* entries of 1933, 1938 and 1940. This suggests that the idea preoccupied him for some time – that it is not merely a transitional notion but is central to the whole of his later conception of what it is to write philosophy and its relation to writing poetry or the literary. But a close look at Wittgenstein's earlier thinking reveals a continuity in at least the connection between the philosophical and the literary.

The profound effect that the *Tractatus* has had on the literary imagination is well known.[8] In his account of the work to a prospective publisher, Ludwig von Ficker, Wittgenstein writes that it "is strictly philosophical and at the same time literary."[9] This suggests that at the time that he was eager to publish the *Tractatus*, Wittgenstein considered the "strictly philosophical" to be simultaneously "literary." The concept of the inexpressible, especially in the distinction between what can be "said" and what can be "shown," is perhaps the most fundamental thought of the *Tractatus*. Its own purpose is in fact to *show* this distinction, for built into the work from the beginning is the principle that its propositions are "senseless." They are themselves an attempt to state what can only be shown:

> This book deals with the problems of philosophy and shows, as I believe, that the method of formulating these problems rests on the misunderstanding of the logic of our language. Its whole meaning could be summed up somewhat as follows: What can be said at all can be said clearly; and whereof one cannot speak thereof one must be silent.

The book will, therefore, draw a limit to thinking, or rather—not to thinking, but to the expression of thoughts; for, in order to draw a limit to thinking we should have to be able to think both sides of this limit (we should therefore have to be able to think what cannot be thought).[10]

This is philosophy conceived not as a prison-house of language, but as a cloister of silence. The *Tractatus* attempts to think both the *limits* and the possibility of representation as one and the same thing, that is to say, that "the picture [*of language*] cannot place itself outside of its form of representation" (2.174), and that "that which expresses *itself* in language, *we* cannot express by language" (4.121). Thus Wittgenstein postulates the unthinkability of the boundary between language and the world:

5.61 Logic fills the world: the limits of the world are also its limits.

We cannot therefore say in logic: This and this there is in the world, and there is not.

For that would apparently presuppose that we could exclude certain possibilities, and this cannot be the case since otherwise logic must get outside the limits of the world: that is, if it could consider these limits from the other side also.

What we cannot think, that we cannot think: we cannot therefore *say* what we cannot think.

The self-reflexive, and paradoxical, motto of the *Tractatus* as a whole is the terse statement which constitutes its final section: "Whereof one cannot speak, thereof one must be silent." (7)

Wittgenstein explained in a letter to Von Ficker that the *second* part of the book, which contains nothing but the single, terse injunction to be silent about that whereof we cannot speak, is by far the most important, more important than the "gassing" of those around him, and more important even than the terse logic of its first six sections.

My work consists of two parts: the one presented here plus all that I have *not* written. And it is precisely this second part that is the important one. My book draws limits to the sphere of the ethical from the inside as it were, and I am convinced that this is the ONLY *rigorous* way of drawing those limits. In short, I believe that while many others today are just gassing, I have managed in my book to put everything firmly in its place by being silent about it. And for this reason, unless I am very much mistaken, the book will say a great deal that you yourself want to say. Only perhaps that you won't see that it is said in the book. For now, I would recommend that you read the *preface* and the *conclusion*, because they contain the most direct expression of the point of the book.[11]

Wittgenstein recognizes that his text transgresses the very principles that it attempts to elucidate in the process of that elucidation itself. The penultimate remark claims that to understand the propositions of the *Tractatus* is in fact to see that they are "senseless," that they are no more than a ladder, disposable once the reader has used them to arrive at the correct vantage point:

> My propositions are elucidatory in this way: he who understands me finally recognises them as senseless, when he has climbed out through them, on them, over them. (He must so to speak throw away the ladder, after he has climbed up on it.) He must surmount these propositions; then he sees the world rightly.
>
> (6.54)

Ladders

The metaphor of the ladder which must be discarded once it has given access to a place from which everything will appear in its proper perspective, is itself troubled and troubling. If one cannot get outside language to see its connection with the world, then where is that place of absolutely clear and commanding vision of the workings and structure of our language? And can the ladder, that necessary but untidy tool, simply be discarded, put behind us, relegated to the subservient, secondary, and menial task of the supplement? When Wittgenstein abandons his concern with the general form of the proposition, does he also let go of the concomitant notions of silence, the unutterable, and the disposable ladder? Yes and no. Although Wittgenstein does not use the metaphor of a ladder explicitly in the *Philosophical Investigations*, he does retain throughout his later work a metaphor that is closely related to the notion of a ladder: the idea or ideal of the "*übersichtliche Darstellung*," commonly translated as a "perspicuous representation." Wittgenstein insists that language requires neither reform nor theory. Rather, it needs to be described in all its dense, intractable, living "hurly-burly."[12] Such description will "teach us differences" which both the forms of language and our own homogenizing myopia prevent us from seeing, despite the fact that they are not hidden, but lie quite openly before us. The problem lies in getting a clear view of the phenomena *and their background* so that we can delineate their relationships comparatively, by "seeing connexions." While we are entangled in the hurly-burly that constitutes living in a language we do not have this clear view. To speak of an *übersichtliche Darstellung*, then, is not merely to seek a "clear" or "perspicuous" view, as the common translations suggest, but also to achieve that clarity by surveying its terrain from on high:

A main source of our failure to understand is that we do not *command a clear view* of the use of our words.—Our grammar is lacking in this sort of perspicuity. A perspicuous representation produces just that understanding which consists in "seeing connexions."...

The concept of a perspicuous representation is of fundamental importance for us. It earmarks the form of account we give, the way we look at things.

(*PI* §122)

The "we" here refers, of course, to the philosopher who wishes to get above the hurly-burly of ordinary language-games in order to see and make the necessary therapeutic connections that will free us from the bewitchments induced by our usual inextricable situatedness in linguistic practice. For the ideal of an elevated perspective is complicated, indeed contradicted, by an equally persistent metaphor in his later work by which philosophy is kept ineluctably down-to-earth, condemned to trace and retrace, over and over again, a landscape where we are both at home and do not know our way about, trying to draw a map of a "multitude of paths" that always "lead off in all directions."[13] Wittgenstein writes in the Preface to the *Philosophical Investigations* that neither a coherent discursive essay nor a complete overview proved to be possible once he had abandoned the search for the single form that informs all language. The divagation of the later investigations offer no more than "a number of sketches of landscapes which were made in the course of...long and involved journeyings" (*PI*, Preface). And this, he claims, is connected with the very nature of the investigation, with the nature of its object of study, which will not be confined by or to any "scientific" point of view.

As early as 1930, Wittgenstein emphatically rejects the idea that he could achieve his philosophical goals via some kind of ladder, thereby discarding the idea that the philosophical perspective that he seeks could be achieved by rising above his immediate situation or surroundings:

If the place I want to get to could only be reached by way of a ladder, I would give up trying to get there. For the place I really have to get to is a place I must already be at now.

Anything I might reach by climbing a ladder does not interest me.

(*CV*, p. 7)

It seems, then, that the later Wittgenstein's search for the overview of the grammar of our language as a therapeutic end to philosophy betrays the most fundamental insight that such an overview is meant to convey, not as therapy but as philosophy, concerning our necessary situatedness within language-games, history, and the world.

The remark immediately following the paragraph in the *Philosophical Investigations* in which Wittgenstein expresses his desire for an overview introduces another metaphor which is only apparently consonant with that of the perspicuous representation: "A philosophical problem," he writes, "has the form: 'I don't know my way about'" (§123). And in another remark he writes: "I am showing my pupils details of an immense landscape which they cannot possibly know their way around" (*CV*, p. 7). This is a metaphor of groundedness, of being in a landscape rather than above it, of having to make one's way through it, rather than simply transcending it, even if it is true that one could find one's way by gaining (how? where?) a total view of the whole terrain.

Gardens and labyrinths

If the need for a ladder is at least implicit in the later Wittgenstein's desire for a clear representation from above, he uses the metaphors of gardens and cities explicitly to explore the problems of achieving such an elevated perspective. Commenting on Macaulay's attempt to offer an account of the "art of fiction," Wittgenstein shows the difficulty of drawing a comprehensive picture of such a diverse practice:

> Macaulay says that the art of fiction is an "imitative art," and naturally gets straight away into the greatest of difficulties with this concept. He wants to give a description: but any picture that suggests itself to him is inappropriate, however right it seems at first sight; and however queer it seems that one should be unable to describe what one so exactly understands.[14]

We may take being "unable to describe what one so exactly understands" as an expression of the central frustration of Wittgenstein's philosophical method, and it is particularly apt that he should speak of it in relation to someone else's attempt to offer a complete theory of fiction. Macaulay is baffled by every general account that he attempts to construct of his object, because there are always cases that fall outside it or do not fit into it. How is this related to the "representation" (*Darstellung*) that Wittgenstein himself seeks? Immediately after this remark, he explicates the puzzle of knowing something intimately and yet being unable to provide a proper picture of it by turning to the metaphor of mapping:

> It is very easy to imagine someone knowing his way about a city quite accurately, i.e. he finds the shortest way from one part of the city to another quite surely – and yet he should be perfectly incapable of drawing a map of the city. That is, as soon as he tries, he only produces something completely wrong.

> (§556)

The problem lies both in the desire to produce the picture in accordance with some system and in the inadequacy of any systematic representation itself:

> Above all, someone attempting the description lacks any system. The systems that occur to him are inadequate, and he seems suddenly to find himself in a wilderness instead of the well laid out garden that he knew so well.

(§557)

We can take this as an acute expression of Wittgenstein's own felt difficulty in providing an accurate map or overview of the grammar of our language. The quotidian familiarity with its homely contours and paths turns to bewilderment and confusion the moment a representation of what is known so well is attempted: the domestic reassurance of a "well laid out garden" is turned into the frightening alienation of a "wilderness." How does one find one's way through such a terrain, let alone offer a perspicuous representation of it?

Despite Wittgenstein's suggestion that the concept of the perspicuous representation or overview is fundamental, both the shape of the *Investigations* and his account of that shape in its Preface eschew the overview and the map for the journey and the sketch. The nature of the investigation, Wittgenstein writes,

> compels us to travel over a wide field of thought criss-cross in every direction.—The philosophical remarks in this book are, as it were, a number of sketches of landscapes which were made in the course of these long and involved journeyings....The same or almost the same points were always being approached afresh from different directions, and new sketches made. Very many of these were badly drawn or uncharacteristic, marked by all the defects of a weak draughtsman.

(p. vii)

If you looked at the sketches, he writes, "you could get a picture of the landscape," but the book "is really only an album" (p. vii). The diachrony inherent in his comparison of language to an ancient city, with its variety and accretions, and the earth-bound situatedness of that simile, means that the synchronic overview – the instantaneous "view from nowhere" – is displaced by the necessity of both place and displacement. In order to show where words have their homes the philosopher must be displaced – he becomes an itinerant sketcher, not a settled cartographer.

This is the story of Wittgenstein's life. Inextricably situated within that process of exile brought about by both the opportunities for cultural and intellectual movement and the cataclysmic upheavals of war in early twentieth-century Europe, Wittgenstein lived his life as a permanent refugee, whether it was from the luxury and decadence of Hapsburg Vienna to the Engineering Faculty at Manchester, from Manchester to the logical philosophy of Bertrand Russell at

Cambridge, from the trenches of the Italian front to a remote cottage in Norway, from the primary schools of remote Alpine villages to the Logical Positivist Circle of Vienna, from Vienna to Trinity College, Cambridge and, finally, to a remote cottage in Western Ireland, before returning to die in Cambridge in 1953.[15] For him, as for so many of the generation that we now equate with Modernism, there was never a home, a *Heimat*: merely a ceaseless series of sketches made from the perspectives of endless, criss-crossing journeyings, back and forth, over the same terrain, in search for the still point which would allow him to stop doing philosophy, to find the "redeeming word." Despite everything that Wittgenstein said and did, he never did manage to find a point of rest, when philosophical problems stopped troubling him, nor did he write in any form other than the sketch or remark rather than the map or the essay.

To keep track of the multitude of linguistic environments that constitute the homes of words, it is thus the philosopher who has to keep on the move, traversing the landscape of the language this way and that, in an effort to find his or her way about. Wittgenstein's account of his own difficulties in presenting a picture of grammar is thus closely related to his metaphorical accounts of the nature of language itself: as a complex terrain, a city, a maze, a labyrinth: "our language can be seen as an ancient city: a maze of little streets and squares, of old and new houses, and of houses with additions from various periods; and this surrounded by a multitude of new boroughs with straight regular streets and uniform houses" (*PI* §19). And the person attempting to provide a representation or map of such a city is incorrigibly earth-bound: one draws the sketches on the ground, in the course of numerous, repeated journeys across terrain that is both familiar and unfamiliar: "Language is a labyrinth of paths. You approach from *one* side and know your way about; you approach the same place from another side and no longer know your way about" (*PI* §203). There is no sense of an *Übersicht* here, rather the bewilderment of discovering that what you thought you knew well has become strange, the familiar alien; a well laid out garden turns out to be a wilderness.

Heimat / heimlich

Following Wittgenstein's extended metaphorical cluster of the ladder, garden, wilderness, city, journey, sketch and home, we can discern relationships in tension among the metaphor of the journey through a well-known, but nevertheless bewildering and alienating, terrain, the ideal of the view-from-above, and the desire to return language, which has wandered off into the wild, to its "original *home*" – "*seine Heimat*" (*PI* §116). The plight of being lost connects most obviously with Wittgenstein's idea that philosophical therapy (against the bewilderment of philosophy itself) involves bringing words that are used out of their usual or proper contexts back to the language-games in which they have their life, back *home*. Philosophical problems arise when words "go on holiday" (*PI* §38). If we keep words safely and properly at home then the bewitchment that they impose upon us will cease and we will see them aright. But Wittgenstein also recognises the ease with which the domestic may become strange, the garden a wilderness, its familiar paths and vistas a maze. It is not as if some actual transformation occurs in the object: rather it is the same object viewed under two different aspects: the *Heim*, where one feels at home, secure in an environment that one "knows so well," and the *heimlich*, which as Wittgenstein's contemporary, Sigmund Freud, teaches us, is furtive, secret, and hidden.[16]

Freud has some telling things to say about the concept of the home. In an essay published in English as "The Uncanny," he draws our attention to the fact that the word *heimlich* "belongs to two ideas, which without being contradictory are yet very different: on the one hand, it means that which is familiar and congenial, and on the other, that which is concealed and kept out of sight."[17] If *heimlich* refers to that which is familiar, known, comfortable – all qualities exemplified by the homely, by what belongs openly and originally in and to the home – then the same word refers also to its opposite: to what is unknown, strange, hidden, alien, out-of-place, even terrifying: the *uncanny* or the *unheimlich*.

This curious doubleness of the concept in Wittgenstein's home language has no place in English, but as Freud has shown us, the notion of the uncanny has deep roots in the idea of the strangeness hidden in the familiar. This is precisely the experience that Wittgenstein traces when he writes of a domestic garden becoming a wilderness, a well-known city a place in which one may lose oneself, a familiar language a "labyrinth of paths," the philosopher being condemned to return to the same place repeatedly, sometimes knowing his way about, at others lost and disoriented by its strangeness. There is a perhaps coincidental but striking parallel in Freud's essay with Wittgenstein's notion of the endless return of the unfamiliar aspects in what Wittgenstein calls *"unsere Sprache"* – "our language." In response to Jentsch's suggestion that the uncanny is a product of intellectual uncertainty or orientation, Freud suggests that there is something incomplete about this definition.[18] He argues that the uncanny arises as much from the recurrence of the "same situations, things and events," and illustrates the argument with an anecdote about having been lost in a deserted street in a strange town. Hastening to leave the street, he found himself retraversing it not once but twice, returning to the very point from which he wished to escape.

The home to which Wittgenstein wishes to restore language so that it will cease to exercise its uncanny bewitchment of our intelligence has precisely the character of the home in the Freudian and (double) German sense: a place of great familiarity in which we dwell without reflection, where everything is "open to view," but which is at the same time and in the same place unknown, unfamiliar, even terrifying. The incompleteness of Jentsch's definition lies in his failure to see the double nature of the familiar, of the home hidden in *Heimlichkeit* (secrecy). And it is in this double sense of the homely that the situatedness of Wittgenstein's philosophy and his philosophy of situatedness expresses itself. Home is never a still point where we can be at peace, least of all the home that is our language. But that does not mean that we are elsewhere, or that we can ever leave it to get a clear perspective on it, in the form of the "synoptic view" for which Baker and Hacker and, to some extent, a part of the later Wittgenstein, continue to put their faith.

Fiction

Like Jacques Derrida in his recent debate with John Searle,[19] Wittgenstein recognizes that what is normally denigrated as "fictional," "non-serious," or "secondary" – marginal in any properly "serious" philosophical enquiry – may in fact be crucially instructive about the linguistic phenomena that are conventionally dubbed "serious" and "primary." Anticipating Derrida's claim that "the possibility of fiction cannot be derived,"[20] Wittgenstein remarks on the importance of fiction for resolving philosophical, or grammatical, problems: "Nothing is more important for understanding the concepts we have than constructing fictitious ones" (*CV*, p. 74).

The suggestion that philosophy may be best pursued through the invention of fictional examples makes two related points: philosophy is concerned not with the phenomena but with the *possibilities* of phenomena, and the meaning of a word is best shown in the ways it is used within the diverse contexts of human practice. If phenomena themselves are to be subjugated to questions about their conditions of possibility, then fictional examples may reveal as much, if not more, than factual ones about such conditions.[21] Also, if the meanings of words are a function of their uses within different cultural practices, then the actual uses may be clarified by two forms of imaginary variation: first, by imagining actual patterns of use, and, second, by imagining completely different kinds of use in order to cast a contrastive light on the actual ones. This process may throw both differences and similarities into sharp relief and also reveal ways in which concepts may develop or change under pressure of changing practices. Wittgenstein's later writings work according to this imaginative pattern, revealing the uncanny familiarity of our everyday linguistic practice through the invention of imaginary examples. In this specific sense they are indeed poetic.

But there is another way in which the poetic may offer the illumination that philosophy seeks: "The contexts of a sentence," Wittgenstein suggests, "are best portrayed in a play. Therefore the best example for a sentence is a quotation from a play. And whoever asks a person in a play what he's experiencing when he's speaking?"[22] This is a strong claim, that a fictional or imaginative context provides the *best* example for philosophical investigation. Why? Because by looking at a quotation from a play we can both clarify the role that context plays in constructing the meaning of an utterance and also rid ourselves of the false but attractive notion that its meaning must lie in the experiential state – some kind of interiority – of the utterer: "what he's experiencing while he's speaking." Far from being an "etiolation" of language, fiction may thus exemplify language in its so-called "proper" state.

Wittgenstein uses both kinds of fictional examples in his own philosophical investigations. This is what sets his work apart from the empirical activity of investigating the actual use of words. Philosophy may be *Dichtung* in part because it *"fictionizes"* (another possible sense of the verb *dichten*), constructing fictitious concepts and their backgrounds. But fiction in the conventional sense of the literary may also show the philosopher something fundamental about the reality of our concepts.

Hamlet

The idea that literature (or "poetry," in the broadest sense) is a kind of grammatical investigation may be illustrated by an example that does indeed come from a play. Shakespeare's *Hamlet* has long been regarded by literary commentators as a watershed in the historical development of our concept of interiority or subjectivity: the sense of an autonomous self that has both the power of interior reflection and expression and also a sense of private depth.[23] That sense is expressed throughout the play in its modes of address. Hamlet's interiority is generally conveyed through the almost obsessive use of soliloquy, and in Hamlet's self-conscious statement of a hidden, "real" self that lies beyond expression:

Hamlet: Seems, madam? Nay, it *is*. I know not "seems".
'Tis not alone my inky cloak, good-mother,
Nor customary suits of solemn black,
Nor windy suspiration of forced breath,
No, nor the fruitful river in the eye,
Nor the dejected haviour of the visage,
Together with all forms, moods, shows of grief
That can denote me truly. These indeed "seem",
For they are actions that a man might play;
But I have that within which passeth show—
These but the trappings and the suits of woe.[24]

(1.2.76–86)

The distinction between "actions that a man might play" and "that within which passeth show" has led some critics to argue that this peculiarly modern sense of self is in some deep sense inexpressible – that Hamlet paradoxically gives full expression for the first time to a real or authentic subjectivity that is essentially hidden from view. The paradoxical nature of this expression is rendered especially significant by Wittgenstein's remark that an utterance from a play teaches us to see the relationship between the meaning of an utterance and the interiority of the utterer from the right perspective because it is clear in such cases that there is no necessary correlation between the speaker's interiority (what s/he's experiencing) and the meaning of the utterance. An actor's utterances exemplify Wittgenstein's fiction of the "beetle in the box" (*PI* §291). Like the supposed beetle that is accessible only to the person who has it in his or her box, the interior state of the actor is irrelevant to what he or she says. But *Hamlet* presents us with the paradoxical case of an actor who, in the name of a character, claims to have "that within which passeth show": something that lies necessarily beyond the capacity of a mere actor to express. How do we resolve this paradox? The best way is to allow Hamlet to do it for us.

In a scene that offers a striking counter-variation on the theme of interiority and expressibility, Hamlet is confronted by a moving display of passion by one of the itinerant actors visiting Elsinore. Witnessing the actor's passionate rendition of Hecuba's lament for her slain husband, Priam, Hamlet is struck by the discrepancy between the mere actor's histrionic intensity and his own culpable passivity:

> O, what a rogue and peasant slave am I!
> Is it not monstrous that this player here,
> But in a fiction, in a dream of passion,
> Could force his soul so to his whole conceit
> That from her working all his visage wanned,
> Tears in his eyes, distraction in 's aspect,
> A broken voice, and his whole function suiting
> With forms to his conceit? And all for nothing.
> For Hecuba!
> What's Hecuba to him, or he to Hecuba,
> That he should weep for her?
>
> (3.1.552–62)

Hamlet confronts here the negation of his earlier disavowal of mere "forms." Whereas he had formerly insisted on the emptiness of outward show in comparison with a profoundly inexpressible interiority, he now struggles to come to terms with the fullness of outward show in the absence of anything "inside." The discrepancy between these in the player's performance horrifies him. It is "monstrous" – inducing a profound feeling of familiarity and strangeness. His first impulse is to persist with his original sense that authenticity resides in an interior self: "What would he do," he asks, "Had he the motive and the cue for passion/ That I have?" (563–4). And his answer is as predictable as it is unsatisfactory:

> He would drown the stage with tears,
> And cleave the general ear with horrid speech,
> Make mad the guilty and appal the free,
> Confound the ignorant, and amaze indeed
> The very faculty of eyes and ears.
>
> (564–8)

Had the player the properly interior emotions that are intrinsically different in kind from all mere "actions that a man might play," such as he himself has, Hamlet speculates that the player's behaviour would be more authentically and overwhelmingly intense. But when he attempts to express that intensity himself, he finds himself becoming no more than a *bad* actor, precisely the kind that he warns against in his advice to the players when he enjoins them to "suit the action to the word, the word to the action, with this special observance: that you o'erstep not the modesty of nature" (3.2.17–19):

> Bloody, bawdy villain!
> Remorseless, treacherous, lecherous, kindless villain!
> O, vengeance!—
> Why, what an ass am I? Ay, sure, this is most brave,
> That I, the son of the dear murderèd,
> Prompted to my revenge by heaven and hell,
> Must, like a whore, unpack my heart with words
> And fall a-cursing like a very drab,
> A scullion! Fie upon 't, foh!—
>
> (582–90)

There are two ways in which one might respond to Hamlet's predicament. One could read it as a confirmation that there is indeed a total discrepancy between what is inward and what may be displayed. The fact that the actor can summon more passion than Hamlet can over the murder of his father may be taken as proof that the two realms are indeed incommensurable. But that leaves us in a curious predicament, in which the genuineness of the "inward man" makes no contact at all with the supposed emptiness of "outward show." But then such interiority, if it exists, plays the role of Wittgenstein's beetle in the box; that is to say, it plays no role at all. The actor's show is not empty: it is strikingly moving and appropriate. It is Hamlet's subsequent expression of his feelings, beginning "Bloody, bawdy villain!" that, as he recognizes himself, is contemptibly hollow. This point is doubly underlined if we take the metatheatricality of the scene into account, expressed by the fact that the problem of interiority and theatricality is being voiced by actors, whose own interiority is irrelevant to the sense of the speeches. Whatever is happening inside the actors playing these parts is irrelevant to the intelligibility of the distinctions between interiority and theatricality that they are making, or, indeed, to the intensity or genuineness of the passion that they express. There is nothing going on inside the actor playing Hamlet that is relevant to the sense or force of what he says. The other response is therefore to take the scene as an indication of the point that Wittgenstein pursues, namely that no matter what we might comfortably assume, language and meaning are not the products of a hidden interiority that is "expressed" via words. And as Hamlet himself discovers when he confronts the "monstrosity" of the player's capacity for moving speech, this discovery about what we regard as the deepest inwardness – that which in ourselves constitutes "home" – is uncanny, disorienting, strange.

This is not to argue, as some literary critics have done, that the concept of interiority evaporates: that the private in *Hamlet* is entirely the function of the public.[25] We need to give it its appropriate place. Shakespeare's play shows that privacy or inwardness needs appropriate public contexts to be viable. Being the products of particular language-games, they cannot survive a society that does not offer the public environments necessary for such games to be played. Denmark is a prison, as Hamlet himself famously observes, because its pathology imposes the public relentlessly upon the private. This is apparent throughout the play, not only in the predicament of the prince, but also his lover, Ophelia, who finds herself so ruthlessly exposed to the public gaze, so unable to engage in the language-games of humane privacy, that she commits suicide.[26] Even in death she is allowed no privacy: she continues to be the object of wider public scrutiny, comment, and suspicion as a presumed suicide. The events at her funeral exemplify the degree to which people inhabiting the Danish court are stripped of the modes for the expression of the personal by rendering impossible the language-games of personal love and devotion. At her grave Hamlet, now himself a spy unable to endure Laertes's public histrionics, exposes himself with an unseemly show of similar histrionics and violence as he wrestles with his beloved's brother over her coffin:

Hamlet: I loved Ophelia. Forty thousand brothers
          Could not, with all their quantity of love,
          Make up my sum.—What wilt thou do for her?
King Claudius: O, he is mad, Laertes.
Queen Gertrude: (to Laertes) For love of God, forbear him.
Hamlet:(to Laertes) 'Swounds, show me what thou'lt do.
          Woot weep, woot fight, woot fast, woot tear thyself,
          Woot drink up eisel, eat a crocodile?
          I'll do 't. Dost thou come here to whine,
          To outface me with leaping in her grave?
          Be buried quick with her, and so will I.
          And if thou prate of mountains, let them throw
          Millions of acres on us, till our ground,
          Singeing his pate against the burning zone,
          Make Ossa like a wart. Nay, an thou'lt mouth,
          I'll rant as well as thou.

                       (5.1.266–81)

I'm not going to call this show "love," Hamlet is declaring, while attempting to establish himself, in contrast, as a paradigm of romantic devotion. But the play as a whole – in its delineation of the circumstances that Wittgenstein indicates are necessary for a concept to take hold at all – constantly calls into question Hamlet's own status as an instance of loving behaviour. This is in a sense not Hamlet's fault, for the representation of those circumstances makes it clear that the social world of Elsinore leaches all meaning from the language-games through which intimacy can flourish. It is therefore understandable that critics should have wanted either to argue that what appears to be the private in the play is in fact public, or that the "real" self resides in an interior realm that is inscrutably impervious to the ravages of the public domain. But the relationship between the private and the public, or the interior and the exterior, should not be decided via metaphysical dogmas that the one is *really* the other. Wittgenstein's argument against the possibility of a private language, which is germane to Shakespeare's tragedy, does not reduce the private to the public. These concepts are distinct; each has a role in the language, even the language that Shakespeare and Hamlet speak. They are embroiled in a multitude of complex ways, but nevertheless belong to different language-games.[27] *Hamlet* shows the debilitating personal and social effects when the one is subsumed or obliterated by the other.

In the light of this brief exploration of the ways in which a play like *Hamlet* highlights the grammatical relationships of the concepts of meaning and inwardness, it may therefore be fruitful to regard fiction, or at least certain kinds of fiction, as being already engaged in this kind of grammatical investigation with which Wittgenstein is concerned in his philosophical work. If he opens the doors of philosophy to fiction, it may be that his kind of philosophy has long been a guest in its house. And following the Freudian insight into the uncanniness of the house or the home, we may return to the notion of the inexpressible in Wittgenstein's philosophy: that which is hidden, secret, veiled, that is to say, *heimlich*.

What cannot be said

Finally, I want to argue that the bewilderment that arises from finding oneself lost in a wilderness rather than at home in a domestic garden arises from what the later Wittgenstein retains of the "inexpressible" from the *Tractatus*. "What is inexpressible (what I find mysterious and am not able to express)," he notes on his return to philosophy, "is the background against whatever I could express has its meaning" (*CV*, p. 16). It is the immense complexity of this background that escapes even the most comprehensive attempts to offer a philosophical *Übersicht* of the broader contexts that allow language to be what it is. Because meaning is possible only against, or within, this "inexpressible" background, our accounts of language cannot be neatly trimmed into manageable, formal patterns: they can neither be covered by a single, comprehensible theory, nor can all the ground be adequately covered in order to "represent all the interrelations between things" (*CV*, p. 12). This background is not inexpressible in the Tractarian sense of being "the logical form of reality" (*TLP*, 4.121). It is, in accordance with Wittgenstein's later contextualism – which expands the early, purely linguistic context of the proposition to the vast domain of "forms of life" – the natural, cultural, social and discursive worlds implicit in everything that may be said in language. Unlike logical form, it does not even show itself in the forms of what can be said: it has to be traced along arduous and confusing paths and "journeyings." This is especially underlined by Wittgenstein's parenthetical qualification "what I find mysterious and am not able to express." He does not state the metaphysical inexpressibility of the "background against which whatever I could express has its meaning" here; he does not set a logical limit, as he does in the *Tractatus*. Rather, he registers a personal sense of bewilderment and limitation. Why should Wittgenstein not be able to "express" this background? And is this limitation limited to Wittgenstein? Is it related to his earlier regret that he cannot write verse? Much depends on what he means by "expressing" this background. Does the problem lie in formulating the nature of the background properly, or describing it?

An answer may be found in the tension that I have traced between the metaphor of the elevated "perspicuous representation" and the earth-bound journey "criss-cross in every direction." The desire for the elevated overview stems from a wish both to see the nature of the background and its relation to any particular concept clearly, and also to map completely the relationships among all concepts in the language and the totality of backgrounds against which they "have their meaning." While there is no logical prohibition against this, Wittgenstein is forced to acknowledge that one can sketch such relationships only from a situated position. Wittgenstein's singular achievement lies in showing us the nature of the relationship, that is to say, in his situated or contextualist philosophy of language. Insofar as he alerts us to the imbrication of background and use, he certainly manages to "express" it. But insofar as the task of mapping the totality of relationships is reduced in specific cases to that of making repeated, iterant sketches, it eludes him.

Wittgenstein's success in the first task (alerting us to the significance of this background) allows us to see that the second is constantly being achieved by the manifold of texts that we call "literature." Wittgenstein's crucial philosophical task is carried out in the vast network of the literary, in which the situatedness of concepts in human life and the world is registered and imaginatively renewed and tested. In this sense poetry (in the broadest sense of the word) is always written as philosophy, and philosophy (as Wittgenstein understands it) takes on the burdens of poetry. Like Wittgenstein's sketches, poetry shows us both our being at home in language and the strangeness of that home. Just as Wittgenstein's poetic traversals of the maze of paths that constitutes our language as practically grounded in the world reveals the uncanny – the *heimlich* – at the heart of our linguistic home, so literature stages and embodies our alternating perceptions of that home – now as a "wilderness," now as a "well laid out garden."

Can Wittgenstein's desire for a synoptic representation of grammar be reconciled with the reality of the "imperfect garden" in which we forge our lives? I have suggested that the first is in fact both inappropriate and impossible – that

Wittgenstein recognizes that impossibility, even if only implicitly, and that the literary is in fact the domain in which that *Übersicht* is offered, if at all. I say if at all, because no single literary work offers a comprehensive survey of the whole of grammar. We would need take it all together, as a complete body, which itself raises the problem of the *Übersicht*. Furthermore, the sketches that the literary offers are in constant transformation, always being supplemented. Like Wittgenstein's writing, it registers the continuous criss-crossing of the vast terrain on which human life and language meet rather than a single, commanding perspective. So the desire for the panopticon betrays the very idea of writing philosophy as poetry. There's no getting around the fact that, as Wittgenstein writes elsewhere, "we must plough through the whole of language."[28] That is what literature does, day by day. But we are then confronted with a paradox similar to the one involving the disposable ladder at the end of the *Tractatus*. The insight that "poetry" or the "literary," with its diverse capacity to engage in such plowing, offers the best kind of grammatical investigation of our concepts, is engendered precisely by Wittgenstein's notion of the *Übersicht*. Without it, we would perhaps not know what it is, in this specific sense, that poetry does. Like the ladder at the end of the *Tractatus*, the very notion of the *Übersicht* needs to be abandoned once we have used it to "see the world rightly." Wittgenstein notes that "my thinking...has sticking to it the shrivelled remains of my earlier (withered) ideas" (*CV*, p. 23). It may be that the desire for the view from above is what (necessarily) remains of philosophy in Wittgenstein's *Dichtung*.[29]

Notes

1 Ludwig Wittgenstein, *Culture and Value*, G. H. von Wright and Heikki Nyman (eds.), trans. Peter Winch, Oxford: Blackwell, 1980, p. 16.
2 Ludwig Wittgenstein, *Philosophical Investigations*, trans. G. E. M. Anscombe, Oxford: Blackwell, 1967, p. ix.
3 *Die Beruhigung in der Philosophie tritt ein, wenn das erloesende Wort gefunden ist.* Ludwig Wittgenstein, *Nachlass* (14 December 1933), item 115, p. 30.
4 I refer here to the quotation from Schopenhauer that P. M. S. Hacker and G. P. Baker use as the epigraph to their commentary on Wittgenstein, *Wittgenstein: Meaning and Understanding*, Oxford: Blackwell, 1980, p. xiv: "Thoughts reduced to paper are generally nothing more than the footprints of a man walking in the sand. It is true that we see the path that he has taken; but to know what he saw on the way, we must use our own eyes."
5 Quoted in Ray Monk, *Ludwig Wittgenstein: The Duty of Genius*, New York: The Free Press, 1990, p. 151.
6 Marjorie Perloff translates the claim as: "Philosophy ought really to be written only as *a form of poetry*." This is preferable insofar as it retains the force of *nur* (only) and avoids Winch's circumlocution, but it (inevitably) misses the force of the verb *dichten*. Marjorie Perloff, *Wittgenstein's Ladder: Poetic Language and the Strangeness of the Ordinary*, Chicago and London: University of Chicago Press, 1996, epigraph.
7 "Wenn ich nicht ein richtigeres Denken, sondern eine neue Gedankenbewegung lehren will, so ist mein Zweck eine 'Umwertung von Werten' und ich komme auf Nietzsche, sowie auch dadurch, dass meiner Ansicht nach, der Philosoph ein *Dichter* sein sollte."

Wolfgang Huemer has suggested the following translation to me:

> If, rather than a more correct way of thinking, I want to teach a new movement of thought, my purpose is a "re-valuation of values," and (with this, or: thus) I come to Nietzsche as well as to the opinion that the philosopher should be a poet.
>
> (*Nachlass* (23 March 1938), item 120, p. 145r.)

8 See Perloff, Chapter 1.
9 Quoted in G. H. von Wright, *Wittgenstein*, Oxford: Blackwell, 1982, p. 81.
10 Ludwig Wittgenstein, *Tractatus Logico-Philosophicus*, trans. C. K. Ogden, London: Routledge & Kegan Paul, 1922, p. 27.
11 Quoted in von Wright, op. cit., p. 83.
12 Ludwig Wittgenstein, *Zettel*, G. E. M. Anscombe and G. H. von Wright (eds.), trans. G. E. M. Anscombe, Oxford: Blackwell, 1967, p. 567:

> How could human behaviour be described? Surely only by sketching the actions of a variety of humans, as they are all mixed up together. What determines our judgment, our concepts and reactions, is not what *one* man is doing *now*, an individual action, but the whole hurly-burly of human actions, the background against which we see any action.

13 Wittgenstein, *PI* §525. See also §203 and the Preface.
14 Ludwig Wittgenstein, *Remarks on the Philosophy of Psychology*, vol. 1, G. E. M. Anscombe and G. H. von Wright (eds.), trans. G. E. M. Anscombe, Oxford: Blackwell, 1980, pp. 555 and 557.
15 See Ray Monk, *Ludwig Wittgenstein*.
16 This argument is related to Perloff's views of the strangeness of the ordinary in Wittgenstein's work.
17 Sigmund Freud, "The Uncanny," *Collected Papers*, vol. 4, trans. Joan Riviere, London: The Hogarth Press, 1948, p. 375.
18

> [T]he uncanny would always be that in which one does not know where one is, as it were. The better orientated in his environment a person is, the less readily will he get the impression of something uncanny in regard to the objects and events in it.
>
> ("The Uncanny," p. 370)

19 The main point of contention is J. L. Austin's exclusion of fictional uses of language as "non-serious" or "etiolated." See Austin's *How to Do Things with Words*, Oxford: Oxford University Press, 1971, pp. 21–2.
20 Jacques Derrida, *Limited Inc*, Evanston: Northwestern University Press, 1998, p. 96.
21 For a more extensive treatment of this argument, see David Schalkwyk, "Fiction as 'Grammatical' Investigation: A Wittgensteinian View," *Journal of Aesthetics and Art Criticism* 53 (1995), 287–98 and also David Schalkwyk, *Literature and the Touch of the Real*, Delaware: University of Delaware Press, 2003.
22 Ludwig Wittgenstein, *Last Writings, Vol. 1: Preliminary Studies for Part II of "Philosophical Investigations,"* G. H. von Wright and Heikki Nyman (eds.), trans. C. J. Luckhardt and M. A. E. Aue, Oxford: Blackwell, 1982, p. 38.
23 See, for example, Ann Ferry, *The Inner Language: Sonnets of Wyatt, Sidney, Shakespeare, and Donne*, Chicago and London: University of Chicago Press, 1983.
24 William Shakespeare, *Hamlet*, in *The Oxford Shakespeare: The Complete Works*, Stanley Wells and Gary Taylor (eds.), Oxford: Clarendon Press, 1994.

25 See Francis Barker, *The Tremulous Private Body: Essays on Subjection*, London and New York: Methuen, 1984.

26 For an elaboration of this argument, see David Schalkwyk, *Speech and Performance in Shakespeare's Sonnets and Plays*, Cambridge: Cambridge University Press, 2002, Chapter 3.

27 See *Philosophical Investigations*, p. 220: "Silent 'internal' speech is not a half hidden phenomenon which is as it were seen through a veil. It is not hidden *at all*, but the concept may easily confuse us, for it runs over a long stretch cheek by jowl with the concept of an 'outward' process, and yet does not coincide with it."

28 Ludwig Wittgenstein, "Remarks on Frazer's *Golden Bough*," James Klagge and Alfred Nordmann (eds.), *Philosophical Occasions: 1912–1951*, Indianapolis and Cambridge: Hackett, 1993, pp. 119–55, p. 131.

29 I wish to thank John Gibson and Wolfgang Huemer for their invaluable help and critical engagement. John alerted me to implications of my argument about the problematic role of the perspicuous representation in the later Wittgenstein, while Wolfgang very generously and patiently helped with Wittgenstein's German and provided me with the quotations from Wittgenstein's *Nachlass*.

4

RESTLESSNESS AND THE
ACHIEVEMENT OF PEACE

Writing and method in Wittgenstein's
Philosophical Investigations

Timothy Gould

My title derives from *PI* §133:

> The real discovery is the one that makes me capable of stopping doing philosophy when I want to. – The one that gives philosophy peace, so that it is no longer tormented by questions which bring itself into question. – Instead, we now demonstrate a method, by examples; and the series of examples can be broken off.[1]

The German word translated as "peace" is "*Ruhe*," which could equally be translated as "rest." A guiding thought of this chapter is that what Wittgenstein's commentators often call (appropriately enough) "disquietude" might well be thought of as a form of restlessness. Such a retranslation already starts to show the connection of the disorder of thought and the kinds of writing in which such disorder finds its appropriate expression. We might then glimpse something of how the achievement of rest from out of our restlessness assumes certain literary forms and philosophical methodologies (e.g., the giving of examples; the breaking off of the series of examples at a certain moment). We can also see why the criticism that the peace Wittgenstein provides is only temporary and provisional is not quite to the point. For some philosophers, "peace," by its very nature, seeks to be everlasting. But a brief period of rest can be quite genuine and provide significant relief, even if it is only temporary.

This chapter consists, first, of an attempt to remove some of the impediments to understanding the goals and achievements of Wittgenstein's writing, followed by an extensive reading of the series of passages that led to the announcement that "A *picture* held us captive" (*PI* §115). The aim of the chapter as a whole is to undermine a particular interpretation of Wittgenstein's view of pictures as a source of philosophical disorder. Since this view is a fairly fundamental part of his teaching, dislodging some common ways of misinterpreting it should be a step toward a more comprehensive view of Wittgenstein's understanding of various philosophical disorders and how they are to be treated.

If my reading of these passages is meant to undermine some of the more standard readings, it is also meant to demonstrate the virtues of a "literary" attention to Wittgenstein's text. For the readings that I have seen seem to me to demonstrate a striking inability to recognize that this particular series of remarks forms a little narrative, and that Wittgenstein's famous remark about "pictures" is best understood as a moment within this story. I suggest that whatever prevents us from reading this story *as* a story is significant in itself and that it also represents a further range of obstacles to our apprehension of Wittgenstein's ways of writing.

It is difficult, but evidently not impossible, to ignore the fact that Wittgenstein was interested in the problems of writing. The evidence for his interest in such issues is pervasively present in the *Philosophical Investigations*, though not always explicitly so. Evidence from unpublished materials and from biographical research has been mounting steadily in the last few decades. The theme is notably present in *Culture and Value*:

> I think I summed up my attitude towards philosophy when I said: Philosophy ought authentically be written as a poetic composition [*dichten*].[2]

It is possible to make too much of this remark. Wittgenstein gives little guidance about how to make the connection that he asserts. But despite his reticence, there ought to be little doubt that this aphorism asserts a connection between what Wittgenstein takes philosophy to *be* and how he imagines philosophy needs to be written in order best to become what it really is.

Some commentators have recently shown a renewed interest in what Wittgenstein means by likening his methods to "therapies." But it seems to me that there has been remarkably little attention paid to the specific relations between the forms of his writing and its various philosophical achievements. Many have noticed that there is something remarkable about the way Wittgenstein writes. And while some have also paid attention to the idea of Wittgenstein's work as therapeutic, very few philosophers have given much thought to the question of how a piece of *writing* can perform tasks analogous to the tasks of therapy.[3] After all, the therapy that Wittgenstein's analogy evidently has in view – something at least partly Freudian in its inspiration – is certainly not conducted in writing.

The title *The Literary Wittgenstein* is ambiguous – as well as provocative. It points toward Wittgenstein's various affiliations with other forms of writing and culture, particularly the forms that surround and infiltrate his literary education and sensibility. (*Culture and Value* makes it clear that these issues were recurrently on Wittgenstein's mind.) And the title also points toward the literary side of Wittgenstein's own writing, an aspect of his work that is almost inevitably referred to as its "style."

I take it that there must be some connection between these two sides of Wittgenstein's attention to the "literary" and perhaps some further connection to something we could call his "literary influence." But despite various writings on the cultural context of his work,[4] not much has been said that would help us connect the culture that Wittgenstein possessed – and was possessed by – and the forms in which he wrote. What we do know – for instance, that he was for the most part alienated from the accomplishments of the last half of the nineteenth century – has so far tended to darken, rather than clarify, the philosophical significance of the literary affiliations of his work.

There is little to be gained in beginning with an investigation of Wittgenstein's literary affinities with other writers (or for that matter with musicians or architects) and in trying to use such perspectives to understand his writing. Looking for similarities between a parable of Wittgenstein's (e.g. about the pictured pot with the pictured steam coming out) and a parable of Kafka's (e.g. about the Chinese Wall) is not likely to be helpful in the absence of a better understanding of the uses to which Wittgenstein and Kafka put their parables. What we need is a precise understanding of his writing that shows what Wittgenstein is up to philosophically, in using these words in these ways.

Acknowledging a certain unfairness in singling out a book that is not intended as a work of philosophy, I want to underscore a striking passage in Monk's biography.[5] Monk attempts to explain an important aspect of Wittgenstein's work by juxtaposing a sentence of Wittgenstein's with a sentence of Hertz's.[6]

> When these painful contradictions are removed, the question as to the nature of force will not have been answered; but our minds, no longer vexed, will cease to ask illegitimate questions.[7]

Monk goes on to cite what he rightly takes Wittgenstein to intend as a "conscious echo" of this sentence:

> In my way of doing philosophy, its whole aim is to give an expression such a form that certain disquietudes disappear. (Hertz.)[8]

But Monk cites this as if Wittgenstein, in echoing Hertz's sentence, had more or less simply taken up Hertz's method and applied it to "[*his own*] way of doing philosophy" with only the barest of modifications. He gives the quotations from Hertz and Wittgenstein, as if there were no differences worth mentioning between them.[9] But even in so small a sampling of Wittgenstein's self-characterizations, and even in a period that is still evidently in transition towards his later work, we can see that something crucial has been altered. Understanding that transformation will put us in a better position to understand the functions of writing in the *Investigations*.

Wittgenstein's sentence speaks of "giv[*ing*]" an expression a certain "form"; and whether we take this to mean something primarily focused on the act of expressing, or something primarily focused on the written expression ("*Ausdruck*," like "expression," could mean either), there is nothing that corresponds to this moment in Hertz's formulation. The disappearance of the contradictions does not depend in any way on finding or giving the appropriate "form" for a certain expression – whether the expression of a thought, an issue, a question, or even a kind of wish. Or rather: Hertz's procedure does not depend on finding such form of expression – unless that simply means finding a form in which the contradiction becomes apparent. Hertz's remark seems to imply that you can get rid of the contradictions before the real work you are engaged in begins. Presumably, the impulse to ask the illegitimate questions will disappear because we can see that they lead to unsolvable difficulties.

If we focus our attention on the way Wittgenstein has modified Hertz's procedure, this leads us to another question: how does Wittgenstein go about finding the appropriate expression?

Among the first places to look for some ways of understanding this question is in the work of Stanley Cavell. Whatever the difficulties that occur in using the work of a difficult writer to elucidate the work of another difficult writer, and without wishing to slight the efforts of those who obviously appreciate the feel of Wittgenstein's writing, I still have not found any commentator[10] who comes close to Cavell's persistent and methodical (if somewhat intermittent) pursuit of the actual structure of Wittgenstein's words and paragraphs. The cost of ignoring Cavell's accomplishment in reading and delineating the structure of Wittgenstein's writing is considerably higher than the cost of putting oneself into Cavell's debt.

It is often useful to go back to the places where Cavell began his excavations. In "The Availability of the Later Wittgenstein," in a section entitled "The Style of the *Investigations*," Cavell has this to say:

> [*Wittgenstein's*] literary style has achieved both high praise and widespread alarm. Why does he write that way? Why doesn't he just say what he means, and draw instead of insinuate conclusions?…The first thing to be said in accounting for his style is that he writes: he does not report, he does not write up results. Nobody would forge a style so personal who had not wanted and needed to find the right expression for his thought.[11]

The critical question is this: How does Cavell think of the connection between "finding the expression of one's thought" and forging a personal style?

Many commentators imagine that the connection is obvious: Someone has a thought and is looking for a way to express this thought that will show that it is hers. She requires a personal style – that is, a style that is especially expressive of her person. The reason for this seems clear enough: Only your personal style can appropriately express your thought *as* yours. Your thought must be expressed in a way that, so to speak, has your name on it. (Perhaps it contains a certain type of metaphor or a penchant for parentheses.) This ambition for one's thoughts is

considered at best a kind of secondary consideration by most academic philosophers. At worst such efforts at writing in so personal a way are likely to be
apprehended as impediments to the clear expression of one's arguments – forms
of thought which are generally thought of as essentially *impersonal*.

There are moments when Wittgenstein approaches such an aesthetic of
personal expression, and consequently where he might seem to deserve the often
simplistic responses that his writing tends to evoke. One certainly cannot ignore
his remarks in the Preface to the *Investigations*:

> For more than one reason what I publish here will have points of
> contact with what other people are writing to-day. – If my remarks do
> not bear a stamp which marks them as mine, – I do not wish to lay any
> further claim to my property.
>
> $(x)^{12}$

It is easy enough to assume that Wittgenstein wants his "remarks" to
display his ownership of them by declaring them to be "expressions" of his
thought. And this would confirm a certain picture of the style of his remarks
as so many signs ("stamps") of his self self-expression. I do not wish entirely to
deny this idea of self-expression so much as to drastically circumscribe the
scope of its application.

The above remark helps to place Wittgenstein at a cultural moment late in the
Romanticism that dominated the nineteenth century. "Romanticism" is
increasingly coming back into philosophical parlance, usually as related to
aspects of Idealism. I am using it to interpret an admonition within Cavell's
characterization of Wittgenstein's modernism: "Self-expression" is no longer
something we can take for granted as a guarantor of the self's ability to
imprint itself on its words. I suggest that Wittgenstein has something to tell us
about the relation of modernism to Romanticism, especially on the mounting
perplexities of self-consciousness concerning the media of human expression.
Without a clearer understanding of self-consciousness and the question of
expression, we will not get very far in connecting Wittgenstein's insistence on
finding the appropriate expression and Cavell's characterization of him as
needing to fashion a personal style.

Without some such understanding of the ways in which Wittgenstein alternately
seeks and dodges his fate as a late Romantic or early modernist, we will have little
hope of characterizing the relation between the details of Wittgenstein's practice as
a writer and his various pronouncements about writing and the ownership of
thoughts and his closely related pronouncements about writing and character. My
sense is that Wittgenstein's self-characterizations of his philosophical practice within
the *Investigations* are far more advanced than his ability to find words to characterize
that practice that do not participate directly in that practice. The self-descriptions
within the *Investigations* are so much a part of the work of that book that the attempt

to bring other material to bear on its power and intricacies – including Wittgenstein's own attempts – seem at best to be out of step with the work they are meant to describe and at worst to smother the originality of the *Investigations*.

Most commentators seem to understand Cavell's focus on the fervor of Wittgenstein's writing as an emphasis on something personal to Wittgenstein. While this cannot be entirely wrong, the difference between Cavell and the more traditional approach to the "personal" is decisive. For most commentators, the personal is *merely* personal, merely the outward expression of somebody's inner self. It is evidently very hard to resist the idea that the primary point of a distinctive style is somehow to express a distinctive self.

In his essay "*The Investigations'* Everyday Aesthetics of Itself," Cavell presents a clue about the role of aphorisms in the *Investigations*, in contrast to their role in *Culture and Value*. He continues to take his explorations of Wittgenstein's writing well beyond the idea of style – even a "personal" style – as essentially the expression of personality and of the aphorism as invariably meant to indicate the quality of a person's mind, for instance, the peremptory authority of a genius:[13]

> in the *Investigations* the aphoristic does not on the whole take the form of free-standing aphorisms (as in the cases of the fly and the fly bottle or the body as the best picture of the soul), but is mostly directed…to reflecting details of its methodicalness, its searching out criteria, articulating grammar, spelling out fantasies, calling attention to a fixated picture, presenting intermediate cases.[14]

This points to one of the more significant ways that Wittgenstein uses aphorisms in the *Investigations*. Wittgenstein's aphorisms gesture beyond themselves to other less spectacular forms of writing. These aphorisms tend to be "embedded" – which here means more than just located within a specific context. The aphorism emerges from a specific moment, and it returns to that moment in various ways. In the case I have in mind, the aphorism emerges as a moment in an all but unnoticed narrative. It is a striking moment to be sure, but a moment that requires the narrative for its full force, and in turn grants to the narrative a kind of climax. We naturally tend to take the sense of climax as voicing the philosophical upshot or denouement of the passage. But there are other reasons for providing the specific sense of climax that goes with such an aphorism.

For Wittgenstein the denouement comes later, as if it is only in getting past the wish for the climax, whether as the conclusion of an argument or as the aphoristic breaking off of conversation or narration, that we arrive at the peace which passes by such forms of breaking off and achieves the peace of examples, the peace of the exemplary.

Reading the *Investigations* demands a respect for the unobtrusive power of the continuities of Wittgenstein's thought and writing. This does not undercut the power of Wittgenstein's discontinuities, for instance, the ways in which he can abruptly bring the reader to a dead stop or point him in another direction:

"Yes, but there is *something* there all the same accompanying my cry of pain. And it is on account of that that I utter it. And this something is what is important – and frightful." – Only whom are you informing of this? And on what occasion?

(*PI* §296)

Here the change of direction or perspective contained in the question "Only whom are you informing of this?" is likely to be found irrelevant by someone in the grip of the skeptical problem. But this feat of Wittgenstein's writing is also likely to be overlooked by someone who "agrees with" what she takes to be the general tenor of his anti-skeptical conclusion. The two sentences following the quotation marks are not aphorisms, and they are not, by themselves, insights into the "problem" of other minds.

It is only if you have allowed yourself to be gripped by the problem of the other, *as* a problem, that you can allow yourself to be instructed by the sheer change of the mind's direction, or his ability to get the mind to track its motions from a different angle. In this case, it is less like a "breaking off" of a series of examples and more like a breaking in of a new kind of self-questioning: What has brought me to this impasse, where I seem to need to assert as news or at least as information something that cannot possibly *be* information – for it cannot possibly inform someone of something he or she does not already know?

What I am calling the abrupt change of direction or perspective in such a passage is not by itself going to achieve the peace that Wittgenstein is aiming for. But quite apart from the fact that it presents us with its own particular form of brilliance, the passage can help us bear in mind that Wittgenstein's writing has more than one way of bringing us to a halt or moving us along. This may in turn help us to remember that not everything that sounds like an aphorism or a magisterial summary of Wittgenstein's position is in fact intended to work in those ways.

I want to offer a close reading of §§113 through roughly 138, intended among other things to undermine more conclusively a standard view of Wittgenstein's use of the idea of a picture:

A *picture* held us captive. And we could not get outside it, for it lay in our language and language seemed to repeat it to us inexorably.

(*PI* §115)

This is often cited, I believe, as if it summarized an entire region of Wittgenstein's thought: (a) language contains pictures; (b) we are unable to avoid these pictures because, presumably, we are unable to avoid (using) language; and (c) we become entangled in our forms of speech at least in part because we are held captive by, entranced by, these pictures. Step (c) is not explicitly stated but it seems to many philosophers that Wittgenstein clearly implies it. And it seems reasonable to present these pictures as one source of our inability to survey our use of words, hence of our lack of a perspicuous representation of our grammar. At the very least, the idea of being "held captive" suggests a kind of immobility – one that would prevent the movement that is required to command the view of language that we need to bring our disquietudes to an end. To get to where we want, we must be able to "arrange" what we have always known (cf. §109). The activity of such "arranging" is incompatible with being immobilized by a picture. Moreover, there is a strong hint that such pictures are, generally speaking, false pictures, blocking a clear view of what we need to know. Such pictures may not be the only source of our "bewitchment" by language, but they must surely figure largely in any account of that bewitchment.

I am not suggesting that there is *no* evidence for such views of the role of "pictures" in the *Investigations*. But I am suggesting that to read these passages in this light is to miss a major aspect of Wittgenstein's writing and, moreover, one that casts light on other regions of the *Investigations*.

Let us ask how Wittgenstein accounts for the presence of these pictures in our language, and how they come to exert a hold on us. Wittgenstein does talk a great deal about pictures throughout the *Investigations*, but only very rarely does he talk about them as "lying in our language." Does this really make sense as something Wittgenstein might have held as a general thesis about the "location" of pictures?[15] As far as I know, he never provides an account of the presence of pictures "in" our language or of how *in general* they are supposed to function or misfunction.

Let us back up a bit. If we attend to Wittgenstein's remark about pictures sheerly as an aphorism, one might also take it to be a kind of general pronouncement, on a par with remarks like "The human body is the best picture of the human soul" or "A foolish consistency is the hobgoblin of little minds." Why take it so? No doubt a sense of a pronouncement is in the air. But that is also true of the pamphlet that begins "A specter is haunting Europe" or the one that asserts "We hold these truths to be self-evident." Neither Marx nor Jefferson nor Wittgenstein seems incapable of turning from a characterization of an apparently general condition to a quite detailed story about the origins of that condition.

Let us place this "isolationist" reading of "A picture held us captive" against the evidence of the surrounding passages. I propose a reading that makes more sense of the aphorism in question. This reading will present in detail Wittgenstein's way of linking an aphorism to the context of perplexity and criteria from which it actually emerges.

The passage occurs in a definite context, beginning at least as far back as §112. The fact is that what is there translated as "simile" [*Gleichnis*] might, in this context, be better translated as "likeness." In that case, the word would explicitly show its affinity for "*Bild*," which is, after, all normally considered a kind of likeness. Then we would be better prepared to see that §112 has everything to do with what Wittgenstein is up to in §115. The standard translation reads:

> A simile [*Gleichnisse*] that has been absorbed into our language, produces a false appearance that disquiets us.

This doesn't tell us *how* this *Gleichnis* became absorbed into the language. But it also doesn't suggest that language (all language?) just happens to contain these misleading "similes." Wittgenstein tells us, to all appearances quite straightforwardly, that something has happened to get the *Gleichnis* absorbed into the language.

Wittgenstein does not declare explicitly that he is about to tell us the story of how that "likeness" got absorbed into our language. But that is the most obvious reading of what he goes on to do. For surely the most striking fact about the sections leading from §112 to §115 is that they form a little narrative. And the most natural way to read this narrative is, precisely, that it tells us how that "likeness" got absorbed into our language in the form of a picture. This fact about these paragraphs has never really been commented on. Yet the marks of narration and other forms of continuity are all in place, requiring only that we be able to read them. We need to know what prevents us from reading what is in front of our eyes.

Section 112 begins with the declaration of a certain event: A *Gleichnis* got absorbed into our language and produces a false appearance that disquiets us. This is already a report on a kind of event. The succeeding passages continue this report:

> "But *this* isn't how it is" – we say. "Yet *this* is how it has to *be!*"
>
> (§112)

It hasn't gone unnoticed that §113 continues §112, by repeating the key phrase *"This is how it is____."* But isn't it equally clear that the disquietude mentioned in §112 as produced by the *Gleichnis* is actually enacted in §113? And isn't it precisely a form of philosophical unrest that leads to this sort of behavior: And isn't this a sort of restlessness?

> I say [*"This is how it is____"*] to myself over and over again. I feel as though, if only I could fix my gaze absolutely sharply (*ganz scharf*) on this fact, get it in focus, I must grasp the essence of the matter.
>
> (*PI* §113)

Moreover, the particular form of disquietude that is here being voiced combines a kind of gaze with a kind of repetition of a particular form of words. The theme of repetition is picked up in the following section, this time referring us to the *Tractatus Logico-Philosophicus*: "The general form of the proposition is: This is how things are____." Perhaps the introduction of the source-text of his own obsession has tended to make readers oblivious to the continuity of the story that Wittgenstein is telling. For he has introduced this earlier work in order, precisely, to continue (and no doubt deepen) the narrative:

> That is the kind of proposition (*Satz*) that one repeats to oneself count-
> less times. One thinks that one is tracing [*nachzufahren*] the outline of the
> thing's nature over and over again, and one is merely tracing round the
> frame [*Form*] through which we look at it.
>
> (*PI* §114)

However we characterize these bits of a story, the connections are clear
enough and the issue of repetition could not be more blatant, Wittgenstein even
goes so far as to use the same words in both sections precisely in his characterization of the act of repetition: "over and over again" in English, and even more
strongly in German: "*wieder und wieder.*" What is repeated is a proposition – a
sentence – about how propositions have to be. (Moreover, what are repeated are
precisely words that signify repetition.) And the outcome is given in §115: A
picture now holds us captive.

There are other indications of the continuity of this little narrative, if they
are needed: The emphasis on the word "this" in §§112, 113 and 114 suggests
that the "likeness" is a kind of image or picture of how the situation has to be,
even though the situation is evidently not like that. What is this "likeness"? In
fact, Wittgenstein speaks of a great many pictures throughout the *Investigations*,
without the slightest suggestion that in our use of these pictures we oscillate
between saying "this is how it has to be" and "the facts are plainly otherwise."
Think of the picture of "blindness as darkness in the soul." If I see it this way, I
will not in general feel that it "must" be like this, and then find myself oscillating
between "this way" and how it really is. This picture of blindness is not likely to
alternate with something else, anymore than it is likely to make me feel that I am
held captive by it, or that it has been imposed on me. If I become alive to other
ways of understanding the blind, these ways are likely to loosen the grip of the
"picture" of darkness in the soul, not produce a disquieting oscillation. Similarly,
if I harbor a picture of Australians as hanging upside down on the other side of
the earth, it is not something I am inclined to oscillate about. Nor do I, in most
circumstances, oscillate between pictures of myself as grasping the meaning of a
word in an instant and the other more painstaking accounts of the "grammar"
of grasping the meaning of a word.

The pictures that are the subject of these other stories show themselves
precisely in the way that we are inclined to take the application of certain words
and a certain picture of the use of these words as *obvious*. It requires work to get
the opposing understanding – for instance, that the use of a word is spread out
over space and time, and is not even a candidate for what could be "grasped in
an instant." And when I have done *that* work I am not then inclined to oscillate
back and forth between, for instance, "it looks like the use isn't grasped in an
instant," and then on the other hand "but it *must* be grasped in an instant." My
perplexity does not present itself as the kind of oscillation we are discussing. (If
you are in the grip of a similar perplexity, you might take this as an invitation to
examine the form it takes.) The two sides of my puzzlement do not possess the

kind of equal weight or force that produces the kind of oscillation that Wittgenstein is here depicting.

For the moment, I am merely claiming, without further evidence than my reading as a whole can supply, that the *obvious* reading of this passage is this: the *Gleichnis* "this is how things must be" and the sentence "A picture held us captive" are meant to apply first of all to the circumstances narrated in the little story that these sentences are embedded in and secondarily to those circumstances that turn out to be analogous. (I say "obvious," fully aware that it will not seem so to everyone. That is another story, one that is also contained in the *Investigations*.)

To recapitulate the story: We begin with a sense of disquiet, an unrest which takes the form of an oscillation. Unable to get away from this oscillation, we repeat the sentence that we feel we need to insist on, as if repetition will fix our gaze, make our focus sharper. And what happens is: after sufficient repetition, language repeats the sentence back to us. It is as if the likeness – which began as a form of words about words – had now become transformed into a picture. This picture, which now seems inescapably part of the language we are examining, repeats back to us the very words we had been repeating, the very words (which constituted a proposition about how propositions had to be) that we had been fascinated by. The outline of the proposition that we had tried to find immovably fixed in the scheme of things has now fixated us.

What is the therapy for such fixation? Without arguing for the correctness of this reading, I will try instead to see where it leads. The first hint of the direction of the therapy occurs in the next section: "What we do is to bring words back from their metaphysical to their everyday use." But how can this "therapy" so much as get a foothold with us? Why would someone in the grip of such a picture of the proposition be interested in the fact that "proposition" and "this is how things are" have perfectly ordinary uses? It is not until §134 that the therapy for this particular fascination seems to pick up again:

> Let us examine the proposition: "This is how things are." – How can I say this is the general form of propositions?

This question confirms one of Cavell's best insights into the issue of skepticism in Wittgenstein, which is closely related to the issue of the general form of what reflects (or fails to reflect) how things are: Wittgenstein is not denying that you can call *this* proposition the general form of the proposition. He is showing us how you *can* make such a claim, what makes it possible to *insist* on such a thought.

Therapy involves the possibility of rest: of coming to a stopping point *somewhere*. This depends on acknowledging that you *can* go further down that path – even under certain circumstances that you *must*. It is the opposite of the kind of therapy that says: "This yields contradictions: keep yourself away from this path." It says rather: "See how you were drawn by a (relatively) normal puzzlement into a kind of fixated repetition. See how your own use of language itself gave you the resources to make you and your words the source of your self-mystification." In this sense, Wittgenstein indeed has created an exemplary vision of a "picture," composed of words, in which I see and hear exactly what I have been repeating to myself. Finally, I have conjured a picture and some words that satisfy my urge to have my thought repeated back to me, as if by the nature of things. I have disguised my own attraction to a certain form of the proposition by means of a philosophical demand for something that will attach me once and for all to what is really there.

Before I say a little more about the kind of therapy Wittgenstein is offering, and about the apparent interruption between the statement of the perplexity and fixation and the beginning (again) of the therapy, I want to say a word about the process of repetition, internalization, and projection that he has described. In a sense, it does not matter whether Wittgenstein is describing a process (for instance, a quasi-Freudian or a quasi-Nietzschean process). As he reminds us, his goal is to replace explanation with description. What he describes is clearly (a) an internalization; followed by (b) a kind of externalization: the picture repeats, what we repeated: we absorbed it into our language: it *seemed* to lie in our language, and language repeats it back to us.

One reading might emphasize the illusory quality of this picture,[16] whereas my reading emphasizes the actual "success" of the internalization via some type of incorporation. But in Wittgenstein (unlike Freud or Nietzsche) the precise version of internalization that is envisioned matters much less than the plain fact that *some* kind of internalization and reversal has occurred and can be described. What had been a process of repetition on the part of the analyzer is now a process of repetition on the part of the "internalized picture."[17] In either case, we are very far from a picture of our language as simply containing random pictures, whose primary function is to trap the unwary philosopher.

If this view about pictures – generalizing the idea that "a picture held us captive" – is as pervasive and tenacious as it seems, dislodging it permits us, literally, to keep reading. We resume our reading at §134, where the preoccupation with "the general form of the proposition" is taken up again. Of course, others have noticed that §134 discusses the "same topic" as §§112–15. I am suggesting that "the proposition" is not merely being addressed again, but that Wittgenstein's self-interruption was intentional – part of the way the passages in question were composed.

Notice that §134 immediately follows the section from which I have drawn my title, a section that forms another climactic summation, this time of what Wittgenstein characterizes as his "methods." I have been suggesting that what he calls "peace" could equally be characterized as bringing rest to this particular kind of philosophical writing. But the irruption of this and other descriptions of method are not themselves the workings of the method. My suggestion is that the bursts of methodological reflection are significant – not just as clues to the kind of therapy he is proposing but as an expression of the wish for health or for peace. These interruptions are at least as significant as the theoretical outbursts of the patient who "interrupts" the analysis to describe the cure that he or she desires. The wish for the cure is not the cure, as the expression of a sense of personhood is not the achievement of personhood. But it is a step.

My last suggestion about these passages is this: What follows, for all the change of tone, is precisely the working out of a therapeutic moment in the *Investigations*. I conclude my reading of §§112–15 with the suggestion that we take Wittgenstein as timing his return to the subject of the form of propositions to achieve a specific effect. He substitutes for his initial narrative of perplexity a presentation in a much lower key of how that perplexity gets dissolved. Unfortunately, this dissolution will seem either flat or tendentious if the reader has not been able to connect the therapy to the initial narrative of the specific fascination and experience the grip of that picture's fascination.

Finally, I want to glance at the question: What does the story of the origin of our captivation contribute to Wittgenstein's methods? One way of answering this would be to ask another question: How do stories end? Normally, stories end with the kind of conclusion we sometimes call an ending. They do not normally just "break off," as Wittgenstein puts it in §133 (and also in the Foreword). This gives at least one further contrast to what happens in the method of examples. One further contrast that comes to the mind of most "analytic" philosophers is that of an argument or a proof, which cannot be "broken off" until it reaches its conclusion (and this is certainly not an irrelevant contrast for Wittgenstein). Yet another contrast is found in our unwillingness to conclude the story of our captivation. For once we have recognized that it is the story of our self-captivation that is being narrated and that seems to climax with the line "a picture held us captive," we are in a better position to learn something from the irruption of Wittgenstein's self-descriptions. For these self-descriptions, on their own, seem to be as potentially (if differently) captivating as any picture, and moreover they seem, in fact, to have abetted our unwillingness to let the story of our captivation be just a story, no less but no more than a story. Then we might let ourselves be done with the story and move on.

When the question of the general form of propositions picks up again at §134 the tone has changed: It begins calmly with, "Let us examine" – as if everything else, including the fabulous bursts of self-description, have been leading to just an examination. ("What stands between us and such an examination of the details?" – as he puts it earlier. It isn't always something irrelevant.) Ask yourself: what good it will do to be reminded that "This is how things are" has a perfectly ordinary use as an English sentence or proposition? What good is supposed to come from recognizing that *this* sentence can work as "the general form of a proposition" only because, in certain circumstances, it *is* an ordinary proposition? For whom will this come as news, much less as therapy? It is only in the realm of the inter-play between what leads to our captivation and the facts that make that captivation possible that therapy becomes both possible and instructive.

Otherwise, the intended therapy is just the flat repeating of something that is intended to be common sense, but more often turns out to be the forced version of common sense employed by philosophers trying to combat a conclusion that seems, from a certain angle, to be inevitable – if unacceptable.

By bringing together the narration of our captivation by a picture of the use of a sentence and the plain series of examples of what we can actually *do* with such a sentence we might become free of this captivation. We might even, in the process of that liberation, learn something. What frees us is not the idea that our captivation is now impossible, because we have seen that it leads to a contradiction. Rather, we are freed from an image of how words represent the world, which seems, in certain frames of mind, to be necessary. (The image that seems necessary is also an image of how things *must* be: it is an image of necessity. This is presumably another aspect of what makes this case so central to the *Investigations*.) The freedom from these false necessities occurs because we see how the image of necessity *became* possible. Therapy is not the elimination of what is impossible. It is what breaks the grip of what seems all too necessary. We are to be liberated precisely from what has come to seem necessary, in order that we may accept what otherwise seems merely, almost accidentally, to be the case.

In this light we can also read the other material in these paragraphs. For instance, we can better understand the claim that "no one is going to call the letter 'p' the general form of propositions," and the apparently more radical claim that "*one* feature of our concept of a proposition is, *sounding like a proposition*" (§134). To the first claim one might say: "Of course not: it was not intended as a representation of the general form of a proposition, it is only a variable standing in for a proposition." Yet this thought is from the same writer who once wrote: "It is obvious that a proposition of the form 'aRb' strikes us as a picture. In this case the sign is obviously a likeness (*Gleichnis*) if what is signified" (*TLP* 4.012). (This passage provides a little further evidence for my re-translation of *Gleichnis* as "likeness" rather than "simile" in the crucial passage in §112: "whatever else it may do, 'aRb' does not strike us as a 'simile.'") When we are in the grip of an idea of what a proposition *has* to be in order to perform its function, it is easy enough to think of aRb as "picturing" a relation between a and b.

No one in the grip of the idea that a proposition has the same form as the facts that it is intended to state – or that it pictures them, or fits them – is likely to be suddenly freed of this conviction by noticing that the letter "p" doesn't have enough structure to picture anything. Such a person is likely to respond: "p" was never intended to have such a structure. (The same philosopher is also not going to be impressed by remarks like "I always know how tall I am. *This* tall"; or by the implication that his careful efforts at verifying something amount to buying two copies of the same edition of the same newspaper.) My point is not that these moments in Wittgenstein – sometimes argumentative, sometimes aphoristic, sometimes using analogies verging on the simplistic – are not doing their job. It is rather that these passages function in a context of writing which we have barely begun to explore. Look for a moment at the way in which two sections later, in the long discussion at §136, he picks up a certain use of the letter "p," now not so much as the form of a proposition, but precisely as some version of a variable "standing for" a proposition:

'p' is true = p
'p' is false = not-p
And he continues by remarking that

> to say that a proposition is whatever can be true or false amounts to saying: we call something a proposition when *in our language* we apply the calculus of truths functions to it…
>
> Now it looks as if the definition – a proposition is whatever can be true or false – determined what a proposition was, by saying: what fits the concept "true", or what the concept 'true' fits, is a proposition. So it is as if we had a concept of true and false, which we could use to determine what is and what is not a proposition. What *engages* with the concept of truth (as with a cogwheel), is a proposition.
>
> But this is a bad picture. It is as if one were to say "The king in chess is *the* piece that one can check." But this can mean no more than in our game of chess we only check the king. Just as the proposition that only a *proposition* can be true or false can say no more than that we only predicate "true" and "false" of what we call a proposition.
>
> (§136)

Here he passes from the question of how "true and false" might "belong" to the concept of the proposition but not "fit" it, in the sense that the picture required – as "being checked" belong to our concept of the king, in our game of chess. (Here we see another reason for the shifts in sections and strings in paragraphs: Now he goes after the idea of "fitting," pointing out that we mean something perfectly ordinary when we say that "checking" doesn't "fit" our concept of pawns, if that implies a game in which the players who lost their pawns lost the game (i.e. on the spot): such a game would be "uninteresting or stupid or too complicated or something of the sort" (§136)).

Again, he is not just giving examples (for instance of how the words are actually used in the everyday language game that is their home or what an expression might actually be used to say in the reverberation of words and world that we might actually possess). He *returns* to such examples, again and again. And the argumentativeness (so often confused with the advancing of theses that he claims he does not have) and the aphorisms form an essential region of what he returns *from*. It is this turning back – not just to the everyday world but to a more ordinary-sounding discursive prose – that gives the plain sentences and propositions of our language, the humble analogies or disanalogies, the ability to be the counter-irritant to our irritated and restless fixations. ("P" is not the form of anything like a sentence; only a real sentence or proposition could so much as seem or pretend to be the general form of propositions; and so on.) In the world of philosophy that Wittgenstein finds himself driven to investigate, only the right match of irritant and counter-irritant produce the balm or relief that his writing pursues. Only after we have known what philosophical discord is about can we know the value of the accord that philosophical writing, from time to time, achieves.

The acceptance of the given – of our forms of life – is not some transcendental accomplishment but the willingness to give up a certain kind of necessity, and a certain fascination with the oscillation between what you know *must* be the case and what the series of examples slowly, almost repetitiously and yet somehow perspicuously teaches you is in fact the case. And that is surely not only part of what it means to know when and how to "break off" the series of examples. It is also part of what it is for us philosophers to learn how to leave everything as it is. Surely that is a form of peace, of restfulness, that resonates between the form of the writing and the life of the writer. What more is there still to ask for?

Notes

1 Ludwig Wittgenstein, *Philosophical Investigations*, trans. G. E. M. Anscombe, Oxford: Blackwell, 3rd edn., 1971, §133. Hereafter cited in the text as *PI*.
2 *Culture and Value*, G. H. von Wright (ed.), trans. Peter Winch, Chicago: Chicago University Press, 1980, p. 14. I have modified the translation to bring out the force of "*eigentlich*" as "authentic."
3 There are some exceptions: see Steven Affeldt, "Captivating Pictures and Liberating Language: Freedom as the Achievement of Speech in Wittgenstein's *Philosophical Investigations*," *Philosophical Topics* 27 (1999), 255–85. This essay refers to an unpublished paper of mine, "Pictures from an Investigation," which first proposed the reading sketched in below, and cites its discussion of the line "A picture held us captive." See also Richard Eldridge, *Leading a Human Life*, Chicago: The University of Chicago Press, 1997, pp. 1–15 and 86–120. This book also raises some issues about the question of therapy and representative autobiography in philosophical writing.
4 By writers such as Heller, Janik, Toulmin, von Wright, and Cavell.
5 Ray Monk, *Ludwig Wittgenstein: The Duty of Genius*, New York: The Free Press, 1990.
6 From the Introduction to *The Principles of Mechanics*, cited by Monk, p. 446.
7 Ray Monk, *Ludwig Wittgenstein*, op. cit., p. 446.
8 Ibid.
9 Similar things used to be said about how Wittgenstein wrote the *Tractatus*. But work by W. Hart, Cora Diamond, James Conant, Eli Friedlander and others has made this a much less attractive reading even for the early work.
10 For instance, O. K. Bouwsma, Rush Rhees, Cora Diamond, Ben Tilghman, James Conant, Arnold Davidson and others.
11 *Must We Mean What We Say?* New York: Charles Scribner's Sons, 1969, pp. 44–72, p. 70.
12 Passages making points about character and style, which can be understood in relation to this preface, are to be found throughout *Culture and Value*, for instance, at pp.18–23. But even in these selections of his thought we find remarks like this: "A present-day teacher of philosophy doesn't select food for his pupil with the aim of flattering his taste, but with the aim of changing it" (p. 17). Here again the emphasis is not on the expression of the writer's selfhood but on the resources – no doubt,

drawn from within – that the writer deploys in order to change something fundamental in the self of *another*, in his receptiveness for instance.

13 Cf. Timothy Gould, *Hearing Things: Voice and Method in the Writing of Stanley Cavell*, Chicago: University of Chicago Press, 1998, Chapters I and II, *passim*.

14 Stanley Cavell, "The *Investigations*' Everyday Aesthetics of Itself," Stephen Mulhall (ed.), *The Cavell Reader*, London: Blackwell, 1996, pp. 376–89, p. 386. (Reprinted in this volume.)

15 I see no evidence that Wittgenstein held the kind of view of language that might make sense of this residue of pictures: originally, some have argued, words were closer to natural aspects of the world. As language progresses, it becomes more abstract, moving away from the physical images, but unable to eradicate their presence and their influence. Cf. Timothy Gould, "Natural Notions, Uncommon Speech," dissertation, Harvard University, 1978.

16 Cf. Affeldt's essay, cited in n.3.

17 For a related view, see Conant's introduction to Putnam's *Realism with a Human Face*, Cambridge: Harvard University Press, 1990.

5

IMAGINED WORLDS AND THE REAL ONE

Plato, Wittgenstein, and mimesis

Bernard Harrison

I

In the closing lines of *To the Lighthouse*, Lily Briscoe makes the final mark on the canvas she has been painting. All she does is to draw a line. Yet it is clearly something which costs her a good deal of effort, and which in her view makes the difference between artistic failure and artistic success.

> Quickly, as if she were recalled by something, she turned to her canvas. There it was – her picture. Yes, with all its greens and blues, its lines running up and across, its attempt at something. It would be hung in the attics, she thought; it would be destroyed. But what did that matter? she asked herself, taking up her brush again. She looked at the steps; they were empty; she looked at her canvas; it was blurred. With a sudden intensity, as if she saw it clear for a second, she drew a line there, in the centre. It was done; it was finished. Yes, she thought, laying down her brush in extreme fatigue, I have had my vision.[1]

The troubling question, now, or at least a question which troubles us a great deal at the moment, is, What is this "vision" supposed to be a vision of? Or, to put it another way, what is supposed to constrain the placing of that final stroke? If the vision is a vision of Reality, we want to say, then the placing of the stroke ought to be constrained by the Real: by the garden, say, of which the painting is supposed to be a painting. But Lily is not looking at the garden; she is looking, and with an "intensity" sufficient to exclude all else, at the painting. So, one is inclined to say, whatever constrains her in placing the stroke must be internal to the painting.

So saying we open our minds to a doctrine central to all that is most radical and "anti-humanist" in present-day critical theory: the doctrine that works of art are not "referential." Lily Briscoe's painting is clearly meant as an analogue of the very novel we are reading: Lily's pains and struggles are, at least in their formal character, indistinguishable from Virginia Woolf's. The problem of knowing where on the canvas to draw, or not to draw, a line is the same problem as the problem of knowing where to insert, or not to insert, a word in the vast tissue of words which is the novel. And there is as much and as little help to be got in either case, in taking these decisions, from "the Real World." F. R. Leavis thought that in *To the Lighthouse* Virginia Woolf had at last managed to write a decent, if not a great, book because in doing so she had followed the welltrodden paths of the autobiographical novel. This makes *To the Lighthouse* to some extent a *roman à clef*. Mr. Ramsey "is" Mrs. Woolf's father, Leslie Stephen, and so on and so forth.[2] This will not do. The novel is not a memoir. Memories of her father will no more tell Virginia Woolf where to place one word in *To the Lighthouse* than looking at the garden will tell Lily Briscoe where to place the final stroke in her painting. Neither novel nor painting is, in that sense at least, a transcription of Reality. But surely, then, if neither is in that sense a transcription of Reality, neither is "referential." However much painting and novel may mimic to the reader a garden or a Georgian upper-middle-class family, however much representations of characteristic features of each of those things may contribute to the fabric of novel or painting (to say, as Barthes says of the barometer, "Je suis le vrai"), the considerations which ultimately determine the placing of a word in the novel must be as internal to the novel as the considerations which ultimately determine the placing of Lily Briscoe's final stroke are internal to the painting.

Arguments of this type have led a large number of literary critics in recent years to conclude that a work of literature is an hermetically self-referential tissue of signs which, though it may exploit for purposes of verisimilitude innumerable commonplace features of the real world, owes its weaving not to any impulse to produce a cognitively adequate representation of that world, but rather to the interaction of a host of more or less "formal" considerations, where "formal" means roughly "internal to literature": genre, trope, topos, the structural oppositions characteristic of myth or of Foucauldian "épistèmes," and so on. I am going to suggest that, while the premises of the argument are perfectly correct, there is a logical gap separating the conclusions which those premises actually yield from the far more radical conclusions which they are frequently taken to sustain. What the argument actually establishes is merely the appositeness of Maurice Merleau-Ponty's observation, "In a sense language never has anything to do with anything but itself,"[3] as a remark about literary language. Literary language has in a sense, like language in general, nothing to do with anything but itself. But can we simply pass, as it seems transparently evident to so many people at present that we can, from that thought to the thought that literature is not concerned with reality? Maybe, if it is evident that being concerned with language excludes being concerned with reality. But is that so evident? It does not seem so to me, and I shall now attempt to make it seem a little less so to you.

II

Our gut feeling as a culture is that a language occupied solely with language cannot be occupied with reality because language itself is empty of reality, is a mere notation, *a flatus vocis*, or a game of marks on paper. It is this conviction, and others parallel to it, which renders our attitude to literature, as to all the arts, so profoundly ambiguous and makes us perennially uncertain whether art in general is one of the glories of our civilization, or something debilitating: a confidence-trick, a delusion or a secret vice. But for literary language to seem to lack, through its self-referentiality, a proper and respectable commerce with reality, we need to be able to contrast it with a kind, a use, of language which does stand in the right, the modest, the genuinely informative relationship with what seems, because extralinguistic, incontestably real. The earliest work that elaborates a rationale for such a contrast is no doubt the *Cratylus* of Plato.

The *Cratylus* introduces three ideas to which particularly voluminous footnotes have been appended by subsequent philosophy. The first is the idea that, while sentences are constructed out of names, the relationship to reality exhibited by a name is not all that dissimilar to that exhibited by a proposition: both can be true or false, for instance.[4] The second, also developed in the *Theaetetus*, is the idea that while the meanings of some names may be verbally explicated in terms of other names, at least some of the names in terms of which these explications are framed must be incapable of verbal analysis because they refer to completely simple things: things which can only be named, but not described.[5] The third is the idea that the question *of what categories of things names are to pick out* is settled wholly by the nature of Reality, with no contribution whatsoever from human convention or practice. Reality just does divide up into certain categories of nameable elements, and it is the business of philosophical enquiry, not of poetry or of linguistic tradition darkly manifesting itself in etymology, to determine the identity and nature of those categories of elements. The philosophically proficient mind, in choosing which elements of the world to name, cuts, like the good butcher, with the joints.

The effect of these three doctrines taken together is, first of all, to promote the idea, potent in the philosophy of both the seventeenth and the early twentieth centuries, of a logically perspicuous language. A logically perspicuous language will be one whose simplest names will denote simple elements of Reality, while the syntactic articulations of simple names into complex names and into sentences will display the actual articulation of simples into complexes. By the standards of a logically perspicuous language, the ordinary language we speak every day lacks clarity. It contains many apparent names, or apparent denoting expressions, which cannot actually denote anything ("The present King of France" is a familiar example of Russell's), while its grammar is notoriously misleading from the point of view of the formal logician.

The second, and perhaps less obvious, tendency of Plato's three doctrines is to promote the idea of language as an epistemically and semantically neutral device for recording the nature of extralinguistic Reality. A logically perspicuous language would, in a certain sense, be transparent to the structure of Reality. Its conventions would not work to mislead us by obscuring the ontological structure of the extralinguistic. It would have lost the power to interpose misleadingly its conventional mechanisms between its speakers and Reality because of the extreme parsimony of the conventional provisions required to set such a language up. Those conventions have often appeared to philosophers to amount to no more than the stipulation of associative links between basic names and simple elements of Reality. It has seemed to many philosophers, including Russell at one stage of his thinking, that once we have associated basic names with simple elements of Reality, or "logical atoms," as Russell called them, the question of what sense a sentence makes, and whether it makes sense, can be left to empirical observation. Russell's logical atoms have logical types: they are, intrinsically, individuals or properties or relations. Strings of the corresponding names thus cohere into sentential structures by virtue of the logical character of the entities they denote. Whether a sentence is true depends upon whether the entities in question are related to one another in Reality as their names stand in relation to one another in the sentence. Whether a sentence makes sense depends on the question of whether the entities picked out by the names that figure in it can, as a matter of empirical fact, stand to one another in the relationship in which the sentence represents them as standing. About the *linguistic* complexities of a logically perspicuous language there is, in short, virtually nothing to know. About the linguistic complexities of the ordinary, or "natural," language we actually speak there is, of course, a great deal to know. But knowing it will tell us nothing about the nature of Reality, since to the exact degree that the linguistic conventions of ordinary language depart from the parsimony of conventional provision characteristic of a logically perspicuous language, ordinary language itself falls away from the perfect transparency to Reality characteristic of a logically perspicuous language, becoming instead a device for generating misleading illusions about Reality. It follows that nothing that has to do only with the exploration of a natural language, including literature if that is what literature does, can contribute in any way to the exploration of Reality.

The three linguistic doctrines Plato sketches in the *Cratylus* contain in germ, in short, the materials for an antiliterary polemic harsher, even, than the one developed in the *Republic*, along the more familiar lines of Plato's critique of artistic *mimesis* in relation to the theory of Forms. It must be said, of course, that few philosophers would nowadays take very seriously the notion of a logically perspicuous language as that which presented itself to Russell, say, in 1918. But the theories of language that have replaced Russell's in the mainstream of analytic philosophy – one thinks particularly of Quine, or Davidson, for instance – preserve features of it which make them equally hostile to any claim to explore Reality on the part of what actually only explores language. There is, however, another major line of attack on the notion of a logically perspicuous language, one which is the more interesting because it goes, in principle if not always explicitly, back to the Platonic roots of such notions, namely, the one due to Wittgenstein. To that I shall now turn.

We could do worse than begin from Peter Geach's insightful remark that "a great deal of the *Tractatus* is best understood as a refashioning of Frege's function-and-argument analysis in order to remove his [*Frege's*] mistaken treatment of sentences as complex names."[6] Among the doctrines Gottlob Frege took over from Plato was one with more than a passing resemblance to the first of the three I extracted from the *Cratylus*. Frege, like the Socrates of the *Cratylus*, held that sentences and names are not dissimilar in their logical functions. In place of the Cratylean doctrine that names can be true and false, however, Frege held that sentences, like names, can refer. For Frege a proposition, like a name, possesses both a sense and a reference; and its reference is a truth-value – the True or the False. Propositions are understood, in effect, as functions from names to truth-values. The assertoric function of a proposition – in plain English, the fact of its *asserting something* – is not considered internal or essential to the notion of a proposition; rather, assertion is taken to be merely one way of employing a proposition, to be shown by the addition of the so-called "assertion sign" ($\vdash$).

In the *Tractatus*, Wittgenstein makes a sharp distinction between propositions and names. The ground of the distinction is that whereas the meaning of a name has to be explained, a proposition is simply understood. And this is so even when the proposition is one that we have never encountered before. "It belongs to the essence of a proposition that it should be able to communicate a *new* sense to us."[7] We don't, that is, come to understand a proposition as we come to understand a name, by identifying the thing, or the kind of thing, it names; rather, we come to understand a proposition by coming to grasp what it asserts. And we grasp that not by having it explained to us, but by simply reading it off from the signs themselves: the words strung in order on the page.

But here, at once, we encounter a difficulty. How am I to know, merely from the sequence of signs, that what the proposition asserts is a possible state of affairs? One answer, of a Platonic flavor, might be that the state of affairs the propositional sign asserts to obtain is not determined merely by the signs themselves, but by the way in which the signs are animated by some mental procedure. Thus Russell's Theory of Judgment envisaged the possibility that whether a given sequence of signs represents (to a given user) the judgment "Othello loves Desdemona; or the judgment "Desdemona loves Othello" might turn on the order in which the mind reaches out and touches the entities which the individual names in the propositional sign pick out.[8] This fails to satisfy Wittgenstein: "The correct explanation of the form of the proposition: '*A* makes the judgment *p*' must show that it is impossible for a judgment to be a piece of nonsense. (Russell's theory does not satisfy this requirement.)"[9]

Whether something is or is not nonsense, in other words, cannot turn upon a mental act. We cannot make a proposition make sense merely by performing an inward gyration with respect to it; but nothing in Russell's theory rules out the possibility of our doing just that.

We still need, then, an answer to the question which struck us a moment ago: how do we know that a propositional sign picks out a possible state of affairs? A plausible answer might be that it does so just in case the propositional sign is formed in accordance with the semantic and syntactic conventions of English. But this fails to move the discussion forward. The problem is that of deciding whether the names in a proposition fit together in such a way as to sketch a possible relationship, out there in the world, between the entities those names pick out. To suppose a *convention* sufficient in itself to decide such a question is just a new form of the absurd supposition, latent, as Wittgenstein has noticed, in Russell's Theory of Judgment, that the distinction between sense and nonsense might turn upon an act of will. The problem cannot be addressed, in short, by any form of conventionalism, but only by an answer which concerns itself in some way with the relationship between linguistic signs and extralinguistic reality. Throughout the period in which the *Tractatus* was conceived and written, Wittgenstein's sense of the range of answers which might be possible appears to have been constrained, despite his rejection of the first of the Cratylean doctrines I distinguished earlier, by his continued acceptance of the other two. Wittgenstein held, in other words, that complex propositions in a language can be systematically analyzed in terms of "atomic" or fully analyzed propositions; that what connects a fully analyzed proposition with the world is the meaning of the names it contains, and that the meaning of a name is simply the real-world entity which it designates.[10] Wittgenstein's name for the real-world entities which the names in fully analyzed sentences pick out is, variously, *Ding* or *Gegenstand*, translated, respectively, "thing" and "object." But if the only relationship that connects a completely analyzed proposition to the world is the relationship between the simple signs that compose the proposition and the "objects" they designate, then simple acquaintance with those objects must be sufficient to determine whether the proposition in question makes sense, sketches a possible state of affairs – and which possible state of affairs it sketches. That, in turn, can only be sufficient if the objects in question actually *compose* states of affairs, and if they have "written into them," as "internal" or essential features, all their possibilities of concatenation into states of affairs, and if these features of objects are not to be discovered *a posteriori* but are evident on acquaintance. These are, of course, just the properties that Wittgenstein ascribes to "objects" at *Tractatus* 2–2.0121.[11]

This solution to the problem did not satisfy Wittgenstein for more than a few years. I have two reasons for having outlined it here. First, to note its general character: intensely logocentric, in Derrida's sense of that term (the role of the logos in this particular variant of logocentrism being performed by the "objects"), and save for Wittgenstein's resistance to the Platonic–Fregean idea that sentences are complex names, intensely Cratylean. Second, because the problem it addresses, of how one can know, just from acquaintance with a propositional sign that one has never encountered before, both that the sign is not nonsense, asserts (unlike, say, "Twas brillig and the slithy toves ...") a state of affairs, the truth of which can be investigated, and which state of affairs that is, is the root problem Wittgenstein is addressing in the *Philosophical Investigations*. The new kind of answer which he evolves there is arrived at in part by dropping, it seems to me, the remaining Cratylean assumptions which partly served to determine the answer he gave to this problem in the *Tractatus*. The dropping of those assumptions represents a profound break with logocentrism, and thus a break with the logocentric presumption that talk about language and talk about reality are, always and necessarily, two different things.

III

The second of our Cratylean doctrines asserts that some of the things with which Reality confronts us are simple things, in the sense of being nameable but not describable, and that the most basic terms of a natural language, those in terms of which any definition of a nonbasic *term* must ultimately proceed, name simples in that sense.

The first seventy-five paragraphs of the *Philosophical Investigations*, although they broach a number of other topics as well, are largely taken up with showing that the Cratylean conception of a simple, also introduced by Socrates in the *Theaetetus*, is unintelligible. The argument proceeds from two directions: from the direction of the world and from the direction of language. A simple, since it is by definition nameable but not describable, would have, if such entities existed, to be locatable without reference to a description. But the distinction between simple and complex can only be drawn relative to a description. Before one can answer the question "Is *x* simple," it must first be determined what is to count as simplicity and complexity in this context. And that can only be done from within language: that is, by specifying verbally some considerations in terms of which the contrast is to be formulated. Extralinguistically – metaphysically, that is – there are no simples because extralinguistically the contrast between simple and complex is without content.[12] Something might still be saved from the Cratylean doctrine if it were the case that experience, just as a matter of empirical fact, presents us with features capable of being named but not described. And it is not implausible to suppose that this is in fact so. Locke's "simple ideas," such as the taste of pineapple, might be regarded as psychological simples in the required sense. What is true about the Cratylean doctrine could now, perhaps, be reformulated thus: the most basic terms in a natural language, in terms of which the analysis of the meanings of nonbasic terms must ultimately proceed, are defined merely by associating them, by the procedure which philosophers have taken to calling, grandly, ostensive definition, perhaps not with metaphysical simples, but at any rate with psychological simples.

Wittgenstein will not accept this weaker doctrine either. His argument, which can seem at first sight too simple to do the job required of it, is that any ostensive definition can be misinterpreted. If someone defines "red" for me by pointing to a red object, am I to take "red" as a name for the color of the object, or its shape, or the material from which it is made, or what? Philosophers wedded to the theory of ostensive definition have sometimes supposed that this difficulty can be solved very simply, by extending the range of indicated samples in such a way as to eliminate specific misunderstandings. The trouble with this is that for every misunderstanding eliminated by a given addition to the array of ostensive paradigms, further possibilities of misunderstanding arise from the addition of the new paradigm. In fact, this reply altogether underestimates the gravity of Wittgenstein's objection. Suppose the sentence "This is a P" is defined for me by reference to one or more paradigms of P-hood (the number is immaterial to the argument). Let this procedure be supposed for the sake of argument to have resulted in my grasping the meaning of "P." How can I manifest that under-standing, except by adding, independently of my teacher but in a manner satisfying to him or her, a further item to the series of paradigms of P-hood? But how am I to set about choosing a further item to fill this role? Which of the many aspects shared by the items already indicated to me as bearers of P-hood must it possess if it is to count as a P?

The imponderability of this question, as long as the materials from which I must elaborate an answer consist merely of acquaintance with a series, no matter how long, of objects guaranteed by someone else to be Ps, is, I trust, evident. If that is all I have to go on, then manifestly, language-learning cannot get off the ground. Yet, equally manifestly, in real life language-learning does get off the ground. What allows it to do so? That question seems equivalent in practice to another: What allows me to add, on the basis of the items already exhibited to me as ostensive paradigms of P-hood, another item to the series?

Wittgenstein's answer to this question is the crux of my concern with him in the present context. His suggestion is the straightforward and evidently correct one that the problems presented by the possibility of misinterpreting an ostensive definition will vanish once the learner knows the logical type of "P": if, that is, the teacher says, or can be taken as saying, not "This is called 'P,'" but "This number is called 'P,'" "This color is called 'P,'" "This length is called 'P,'" "This chess piece is called a 'P,'" and so on. But what is it to know the logical type of a term, in the sense which such examples suggest? It is to know how the term fits into a practice: the practice of one-to-one correlation of the members of sets, the practice of comparing and sorting shades of color with respect to named paradigms, the practice of measuring, the practices which define the game called "chess," and so on. To show how a term fits into a human practice is to show "the post at which we station the word" (*PI* §29). That is, at one and the same time, both to grasp how to make use of an ostensive definition to fix the refer-ence of the term in question, and to grasp how to set about determining the truth-values of sentences in which that term occurs and in which the determina-tion of truth-value depends crucially on the reference of that term. Suppose, for instance, someone attempts to enlighten me concerning the sense and reference of the expression "three inches long" by showing me a variety of objects of which the proposition "X is three inches long" is true. *Ex hypothesi*, I know nothing of measuring. Naturally, I try to associate the expression "three inches long" with some perceptible common feature of the objects exhibited. Equally naturally, I fail. The significance of my failure is that I am unable to extract from bare contemplation of the objects comprising the set any criterion which would allow me to add, to the satisfaction of my teacher, a further object to the set: an object chosen by me, that is, of which "*X* is three inches long" would also be true. What can be done to help me in this impasse? What is required, plainly, is that I grasp the logical category of the component expressions of "three inches long": that "three" is a name for a *number*, that "inch" is a name for a *modulus of measurement*, and that the whole expression designates a *length*. But being taught to recite dictionary definitions of those terms would hardly help me. What I need to grasp is the practical implications of the terms in question possessing those functional roles. And I can only be taught *that* by being taught the point of measuring, and how to measure, using a ruler or tape with a modulus of one inch. Once I am familiar with the practice of measuring – once I grasp *how in general one arrives at* a statement of the form "*X* is *n* inches long" – I shall be in a position to distinguish true from false statements made by asserting the proposition "*X* is three inches long" of a given object. So I shall be in a position to understand the intention of the person who originally tried to enlighten me about the reference of the expression "three inches long" by ostensively indicating sample objects of that length; and I shall be in that position by adding to the series objects of my own choosing of which the assertion "This is three inches long" is also true.

Seeing how expressions like "inch" or "three inches long" fit into the practice of measuring offers, I think, a good instance of what Wittgenstein calls "mastering a language-game." Wittgenstein's thoughts on "language-games" have seemed to many interpreters both puzzlingly remote from the very different thoughts about meaning, truth, and reference which occupy the *Tractatus Logico-Philosophicus* and also strangely unmotivated, or at least undermotivated, in their context. The answer to this puzzle, it seems to me, is that they are motivated by exactly the considerations which motivate Wittgenstein's earlier theory of meaning. These are (1) the wish to retain Frege's insight that to understand the meaning of a term is to grasp what is involved in establishing the truth or falsity of sentences in which that term figures; (2) the need to give some account of how what is asserted by an unfamiliar sentence can be read off from its signs. The new account, arrived at in part by dropping the second Cratylean thesis, satisfies these requirements. By the manner in which it does so it entails the abandonment of the third. On Wittgenstein's new account the reference of an expression is not determined by a convention linking it associatively to some extralinguistically individuated element of Reality. What items are picked out by a sentence like "This is [*an*] *n*" are determined by criteria which can only be made clear by explaining a practice. That the word "*n*" refers to n's is a function of "the post at which the word [*'n'*] has been stationed" relative to that practice. And, while it is, of course, possible to locate instances of n's in the world (one point of the practice, after all, is to make it possible to single out those occasions on which "This is an *n*" has been used to make a true assertion), it is not possible to locate them extralinguistically, that is, without reference to the practice in relation to which n has acquired its meaning. Objects indeed have lengths; but it is not possible to locate lengths as constituents of reality without reference to the practice of measuring. So it isn't possible to treat length as one category out of the many categories of objects into which, according to the perspective of the *Cratylus*, Reality, antecedently to the institution of any human practice or linguistic convention, divides up.

<h1 style="text-align:center">IV</h1>

The arguments which we have briefly sketched are in principle completely general and, if sound, are fatal to the ideal of a logically perspicuous language. If the position they outline is defensible, then, although the true sentences of a natural language are descriptive of Reality, there is, in a natural language, no category of "basic names" referentially associated with "simples," in the sense of prelinguistically individuated basic elements of Reality. Nor does the logical syntax of a sentence in a natural language reflect extralinguistically given modes of articulation of "simples." The logical form of sentences, like the references of the names in them, is always in part a function of specific human practices.

What is important about this account of things from our point of view is what it does to the notion of "referentiality," as that has been understood by literary theorists. It has been fairly widely assumed, first of all, that to abandon the claim that a use of language, for instance literary language, is not "referential," is to abandon the claim that that use of language is directly revelatory of the nature of anything extra-linguistic. It has seemed evident to many minds, moreover, that abandoning that second claim commits us to the view from which we started out: the view that the serious study of literature can reveal only the web of intraliterary or intrasocietal constraints, of ideology or intertextuality, which determine the production of literary works; and that the pretense of a literary work to offer, or of critics to discover, more than that is sustained only at the expense of those internal contradictions which it is the aim of deconstruction to uncover. And, second, it has been widely assumed that the notion of "referentiality" is to be explicated, broadly speaking, in terms of something like the philosophical notion of a logically perspicuous language.[13]

Wittgenstein's later views on meaning should be of interest to the literary theorist, it seems to me, precisely because they disturb these certainties. If they are correct, there neither is nor could be any such thing as a logically perspicuous language. Hence the linkages between an actual natural language and Reality cannot run by way of "referentiality" as that is ordinarily envisaged. In the philosophy of Wittgenstein's later view there are, roughly speaking, two ways in which language is connected to reality. On the one hand, the true sentences of a natural language truly describe reality, in the trivial sense that, for example, to say truly of an object that it is three inches long is to describe it correctly. On the other hand, what makes it possible to formulate sentences that correctly describe reality is the multifarious range of ways in which reality is engaged by the web of practices that determine the sense and reference of the terms employed by those sentences. A natural language does not, that is, encounter reality only by way of the relationship between a referring expression and its referendum: it is *already* multifariously connected to reality at the level of the practices which are what alone enable us to make the relationship between referring expression and referendum, proposition and truth-value, determinate in the first place.

If the line of argument we have followed here is to be trusted, then, it offers a way of making sense after all of the thought that a language occupied solely with itself might, just in virtue of doing that, be occupied with exploring reality. A language occupied with bringing to consciousness the structure and rationale of the practices underlying its possibilities of reference and description will be a language occupied with language: with itself. But at the same time it will be concerned with reality, because it will be concerned with the specific modes of engagement of language with reality via the practices which ground its possibility as language by furnishing its speakers with criteria allowing them common access to the reference of names and the truth-conditions of sentences. All of Wittgenstein's later writings are taken up with just such a double investigation.[14]

But supposing this much of the argument to be sound, what bearing, exactly, can it have on literature? The Wittgensteinian reflections I have been pursuing may throw light on the foundations of language, but can hardly serve, as Wittgenstein himself is always careful to emphasize, to establish any factual claim about what is altogether outside language.[15] "Humanist" critics, however, have generally wanted to claim that literature is a "study of man," or "human nature." And human nature is, surely, something as altogether outside language as the natural world of trees and rocks.

A modest extension of Wittgenstein's argument, however, renders this questionable. The philosophy which conceives the mind not merely as a part of nature, but as an essentially independent counterpart of physical nature, is, of course, Cartesianism. Part I of the *Investigations* constitutes an impressive assault upon precisely that view of how things stand with us. Earlier, following Wittgenstein, I suggested that one of the logical roles of the practice of measurement is to give us the means of establishing whether someone has understood the sense of the remark "This is three inches long." Someone displays that understanding by producing further instances of three-inch-long objects, and that in turn involves a display of the ability to measure using a rule or tape. When that can be done we say "*A* has understood." But what, and where, exactly, is *A*'s understanding? The Cartesian tradition in philosophy tempts us to think of it as a mental state: a special sort of object existing in that dimensionless immaterial realm which the late Gilbert Ryle was wont to refer to as the Cartesian Theatre of the Mind. But because it is central to Cartesianism to conceive of mind and body as essentially distinct, and thus in principle disconnectable entities, that move into Cartesian inwardness involves the abrogation of the body and the physical world, and with them the abrogation of the practices which gave sense to the notion of understanding, and so led to our wanting to postulate the existence of an inner process corresponding to that term in the first place. Suppose A is, and has always been, a disembodied mind? Could that mind contain a state describable as that of understanding what "three inches long" means? A disembodied mind cannot learn how to measure physical objects, after all. Perhaps such a mind could learn to measure in imagination? But the notion of learning to measure by measuring imaginary objects is flawed just because such "measuring" cannot be performed clumsily or wrongly, haltingly or with increasing confidence and accuracy. There is thus no place in it for the notions of error or correction, and thus no place in it for the notion of learning. Only someone who has learned to measure in the ordinary way, that is, in the physical world, can *imagine measuring*. "An 'inner process' stands in need of outward criteria" *(PI* §580). Wittgenstein's thought here is not, as has often been supposed, that there are no mental states, but that if we treat the mind as an essentially separate realm, in principle disconnectable from the physical world and the body, the possibilities of reference to, and description of, mental states which we ordinarily enjoy as *embodied* minds collapse into vacuity. The burden of these arguments of Wittgenstein's is that the possibility of reference to and description of ourselves and our inner states is just as much dependent on practices which secure the sense and reference of the terms we employ in those descriptions as is the possibility of reference to and description of the physical world. But this is to say that what we are as human beings is essentially bound up with the nature of the practices which give sense and reference to the language in which we attempt to formulate our understandings of ourselves and our situation. We are creatures of language – in Wallace Stevens's phrase, "men made out of words." Insofar as it is a mode of self-examination undertaken through the examination of the language which, through its underlying practices, constitutes us, literature is necessarily taken up with the double investigation I spoke of a moment ago: of its own inherited language and of reality (our reality; human reality) through the investigation of the modes of engagement with the world involved in the founding practices of that language.

So perhaps there is a sense – the one just outlined – in which philosophy of the sort that Wittgenstein did in his later years really is to be read, as he himself suggested, as poetry: a sense, also, in which saying that sort of thing need not involve, as is so often assumed, the abandonment of all claim to cognitive content for either poetry or philosophy. Both, at least if we are speaking of major literature, represent forms of linguistic self-consciousness mobilized in the service of deliverance from misleading images and theoretical schemata, from sentimental oversimplification, from error in our self-descriptions. Both, at their best, thus serve ends traditionally considered humane and central to what is of value in the study of the humanities.

V

Let me conclude by attempting a concrete illustration of the literary application of the arguments I have somewhat sketchily outlined, drawn from the novel from which we started out, Virginia Woolf's *To the Lighthouse*. Mr. Ramsey, after a half-serious little quarrel with Mrs. Ramsey about whether the masculine intellect is capable of a dominating grasp of tomorrow's weather, has retired to the garden. A voice, which may be Mrs. Ramsey's or may be Virginia Woolf's or may be his, takes up the story.

> He was safe, he was restored to his privacy. He stopped to light his pipe, looked once at his wife and son in the window, and as one raises one's eyes from a page in an express train and sees a farm, a tree, a cluster of cottages as an illustration, a confirmation of something on the printed page to which one returns, fortified, and satisfied, so without his distinguishing either his son or his wife, the sight of them fortified him and satisfied him and consecrated his effort to arrive at a perfectly clear understanding of the problem which now engaged the energies of his splendid mind.
>
> It was a splendid mind. For if thought is like the keyboard of a piano, divided into so many notes, or like the alphabet is ranged in twenty-six letters all in order, then his splendid mind had no sort of difficulty in running over those letters one by one, firmly and accurately, until it had reached, say, the letter Q. He reached Q. Very few people in the whole of England ever reach Q. Here, stopping for one moment by the stone urn which held the geraniums he saw, but now far, far away, like children picking up shells, divinely innocent and occupied with little trifles at their feet and somehow entirely defenseless against a doom which he perceived, his wife and son, together in the window. They needed his protection; he gave it them. But after Q? What comes next? After Q there are a number of letters the last of which is scarcely visible to mortal eyes, but glimmers red in the distance. Z is only reached once by one man in a generation. Still, if he could reach R it would be something. Here at least was Q. He dug heels in at Q. Q he was sure of. Q he could demonstrate. If Q then is Q–R–Here he knocked his pipe out, with two or three resonant taps on the handle of the urn, and proceeded. "Then R…" He braced himself. He clenched himself.

This, as self-examination allows some of us to certify, is a marvelous and discomforting portrait of an abstracted, over-intellectual man whom a mixture of genuine intellectual capacity and intellectual vanity renders habitually and rather culpably indifferent to others and to the lived texture of his days. But is "portrait" quite the right word? As I noted at the beginning of this essay, some people, notably F. R. Leavis, have assumed it to be a portrait of Leslie Stephen,

Virginia Woolf's father. I expressed some doubt, earlier, whether it would actually have been much help to Virginia Woolf, in resolving the anguishing issue of
which words to set down in order on a blank sheet of paper, to contemplate the
existent person or character of her father. And certainly it is not much help to
the reader. We have to deal not with Leslie Stephen but with Mr. Ramsey, and
rushing for help to a biography of the former, as if by the light of some bizarre
extension of the Method of Sainte-Beuve, would not be a useful way to confront
any problem that we might encounter in our dealings with the latter. So we may
as well grant that what Virginia Woolf has to say about him is not a "portrait": is
not "referential" in the sense of describing, accurately or otherwise, an existent
particular. Nor does it seem overly plausible to attempt to save the "referentiality" of the passage by making it out to describe, or to manifest, a universal
(perhaps a Concrete Universal); or a Theophrastan "Character" – The Over-
Intellectual Man. Mr. Ramsey is *sui generis*: too much himself to be identified
with any kind of universal. Let us, then, admit it: the chunk of text before us is
not "referential" in any sense, no matter how strained; it is not "referential" at
all. Mr. Ramsey is a creature of pure textuality. He is an insubstantial pageant.
His tissues are the tissues of words which have conjured him up. Must we then
treat him as having nothing at all to do with reality? Well, not necessarily. For the
tissues of words which constitute him are not just tissues of words. Behind the
words are the systems of practices which give life and meaning to the words.
Those practices interact with reality in multifarious ways. They link us to the
complex, commonplace world to which we all share a common access. Whether
we do share common access to a common world is widely reckoned to be philosophically controversial, on all sorts of levels, but in fact each of us tacitly admits
to a wide measure of access to the world taken for granted by others, by the
effortless facility with which he or she masters the shared practices which
underlie his or her native language. The textuality which constitutes Mr.
Ramsey's personality is, then, not a textuality of words alone, but a textuality of
practices. And since we share those practices, and are also in part constituted as
individuals by them, the practices out of which Mr. Ramsey is constructed link
him not merely to the reality of the prelinguistic world present to all of us as the
condition of our speaking a common language, but to the reality which we
constitute: to us, as readers.

Let me attempt to dispel the somewhat liturgical atmosphere with which
frequent repetition may have begun to invest the word "practice," by getting
down to the detail of the passage. The word-play with Ps and Qs conjures up,
does it not, the use of those letters in formal logic, and beyond that the whole
apparatus of letters and numbers which mark the progress of the argument in
learned writing of the more strenuous sorts? Mr. Ramsey's meditations on the
passage from P to Q, which may be mimetic or may be diegetic (we can't quite
tell), are not just the chance meditations of an existent individual man. (That, I
take it, is why Virginia Woolf sees to it that the reader can't quite tell whether
the ruling mode of the passage is mimesis or diegesis.)[16] Rather, they sketch out

a possible *route*; a route by which someone much given over to the kind of learned enterprise which cannot proceed without P's and Q's might, though he need not, find his personality elaborating itself in certain ways, hardening into a certain shape around the armature provided by the practice of such an enterprise. "Fortified and consecrated his effort." The words make present to us the striving which must go into the production of the kind of intellectual advance such enterprises at their best produce. The thought that such, rather exhausting, striving constitutes the groundswell of Mr. Ramsey's days, serves to make it quite intelligible and understandable that his favorite poetry, shouted and muttered throughout the novel, should be the more vacuously and sonorously energetic bits of Tennyson. But the strenuousness of his life also makes understandable the possibility of a certain temptation, internal to the practice which centrally constitutes his life, towards vanity and self-absorption. Take that phrase "the energies of his splendid mind." Even if the phrase is his, it is one to which he has a certain right. Only a splendid mind will be fitted to reach, let alone pass, Q. But, grasping and forgiving in this way the innocent urgency of his desire to reach Q, we also grasp why his wife and child too often appear to him only in relation to such urgencies, as fortifying, as satisfying, as consecrating his life's endeavor (and in virtue of that deserving the protection of a splendid mind engaged upon the road to Z); too seldom in the light of their own concerns, their own proper persons. The three resonant taps of his pipe which signal his decisive turning towards the real world of intellectual enquiry, signal also now, to us as readers, his turning away from another world, equally real, which cannot be brought before us by the methods of the kind of intellectual enquiry that leads one from P to Q, but only by those of the novel we are reading: the double investigation, through language, of that common fabric of language and practice upon the foundation of which Mr. Ramsey erects his mode of being, and we erect ours.

If you like, Derrida is perfectly correct: Mr. Ramsey is no more than an *effet de différence*. That thought also has seemed to many to disable literature from having any bearing upon reality. But it suggests a complementary thought: what more are we? We also fabricate personalities for ourselves by living our way through the web of practices that constitute the social environments into which we are born, succumbing to a temptation here, resisting one there, until, as Nietzsche puts it, we become what we are.[17] The practices embedded in social life which allow us to elaborate intelligible roles for ourselves as individuals are also, on the Wittgensteinian view we have been exploring, what render intelligible, what make possible the passage from words to referents and to truth-values in our everyday language. That language, being all we have, is necessarily the language in which we have to formulate whatever self-descriptions, whatever narratives of our own lives, we manage to achieve. And, of course, to the extent that we ourselves fail to grasp how we have arrived at those narratives, how the linked process of self-making and self-describing has gone, we are constrained by them, in the way that we are constrained by unexamined habit. What is brilliant about the passage I quoted earlier is that in it this habitual constraint dissolves. The floating voice, uncertainly mimetic or diegetic in its mode, allows Mr. Ramsey to constitute himself out of the practices and enterprises of intellectual enquiry, and does that precisely through its refusal to uphold the conventions of overtly "referential" narrative in a way which allows us to see exactly how he is doing it. "Becoming himself" before our eyes he allows us to see, perhaps for the first time, how that sort of thing is done.

What we have before us, in short, is not a *representation*, either of an actual person or of the Platonic Form of a kind of person, but an exploration of the constitution of a possible person on the basis of the practices that uphold our language and link all of us, through it, to the world. The vision Virginia Woolf offers us is a vision of ourselves as beings self-created from the materials offered by language and the practices underlying it. Sometimes, where the patterns of being she explores are shared between several characters, as in her exploration of the different structures of female being that Mrs. Ramsey and Lily Briscoe have erected for themselves on the basis of different choices about how each is to relate to men, and the way in which those structures dominate and show themselves in how each responds to words in the context of conversation, one has an odd sense that one is indeed being brought face to face with Platonic Ideas. In the scene in the second part of the book where Lily finds herself seriously tempted, if only for a moment, to enter with Mr. Ramsey the specific dance of male–female relationship in which Mrs. Ramsey has chosen to engage with him throughout their marriage, that dance does seem almost to take on the status of a separable entity, a Form of Relationship which could be realized by many different male/female pairs. But in the end such a Form is not an element of Platonic reality, any more than a dance is, but like a dance, an entity individuated, primarily at least, structurally and in terms of practice, and only secondarily in terms of the features of the world which allow such practices to be set up.

This brings me back finally to my beginning. I began by asking what Lily Briscoe can be supposed to be looking at. What *constrains* her in making that final mark upon her canvas? The constraint upon Virginia Woolf's enterprise, the *work* involved in it, is not that of accurately describing something external to language, but that of finding ways of exhibiting something internal to the very language (considered, in the manner of Wittgenstein, as a form of life) in which one exhibits it, and which has to do with the hidden ways in which that language, which is also our language, engages, through practice, with reality.

Similar things could, I suppose, be said of Lily's enterprise. When one visits the garden at Giverny for the first time, one is initially surprised by the evident disparities between the garden, admittedly reconstructed, and Monet's paintings of it. But as one looks, the problem resolves itself. Monet is painting not the garden but his own eye passing over the garden. The painting enables us to follow and grasp the visual delight in Monet's contemplation of the garden. The original of Lily's concluding stroke is something she has to find, neither "in the world" nor "in herself," but in the practical union of eye and brush: "her vision," as Virginia Woolf's conjuring of Mr. Ramsey "merely" out of the commonplace language we share with her is her vision, and Wittgenstein's conjuring out of that same language his account of the inseparability of ourselves and our linguistic practices is his.

Notes

1 Virginia Woolf, *To the Lighthouse*, New York: Harcourt, Brace and World, 1981, pp. 208–9.
2 F. R. Leavis, "After *To the Lighthouse*," *Scrutiny 10* (1942), 295–8.
3 Maurice Merleau-Ponty, *The Prose of the World*, trans. Claude Lefort and John O'Neill, Evanston: Northwestern University Press, 1973, p. 115.
4 See *Cratylus* 385 c–d. *Collected Dialogues of Plato*, Edith Hamilton and Huntington Cairns (eds.), Princeton: Princeton University Press, 1961, p. 423.
5 Ludwig Wittgenstein, *Philosophical Investigations*, trans. by G. E. M. Anscombe, Oxford: Basil Blackwell, 1953, §46, identifies this as the source of one of the main doctrines of the *Tractatus*, and one which at that point – the early 1930s – he considered to have been badly mistaken.
6 P. T. Geach, "Saying and Showing in Frege and Wittgenstein," Jaakko Hintikka (ed.), *Essays on Wittgenstein in Honour of G. H. von Wright*, Amsterdam: North-Holland Publishing Company, 1976, p. 64.
7 See Ludwig Wittgenstein, *Tractatus Logico-Philosophicus*, trans. D. F. Pears and B. F. McGuinness, London: Routledge & Kegan Paul, 1961, 4.026–4.03.
8 See David Pears, "The Relation Between Wittgenstein's Picture Theory of Propositions and Russell's Theory of Judgment," *Philosophical Review* 86 (1977), 177–96.
9 Wittgenstein, *Tractatus* 5.5422.
10 See Wittgenstein, *Tractatus* 3.2–3.203.
11 Wittgenstein develops this point at *PI* §§46–49.
12 Wittgenstein, *PI* §29.
13 This term, admittedly, is seldom used by continental philosophers, or by literary theorists. Merleau-Ponty in *The Prose of the World*, for instance, speaks of "algorithmic language," but means by that very much what early analytic philosophers had in mind when speaking of a logically perspicuous language.
14 The account of the development of Wittgenstein's thought briefly sketched in this and the preceding section is amplified and defended in Bernard Harrison, "Wittgenstein and Scepticism," Klaus Puhl (ed.), *Meaning-Scepticism*, Berlin: Walter de Gruyter, 1991, 34–69, "Truth, Yardsticks and Language-Games," *Philosophical Investigations* 19 (1996), pp. 105–30, and "Criteria and Truth," *Midwest Studies in Philosophy*, v.xxv, Peter A. French and Howard Wettstein (eds.), Oxford: Blackwell, 1999, pp. 207–35; and in Patricia Hanna and Bernard Harrison, *Word and World: Practice and the Foundations of Language*, New York and Cambridge: Cambridge University Press, 2003.
15 See *PI* §109 and §126.
16 Erich Auerbach, in Chapter 20 of *Mimesis*, Princeton: Princeton University Press, 1953, notes at length the insistent ambiguity in the book as to who is speaking at any given moment.
17 Friedrich Nietzsche, *The Gay Science*, §270: "Du sollst der werden, der du bist."

6

READING FOR LIFE

John Gibson

People nowadays think that scientists exist to instruct them, poets, musicians, etc. to give them pleasure. The idea that *these have something to teach them* – that does not occur to them.

(Wittgenstein, *Culture and Value*)[1]

Do not forget that a poem, even though it is composed in the language of information, is not used in the language-game of giving information.

(Wittgenstein, *Zettel*)[2]

One of the more distinctive features of Wittgenstein's philosophy is his belief that when philosophy steps on the scene – good intentions notwithstanding – it tends to create the very conceptual messes it claims to have come to clean up, and is in the end responsible for that from which it styles itself as a liberator: confusion.[3] This, I will argue, is especially true of a small but important area of philosophizing about works of literature. The confusion I will discuss concerns two basic but evidently contradictory views we have about the nature of the literary work of art. One view emphasizes the social and cognitive value of literature, and it tells us that literature offers the reader a window on the world. It is the idea, familiar to all of us in some respect, that literature is the textual form to which we turn when we want to read the story of our shared form of life: our moral and emotional, social and sexual – and so on for whatever corners of our world literature brings to view – *ways of being human*.[4] The second view emphasizes, simply put, the fiction that goes into a work of literary fiction. For it seems equally intuitive to say that the imaginative basis of literary creation presents to the reader not her world but *other* worlds, what we commonly refer to as *fictional* worlds. Works of literary fiction trade in aesthetic creation rather than factual representation. They speak about people made of paper, who inhabit worlds made only of words. And from this it seems quite natural to conclude that literature is therefore essentially and intentionally silent about reality, choosing instead to speak about worlds none of which are quite our own. The confusion, then, concerns how we might make sense of this basic vision of literature as somehow

109

at once, as it were, both thoroughly our-worldly and otherworldly, how we might reconcile these two very different ways of speaking about the nature of the literary work of art.

Of these two views, the first has suffered most in contemporary philosophy of literature. In the last twenty-five-odd years philosophers and literary theorists have developed rich theories of the logic and semantics of fictional discourse, of the nature of the imagination, of how talk, thought, and texts can be "of what is not."[5] But literary aesthetics has largely done so at the expense of the worldly interest we take in literature, developing theories of fiction that often leave no room for speaking sensibly about one of the reasons we so value the literary work of art: that it can be read, not only for fictions, but also for life. And if we are to develop a reasonable model of how we might read literature for life, we will need to find a way of understanding fictions that grants them the independence from reality much current philosophy gives them (as we must, since fictions are not, after all, real), but not such utter emancipation that we end up creating a gap between literature and life we cannot bridge. I will argue in this essay that Wittgenstein's remarks in *Philosophical Investigations* on the nature of linguistic representation – on how we are able to render ourselves and our world in words – make such an understanding possible. Wittgenstein himself never addressed the confusion I discuss in this essay (though the above quotations indicate that he was at least in possession of each of the views that are together responsible for it), but, I hope to show, we can find in his work a novel suggestion for how to go about dispelling it.

LITERATURE WITHOUT LIFE

I will begin by offering a more detailed analysis of the problem just mentioned, since a fuller understanding of it is needed before turning to a discussion of how we might use Wittgenstein to solve it. What I intend to show in this section is that unless we find some alternative to common ways of speaking about the fictions we find in literature, we will have great trouble avoiding a position I trust no one except the most recalcitrant formalist would willingly embrace, what I will call *literary isolationism*. Literary isolationism is not so much one theory among many we might endorse as it is a position we invite, by default as it were, when we find ourselves unable to say something sensible about how we might read literature for life. For if we cannot explain how a work of fiction can bring reality to view, we will be extremely hard-pressed to state exactly *where* in a novel we can find this life we want to read for. We will, that is, have invited a picture of literature, not as without *any* connection to reality (a claim that would likely be incoherent as well as mad), but as at least without a point of contact significant enough to make the idea of reading for life appear worthwhile.

Below I consider two standard approaches to the problem. Neither, we will see, helps us stave off isolationism; but by seeing where they go astray we will be able to get a clear idea of what needs to be done if we are to provide a plausible response to the problem. I take the two approaches I discuss here to bring to view what at first might well appear to be the *only* two options for giving sense to the idea that fictions can be read for life, for between them there does not seem to be anywhere else to look for the reality we want to claim literature can show us. One approach, which I will call the "direct" approach, attempts to locate a layer of reality *within* the literary work, thus making the life one reads for a proper feature of literary content itself. The other approach, which I will call the "indirect" approach, accepts that literature is thoroughly fictional – that reality is, so to say, always extra-literary – but argues that *the reader* builds the bridge between fiction and reality, that our appreciation of literary content unites what the work itself does not.

Life through literature?

I will start with the indirect approach, since it is the most common (and arguably intuitive) way of addressing the problem. Indeed, there are a considerable number of philosophers who appear to have no trouble at all claiming what I just said is so difficult to claim, namely that literary content is both thoroughly fictive *and* capable of revealing reality. The argument typically offered for this is gracefully simple. It asks us to admit something few of us would deny: that literary works, while not speaking about reality, can at least invite modes of reflection, simulation, and imagination which can in turn lead us to a better understanding of our world. It is not that literature, speaking about fictions as it does, *tells* us how the world is. But it can suggest ways of regarding it, presenting us with possibilities of worldly understanding and involvement. Literature offers – to put it vaguely at first mention – conceptions, stances, and perspectives. They are, in their proper literary mode of presentation, perspectives on purely fictional states of affairs. But when we read, we are drawn into these perspectives, we think from *within* them (the confessor's view of the pleasure of suffering in Dostoevsky's *Notes From Underground*, for example). Once we have done this, we need only state the obvious fact that we can then take the conception we find in a story and use our reflective and imaginative capacities to transform it into a tool for approaching reality. As Catherine Wilson puts it, giving substance to this line of thought requires only that the reader

> (a) recognizes the conception presented in the novel as superior to his own and (b) adopts it, in recognition of its superiority, so that it comes to serve as a kind of standard by which he reviews his own conduct and others'.[6]

One might object that many literary works do not offer anything like *a* stance on, or *a* clearly articulated conception of, experience (for example James Joyce's *Finnegans Wake*), and that of those which do, we often find, for reasons moral and otherwise, that we would not want to turn the perspective they offer into a way of regarding worldly affairs (for instance Henry Miller's view of sexuality in *Tropic of Cancer*). But notice how flexible the above line of reasoning is. All that is crucial to the indirect theorist's position is the claim that we can treat literature as offering the raw material out of which we can build ways of understanding our world. The indirect theorist can discard the idea that literature leads us to life by way of offering distinct and morally (etc.) attractive conceptions of experience, and in its place he can put all of the emphasis on what we can take out of our imaginative participation in fictional worlds.[7] Gregory Currie offers one such expression of this approach:

> A really vivid fiction might get you to revise your values. Sometimes we suspect that our values are the wrong ones, and we may then desire to value differently. But fictions serve not only to change our current values; they can, more modestly, help us to reinforce or test our commitment to those own values....Fictions can help here by inviting us to imagine ourselves more committed than we really are to our values and then to see ourselves, in imagination, flourishing as a result.[8]

"Real life" rarely presents moral (or social, psychological, and so on) circumstance with the depth and precision of detail we find in works of literary fiction, and so novels offer us an opportunity to explore what life never quite gives us (or not, at any rate, as risk-free as literature does). None of us, one would hope, has ever witnessed a lynching. Yet, for that reason, none of us has been given the occasion to examine the shock of one, and so to engage in that refinement of moral response, of ideas of human dignity, of commitments to social change, that would naturally arise from witnessing something horrible of this order. It is a good thing that life rarely compensates for this lack. But it is also fortunate that we do not remain altogether innocent for it. We can, for example, read James Baldwin's "Going to Meet the Man," and thus find occasion to examine, through our imaginative involvement with Baldwin's creation, the *possibility* of such an event, and the significance it would carry for the entire spectrum of moral, social, and philosophical concerns that such a horror would touch upon. In short, though speaking about fictions, literature can play an important role in getting us to examine questions of vital worldly interest. Literary works do not need to answer these questions if we are to find a way to connect them with life; they do not even need to raise the questions themselves. It is enough that they give us an occasion for this sort of exploration, a ground upon which to carry it out. And this exploration, of course, is not just for the reader's private enjoyment. Moral philosophy, for fairly obvious reasons, could make great use of such a practice, as could any area of human concern that requires exempla, illustrations, and anecdotes.

It would be difficult to exaggerate how frequently one runs into arguments like the above. Indeed, in light of some of the more rigidly formalist theories of literature, it is likely worth shouting the indirect theorist's argument. But thinking that we can turn this into a viable account of how we might *read* literature is another matter altogether. The basic problem is that if literary texts offer suggestions, if they whisper possibilities and otherwise hint at new ways of approaching reality, it will always be the world that answers and not the literary work; it will always be reality (or our consideration of it) that determines whether the conceptions and perspectives we find in literature can be turned into cognitively adequate, world-directed attitudes. The indirect theorist admittedly concedes so much. But he fails to see the consequence of this admission, namely that when we consider these new ways of perceiving and knowing reality, we have turned away from precisely that to which we want to be brought closer: an understanding of the literary work and the array of ways in which we encounter *it* (rather than some external thing to which it might lead us). Literary texts obviously do present the reader with objects of contemplation, namely the world of the story. But beyond what is asserted, proposed, and stated in the literary text *about the world of that text*, literary works do not provide a further claim to the effect that *this is how the world is as well*. We may of course take what we find in a literary text and ask whether it holds true in the real world, whether, if we apply it there, we can acquire a better understanding of worldly affairs. But as soon as we have done this we have left aside literary appreciation and stepped into something more like social science: we are now investigating the world and not the literary work. These questions may be infinitely important to us, and the indirect theorist is right to emphasize ways of using literature to engage in non-literary investigations; but they ultimately say nothing about how we experience literary works, and thus they will fail to help us understand the ways in which we can read the literary work of art.

This is a lesson literary theory learned quite some time ago. We find it in the old New Critical argument for the so-called heresy of paraphrase. As Cleanth Brooks asked us to see, the idea of a work of literature presupposes some degree of inseparability of form and content, some unity of what a literary work says and how it says it.[9] The literary work of art enjoys a certain sanctity, for a presentation of its content in another form – to render it in "other words" in any way – is a violation of the work, a loss of the work itself. In this respect literary texts are unlike "argumentative" texts such as philosophical works. If one can show that there is a paraphrase of Hegel's *The Science of Logic* that expresses his insight in fewer and clearer terms, we would with good reason prefer it to his work, for it would capture the value we would presumably find there (his philosophical insight) in considerably less than the treacherously worded eight hundred pages in which he presented his arguments. Yet if one values Faulkner's writing, there is just nothing like reading Faulkner. Indeed there is no alternative. To say that Faulkner is a valuable writer of *literature* implies that a paraphrase of his writing is a loss of the very thing that expresses the value of his literary efforts, namely the specific intermingling of form and content we find in his written works. To generalize this, while it may be true that through our imaginative engagement with literary content we can derive positions, perspectives, and stances that say something of significance about reality, when we examine these derivations we are no longer really talking about literature, and so no longer specifying ways in which we can read the literary work of art. We quickly find that these positions and perspectives are aesthetically impure, literarily heretical, for they in no way can stand in substitution for the proper object of literary experience: the text itself. To think otherwise is to fail to take seriously, we might say, the literature we find in literary works, which is a rather unpardonable sin if our intention is to say something about the nature of our engagement with a novel.[10]

Life in literature?

Something important comes to view at this point, a restriction on how we can cast the relationship between literature and reality if we are to give a viable account of reading for life. The indirect theorist accepts that there is a divide between reality and literary content and tries to bring them closer through the activities of imagination, reflection, simulation, and so forth. But – and this is the core of the problem with *any* approach that treats the relation between literature and life as indirect – as long as a divide between literature and life is countenanced, one can always point to this divide and show that reading for life always leads us to the wrong side of it, the side of the world and not the literary work. And so the moral of the failure of an indirect approach is that we can give sense to the idea of reading for life only if we find a way to locate reality in some sense *directly* within the literary work, as part of its interior. And this is where the problem might very well begin to look like a paradox, for when we look within a literary work, we only find fictions. As Peter Lamarque puts it:

> The particulars presented in a novel are *fictional*, and how can any view, however objective, of *fictional* particulars, give us truth? Ex hypothesi, it is not a view of the real world.[11]

Implicit in the distinction between literary fiction and non-fictional forms of writing is a contrast between "world-constructing" and "world-imaging" texts and discourse forms, in effect a distinction between texts which attempt to describe the world and those which attempt to create one.[12] Works of literary fiction are not empirically adequate statements of fact. They make no claim to being transcriptions of the actual. Indeed it is built into our idea of reading something *as* fiction that we do not take the text to be constrained, like a journalist's report, by the facts, by an attempt to offer true (or false) statements about how things stand in the world: it is built into our understanding of its sentences that they are "beyond truth-valuation" in this sense.[13] With slight but instructive exaggeration we might put it like this: *literary works describe their own creations.* In the very act of describing the happenings of the story, in the very act of creating literary content, literary works generate the characters and events to which the sentences of the text "refer." The representations we find in literary texts are "representations" of constructs of language: Othello, at least the character found in Shakespeare's *Othello*, does not exist outside the work. So when the words of that work describe Othello and his actions they do not reach beyond the text to any particular bit of reality. Works of literary fiction are at root world-constructing, engaged in the creation of imaginary worlds rather than in the building of mirrors held up to the actual world. And thus it is quite unclear what it might even mean to say that the words that run through a literary work attempt to generate a *direct* view of how things stand in *our* world.

Interestingly, the argument against the idea of having a direct vision of reality in a literary work is one of those few that remain strong even if we drastically weaken its central claims: that literature speaks about fictions rather than about how things stand in our world. We might accept, if only for the sake of argument, that the sentences of a literary work are descriptive not only of the contours of fictional worlds but also, and directly, of the actual world – at least in those cases where we find that what is said in a work of fiction also holds true in reality (consider the sundry accurate historical and geographical details we find in literary works). Stronger still, we can accept, again for argument's sake, that literary works, though largely composed of fictive content, can also engage in straightforward psychological, political, and theological commentary; that novelists, when so inclined, can do exactly what historians or philosophers do. We can accept all of this. But it is of no use in answering our question. This is because the idea of reading for life requires us to look at literature *just* when it strikes us as fictional. We are not asking whether it is possible that there be a text – *any* – that blurs the boundary between fictional and non-fictional forms of writing. Surely there are many, but finding examples of them will not help us. We are asking a very precise question, one which concerns our *actual* literary heritage, specifically about all those works within it that are content to speak about fictions. We are asking why we give such status to – why we take so *seriously* – Medea's madness, Othello's jealousy, Baldwin's depiction of a lynching (a fictional lynching, but, for all that, a horrible fiction).

We might recall a fairly common experience when teaching and attending conferences on aesthetics, that of the student or colleague who believes to have solved the problem by pointing out that certain well-known science fiction serials speak (directly, perhaps truthfully) about the possibility of time travel, the difference between minds in humans and "minds" in machines, even the feasibility of communication with a cosmic Other. Perhaps they do, but – one always wants to say – so what? For unless one wants to offer a response that gives, say, a *Star Trek* novel pride of place among those works of fiction that can be read for life and no place at all to Shakespeare's tragedies, Faulkner's novels, Nabokov's satires, responses of this sort will prove to be thoroughly unhelpful. This might strike one as a deliberately ridiculous example. But it is worth noting that *any* attempt to respond to the question by finding a layer of non-fiction in works of literary fiction will be every bit as silly, and for quite the same reasons.

Literary isolationism

The upshot of all this is that we *must* take a direct approach to the problem, and that this appears to be exactly what we cannot do. So we might well seem to be silenced, left without a word to say about how a work of fiction can be read for reality in any literarily respectable manner. Yet it is precisely this word we need if we are to explain why a thesis as unattractive as that of literary isolationism is also unsound. I take the preceding observations to offer a fair (albeit condensed and cursory) example of a very common way of speaking about fiction; and by briefly running through it a question as simple as that of how we might read literature for life, we can identify a very clear limitation to this vocabulary. This is not to say that this vocabulary is all wrong; but it does not allow us to say something we want, indeed *expect*, to be able to say, and that is surely a limitation. Something is amiss, and we would like to know exactly what it is.

REALITY WITHOUT REPRESENTATION

As with many cases in which we find ourselves unable to say something it would seem perfectly natural to say, there is an unspoken commitment, lurking somewhere in the background, preventing us from speaking sensibly. This is what I believe is happening here. There might be many ways of bringing to view the commitment that is causing us trouble, but I think that it begins to surface most clearly if put in terms of an implicit acceptance of a certain picture of how language is able to connect to reality. It is, I suggest, at root a general commitment to the essential role of the notion of *representation* in explaining how a use of language, a description, an image, can be *about* the world.

This is a quite natural commitment, given how much philosophy of language endorses it in one form or another. But it is also extremely dangerous, especially if taken to mark the exclusive means of building a bridge between a sentence or an image and reality. In the philosophy of language, this can easily lead to the belief that there are two basic uses of language, that in which language represents some actual state of affairs and is therefore informative of how things stand in the world, and that in which it does not, in which case it is, if not just so much nonsense, at least not revelatory of anything that could go by the name of reality (something many verificationist and positivistic strands of twentieth-century philosophy were content to claim). In aesthetics, this commitment to representation surfaces in a strikingly similar sense that we have two and only two alternatives. Consider the following passage from J. Hillis Miller's most recent book:

> A literary work is not, as many people may assume, an imitation in words of some pre-existing reality but, on the contrary, it is the creation of a new, supplementary world, a metaworld, a hyper-reality.[14]

116

What Miller describes as the assumption that literature is an "imitation of pre-existing reality" is what the history of aesthetics calls the *mimetic* theory of art, namely the theory that casts art as a representation of extra-literary reality, the so-called "mirror view" of art. And notice what the alternatives are, at least as Miller frames them: either literature is mimetic, in which case it shows us our world; or it brings to view a newly created world, a *hyper*-reality, which, whatever else it might be, presumably is not quite *our* reality. How odd that there shouldn't be anything between the two.

Since the 1960s there has hardly been anyone willing to endorse a genuinely mimetic theory of literary fiction, to claim that fictions in any proper sense of the term *represent* reality.[15] Indeed the arguments I gave in the last section are really just abridged versions of common ways of dismissing mimetic theories of literature. But the problem – indeed the core of the problem, I believe – is that we tend to hear the rejection of the mimetic theory as an implicit denial of the idea that literature can be in any significant sense "about" the world. This is what claims such as Miller's play upon. For in giving up the representational picture of literature, we abandon the very thing so much aesthetics and literary theory tells us we need if we are to give support to the idea that literature can be revelatory of life. What we need, then, is an alternative to this picture that tells us that in the absence of representation we have words with no worldly point of contact, a case of a text isolated from reality. This is where Wittgenstein can help us.

The Paris archive

To see what is liberating in the alternative Wittgenstein opens up for us, it might be wise to begin by situating a discussion of it in a more basic matter of philosophical interest, what we might refer to, initially at least, as *the wonder of agreement*. We share, to a rather astonishing degree, similar patterns of linguistic response and description. We by and large call the same things by the same names, and we perceive the world in the same general hues: *this* expanse of sky is blue, *that* patch of earth is lush, *this* gesture counts as an expression of delight, *that* shrug announces indifference. This does not mean that we always say the same things about the world. We differ as a matter of daily course in how we describe various regions of our world. But, as Wittgenstein shows us, the very possibility of disagreement points up the existence of a broad backdrop of agreement, of a shared stage upon which we can rehearse our differences: "In order to make a mistake, one must already judge in conformity with mankind."[16] In what, then, does this "conformity" consist? What, exactly, is it that we possess in common that accounts for this general alignment with one another in speech?

One of the ways of expressing the attraction Wittgenstein has held for so many philosophers of an anti-metaphysical bent is that he offers what is arguably the first thoroughly *cultural* response to this question. I would not think it an overstatement to say that it is among Wittgenstein's chief contributions that he saw that much philosophy goes astray – becomes a form of nonsense – in response to the question of how this general alignment is possible. If a proper account of the wonder of agreement requires that we explain precisely *what* is shared among us, the standpoint philosophy has baptized "platonism" might be seen as attempting to explain this in terms of metaphysical entities, say a common grasp of an Idea or of an item in the Realm of Sense. Not only platonism, but what we often take to be its contrary, empiricism, is often guilty of a similar offense, positing something "given" in experience, for example "sense-impressions" that produce common concepts in each of us. Wittgenstein saw that if we are to exorcise philosophy completely of its traditional reliance on metaphysical theses, no occult entities, nothing "hidden," may be allowed into the story we tell of what makes this agreement possible:

> Philosophy simply puts everything before us, and neither explains nor deduces anything.—Since everything lies open to view, there is nothing to explain. For what is hidden, for example, is of no interest to us.
>
> (*PI* §126)

It is because we are held captive by a certain picture – a *theory*, as Wittgenstein often puts it – that we are unable to see what is already in plain view; our metaphysical commitments prevent us from seeing our world aright. So the question becomes: how do we find that feature of our world which is already open to view but which we somehow fail to see; how do we come to identify that aspect of our form of life which can bring to clarity what we once thought only a metaphysical thesis could explain? The closest thing Wittgenstein offers philosophy as a method for achieving this clarity is the idea of a "perspicuous representation":

> A main source of our failure to understand is that we do not *command a clear view* of the use of our words.—Our grammar is lacking in this sort of perspicuity. A perspicuous representation produces just that understanding which consists in "seeing connections." Hence the importance of finding and inventing *intermediate cases*....The concept of a perspicuous representation is of fundamental importance for us. It earmarks the forms of the account we give, the way we look at things.
>
> (*PI* §122)

The "failure to understand" is remedied by presenting an example of a way of engaging in the activity in question (for example, a way of applying a concept, of following a rule, of grasping a new sense) but in such a way that *nothing* seems strange, nothing appears to stand in need of explanation. Indeed a perspicuous representation does not *explain* anything. It rather demystifies what we once found "queer" – a perspicuous representation takes, if you like, the wonder out of our wonderings. It does not do so by revealing what goes on in *every* instance of the activity we want to understand clearly, as though a perspicuous representation offers a God's-eye view of our practices, an insight into something like their common core.[17] They haven't one. This search for a comprehensive overview is anathema to the thinking of the later Wittgenstein, a symptom of the very metaphysical sickness he sees himself as attempting to cure. Perspicuous representations rather act as "intermediate cases" in the sense that *in* them we see presented a picture of human activity that appears to be of a piece with the practice that once seemed problematic, only now without the attendant sense of wonder, only now without the sense that something stands in need of explanation. We thus see suggested in a perspicuous representation a possibility for how we might regard our *own* practices in a similar light, for how to turn back to them and see them *clearly*.

To return to the question of agreement, and to begin to build a bridge back to literature, I want to offer a few words on the so-called "Paris archive" passage in the *Philosophical Investigations*, which I take to offer a model case of a perspicuous representation. "There is *one* thing," Wittgenstein tells us,

> of which one can say neither that it is one metre long, nor that it is not one metre long, and that is the standard metre in Paris. —But this is, of course, not to ascribe any extraordinary property to it, but only to mark its peculiar role in the language-game of measuring with a metre-rule. —Let us imagine samples of colour being preserved in Paris like the standard metre. We define: "sepia" means the colour of the standard sepia which is there kept hermetically sealed. Then it will make no sense to say of this sample either that it is of this colour or that it is not. We can put it like this: This sample is an instrument of the language used in ascriptions of colour. In this language-game it is not something that is represented, but is an instrument of representation....It is a standard in our language-game, something with which a comparison is made. And this may be an important observation, but it is nonetheless an observation concerning our language game – our method of representation.
>
> (*PI* §50)[18]

What we find in this passage is a thoroughly demystified picture of how we come to possess commonly what is required for the existence of a representational practice. If the fact of agreement appeared incredible, a thing of wonder, the above example presents it as something altogether mundane. We are able to represent our world as counting as a meter long not because all those who engage in this practice have access to a common metaphysical item. It is because of a prior cultural act, an initial moment of social production, that this is possible: the creation of public *standards* of representation, the construction of common cultural instruments with which we can then go on to engage in the building of representations of our world.

What is crucial in the above passage, what makes it perspicuous, is that the standard meter is *archived*. This is what brings to clarity what it once seemed only a theory could explain. For the idea of an archive shows us how to tell the story of agreement without invoking anything "queer," anything extra-cultural. It shows us the *institutional* setting of language, that agreement is grounded in something fully public. When Wittgenstein goes on to imagine a "standard sepia" in the Paris archive, we are not asked to see our practice of representing the world in colors as resting upon samples preserved in any one archive, of course. Wittgenstein here draws attention to the fact that he is describing an "intermediate case," and we are expected to turn from it and see that explaining our representational practices generally can be carried out in a similar fashion. That is, we are expected to go on and consider *our* archives, or those features of our public world that amount to them. We are expected to look for the *actual* places in which we store our instruments of representation. We are not asked to consider some oddity such as a "color archive" but to recall, for example, that a standard color chart can be found with ease in art supplies and hardware stores.

One final point about this passage. When Wittgenstein describes the standard meter as neither a meter long nor *not* a meter long, he is not ascribing "any extraordinary property to it" because he is not speaking of a property at all. He is rather describing the *role* the standard meter has in the practice of measurement. There is nothing more to say about whether a certain length counts as a meter if we hold it up to the standard in the Paris archive. And there is nothing more to say precisely because the standard meter is not a representation of some further thing that accounts for its being a meter long: it is the *very* thing that explains what it means to be a meter long. We cannot call it a "real instance" of a meter because it is not an *instance* at all. But, for all that, it is not *unreal*, a *fiction* of a meter. It is crucially real: its existence explains the possibility of an entire – as Hayden White might say – tropic of discourse, namely talk of measuring the world in terms of meters. To make explicit the general point this announces, when we examine our instruments of representation, when we inspect the standards we archive, we are looking at things that are obviously real though not representations of anything real at all.

Literature as archive

To return to the question of how we might read for life, it is first worth pointing out that we can now see that a textual form such as literary fiction which offers no representations of reality – which is in no way mimetic – will not on that count alone be isolated from reality. There are, that is, other possibilities of worldly involvement, and this is at least half of what Wittgenstein helps us to see. But there is more to it, of course. For Wittgenstein not only frees us from the picture that holds much literary theory captive – the picture that leads us to think that literature *must* be representational if it can be read directly for life. He also helps us to see what we might replace this picture with, how we might go on to offer a positive statement of the ways in which literature can engage reality.

To see this, consider for a moment not our practice of measuring with meters or representing the world in color but something much more complex. Consider those words that are crucial to our more cultural – our more "humanistic" – renderings of our world. Think of those terms and concepts that describe significant sorts of human activity and response, that bring to view ways in which human lives can assume significance, come undone, thrive, and so on. Think, for example, of "love" or "suffering," of "exploitation" or "devotion." Consider our ability to cast ourselves as in possession of this or that sort of self, of our ability to depict others in very precise shades of moral, political, and cultural identity. How is it that we can represent reality in *these* hues, that we can describe features of our world as expressive of or otherwise falling under *these* concepts? Unlike the standard meter, these words – rather, these features of human circumstance (for they are much more than just words, of course) – would seem to have no corresponding "object" that could be archived. They designate extremely complex representational practices, at any rate sufficiently more complex than measuring with a meter-rule. And if the story of agreement, of how we can come to represent the world commonly, requires the existence of public standards of representation, what could possibly act as our standards for terms and concepts such as *these*? They are grounded on not "things" or "objects" at all but very elaborate visions of human life. And how could something like *that* be archived? How could we make something like that public such that a shared way of representing – of *seeing* – our world could be built upon it? We can imagine a sample of sepia being placed next to the standard meter in the Paris archive. But what could we possibly imagine placing there to ground the practice of depicting certain items in the world as *oppressed*, as *flourishing*, as counting as an instance of *joy*?

If the Paris archive is a perspicuous example of what makes representing the world in measurement and color possible, what would bring to clarity our understanding of how we can represent our world in these more human terms, of how we can offer such complex renderings of – for want of a better phrase – our way in the world? The claim I want to urge is that it is *the fact* of literature that most perspicuously represents this possibility. It is our culture's possession of a textual tradition which documents the various stories we have to tell of ourselves that shows us how this could be. As soon as we recall what it means to have a literary heritage, we see that we have a culture full of "objects" we can use to archive these stories. We have, that is, novels, plays and poems. And we have places where we put them, public places, namely libraries, bookstores, etc. Indeed, the idea of a novel is the *clearest* picture we have of how a culture can enjoy such refined, varied, and complex possibilities of perception and description. It is the fact of literature that explains how we can distil into a simple public object and thus make available to a culture generally something as intricate as, say, a vision of life undone by jealousy and ambition. For we have *Othello*. Literature is not the only institution that plays a role in archiving these instruments of cultural representation – there are other art forms, for instance, and other ways of telling stories. But I would think it fair to say that literature brings to view the *possibility* of having such complex representational practices more clearly than any other institution in our culture.

This is not to ascribe any extraordinary property to literature. It is, ultimately, just to mark the role – or at least one crucial role – literature plays in our form of life. It is to say that if we want to understand what we are talking about when we represent some item in the world as, for example, suffering, we will do no better than to look at *Notes from Underground*. For there Dostoevsky created not merely fictions but fictions that draw together at such a level of clarity and order all that goes into what we call "suffering" that there is no wedge to be placed between his work and what our idea of suffering most basically is. Dostoevsky's creation represents no *actual* case of suffering, but, for all that, it is not *nothing* we see when we read it, anymore than a view of the standard meter in the Paris archive would be a glimpse of a purely imaginary meter. When we look at Dostoevsky's creation, we are regarding an object that is *constitutive* of a way in which we can see our world rather than a representation of it. Of course *Notes from Underground* does not mark the only way in which we can conceive suffering; but if we want to identify the various visions of suffering our culture makes available to us, the claim I am advancing is that we will do best to examine those texts that comprise our literary inheritance (we might begin, for example, with our tradition of tragic literature). Without Dostoevsky's creation, and without our literary heritage more generally, we quite literally would not be able to see the world as we do, for it is literature that offers us a shared fabric out of which we can weave such intricate visions of our world. This is what it means to claim that something – some object, some image, some narrative – is a standard of representation. It is to claim that it opens up a way of seeing the world, and all that this implies.[19] We require the archive that is in effect our literature heritage to be able to develop and sustain such evolved and sophisticated representational practices.

I would like to think that this accounts rather nicely for the sensation we often have of being able to see our world so clearly in a literary work while all the while knowing that we are witnessing nothing actual. Literature shows us reality, but at a level we might call *foundational* rather than *representational*, placing before us those narratives that hold in place and in so doing structure our understanding of large regions of cultural reality. We see nothing actual in literature. But we do see something just as crucial from the worldly point of view: those stories in virtue of which entire expanses of human experience and circumstance are made visible to us. And if this is so, the idea of reading for life can be seen as resting upon a perfectly legitimate picture of literary appreciation. For it is nothing but the words that run through a literary work that generate these narratives that are so essential to a culture's ability to articulate to itself a sense of its world. There is, as far as I can see, no threat of literary isolationism on a model such as this, for the life we read for is a proper feature of literary content itself, in fact is in no significant respect distinguishable from it.

What I hope these claims bring to view, if only in outline form (for there is much more one could say), is a model of reading for life that shows us that we can accept the "fictionality" of literature – that a fiction is, after all, just that – yet maintain without contradiction that literature offers the reader a vital encounter with her world. What is barred from the idea of reading for life on this account is an appreciative stance that casts literary content as *merely* fictional, that regards a work of fiction as a sort of imaginative reduplication of empirical discourse, a place where we just find "facts" stated about made-up people and events. But it also asks us not to reawake the mimetic theory of literature to explain what this something more than *mere* fiction we find in literature might be. It asks us to see that calling (say) Othello a fiction is to acknowledge that he represents nothing real. And it tells us that to go on to read Othello for life is to recognize that we nevertheless can see *in* this creature of fiction – and literature more generally – our *standards* of representation, those sense-bestowing narratives in virtue of which we are able to narrate our own way in our world. And we read for this life not as the indirect theorist says we must, by looking away from the literary work and towards something external to it. It is precisely by exploring the interior of the literary work, by looking directly within it – *by reading it* – that we come into contact with the life it has to show us. This, at any rate, is what I believe Wittgenstein can help us see.[20]

Notes

1 Ludwig Wittgenstein, *Culture and Value*, G. H. von Wright and Heikki Nyman (eds.), trans. Peter Winch, Chicago: University of Chicago Press, 1985, p. 36.

2 Ludwig Wittgenstein, *Zettel*, G. E. M Anscombe and G. H von Wright (eds.), trans. G. E. M. Anscombe, Berkeley: University of California Press, 1967, §160.

3 See the series of remarks in the *Philosophical Investigations* running from §106 to §133 (*PI* henceforth). All references follow the 3rd edn., translated by G. E. M Anscombe, Oxford: Blackwell, 2001. See also *The Blue and Brown Books: Preliminary Studies for the* Philosophical Investigations, Oxford: Blackwell, 1969, pp. 17–18.

4 Following fairly standard procedure in the debate, throughout this essay I use "literature" to refer to works of narrative fiction (which would include many plays, poems, and novels, but certainly not all). There are, of course, texts we treat as examples of literature whose content is in no clear sense fictional (some philosophical and historical works, for example). Should it require mentioning, I do not take the arguments I advance here to touch on texts that are examples of literature in this more expansive sense.

5 Consider, for example, the various "pretense," "possible world," and "make-believe" approaches to fictional discourse, initiated in the late 1970s and early 1980s with the work, most notably, of John Searle, David Lewis, and Kendall Walton, respectively.

6 Catherine Wilson, "Literature and Knowledge," *Philosophy* 58 (1983), 486–96, p. 495.

7 As, most notably, do many philosophers who make simulation central to their account of how we appreciate works of fiction. Susan Feagin offers the most fully developed account of this in *Reading with Feeling: The Aesthetics of Appreciation*, Ithaca: Cornell University Press, 1996.

8 Gregory Currie, "The Moral Psychology of Fiction," *Australasian Journal of Philosophy* 73 (1995), 250–9, pp. 254–5.

9 See Cleanth Brooks, *The Well Wrought Urn: Studies in the Structure of Poetry*, 2nd edn., New York: Harcourt, 1968.

10 One might object that my argument against the indirect approach makes use of a too literal notion of reading, one which suggests that our appreciation of a literary work consists only in what we can glean from it when examining its pages, excluding what

is often called "reflective aftermath" of aesthetic appreciation. This is a reasonable point, for it might take, for example, a career to answer adequately why Hamlet hesitates, and surely the scholar who ponders this question not while actually reading the work but during a sleepless night is having what we would call a proper literary encounter. All the argument asks us to accept is that he is "reading" *Hamlet* just as long as he has as his object of reflection the content of *Hamlet*. This is a rather inclusive sense of reading, but I would be happy to accept it. We should notice, however, that it still is unable to accommodate the indirect theorist, for however expansive we make the notion of reading, it will always require that we have the text, and not what is external to it, as the object of attention.

11 Peter Lamarque, *Fictional Points of View*, Ithaca: Cornell University Press, 1996, p. 105.

12 Lubomír Doležel, *Heterocosmica*, Baltimore: Johns Hopkins University Press, 1998, p. 24.

13 Lubomír Doležel, op cit., p. 24.

14 J. Hillis Miller, *On Literature*, London: Routledge, 2002, p. 18.

15 For an interesting and well-argued exception, see A. D. Nuttall, in *A New Mimesis: Shakespeare and the Representation of Reality*, Oxford: Oxford University Press, 1983.

16 Ludwig Wittgenstein, *On Certainty*, Oxford: Blackwell, 1969, §156. We might also consider *PI* §242: "It is what human beings say that is true or false and they agree in the language they use. That is not agreement in opinions but in forms of life."

17 I thank David Schalkwyk for bringing to my attention the difficulties of offering a genuinely anti-metaphysical interpretation of Wittgenstein's notion of a perspicuous representation.

18 In developing my interpretation of this passage I profited immensely from reading Cora Diamond's "How Long Is the Standard Meter in Paris," in Timothy G. McCarthy and Sean C. Stidd (eds.), *Wittgenstein in America*, Oxford: Oxford University Press, 2001.

19 David Schalkwyk and James Guetti have each discussed the importance of the idea of Wittgenstein's distinction between representations and standards of representation for literary theory, and I am indebted to their discussions. See David Schalkwyk's "Fiction as 'Grammatical' Investigation: A Wittgensteinian Account," *The Journal of Aesthetics and Art Criticism* 53 (1995), 287–98, and James Guetti's *Wittgenstein and the Grammar of Literary Experience*, Athens: University of Georgia Press, 1993 (see pp. 81–3).

20 I would like to thank Simona Bertacco, Bernard Harrison, Wolfgang Huemer, and Sonia Sedivy, for extremely helpful comments on this essay or one of its earlier incarnations. I am also very grateful to Susan Feagin, who offered a number of helpful last-minute suggestions.

Part II

READING WITH WITTGENSTEIN

INTRODUCTION TO "HAVING A ROUGH STORY ABOUT WHAT MORAL PHILOSOPHY IS"

Cora Diamond

"Having a Rough Story" was written originally as a commentary on papers in a special issue of *New Literary History*, on "Literature and/as Moral Philosophy."[1] In this introduction, I shall try to bring out some connections with "the literary Wittgenstein." To make those connections clear, I shall begin with the contrast between two ways of seeing the philosophical interest of *Tom Jones*.

In the essay of D. D. Raphael's on which I was commenting, Raphael had located *Tom Jones* in the context of eighteenth-century moral philosophy. Fielding's novel, he says, "[*makes*] a genuine contribution to moral philosophy...in that its instances of goodness and innocence contradict the theory of Mr. Square (a caricature of rationalist moral philosophers such as Samuel Clarke and John Balguy), while implying support for the 'sentimentalist' theories of their opponents, notably Lord Shaftesbury and Francis Hutcheson."[2] The philosophical interest of *Tom Jones* thus lies, on Raphael's view, in the views it represents, one of which it supports, and the other of which it is concerned to refute. I contrasted Raphael's reading with that of Wolfgang Iser. Iser sees the reader of *Tom Jones* as coming to recognize the inadequacy of all of the philosophical viewpoints represented by the various characters in the novel. But what is thus recognized is not something that is "in" the novel in the same sort of way as is the caricature, say, of rationalism, in the person of Mr. Square. My contrast, then, between Raphael and Iser is a contrast between taking the philosophical interest of a text to lie in the ideas in it, on the one hand, and, on the other, taking the philosophical interest to lie in what is not in the text. The contrast extends also to the kinds of demand on readers which go with the two different understandings of the philosophical interest that a text may be thought to have.

The idea of what is not in a text is what I now want to turn to. The connections with Wittgenstein are more extensive and deeper than is suggested in "Rough Story." "Rough Story" makes the connection with Wittgenstein by referring to *Tractatus* 6.53, where Wittgenstein lays out "the correct method in philosophy." In "Rough Story," I speak of what Wittgenstein describes as if he were recommending that one write a certain peculiar kind of philosophical text, but what can I have meant by that? What Wittgenstein says is that one should say nothing except what can be said, that is, nothing to do with philosophy, and one should respond to people who come out with metaphysical remarks by demonstrating to them that they have used a word without meaning. But, if one followed his instructions, where is the philosophical text? If one wrote a book of ordinary non-philosophical propositions, that wouldn't (it seems) be a philosophical text, and if one drew someone's attention to her failure to give meaning to a word in some would-be metaphysical claim that she had made, doing so might or might not help the person, but this kind of demonstration might well be something one did in discussion with her. Why talk of "texts"?

To cast some light on these issues, we should look at an earlier point in the *Tractatus*, at which the idea first comes up of a text that is no philosophical text but that does have a philosophical point. This is 5.631. Wittgenstein first straight out says "The thinking, presenting subject; there is no such thing," and he then goes on:

> If I wrote a book *The World as I found it*, I should also have therein to report on my body and say which members obey my will and which do not, etc. This then would be a method of isolating the subject or rather of showing that in an important sense there is no subject: that is to say, of it alone in this book mention could *not* be made.

Here we have the idea of a text which has a philosophical use, a philosophical point, through what is not in it, and not through the philosophical significance of anything that is actually said in it. The philosophical method that Wittgenstein calls "the correct method" could indeed consist in handing a copy of the book to someone who was in the grip of the idea of the philosophical self (or in writing the book with the intended use of handing it to someone in the grip of such an idea). While Wittgenstein says of "the correct method" that those on whom it is tried may not have the feeling that they are being taught philosophy, the point at 5.631 is certainly that one can learn philosophy in "getting" the philosophical point of *The World as I found it*. But there is decidedly here an idea that, although one can learn philosophy from the book, one has oneself to make of it something from which philosophy can be learned. One has not only to understand what is absent in it, but also to turn that absence into something that can transform one's conception of one's philosophical difficulties. The book doesn't "teach" one philosophy, in the sense that it has no teachings on offer; and as long as one restricts oneself to looking for teachings, one will be unable to learn anything philosophical from it.

Wittgenstein makes a parallel kind of point about the ethical significance of the *Tractatus* itself. Writing to Ludwig von Ficker about his book, which he hoped Ficker would publish, Wittgenstein said that the point of the work was an ethical one. He said that he had once meant to include in the preface a sentence, which he would write out for Ficker in the hope that it might provide a key to the work for him. He went on:

> My work consists of two parts: the one presented here plus all that I
> have *not* written. And it is precisely this second part that is the important
> one. My book draws limits to the sphere of the ethical from the inside
> as it were, and I am convinced that this is the ONLY *rigorous* way of
> drawing those limits. In short, I believe that where *many* others today
> are just *gassing*, I have managed in my book to put everything firmly
> into place by being silent about it.[3]

The *Tractatus*, then, has an ethical point in something like the way in which
the imagined work *The World as I found it* can have a philosophical point. That
book has nothing philosophical in it, but one can learn philosophy through
reading it; so too his book has nothing of the ethical in it, but one can come to
understand something about the ethical from it, precisely from what is not in it.
But just as the former book can help one to learn philosophy only if one turns
the absence of anything philosophical into something that can transform one's
understanding, so too the *Tractatus* can help one to understand the ethical only if
one oneself turns the absence of the ethical in it into something that transforms
one's understanding.

Wittgenstein went on, in his letter to Ficker, to say that Ficker should read the
Preface and the *Conclusion*, because "they contain the most direct expression of the
point of the book." The book, he says in the preface, is not a *Lehrbuch*. This
means that, so far as there is anything to be learned from it, what one is to learn
is not a matter of *Lehre*, of philosophical doctrines, or of doctrines about how to
be in a right relation to the world. At the end of the *Tractatus* (6.52), we are in a
position to imagine a whole library of books containing all sorts of true learning
about the world and what is in it, the answers to every imaginable question. But
all these books have in them an absence. There is nothing in them that answers,
or bears on, the problems of life. But the very fact that in these books, as we may
imagine them, there are answers to every imaginable question can help us to
transform our own desire for an answer to the problem of life. This can be done
by transforming also our desires with relation to the *Tractatus*, the "philosophy
book" before us, that is, by giving up our desires to read its propositions as
providing a kind of knowledge. To take a book like *The World as I found it* philosophically is not to learn from anything it says but to use it in transforming one's
understanding; similarly, to take Wittgenstein's book philosophically will not be
to learn from anything it says but to use it in transforming one's understanding.

Throughout his life, Wittgenstein greatly admired Tolstoy's *Hadji Murad*. He
wrote about it with great enthusiasm to Russell in 1912, and to Norman Malcolm
in 1945. Tolstoy, he said to Malcolm, impressed him infinitely more when he
turned his back to the reader and just tells a story, as opposed to the Tolstoy of
Resurrection. We can put his remarks about *Hadji Murad* alongside his earlier
remarks about Ludwig Uhland's poem "Graf Eberhards Weissdorn." Speaking
about the Uhland poem with Engelmann, he said "if only you do not try to utter
the unutterable then *nothing* gets lost. But the unutterable will be – unutterably –

contained in what is uttered."[4] In both the Tolstoy story and the Uhland poem, the ethical is, as Wittgenstein saw it, in a sense contained in the work, but not by being spoken in it, not by being told. The ethical character of the story and that of the poem depend on the absence in them of the explicitly ethical. This, though, is complicated; one cannot say simply that Tolstoy keeps his ethical views unsaid. The Tsar, in *Hadji Murad*, is presented with his vices etched very sharply indeed; and Tolstoy has his usual comments on the fashionable exposure of breasts. What Tolstoy does not tell us is how to think about Hadji Murad himself, his life and his death, or how to make what we think of Hadji Murad alive in our own lives. And in that respect the story resembles Uhland's poem. While Graf Eberhard is described as faithful and good, what we see in the poem itself is rather only the role in his life of the hawthorn. How to make that a reflection of a life is not said; what it might be to take that to heart is not said.[5] Wittgenstein's reading of the story and the poem can be seen to be connected with the way he wanted his book to be read. What links his *Tractatus Logico-Philosophicus* with those two works of literature is the kind of demand that Wittgenstein places on readers: that they respond to what is not there by making of the work something that can be significant in the spirit in which they meet what happens, what needs to be done, and what has to be suffered.

In "Rough Story" I barely touched on Wittgenstein's later writings. I mentioned P. F. Strawson's remark that only a "very specialised view of the nature of philosophical understanding" would stand in the way of attempting to present the thought in the book in a more conventional philosophical form, as arguments for this or that specific philosophical conclusion. I am not sure what he meant by a "very specialised view of the nature of philosophical understanding," apart from "not the usual view." Here I want only to suggest that we can see the *Investigations* also as a book to be read through attention to what is absent in it. Strawson, for example, sees Wittgenstein simply as extremely averse to providing any kind of systematic setting out of the logic of the various "regions" of discourse with which he is concerned.[6] The absence of such systematic layings out of logic is not itself seen to be something like the absence of the "philosophical subject" from *The World as I found it*. That is, for Strawson, the absence isn't seen to be something from which the reader is meant to learn, something essential to the intended philosophical use of the book. So far as that might be taken to be a possible understanding of how the book should be read, Strawson has already dismissed it as reflecting a "very specialised" view of the nature of philosophical understanding. In some of his last papers, Gordon Baker developed a reading of Wittgenstein's later philosophy which emphasized "the *spirit* in which [*Wittgenstein's*] remarks are to be read."[7] Baker sees Wittgenstein's philosophy as involving "negotiations" with his readers about such pictures as Augustine's picture of language. Baker's Wittgenstein offers us pictures, alternatives to be set alongside those to which we may already be attracted, those by which we may be transfixed. His Wittgenstein then differs from Strawson's in that Strawson's is simply constitutionally unhappy with providing plain arguments, which can however be developed on the basis of what is present in the *Investigations*, while Baker's is engaged in a different sort of project altogether, and the absence of ordinary philosophical arguments and conclusions is important in understanding what that project is. The contrast between Baker's Wittgenstein and Strawson's lies also in what they see as the continuation of the line of philosophy in the *Investigations*, Strawson seeing as a continuation the systematic laying out of the facts of language-use, while for Baker, such a conception fails to recognize the character and depth of the pictures with which Wittgenstein was concerned (their unassailability by argument based on grammatical description). What we should connect with "the literary Wittgenstein" is this: Baker's reading of Wittgenstein can be seen as a response to a literary feature of the text of the *Investigations*, namely "significant absence," absence which belongs to the way the text is meant to be read, a feature which it shares with *Hadji Murad* and "Graf Eberhards Weissdorn" as Wittgenstein read them, and with *The World as I found it* as Wittgenstein imagined it. Strawson does recognize the power and concentration of *The Philosophical Investigations* to be dependent on its unconventional form and the absence of systematic development of arguments, but he explicitly rejects the idea that we should consider that form to be relevant to the philosophical use of the book, or the interest of what it contains. My suggestion here is that we can see disputes about how to read Wittgenstein's later philosophy, and about what the philosophical significance is of grammatical description of parts of our language, as tied to the way in which the *Investigations* itself is seen as a literary work, or not. Wittgenstein's own "habit of reading," as we might put it, was a reading for absences; and he writes absences, or so I am suggesting.

In "Rough Story," I picked up from Iris Murdoch the idea that one difficulty about what moral philosophy is is a difficulty about the character of the world. She takes the usual understanding of the subject of moral philosophy to reflect an idea of the world as fundamentally comprehensible, an idea which for her is contrasted with the idea of the world and life as ultimately mysterious. Of all of the stories and novels of Tolstoy, none gives more deeply a sense of the mysteriousness of life, and of the ways life goes, than does *Hadji Murad*, and that is part of what Wittgenstein was responding to in the story. For him, philosophy too, if it was worth engaging in, had to connect with that sense of life. The connection can be seen in various remarks of his, including one quoted by Norman Malcolm, "The joy of my thoughts is the joy of my own strange life."[8] Philosophy was for him the hawthorn tree with which his life was lived, and which gives his life its unity and joy. People sometimes wonder why there are no remarks about ethics in the *Investigations*, or his other later writings. And we are given his "views on ethics" (from conversations, e.g.) to make up for the unfortunate lacuna. But it is usually a mistake to try to make up for an "unfortunate lacuna" in Wittgenstein. It's there on purpose; and *it* is the point. His philosophy has in it his response to life and the world, in it in the only way it could be.[9]

Notes

1   Vol. 15, no. 1 (Autumn 1983).
2   "Can Literature be Moral Philosophy?" *New Literary History* 15, 1–12, p. 10.
3   The letter is quoted in full, on pp. 15–16, by G. H. von Wright in "Historical Introduction: the origin of Wittgenstein's *Tractatus*," Ludwig Wittgenstein, *Prototractatus*, B. F. McGuinness, T. Nyberg and G. H. von Wright (eds.), Ithaca, NY: Cornell University Press, 1971, pp. 1–34.
4   The remark is in a letter of Wittgenstein's to Paul Engelmann; see Engelmann, *Letters from Ludwig Wittgenstein. With a Memoir*, New York: Horizon Press, 1968, p. 7.
5   See, on this matter, Michael Kremer, "The Purpose of Tractarian Nonsense," *Noûs* 35 (2001), 39–73, at pp. 62–4, and William Brenner, *Wittgenstein's* Philosophical Investigations, Albany: State University of New York Press, 1999, pp. 151–2.
6   Critical Notice of Ludwig Wittgenstein, *Philosophical Investigations*, *Mind* 63 (1954), 70–99, p. 78.
7   See, for example, Baker, "Wittgenstein: Concepts or Conceptions?" *Harvard Review of Philosophy* 9 (2001), 7–23. The whole essay is relevant but see especially pp. 14–15.
8   Malcolm, *Ludwig Wittgenstein: A Memoir*, Oxford: Oxford University Press, 1984, p. 84.
9   For a discussion of the significance for ethics of Wittgenstein's later writings that takes absence as central, see Stephen Mulhall, "Ethics in the light of Wittgenstein," *Philosophical Papers* 31 (2002), 293–321.

7

HAVING A ROUGH STORY
ABOUT WHAT MORAL
PHILOSOPHY IS[1]

Cora Diamond

If we are to say anything about the relation between moral philosophy and literature we must, as Professor Nussbaum makes clear, "have some rough story about
what moral philosophy and the job of moral philosophy are" (p. 40). I propose to
discuss why it is difficult to characterize moral philosophy – and in particular difficult when what we are aiming at is clarity about its relation to literature.

Professor Raphael alludes to one of the difficulties, quoting A. J. Ayer's
Editorial Foreword to P. H. Nowell-Smith's *Ethics*: "There is a distinction
...between the activity of the moralist...and that of a moral philosopher."[2] For
Ayer that distinction was a straightforward one. The moral philosopher as such
makes no moral judgments; the moralist, on the other hand, "sets out to elaborate a moral code, or to encourage its observance." Thus Ayer went on to
describe Nowell-Smith as a moral philosopher: he "shows how ethical statements
are related to, and how they differ from, statements of other types, and what are
the criteria which are appropriate to them." Ayer's idea was that this could be
done without the philosopher's taking sides on any moral or practical issue. For
Ayer, then, three things were closely linked: the distinction between moralist and
moral philosopher, the ethical neutrality of the philosopher, the characterization
of his aim as linguistic or conceptual clarification. It has now gone out of fashion
to hold that the moral philosopher as such makes no moral judgments, and
Nowell-Smith himself in that very book (back in 1954, when it *was* fashionable)
rejected any such idea: "Moral philosophy," he said, "is a practical science; its
aim is to answer questions in the form 'What shall I do?'"; to help you answer
such questions, it can "paint a picture of various types of life in the manner of
Plato and ask which type of life you really want to lead."[3] There is clearly no
suggestion there that the philosophical task requires ethical neutrality; and
indeed Nowell-Smith's remarks leave open the possibility that such "painting"
might be carried on as well in literature as in explicitly philosophical works.
Going along with fashion, then, we give up ethical neutrality, and recognize it to
be neither desirable nor indeed possible. With it, we drop the idea that the aim of
moral philosophy is limited to conceptual clarification. But there is still the
matter of the distinction between the activity of the moralist and that of the

moral philosopher. If it is no longer to be drawn in Ayer's way, do we still want to draw it, and if so, how? This is a question not only for Raphael, who has an explicit answer, but for Martha Nussbaum, who has a different but largely implicit one. Hers reflects a willingness to let works of literature teach us something about what moral philosophy can be. But that conclusion I shall need to argue for later.

Why is it a question for her? She wants to argue that *The Golden Bowl* may be regarded as a text in moral philosophy; and for that purpose she needs (or thinks she does) a characterization of moral philosophy which will be widely acceptable. She offers us one derived from Aristotle: "Ethics is the search for a specification of the good life for man" (p. 40). An objection that some philosophers would surely bring is that the characterization includes too much. For (it will be said) a *moralist* may engage in just such a search; and if she shows us that Henry James in *The Golden Bowl* communicates something about how to live well, she will not thereby have shown that he is to be taken seriously as a moral philosopher but will merely have illustrated his powers as a moralist. I think that this objection misses the point, but it serves in any case as an illustration of the difficulties here.

Let me turn back to Raphael, to *his* way of handling the distinction between moralist and moral philosopher. He first contrasts the activity of the moralist with that of the moral philosopher, then makes (as if it were the same) a contrast between moral*ism* and moral philosophy, and later (as if it were the same again) a contrast between moral*izing* and moral philosophy. It may by now be unclear quite *what* should be distinguished from moral philosophy – but let us turn to Raphael's actual way of drawing his distinction. *Mere* preaching of moral doctrine goes on one side; moral doctrine presented as the outcome of structured argument he puts on the other, the moral philosophy, side – and that leaves him with some significant cases undecided, cases in which moral doctrine is presented in a new perspective. If the author uses *rational* methods of persuasion, we should, Raphael thinks, recognize his work as moral philosophy. It is not the label, though, that matters, on his view: it is the points of resemblance to clear examples of moral philosophy. Applying this distinction, Raphael is then willing to claim that literary works can contribute to moral philosophy.

There are still difficulties here, and one is what is supposed to be at stake. What does it matter whether we say that literature can be moral philosophy, or moral philosophy literature? Let me pursue this further.

Raphael supports his claim that moral philosophy may be done in literature by discussing three examples, the *Oresteia*, *Tom Jones*, and *Erewhon*. He argues that the *Oresteia* explores the concept of justice, develops it – and that it thus shows there to be *room* for the kind of conceptual exploration we see when moral philosophy proper, "the real thing," comes into existence. The possibilities for moral philosophy in literature are different once "the real thing" does exist (p. 9). A novelist like Fielding, aware of the ideas of contemporary moral philosophers, can in a novel take sides in a philosophical dispute. Thus we can see the rationalist/sentimentalist controversy pursued in *Tom Jones*. Rationalism in the person of Mr. Square is satirized, and sentimentalism supported. And, finally, Raphael discusses both the explicit philosophizing in *Erewhon* and the use in it of satirical transposition to make philosophical points.

To bring out the limiting assumptions in Raphael's account, we may contrast his view of philosophy in *Tom Jones* with Wolfgang Iser's.[4] Iser sees the relation of the novel to the philosophical systems of the day as much more "indirect" than does Raphael. Rationalism is indeed embodied in Mr. Square, and other philosophical positions are associated with Allworthy, Thwackum, Squire Western, and Mrs. Western. The inadequacies of any such systematic account of human nature, of any such attempt to fix it in some single principle, rationalist or sentimentalist or whatever, can be brought to light by literature, Iser suggests, "not by systematic discourse." Through a reading of the novel, we can come to recognize the gulf between all such systems and the "fluidity" of human experience, as we repeatedly encounter the limited character of each of the principles, bearing in mind each time the previous encounters.[5] What we learn of human nature is not the truth or falsity of any particular view in the repertoire; rather, reading the novel teaches us how to think about human nature by making us think about it, in response to its "constant intertwining" of perspectives.[6] Its criticism of philosophical views is not separable from the very different sort of demand it makes on the reader from that made by ordinary philosophical works. If we can say that it makes a contribution to philosophy, the argument would be different from Raphael's and would have to reflect a different view of moral philosophy, including a different view of the reader of moral philosophy. In philosophy as Raphael sees it, we are concerned to develop certain ideas, to work out their consequences and systematic relations, to see their rational justification. The training a reader of philosophy needs will develop in him the capacity to grasp, formulate, and examine critically the philosophical ideas present in a text. The differences between Raphael's reading of *Tom Jones* and Iser's are not just differences about that novel. If Raphael does not see what Iser does, if he describes differently the relation of the novel to the philosophical systems of the day, it is partly because he is not looking for, or even looking at, the same thing. He is looking for ideas in the text, for the views it presents, while Iser looks at what the reader – of a certain sort – *does* because certain things are *not* in the text. For Raphael, if some of the ideas or issues in the three works he discusses are philosophical, their definition as philosophical issues lies outside the works; one might say that their validation as philosophical is external. Our experience is, for Raphael, the touchstone of the rationality of the perspectives they employ: their philosophical seriousness does not lie in what they can do, as works of art, to make us reshape that experience.

We can approach the same questions by turning to Raphael's brief remarks about Kierkegaard and Nietzsche. One of the reasons he gives for allowing that literary works may count as philosophy is that "there are acknowledged philosophers who make their mark by means of novel perspective rather than structured argument"; he is referring to Nietzsche and Kierkegaard (p. 5). But even so, Raphael is not happy calling them philosophers, because the novel perspectives their work depends on are not rational ones. But if he will not himself call what they do philosophy, what weight has their acknowledgment by others as philosophers? To take that acknowledgment as a reason for shaping the definition of moral philosophy one way rather than another leaves the whole issue pretty muddy.

Let us ask whether a philosopher may invite philosophical thought in his readers by defeating some of their expectations of a philosophical text. Wittgenstein, interestingly, once claimed that that is *all* a philosopher should do: "The correct method in philosophy would really be this: to say nothing except what can be said, i.e., propositions of natural science – i.e., something that has nothing to do with philosophy – and then whenever someone else wanted to say something metaphysical, to demonstrate to him that certain signs in his propositions had been given no meaning. This method would be unsatisfying for the other person – he would not have the feeling that we were teaching him philosophy – but *this* method would be the only strictly correct one."[7] What is to be learned by the reader of such a philosophical text would not be anything in the text; the person to whom such philosophy is addressed must take philosophically seriously the use of a literary technique, that of *not* enabling the reader to find what he expects in a certain sort of work. Just as Iser, reflecting on *Tom Jones*, emphasizes that the novel teaches us how to think about human nature by making us think about it and not by giving us *what* to think, so a philosophical text may aim to make us think about things in a new way, not by giving us *what* to think about them, not by presenting new views or doctrines. What philosophical readers, trained to extract and examine critically the ideas and arguments in a philosophical text, make of such works might easily be guessed, though there is no need to. An important example is P. F. Strawson's review of Wittgenstein's *Philosophical Investigations*. Only a "very specialised view of the nature of philosophical understanding" would, he thinks, block the attempt to treat that text as containing extractable views on a set of philosophical topics.[8] The "very specialised view" would be one which regarded as *part* of the philosophy of Wittgenstein the distance between the way it is written and the way academic philosophers write; it is to be connected with Iser's remark that only literature and not systematic discourse can bring to light the inadequacy of certain philosophical ways of thinking about human life and with Martha Nussbaum's claim that clarity about the role of mystery and risk in the "stories" of our moral lives requires the abilities and techniques of a teller of stories and cannot be done through the "plainness" of traditional moral philosophy (pp. 43–4).

Raphael says that a philosophical work may "have merit as a work of literature," and he gives examples, including several of Plato's dialogues (p. 2). We may ask what the interest is of the literary quality of such works. Is it that the response demanded or invited by the work as a work of literature contributes to what we may learn from it as moral philosophers? The only example Raphael goes into is that of the *Phaedo*, which leaves the matter obscure. That is because Plato's philosophical aim, as Raphael describes it, is so very different from the aim of most moral philosophers. The *Phaedo* was intended, he says, to be a sort – a new, reformed sort – of tragic drama: "philosophical" tragedy *replacing* "poetical" (pp. 3–4). We may be able to see how literary features of the work are necessary for the fulfillment of that aim – but that does not help us much to see their bearing on moral philosophy when it is not taking over, or trying to, the place of poetry.

Raphael's remarks about possible literary merits of philosophical works leaves unasked a significant question: What about literary weaknesses and their relevance to philosophical aims? May failings of a sort we can come to notice through what we might refer to vaguely as literary sensibility (i.e., whatever those abilities are we need to read literary works adequately, whatever it is to do that) be relevant to a philosophical evaluation? Can a literary critic draw to our attention signs of *philosophical* trouble? Dorothea Krook's critical remarks about Hume's *Enquiry Concerning the Principles of Morals* may serve as an example.[9] She tries to make clear the unreality of Hume's vision of the good life, bringing to his philosophical writings the sensibility and tools of a student of literature. Perhaps we may see here again, in Raphael's not raising such questions, evidence of the view of philosophy I ascribed to him earlier: that the essential thing in it is the development and criticism of ideas. Literary skill, if a philosopher has it, may then make his ideas strike us more forcefully (if we have the requisite sensibility as readers), but the important thing for a philosophical reading is the ideas themselves, and whatever considerations may rationally support them. Such a view of philosophy may then go with a *narrow* conception of the kind of weakness we need literary sensibility to see: a narrowing of the notion to weaknesses of style in a fairly superficial sense, which might make philosophical ideas less striking, less immediately attractive, but not less *cogent*. Failure of style as *philosophical* failure has then no place.[10] Perhaps I have pushed too far the attempt to make Raphael's remarks the expression of a particular view of moral philosophy. But it is the prevalent view, even if he himself is not as committed to it as I have suggested.

Let me turn now to some other features of the prevalent view of moral philosophy, important for understanding its relation to literature. Earlier I quoted P. H. Nowell-Smith's remarks about the aim of moral philosophy being to help us answer questions about what to *do*. It is a striking fact that many moral philosophers wish to define the sphere of the moral by tying it in some such way to action. How deep a difference is there between such accounts and characterizations like Martha Nussbaum's, in which the central notion is not action but the good human life? It might be argued that the difference is not significant. Those philosophers – so the argument might begin – who define the subject matter of moral philosophy in terms of action may, like Nowell-Smith, assign an important place to philosophical description of types of human life. Such descriptions subserve the end of moral philosophy by helping us to act and choose as well as we can. On Nowell-Smith's own view, we come, through philosophy, to see what kind of life we want to lead, and we then act, or try to act, in accordance with the decision to live so. Or that part of the story might go somewhat differently: we come to know, through philosophy, what makes a good human life, and that knowledge is what enables us to answer questions about what to do, how to act, how to choose. The argument might then continue: just as philosophers who define the moral sphere in terms of *action* might give a central place to the description of kinds of life, or to the attempt to specify the good human life, so philosophers whose definition links moral philosophy or moral thought directly to the specification of *the good human life* must give a central place to principles of action. For it is our actions, our choices, which give a particular shape to the life we lead; to be able to lead whatever the good life for a human being is *is* to be able to make such choices well. So the argument concludes that there is no real difference between the two types of definition: specifying the good life for human beings and enabling us to answer questions of the form "What shall I do?" are inseparable or perhaps even equivalent.

But the argument begs the question – and might serve as a perfect example of something Iris Murdoch warned us of. There is, she argued, a peculiar difficulty in ethics (in contrast with other parts of philosophy) in specifying the phenomena to be studied. Our moral judgments themselves shape our conception of the field of study. We thus come up with a "narrow or partial" selection of phenomena; that selection then suggests particular philosophical approaches, which in turn support the initial selection: "A circle is formed out of which it may be hard to break."[11] The argument of the last paragraph illustrates these dangers: it reflects a particular evaluation of action, and accordingly represents what is morally significant in life in terms of actions and choices.

"A particular evaluation of action" – but action as opposed to *what*? What is being left out, ignored, played down? We may look for an answer to Miss Murdoch – but in the essay I have quoted she puts her answer in several different ways.[12] She points out that when we use the notions of action and choice to specify the sphere of morality, it may be action as what is observable, public – opposed, then, to what is private, to the "inner life." But "inner life" itself may be understood to mean what goes on in our minds and is knowable through introspection – or to mean "private or personal vision which may find expression overtly or inwardly." There are already then two contrasts: between the publicly observable and the inner world, and between action and vision. There is a third, brought in as part of her explanation of the second:

> When we apprehend and assess other people we do not consider only their solutions to specifiable practical problems, we consider something more elusive which may be called their total vision of life, as shown in their mode of speech or silence, their choice of words, their assessments of others, their conception of their own lives, what they think attractive or praiseworthy, what they think funny: in short, the configurations of

their thought which show continually in their reactions and conversation. These things, which may be overtly and comprehensibly displayed or inwardly elaborated and guessed at, constitute what, making different points in the two metaphors, one may call the texture of a man's being or the nature of his personal vision.[13]

The two metaphors do indeed make different points, different contrasts with action. Iris Murdoch is herself more interested in the second metaphor. In *The Sovereignty of Good* she connects the significance of vision in moral life with Simone Weil's use of the word *attention* "to express the idea of a just and loving gaze directed upon a particular reality," and she takes such attention to be "the characteristic and proper mark of the active moral agent."[14]

But we need also to turn to the other metaphor if we are concerned with the relation between moral philosophy and literature. Moral philosophers have been obsessively concerned with action and choice, and do occasionally refer to moral vision. But "texture of being" hardly gets a mention; and yet it is surely enormously characteristic of many novelists that *that* is what they give us – and out of an interest we may properly call moral. The opening chapters of *Anna Karenina* – what do they give us so much as the texture of Stiva's being? His good-hearted, silly smile when he is caught at something shameful, his response to the memory of the stupid smile, the failure of his attempt to look pathetic and submissive when he goes back to Dolly – what he blushes at, what he laughs at, what he gives an ironical smile at, what he turns his eyes away from: this is Stiva. Such things, as Iris Murdoch points out, are what we consider when we "apprehend and assess" another person; but if we refer to them as the person's "total vision of life," the word "vision" is used in a far looser sense than she gives it elsewhere. I could put the problem here this way. One may properly be concerned how one sees another person, whether one's mode of vision is just – and Iris Murdoch has described such a case in detail, showing the significance both of the inner life (as contrasted with observable actions) *and* of vision (as contrasted with action).[15] Many philosophers might be willing to be persuaded that vision in such a case *is* morally assessable – but what a man finds funny? What kind of blushes he gives? His precision of expression? Here they would find it far harder to see that they are dealing with something of moral interest. If a case can be made it will be a different one, a harder one, because it runs up against deeper prejudices. But we cannot see the moral interest of literature unless we recognize gestures, manners, habits, turns of speech, turns of thought, styles of face as morally expressive – of an individual or of a people. The intelligent description of such things is part of the intelligent, the sharp-eyed, description of life, of what matters, makes differences, in human lives. Martha Nussbaum's Aristotelian specification of ethics leaves room (or is intended to leave room) for attention to these things; an account of ethics, or of moral philosophy, which takes action as definitive of the moral does not.

"Texture of being" is a useful expression for this area; it also allows for an extension of Miss Murdoch's general point. Moral reflection may be directed not just towards individual human beings but towards forms of social life. The social phenomena that are usually regarded by moral philosophers as their concern are familiar enough; they do *not* include what corresponds on the social side to "texture of being" *or* "vision" on the individual side. Income distribution or the death penalty count for moral philosophers as properly of concern to them; styles of furniture, for example, as expressive of the "texture of life" do not. Yet surely Henry James's interest in furniture in *The Europeans* is an interest in it as expressive of attitudes to life. Just as what a person is *like*, his complex attitude to life, shows continually in how he thinks, what he says, what he laughs at, and the like, so the complex attitudes of a people to life show continually in their manners, habits, styles of utterance, dress, architecture. Martha Nussbaum touches very briefly in her discussion of *The Golden Bowl* on the "international theme" in that novel: the significance of the fact that moralism and excessive simplicity characterize an *American* character. Her main interest, though, is what the novel shows about human moral experience and whether we need such texts in moral philosophy – and here the "international theme" drops out of sight, or seems to. There is a further question then whether the same kind of argument she makes about James's explorations of the lives of individual human beings can be made about his explorations of contrasting forms of social life. I thought at first that she implied that it could: ethics, understood as she proposes, cannot "in any way be cut off from the study of the empirical and social conditions of human life" (p. 40). But the question remains how *particular* the things may be that ethics is concerned with. Is its concern limited to what *generally* belongs to the empirical and social conditions of human life? Can it include in its phenomena the contrasts between European and American life, not taking these as examples of anything more generally human? Professor Nussbaum remarks that even in order to raise the question whether *The Golden Bowl* can be regarded as an important text for moral philosophy, we need to drop the Kantian insistence that moral philosophy as such (as opposed to "practical anthropology') be concerned only with what is independent of specifically *human* experience (p. 40). The Kantian definition even more obviously rules out James's explorations of his "international theme'; they do not even make it (as far as I can see) into practical anthropology.

There may even be a tension between Martha Nussbaum's account of ethics in terms of the good life for human beings and James's interests. His description of his aim (the production of an "intelligent report" of experience, i.e., of "our apprehension and measure of what happens to us as social creatures") brings him, she says, "into intimate connection with the Aristotelian enterprise" (p. 40). But is the relation so close? That James and Aristotle can both be described as concerned with the "appearances," with people's "experiences and sayings," does not settle the question. James's interest is that of a "painter'; his "report of people's experience" is essentially his "appreciation" of it, and to appreciate is to avoid as far as possible all simplification (simplification which would be in place if one's concern were action and practical application), to convey the sense and taste of a situation through intimacy with a man's specific behavior, intimacy with his given case, and so to see that case as a whole.[16] He certainly does not explicitly say anything about the good life for human beings, nor even imply that there *is* such a thing. And even if he did believe that there is such a thing, an interest in moral features of human life need not (in general) be an interest in what the good human life would be.

I have argued, following Iris Murdoch, that any specification of the sphere of morality, of the phenomena of interest to moral philosophy, in terms of action and choice is a limited and limiting one. How we define the sphere of the moral bears in several different ways on the relation of literature to moral philosophy.

It bears first of all on the question *where* in works of literature a moral philosopher can see an exploration of something of moral significance. A narrow definition of the moral will, for example, enable us to recognize a moral interest in the account, in *Portrait of a Lady*, of Isabel's decision to return to Osmond, but not in the description of architecture and furniture in *The Europeans*. It may also lead to crude views of the moral implications of literary works.

Secondly, if we say that the sphere of the moral is not limited to action but includes thought and imagination, the moral significance of works of literature is not reducible to their connection, direct and indirect, with action, but includes also what kind of thought and imagination they express and what they invite. Take as an example Martha Nussbaum's argument that *The Golden Bowl* elicits from us as readers an acknowledgment of our own imperfection. We are, she says, repeatedly struck, while reading it, by the inadequacies of our own attention and thus learn something of ourselves (p. 46). This self-knowledge may itself be regarded as a good thing for us, irrespective of any bearing it may have on what we go on to *do*.

There is a third point. Any discussion of a practical issue, of what to do, exhibits thought or thoughtlessness. Regardless of the right or wrong of what is argued for, the thought itself may be criticized. If we limit the sphere of morality to action, we leave no room for criticizing thought about action except so far as it involves mistakes of reasoning or premises against which some rational argument may be brought. On the other hand we may treat, let us say, a too great knowingness, a refusal to acknowledge mystery or adventure in deliberation (to use once more Martha Nussbaum's discussion of *The Golden Bowl* [p. 44]), as failures of thinking, failures subject themselves to moral criticism. Here the significance of works of literature for moral philosophy is that we may learn from our reading of such works, and from reflection on them, terms of criticism of thought applicable to discussions of practical issues and to moral philosophy itself.

I want to turn to one last difficulty about what moral philosophy is – a difficulty about the sort of world it goes on in. Again I shall begin from something

Iris Murdoch has said. If we treat action as the central notion in defining the sphere of morality, this may, she suggests, have as one of its sources a view of the world as in a fundamental sense comprehensible, and of the facts constituting the situations in which we act as straightforwardly describable.[17] Comprehension, description, appreciation of the facts will not be seen as tasks for which moral energy, discipline, imagination, creativity, wit, care, patience, tact, delicacy,…may be required. The problem here should be treated separately from the last. What sort of subject we think moral philosophy is depends on whether we accept or not some such view of the world. Is there not a taking for granted that whatever philosophical questions there may be about knowing what the world is like, they belong to epistemology (as traditionally conceived) or philosophy of science and are not seriously troubling ones for moral philosophy? Is there not a taking for granted that *saying* what the world is like, what the situations are in which we find ourselves, is a "plain" business, in that sense of "plainness" which Martha Nussbaum used in speaking of traditional moral philosophy? If in philosophy we see the moral life of human beings against such a background, we shall surely greet with disbelief the idea that the *un*-plainness of literary works is itself important for moral philosophy.

Consider Professor Raphael's remarks: "If someone says that literature feeds moral philosophy, he may mean that characters or situations in a work of literature can be used as evidence for some issues in moral philosophy. This is the most obvious, the richest, and the most satisfying way in which literature and moral philosophy are connected" (p. 1). It is the most obvious; to suggest that it is the richest and most satisfying reflects a particular view of moral philosophy, of how far it is concerned with a world whose deepest difficulties include difficulties of description. What, let us ask, is it to use a character or situation in a novel as evidence for an issue in moral philosophy? Prior to reading it, we may, as philosophers, have been concerned with questions, for example, about the significance of rules; the novel, let us imagine, describes a situation involving adultery and marriage, and we may take the novel to bear upon the general questions we had had. After reading it, we may recognize that our previous answers to those questions were inadequate, that we had failed to take into account certain human possibilities or what we can now see to be likelihoods, certain ways in which situations may be resolved or possible explanations for their being irresolvable, possible kinds of background or complications of character – and we may accordingly modify or refine our general principles or our systematic account of how principles bear on cases. The contribution of the novel is then a greater understanding of how things can and do happen – an understanding which could also have come from keeping one's eyes open to similar things happening in the world. What is here "food" for moral philosophy is the story itself, what happens, and to what kind of people, in what sort of situation; what plays no role is *how* the story is told, the "unplainness" of the telling, its "density," the kinds of demand that that makes on the reader. Here I am going over Professor Wollheim's line of reasoning (in his commentary on Martha Nussbaum's piece);

such a contribution by a novel to philosophical thought is, for the reasons he gives, not *specifically* a contribution as novel but rather as Story, in his sense (p. 186). The Story provides evidence, bearing on issues and questions already there in moral philosophy; the effect of reading is the difference the evidence makes to judgments, conclusions, answers we reach.

An argument for a richer kind of connection between moral philosophy and literature is provided by Martha Nussbaum; what I want to bring out is that her argument supposes a different view of moral philosophy from Professor Raphael's. What we are to get from the experience – the "adventure" – of reading such a text as *The Golden Bowl* is not *evidence* bearing on philosophical conclusions about the nature of deliberation. What philosophical thought does a novel like that call for, then, if she is correct? It calls for an attempt to connect features it has specifically as a novel with the character of what in human life the novel is about; it calls, that is, for an attempt to show the relation between the thought it invites and the author's relation to his characters, the ambiguity, the "dissonance," the complications it presents of possible treatings as salient, and so on. The task is not one belonging to the philosopher as such, drawing on things in the novel, as opposed to that of a literary critic, nor that of a critic as opposed to that of a philosopher. The question being thought about is of the form, "How is it that *this* (whatever feature of the novel it may be) is an illuminating way of writing about *that* (whatever feature of human life)?" And what we can see in Martha Nussbaum's essay is the combination of that question with, "How is it that *this* is so much more illuminating a way of writing about it than are the familiar ways of moral philosophy?" The implication is that it is no plain business finding how to write illuminatingly about human experience – and no plain business reading about it either. But these are not issues or questions which belong to moral philosophy on the prevalent view of the subject; if they are questions for it, it is only through our familiarity with unplain ways of using language, through our responses to those ways of using language, that we can recognize them as such questions.

Let me put the matter with a different kind of example. Lawrence spoke of *the novel* as a great discovery: "…it won't *let* you tell didactic lies"; it shows them up, shows *you* up if you try to put them in.[18] Here is a view (true or false does not matter for my present concerns) about the relation between forms of thought and expression, and what we try to think about. But it is not on every view of philosophy that what Lawrence says will seem to call for philosophical discussion. Philosophers can easily see as a conceptual innovation relevant to their concerns a new way of thinking about justice (let us say); but that *the novel* (or particular forms, particular kinds of novel, styles of narration and the like) might be thought of as a kind of moral discovery, that modes of describing or presenting life are significant from the moral philosopher's point of view: this is not something that fits into their current conception of their subject matter.

I have two points in conclusion. First, that Martha Nussbaum's attempt to take as a starting point a widely agreed and inclusive notion of the aim of moral philosophy is pretty much doomed. No one knows what the subject is; most widely agreed accounts of it depend on suppositions that are not obvious and that reflect particular evaluations and views of the world, of human nature, and of what it is to speak, think, write, or read about the world. The more inclusive an account is, the more likely it will include what many philosophers would not dream of counting as part of their subject. Fortunately, her essay and more particularly her attempt to show us how we may take *The Golden Bowl* as a text of moral philosophy, do not depend on finding such an agreed account. By thinking philosophically about literature in a way that breaks the rules of what counts – on many views – as moral philosophy, she goes some way toward showing, that we should not take those rules seriously, or the conception of moral philosophy which they determine.

In the essay I quoted earlier, Iris Murdoch said of the moral philosophy of the 1950s: "What these linguistic analysts mistrust is precisely language."[19] She had in mind their idea of philosophy as mere analysis of moral concepts, in contrast to the development of new modes of understanding, new moral visions. As they saw matters, the moralist or the ordinary man, in making moral judgments, labels certain things "good" or "right"; the moral philosopher then shows how the use of such terms is related to the facts on the one hand and to action and choice on the other. It is striking that, although such an approach in moral philosophy has virtually disappeared, although the notion of neutral analysis of moral terms is dead or moribund, what she meant by "mistrust of language" is as present as ever it was; and that is the second point I wanted to reach. The focus is *still* on "evaluations," "judgments," on explicit moral reasoning to conclusions that something is worthwhile, or a duty, or wrong, or ought to be done; our conception of what are "issues" for moral thought is still "x is wrong" versus "x is permissible"; the abortion debate is our paradigm of moral utterance. "Mistrust of language" is a reluctance to see all that is involved in using it well, responding well to it, meeting it well, reluctance to see what kind of failure it may be to use it badly. How do our words, thoughts, descriptions, philosophical styles let us down or let others down? How do they, used at full stretch – and in what spirit or spirits – illuminate? Moral philosophy may no longer be called "linguistic" (it rarely called itself that anyway), but the narrowness of focus has not changed.

Notes

1 This essay comments on papers in an issue of *New Literary History* 15, no. 1, Autumn 1983, on Literature and/as Moral Philosophy. The papers to which I refer are Martha Nussbaum's "Flawed Crystals: James's *The Golden Bowl* and Literature as Moral Philosophy," 25–50, reprinted in Nussbaum, *Love's Knowledge*, Oxford: Oxford University Press, 1990, 125–47; D. D. Raphael's "Can Literature be Moral Philosophy?" 1–12; and Richard Wollheim's "Flawed Crystals: James's *The Golden Bowl* and the Plausibility of Literature as Moral Philosophy," 185–91. Page references in the text are to that issue of *New Literary History*.

2 Raphael (p. 3) quotes A. J. Ayer, Editorial Foreword to P. H. Nowell-Smith, *Ethics*, Harmondsworth: Penguin, 1954, p. 7.
3 Nowell-Smith, p. 319.
4 Wolfgang Iser, *The Act of Reading*, Baltimore: Johns Hopkins University Press, 1978; Iser, "Interaction between Text and Reader," S. R. Suleiman and I. Crosman (eds.), *The Reader in the Text*, Princeton: Princeton University Press, 1980, pp. 106–19.
5 Iser, *The Act of Reading*, pp. 76–7.
6 Iser, "Interaction between Text and Reader," p. 113.
7 L. Wittgenstein, *Tractatus Logico-Philosophicus*, London: Routledge, 1961, 6.53.
8 P. F. Strawson, "Critical Notice: L. Wittgenstein, *Philosophical Investigations*," *Mind* 63 (1954), 70–99, p. 70.
9 Dorothea Krook, *Three Traditions of Moral Thought*, Cambridge: Cambridge University Press, 1959, Chapter 6. See also Michael Tanner, "The Language of Philosophy," L. Michaels and C. Ricks (eds.), *The State of the Language*, Berkeley: University of California Press, 1980, pp. 458–66.
10 On these issues, see W. Hart, "How are we to read philosophy?" *Haltwhistle Quarterly* no. 3 (1975), 47–56.
11 Iris Murdoch, "Vision and Choice in Morality," *Proceedings of the Aristotelian Society*, supplementary vol. 30, 1956, 32–58, pp. 32–3.
12 op. cit., pp. 35–40.
13 op. cit., p. 39.
14 Iris Murdoch, *The Sovereignty of Good*, London: Routledge & Kegan Paul, 1970, p. 34.
15 op. cit., pp. 17–40. The importance of this notion of vision is emphasized in Martha Nussbaum's recent work. See especially "The Discernment of Perception: An Aristotelian Conception of Personal and Public Rationality," revised version in Nussbaum, *Love's Knowledge*, Oxford: Oxford University Press, 1990, pp. 54–105, "'Finely Aware and Richly Responsible': Moral Attention and the Moral Task of Literature," revised version in Nussbaum, *Love's Knowledge*, 148–67, and Section E2 (pp. 37–40) of the Introduction to *Love's Knowledge*, with further bibliographical references. My comments on an earlier version of "'Finely Aware'" are in "Missing the Adventure," *The Realistic Spirit*, Cambridge: MIT Press, 1991, pp. 309–318.
16 The remarks are drawn from the Preface to *The Princess Casamassima*, Harmondsworth: Penguin, 1977, p. 12; the paragraph from which they are drawn follows that quoted by Martha Nussbaum.
17 Murdoch, "Vision and Choice," pp. 49–50; see also pp. 42–3.
18 D. H. Lawrence, "The Novel," Lawrence, *Phoenix II*, London, 1968, pp. 416–26, at pp. 416–17.
19 Murdoch, "Vision and Choice," p. 42n.

8

"THE LIFE OF THE SIGN"

Wittgenstein on reading a poem

Joachim Schulte

Hardly anything was of greater importance to Wittgenstein than reading poetry, plays and novels except, perhaps, for listening to and thinking about music and doing philosophy. The fact that among the six or seven mottos he took into consideration for his later work three were lines taken from poets (Goethe, Matthias Claudius, and Longfellow) is testimony of the great significance poetry had for him.[1] He had fairly clear preferences for certain authors,[2] but it is unlikely that he believed his personal taste ought to form the basis of a general canon. Although he evidently thought a great deal about aesthetic questions, he surely did not develop anything like an aesthetic theory or a general view of literature or a systematic discussion of problems arising from philosophical reflections on poetry. Nevertheless, certain insights articulated in the context of his later philosophy can, in my opinion, assist us in our attempts to understand what it means to come to grips with or master the content of a poem. I think it is useful to see these insights into what it means to read a poem against the background of Wittgenstein's remarks on the "life" of signs. And I am furthermore convinced that whatever can be learned from these considerations may help us get a better grasp of Wittgenstein's own way of writing as well as certain basic ideas that informed his thinking.

It may be profitable to approach our subject by way of an interesting misunderstanding. Michael Dummett, in his magisterial book on Frege's philosophy of mathematics, chastises Wittgenstein for having misrepresented, underrated, and foolishly criticized Frege's views on the application of mathematics. Dummett says:

> He [*Wittgenstein*] criticized Frege in this connection, without, apparently, having understood him, and certainly without appreciating how far more sophisticated Frege's view was than his own. He described Frege's view, maintained against the formalists, as being that "what must be added to the dead signs in order to make a live proposition is something immaterial, with properties different from all mere signs", | "But if we had to name anything which is the life of the sign, we should have to

say that it was its *use*" [*Wittgenstein*, Blue and Brown Books, *p. 4*]. As a critique of a passage in which Frege said that it was applicability alone that raised arithmetic above the rank of a game,[3] this remark is astonishing; but equally astonishing is the crudity of Wittgenstein's conception of the application of mathematics...[4]

If, upon reading this passage and mindful of the respectful tone of Wittgenstein's discussion of Frege's objections to formalism,[5] one turns to the *Blue Book* to read the passage quoted by Dummett, one will soon be surprised to learn that, in this context, Wittgenstein does not discuss Frege's philosophy of mathematics, expresses no criticism of Frege and, indeed, does not ascribe the view cited by Dummett to Frege. This remarkable misunderstanding of Wittgenstein's words indicates that the passage in question is not easy to read and that, in particular, it poses a problem of how to attribute the ideas articulated there.

The passage alluded to and partly quoted by Dummett can be found near the beginning of the *Blue Book*, which opens with the question "What is the meaning of a word?" Wittgenstein soon examines various ways in which it appears tempting to connect questions of meaning with questions regarding the occurrence of mental processes. In doing so he of course tries to point out that this sort of temptation tends to mislead us into proposing or accepting erroneous conceptions of meaning. What may prove especially dangerous here is the observation that utterances may require interpretation to fulfill a function in situations involving linguistic exchanges. In that kind of situation, Wittgenstein remarks, one may easily get the impression that the working of language depends on the occurrence of "*certain definite* mental processes...of understanding and meaning. The signs of our language seem dead without these mental processes; and it might seem that the only function of the signs is to induce such processes, and that these are the things we ought really to be interested in."[6]

The metaphorical contrast between dead and live signs is not the only one Wittgenstein employs in this context. A similar role is played by the pair of opposites "organic/ inorganic,"[7] which is invoked to bring in the notion of an occult "mechanism" that might be supposed to serve as the medium of the relevant processes of understanding, meaning, etc.: "We are tempted to think that the action of language consists of two parts; an inorganic part, the handling of signs, and an organic part, which we may call understanding these signs, meaning them, interpreting them, thinking. These latter activities seem to take place in a queer kind of medium, the mind" (ibid.). One way of getting rid of the idea that understanding and meaning are essentially obscure mental processes in an occult medium of strange mechanisms of association etc. consists in replacing presumed processes of that sort with public processes involving observable and tangible objects like material pictures or models.

It is at this point of his considerations that Wittgenstein mentions Frege and his confrontation with formalism. The entire passage, which contains the words quoted by Dummett, reads as follows:

147

Frege ridiculed the formalist conception of mathematics by saying that the formalists confused the unimportant thing, the sign, with the important, the meaning. Surely, one wishes to say, mathematics does not treat of dashes on a bit of paper. Frege's idea could be expressed thus: the propositions of mathematics, if they were just complexes of dashes, would be dead and utterly uninteresting, whereas they obviously have a kind of life. And the same, of course, could be said of any proposition: Without a sense, or without the thought, a proposition would be an utterly dead and trivial thing. And further it seems clear that no adding of inorganic signs can make the proposition live. And the conclusion which one draws from this is that what must be added to the dead signs in order to make a live proposition is something immaterial, with properties different from all mere signs. But if we had to name anything which is the life of the sign, we should have to say that it was its *use*.[8]

Here we are offered quite a collection of contrasts: "unimportant," "sign," "dead," "uninteresting," "trivial," "inorganic" on one side, "important," "meaning," "life," "sense," "thought," "immaterial" on the other. It becomes clear that Frege's attack on formalist interpretations of mathematics is only mentioned as an example, illustrating a certain attitude towards uses of signs. And surely this much is true: Frege regarded it as a shortcoming of certain formalist conceptions that according to them the signs occurring in (mathematical) sentences were to be seen as "mere signs" – as objects on a par with physical chess pieces.[9] The moment Wittgenstein says that "Frege's idea could be expressed thus" he is no longer reporting Frege's own view but describing an aspect of his attitude in such a way that it fits in with a whole cluster of ideas represented by the life-organism side of the general contrast developed in the passage quoted. Accordingly, Wittgenstein's statement about the "life of the sign," namely, that it consists in the use of the sign, is not (as Dummett claims) part of a "critique" of Frege but Wittgenstein's way of suggesting (a) that there is something odd about the picture behind the life–death opposition if this is understood in a certain way and (b) that whatever is sound in the intuition that, seen from a particular perspective, signs may appear dead or alive ought to be elucidated, not by means of invoking "a queer kind of medium," but in terms of a helpful notion of use.

In the *Blue Book*, this notion of use is still conceived in terms of a "system" (the successor concept of Wittgenstein's earlier idea of a "calculus" and, in its turn, the predecessor of the far more heterogeneous omnium-gatherum often indicated by his later term "language-game"[10]):

The sign (the sentence) gets its significance from the system of signs, from the language to which it belongs. Roughly: understanding a sentence means understanding a language.| As a part of a system of language, one may say, the sentence has life.

(p. 5)

This shows that Wittgenstein regards the idea of live signs as an innocuous metaphor as long as it can be understood to be firmly anchored in a tenable conception of meaning as use. But the contrast between dead and live signs can be fatally misleading if it is employed in such a way that it engages with tricky notions of mental processes and obscure images involving mental mechanisms. All in all, from reflecting on these pages of the *Blue Book* one gains the impression that while Wittgenstein does not really object to the idea of live or dead signs in a general way, he does want to warn us that this idea *can* lead to confusion and error.

The *Blue Book* was dictated during the academic year 1933/34. Thus it is no accident that the only other writings where the life–death contrast is frequently used in a way similar to its employment on the first pages of the *Blue Book* are Wittgenstein's manuscripts from the same time, in particular *Band* X (MS 114).[11] The relevant part of this (as well as the following) volume contains revisions of the so-called "Big Typescript" (TS 213) large chunks of which found their way into *Philosophical Grammar*, a book assembled by Rush Rhees.

A particularly interesting passage involving the metaphorical idea of something dead deals with the concept "intention" ("meaning"). As in the *Blue Book*, Wittgenstein recommends substituting talk about inner pictures with talk about publicly accessible pictures. But when it comes to describing "the process of intention" the picture one sketches to convey the content of an intention seems isolated, open to all kinds of different interpretations, lifeless, dead:

> When one has the picture in view by itself it is suddenly dead, and it is as if something had been taken away from it, which had given it life before. It is not a thought, not an intention; whatever accompaniments we imagine for it, articulate or inarticulate processes, or any feeling whatsoever, it remains isolated, it does not point outside itself to a reality beyond.[12]

Now one may try to get around this difficulty by pointing out that it is not the picture itself which does the intending; that it is ourselves who intend by means of it. And in that sense one might want to observe that "Meaning is surely essentially a mental process, a process of consciousness and life, not of dead matter" (ibid.). But this does not get us anywhere, Wittgenstein says: there is something wrong with the whole approach. And what is wrong is connected with the fact that we are tempted to use the notion of a process. "For what we are dissatisfied with here is the grammar of *process*, not the specific kind of process. – It could be said: we should call any process 'dead' in this sense." What we need is a change of perspective. Instead of thinking about intending (or wishing) in terms of a process taking place in, or exemplified by, an individual person, we should look at *expressions* of intentions. It is then that the problem may seem solved "because the system of language seems to provide me with a medium in which the proposition is no longer dead" (*PG*, p. 149, §101).

This idea, however, should not be confused with the notion that the system of language actually does the work of turning lifeless signs into live thoughts. The question "Is the sign dead or alive?" does not present itself when one is using language to articulate thoughts or intentions. It only arises if one begins to ponder and actually ponders the question why sentences and what they are used to express do not normally appear dead. The idea of the system of language, of "the whole network to which the sentence belongs" (ibid., §102), as that which lends our sentences life is useful inasmuch as it suggests an answer to that question.[13] But it does not *explain* the life of the sign for the simple reason that there arises no question about that in a way analogous to e.g. biological questions about the conditions rendering possible the life of certain organisms. To speak of life and death in the context of signs, language, thinking, intending and meaning is, after all, a metaphorical use of this contrast. And it can only lead to confusion if one uses this sort of figurative language when trying to explain what is really happening. It is an "odd way of looking at things" which can inspire people to say things like "thought isn't something dead, because *for me* what I think *really* happens" (*PG*, p. 154, §105).

It is important to avoid connecting the image of a dead thing (in contrast to a live organism) with certain other kinds of metaphor. Thus it can only mislead us if we think of meaning or intending something as a specific process of experiencing something or as an event involving, or happening to, us. Here the impression that what is happening to us is dead may signal danger but it may also suggest deceptive questions about why intending (or meaning) something does not seem dead if you are directly involved.[14] Direct involvement (live activity) is seen as opposed to the experience of an external event (dead phenomenon). But this opposition rests on linking our complex concept of experience with a misleading image which in turn feeds on the metaphorical contrast "live–dead":

> what we are speaking of is a case in which contrary to experience the subject is linked like an element in a chemical compound. But where do we get this idea from? The concept of living activity in contrast with dead phenomena. |...| We want to say: "When we mean something, there isn't a dead picture (of any kind); it's as if we went up to someone. We go up to what we mean." | But here we're constructing a false contrast between experience and something else, as if experience consisted of sitting still and letting pictures pass in front of one.
>
> (*PG*, pp. 156–7, §107)

To appreciate the extent to which the live–dead contrast may be used figuratively it can be helpful to look at constructed, artificial cases. It is a fact about *us* that in reading a story we entertain certain impressions, pictures that pass before our inner eyes in a way similar to that in which the cartoons forming a comic strip pass in front of our outer eyes. Pictures and sentences can be similar in evoking certain impressions on the part of those who read or "read" them, e.g. impressions of satisfaction (*PG*, p. 171, §125). This is a fact about us and our use of language. But things could be different:

> We can...imagine a language in whose use the impression made on us by the signs played no part; in which there was no question of an understanding, in the sense of such an impression. The signs are e.g. written and transmitted to us and we are able to *take notice of them*. (That is to say, the only impression that comes in here is the pattern of the sign.) If the sign is an order, we translate it into action by means of rules, tables. It does not get as far as an impression like that of a picture; nor are stories written in this language. But there is perhaps a kind of reading for entertainment which consists in certain series of signs being translated into bodily movements to make a kind of dance ...| In this case one really might say "the series of signs is *dead* without the system."
>
> (*PG*, pp. 171f, §124)

This would be a case in which the existence of the system literally is a condition of the life of those signs: without the system they would be dead, not only if looked at from a certain perspective, but straightforwardly dead in the sense of having no use. This consideration serves to clarify the metaphorical aspect of the live–dead contrast, and by illustrating a non-figurative use of this notion it helps us to understand the difficult passage from the *Blue Book* quoted earlier. The sense of the live/dead contrast in which we are prone to respond by using further contrastive pairs like "important/unimportant, trivial," "organic/inorganic," "interesting/uninteresting" and by expressing our wish "to breathe life into those signs"[15] is clearly on the figurative side. But metaphorical or figurative speech is a kind of use which in its turn depends on the existence of what one may want to call an "established use." And it is this established use – a use to which Wittgenstein (also) refers in the short paragraph concluding the quotation from p. 4 of the *Blue Book* – which gives life to signs both in the straightforward sense illustrated by the constructed example from *Philosophical Grammar* and in all those derivative senses involving "dependent" uses.[16] One of the difficulties presented by the quotation from the *Blue Book* is this: that in it apparently there occur established and dependent uses at the same time.

It is not easy to spell out what might be meant by speaking of simultaneous occurrences of established and dependent uses.[17] But the idea is an important one, and it is connected with one of the main themes of Wittgenstein's late philosophy, in particular with his remarks on the philosophy of psychology written in the second half of the 1940s. The idea of the "life" of signs is mentioned in these remarks, but it does not play a prominent role. However, there is a more general idea behind it which might be regarded as the leading concept inspiring a great deal of Wittgenstein's thinking during those years. This is the idea of aspect change or, to be more specific, the *experience* of aspect change. The questions Wittgenstein raises in this context can in many cases be seen to be connected with the contrast between live and dead signs he discussed at the time of dictating the *Blue Book*.

As I said, the word "life" (and its cognates) in its figurative use does not occur very often in Wittgenstein's writings of the relevant period, but it is striking that what one might regard as the very first remark of this long sequence of reflections on the philosophy of psychology does employ that image. The last part of the important manuscript book 116 (dated "May 1945") opens with the invitation to imagine people who, whenever they *mean* what they say (in contrast with e.g. practicing or rehearsing words), *sing* their sentences. Of a sung sentence they claim that "it is alive" while sentences which are not sung are declared to be "dead." And if these people started to philosophize about the concept "to mean," then, according to Wittgenstein, they would be tempted to say "to mean is to sing."[18]

There are various obvious ways in which this thought experiment is connected with central ideas of Wittgenstein's later philosophy. For one thing, singing is not easily confused with an accompaniment, let alone an *inner* accompaniment, of words: it is a way of expressing something, a kind of performance bound up with a certain repertoire of means of expression. *Our* concept of meaning, on the other hand, tempts us to say completely different things. And it is one of the points Wittgenstein wishes to make by means of this juxtaposition that our concept of meaning something is, or should be seen to be, in certain respects more similar to the concept of singing than we expected: it is helpful to notice in which ways talk about meaning something involves talk about forms and repertoires of expression.

A year and a half later Wittgenstein used the image of the life of words in the context of a series of remarks on words which can be interpreted in two radically different ways. An example is provided by one of Wittgenstein's favourite jokes: The word "*weiche*" as it occurs in the Wagnerian sentence "*Weiche, Wotan, weiche!*" can be read either as the imperative of the verb "*weichen*" or as the plural form of the adjective "*weich*." Accordingly, the sentence can be understood as meaning either that Wotan should retreat or that he is requested to prepare soft-boiled eggs.[19] What Wittgenstein says sounds a little like a variation on the same theme as was intoned in the remark on singing/meaning. Instead of mentioning singers he now talks about a tribe of doodlers:

> Imagine that people had the custom of doodling while they spoke; why should what they produce in this way while talking be less interesting than accompanying processes in their minds, and why should our interest in *these* be of any different kind? | Why does one of these processes *seem* to give the words their peculiar *life*?[20]

And he goes on to ask how it is possible for an illustration to "give the sentence a *particular* life, if language doesn't do so? How is it supposed to manage to be more specific than the language of words?" (ibid., §677). But now the discussion moves into a different area. The question is, How is it possible to experience, and to express the experience of, one rather than another meaning of a word? How, for example, can we deprive a word of its felt meaning by repeating it several times over (cf. ibid., §680)?

In these and other respects words and their meanings are like pictures[21] and corresponding ways of seeing them (aspects). Wittgenstein emphasizes the importance of the fact that meanings and aspects *can* be experienced: it is not our usual way, but in certain contexts – and especially if we are dealing with ambiguous words or pictures – we express our understanding of linguistic or visual items by clarifying (or "illustrating") which meaning or aspect out of several possible ones we experienced. In such cases understanding may involve *savoring* a specific tone, aroma or facet of the object (song, coffee, drawing etc.) in question, and the activity of savoring something as well as the results of that activity can be expressed in typical ways belonging to a limited repertoire of ways of showing what was felt.[22]

The ability to savor or experience kinds of tone or shades of meaning may be developed to a higher or lower degree. At least in certain cases it can perhaps be imagined to be totally absent. And this is another context where Wittgenstein exploits parallels between the experience of word meanings and the experience of visual aspects:

> What is lacking to anyone who doesn't understand the question which way the letter F is facing, where, for example, to paint a nose on? | Or to anyone who doesn't find that a word loses something when it is repeated several times, namely, its meaning; or to someone who doesn't find that it then becomes a mere sound? |...| Is it that such a person is unable to appreciate a sentence, judge it the way those who understand it can? Is it that for him the sentence is not alive (with all that that implies)? Is it that the word does not have an aroma of meaning? And that therefore he will often react differently to a word than we do? – It *might* be that way.[23]

These questions are then given a more specific content by looking at the example of listening to a piece of music "with understanding" and pointing out that there are ways of indicating the presence of such understanding which are better (more instructive and assessable) than "uncouth" or "fatuous" ("*abgeschmackte*") attempts at conveying what is going on in myself while listening with understanding.

Of course, this is not the place to go into all the questions raised by Wittgenstein's discussion of experiencing shades of meaning, tones of voice, aspects and aspect changes. But it may be useful to bear this sort of question and Wittgenstein's illustrations in mind when we look at some remarks where he mentions the example of reading a poem. It is an intriguing fact about a number of passages where Wittgenstein highlights peculiarities of our comprehension of language that he compares language with music and our understanding of linguistic utterances with our understanding of songs, tunes and musical phrases.

Some of these comparisons bear on the deepest aspects of his philosophy of language. What concerns us here, however, might be characterized as "superficial" features of language and music: music can speak, and speech can be musical. Music can speak in at least two different senses. On the one hand, he who performs a piece of music can speak by playing this work in a certain way,[24] on the other hand, a work of music can speak in the sense of containing quasi-linguistic elements. In this second kind of case many different types of quasi-linguistic features can be distinguished: they may be a matter of form or harmony (grammar, syntax), but probably more often they will be a matter of rhythm, accentuation, phrasing (rhetoric, elocution). A particularly striking parallel is mentioned in the following passage:

> The way music speaks. Don't forget that even though a poem is framed in the language of information, it is not employed in the language-game of information. | Might one not imagine someone who had never known music, and who came to us and heard someone playing a reflective piece of Chopin, being convinced that this was a language and people were merely keeping the sense secret from him? | Verbal language contains a strong musical element. (A sigh, the modulation of tone for a question, for an announcement, for longing; all the countless *gestures* in the vocal cadences.)
>
> (*RPP* I, §888)

The observation on the language-game of information or communication (*Mitteilung*) is easily misunderstood. First of all, here the phrase "language-game" is not used in any of the more specific senses employed by Wittgenstein ("primitive" or "invented" language-games, language-games "with certain words" etc.).[25] Second, this passage should not be taken to suggest that Wittgenstein believes that there is such a thing as a delimitable, surveyable "language-game of information." The terms "information" and "communication" are far too comprehensive and too vague to permit any drawing of boundaries around uses for the purpose of information or communication. I think that Wittgenstein merely wants to say that poetry, even though it employs the same building-blocks as ordinary ("prosaic") speech, is subject to different conventions from those regulating the manifold kinds of uses of language which serve to impart information and to communicate facts. And of course Wittgenstein does not want to deny that poetry can be used to communicate all sorts of information. He only reminds us of the fact that if poetry is used *as poetry* it is not (mainly) used to give information; and that if it is chiefly used to convey information it is not really used *as poetry* – it may, for instance, be employed in an, as it were, "quotational" way.

The example of the "reflective piece of Chopin" is particularly well chosen. It immediately reminds one of the fact that the degree to which music can compare with language varies a great deal with different composers. It also brings out that, if our visitor from a culture without music is to mistake a reflective piece (*pensieroso*) by Chopin with utterances in a secret language hiding certain thoughts, the performer will have to play it in a reflective manner (*pensierosamente*). Similarly, the musical element contained in verbal language will only come to the fore if the relevant *gestures* are performed with sufficient competence, that is, if rhythm, cadences, accentuation etc. are such that the gestures can be perceived as gestures of certain kinds.[26] Complications can be introduced by thinking of those cases where we play music or recite poetry in our imagination. But this is one kind of problem where the typical and conventional element in music and language or speech (the varied but limited repertoire of forms of expression stressed by Wittgenstein) can be helpful in trying to sort out what is meant by referring to such types of inner performances.

It is a commonplace that often the language of poetry is, or can be, treated like music. In the case of certain poems we up to a point abstract from the meanings of the words used and the sense (if any) expressed by the poems' sentences. What seems to matter is a poem's sound, its rhythm, the melodiousness of its "voice" and, perhaps, the harmony of its rhymes. This may be one of the reasons why some authors and many admirers of poetry insist that it can be understood properly only if read aloud.[27] To read the lines aloud can be a means of understanding or interpreting (helping others understand) a certain poem. Even imagining that I am reading the lines aloud may assist me in grasping what the poem is meant to suggest.

Reflections on the reading of poetry contribute to finding out about things that only poems can do or which certain poems can do much better than others or than other uses of language:

> But how about this: when I read a poem, or some expressive prose, especially when I read it out loud, surely there is something going on as I read it which doesn't go on when I glance over the sentences only for the sake of their information. I may, for example, read a sentence with more intensity or with less. I take trouble to get the tone exactly right. Here I often see a picture before me, as it were an illustration. And may I not also utter a word in such a tone as to make its meaning stand out like a picture? A way of writing might be imagined, in which some signs were replaced by pictures and so were made prominent. This does actually happen sometimes, when we underline a word or positively put it on a pedestal in the sentence.
>
> (*RPP* I, §1059)[28]

155

As we have seen, getting the tone exactly right matters because (a) it helps us understand the poem, (b) it helps others understand the poem a certain way, (c) it helps others grasp what we feel (or think ought to be felt) when reading it.

The fact that one can take trouble to get the tone exactly right shows that here there is something one can try to do *well*, something which one may fail to do well. This suggests that getting it right is something one may be able to learn, something involving certain techniques which can be taught, comprehended and acquired and which some people are better equipped to acquire than others. And thinking through these possibilities one may come to notice that poetry can do something other forms of language use cannot achieve or, at any rate, cannot achieve in the same fashion: it can exhibit individual words and phrases in such a way that their meanings stand out and function like pictures – like icons, symbols, illustrations and other kinds of image. The way poetry is capable of achieving this is by "positively putting a word on a pedestal in the sentence"; and this is something poetry can do because it is governed by, and may exploit, conventions that play no role, or minor roles, in other domains of language use.

One of these conventions is bound up with the savoring of aromas mentioned above. Another one involves paying attention to the musical side of language. Others imply an awareness of the peculiarity of the institution of poetry, the custom of reciting it and its almost ritual functions. However, all these conventions and the techniques the mastering of which makes possible their rule are no guarantee that the intended effects will really be brought about. For these effects to come about many things are needed besides those conventions – receptivity, experience, certain kinds of upbringing etc. What failure to produce the relevant effects amounts to is indicated by the first sentence of the passage quoted, which (in its revised version printed in *PI*) underlines the contrast between "reading with feeling" and "merely skimming the lines for information." This is the contrast between falling flat and resonating with people's feelings, engaging their powers of imagination. And of course one might characterize this contrast by saying that the words of a poem may come alive or remain dead.

This sort of contrast is alluded to in a later passage (*RPP* II, §§501ff.) which begins by mentioning feeling certain sensations when listening to music and then goes on to consider parallel experiences in the case of reading a poem:

> [1] A poem makes an impression on us as we read it. "Do you feel the same while you read it as when you read something indifferent?" – How have I learnt to answer this question? Perhaps I shall say "Of course not!" – which is as much as to say: *this* takes hold of me, and the other not. "I experience something different."...| [2] But now you remember certain sensations and images and thoughts as you read, and they are such as were not irrelevant for the enjoyment, for the impression. – But I should like to say that they get their correctness only from their surroundings: through the reading of this poem, from my *knowledge* of the language, with its metre and with innumerable other things. (These

eyes smile only in *this* face and in *this* temporal context.) |...| [3] But isn't understanding shown, e.g., in the expression with which someone reads the poem, sings the tune? Certainly. But what is the experience during the reading? About that you would just have to say: you enjoy and understand it if you hear it well read, or feel it well read in your speech-organs. | [4] Understanding a musical phrase may also be called understanding a *language*.[29]

This sequence of remarks contains many allusions to various problems and insights developed in Wittgenstein's later philosophy of psychology. Here, however, I should like to concentrate on just a few points which may serve to summarize some of the things said above and pave the way for my concluding observations.

[1] points out that a poem which does make an impression on me produces a different kind of experience in me from the experiences (if any) resulting from reading something indifferent. This contrast may as well be described in terms of the image of live versus dead signs. [2] emphasizes what one might call the "institutional preconditions" for experiences of the kind involved in reading poetry as well as listening to music and appreciating paintings. If I am to make something of a poem I have to know its language extremely well, for I have to be alive to unobvious features of metre and "innumerable" other kinds of details. In the case of music the parallel is clear, since understanding music is understanding a special sort of language [4]. And to appreciate a painting it is not enough to look at it in a casual way: you must have learnt a number of things and be open to the expressive powers of pictures. ("I might say: a picture does not always *live* for me while I am seeing it. | "Her picture smiles down on me from the wall.' It need not always do so, whenever my glance lights on it."[30]) [3] is a difficult remark. What is clearly correct is that the expression (accentuation, rhythm, intonation) with which I recite or repeat or perform a poem or a tune is a criterion for whether and how I have understood the poem or the tune. But the cited answer to the question about the experience during the reading must be wrong. Surely the circumstances and feelings mentioned in this answer are not essential to appreciating and understanding a poem or a tune.

Here, however, we must ask ourselves in what sort of case it may be important to wonder about experiences had *while* reading certain words (looking at a picture, listening to a tune). From Wittgenstein's point of view the answer is that these experiences matter when our understanding of those words (etc.) depends on the felt presence of a particular aspect, especially if this involves choosing between two or more different aspects suggesting themselves.[31] For you, a certain aspect, a certain meaning (remember the meaning of a word "put on a pedestal"!) can come alive only if you are alive to it, and that may involve striving to notice this aspect or meaning where its presence can be felt merely as a potential one. This kind of case is reminiscent of puzzle-pictures hiding their "solutions" which after a certain amount of looking for e.g. a face all of a sudden reveal it and can from now on be seen as "containing" this aspect.[32] Seeing the solution "in" the picture requires talent, effort and training. A different kind of aspect-seeing is involved in experiencing a change of aspect, for example, the switching from the duck-aspect to the rabbit-aspect in the famous duck–rabbit picture (cf. *PI*, p. 194). What matters in this latter kind of case is that one be able to feel the change as a momentary one and to indicate one's understanding of this change by means of appropriate words and gestures.

It is an interesting fact about that sort of experience that intelligent people may be unfamiliar with it. This sort of possibility is examined by Wittgenstein under the headings "aspect-blindness" and "meaning-blindness."[33] In the case we have been discussing this could amount to either of two possibilities: (a) Someone may be unable to notice the potential life contained in the dead (indifferent) signs he is perusing. Such a person will, for example, be incapable of accompanying his reading of those signs with the gestures suggesting themselves to someone who can see these signs come alive. (b) Someone may be unable to experience, or savor the aroma of, the change from live to dead signs and back again. Such a person will, for example, be incapable of correctly using words like "the flashing of an aspect (or an unexpected meaning)" (cf. *PI*, p. 197).

I think it may safely be claimed that the understanding of some (but not all) poems presupposes that one be alive to the presence of different aspects or meanings as well as capable of experiencing changes of aspect or meaning. That is, no one will be able to understand certain kinds of poetry if he is aspect- or meaning-blind in ways (a) or (b). A wonderful instance of the requirement to be alive to unobvious aspects or meanings is described by Wittgenstein in the first of his *Lectures on Aesthetics*:

> Take the questions: "How should poetry be read? What is the correct way of reading it?" If you are talking about blank verse the right way of reading it might be stressing it correctly—you discuss how far you should stress the rhythm and how far you should hide it. A man says it ought to be read *this* way and reads it out to you. You say: "Oh yes. Now it makes sense." There are cases of poetry which should almost be scanned—where the metre is as clear as crystal—others where the metre is entirely in the background. I had an experience with the 18th century poet Klopstock. I found that the way to read him was to stress his metre abnormally. Klopstock put ∪—∪ (etc.) in front of his poems. When I read his poems in this new way, I said: "Ah-ha, now I know why he did this." What had happened? I had read this kind of stuff and had been moderately bored, but when I read it in this particular way, intensely, I smiled, said: "This is *grand*," etc. But I might not have said anything. The important fact was that I read it again and again. When I read these poems I made gestures and facial expressions which were what would be called gestures of approval. But the important thing was that I read the poems entirely differently, more intensely, and said to others: "Look! This is how they should be read."[34]

Wittgenstein's reflections on what is involved in reading a poem are surely helpful, not only when we are trying to understand what it means to talk about the *experience* of reading poetry, but also when we are examining the question how a poem can manage to mean what we may read it as meaning – especially if what it appears to mean is not what it appears to say. The tools Wittgenstein supplies for examining this sort of question are fashioned from his inquiries into our concepts of seeing and noticing aspects or (unobvious) meanings, experiencing changes of aspect or meaning, and aspect- or meaning-blindness. One of the philosophically challenging features of Wittgenstein's investigations is his way of connecting the inner and the outer by, as it were, making us see talk about the outer as containing, or amounting to, talk about the inner: the outer is the sphere in which objectivity, checkability (criteria) and communicability are anchored while the inner is allowed full rein to the extent it can be understood as finding expression.

One point of starting my account with a glance at the *Blue Book* and Dummett's misunderstanding of the quoted passage mentioning Frege was to suggest that one might fruitfully look back from Wittgenstein's late philosophy of psychology to his earlier investigations. It is not only possible to see his thoughts about the experience of aspect change as naturally growing out of his concerns about the life of signs; it is also possible, and likely to be profitable, to regard his use of the live–dead contrast as exemplifying or anticipating his later insights into experiences of aspect change. Thus, for example, to see dead signs as harboring live signs is quite obviously reminiscent of seeing a rabbit-picture as containing a duck-picture; and noticing that live signs could any minute turn into dead ones is evidently an instance of what Wittgenstein would later call spotting an aspect. Similarly, the challenge of the *Blue Book* passage lies in this: that at the same time it exploits and plays with what we have called "established" and "dependent" uses. The life of the signs employed in mathematics literally rests on an established use; at the same time we understand the idea of the life of signs in a figurative, and hence in a dependent, sense. This fact helps us see the established use, not only as based on, but also as containing the dependent use; and this in turn alludes to an however far-fetched possibility of perceiving the established use as contained in the dependent one – a possibility which may after all mirror the order of understanding the different levels at which these uses come into play in the quotation from the *Blue Book*. If a reading of this kind points in the right direction, then it also explains why it is so easy to misunderstand this passage: comprehending it requires an approach similar to one often necessary for understanding poetry – you have to see it the way you would scrutinize a puzzle–picture, as exhibiting more than one face at a time.

What is of great interest in those cases of aspect–seeing is, as Wittgenstein makes clear, the way certain conventions and institutional preconditions come into play and render talk about aspect–seeing and experiences of meaning intelligible. And it is exactly in the context of Wittgenstein's discussion of Frege's criticism of formalism that he uses the phrase that we *project* rules that cannot be expressed by propositions *onto* equations (*WVC*, p. 152) – the rule is so to speak an aspect of certain equations, and what the rule amounts to is shown by the use of these equations. Similarly, he says: "Generality shows itself in application. I have to read this generality into (*hineinsehen*) the configuration…I have to read the rule into the expression with letters in the same way as into the expression with numbers, and if I do not do it, the letters do not help me at all" (*WVC*, p. 154), that is, the signs will remain dead. This notion of "*hineinsehen*," of projecting something onto or reading something into something else, is not clear in this context; and as it stands it might yield reasons for worries of the kind mentioned in the *Blue Book* context where the image of the life of signs is observed to contain the seeds of misunderstandings that might lead us to posit an obscure medium and strange mechanisms. But with the wisdom of hindsight it may also be understood to contain the seeds of enormously fertile conceptual insights of the kind adumbrated in Wittgenstein's later philosophy of psychology.

Another important idea which may be seen as connected with this whole set of considerations is Wittgenstein's early distinction between showing and saying. The two terms of this distinction are like two faces: they are incompatible in the sense that when you are seeing one you cannot be seeing the other – what can be shown cannot be said (*Tractatus*, 4.1212). On the other hand, it is by way of saying something, by way of making meaningful statements, that ineffable features of logic and the world show themselves. In a sense, what is said can be seen to contain another aspect, viz what can only be shown. But what cannot be expressed by, but only manifests itself in, meaningful statements can be alluded to only if it is possible to see what is shown, or manifests itself, as an aspect enshrined in what is meaningfully stated (and hence intersubjectively accessible). The extent to which Wittgenstein believed it possible to get anything across by means of indirection is a matter of exegesis and of much recent controversy.

One of the issues discussed by participants in this controversy is the question of what to make of Wittgenstein's comments on a poem by Ludwig Uhland. While some of the poems of which it is known that Wittgenstein esteemed them sufficiently to quote them to friends or pupils are characterized by a marked degree of didacticism (and were probably quoted by him with didactic purposes in mind),[35] the Uhland poem distinguishes itself by its lyrical qualities, the naturalness of its tone and the straightforwardness of its narrative. The poem had been sent to Wittgenstein by his friend Paul Engelmann, who, in his account of the matter, quotes Karl Kraus's words to the effect that it is "so clear that no one understands it." In his reply to Engelmann's letter Wittgenstein agrees that "the poem by Uhland is really magnificent."[36] He continues to say: "And this is how it is: if only you do not try to utter what is unutterable then *nothing* gets lost. But the unutterable will be – unutterably – *contained* in what has been uttered!"

It is evident that in this remark Wittgenstein is in some way employing the distinction between showing and saying. What remains unclear and a bone of contention between various authors trying to make good sense of that distinction is the extent to which it is possible to say something about the supposedly ineffable second face of the poem. Brian McGuinness points out how Wittgenstein's admiration for this poem fits in with his other known preferences in the domain of literature (Mörike, Keller, Tolstoy etc.).[37] Peter Hacker observes that if Wittgenstein's comment is to be taken seriously, then the saying–showing distinction must be understood as ascribing to the "showing" side a modicum of appreciable content.[38] But surprisingly no one seems to go further than Michael Kremer, a severe critic of Hacker's reading of the saying–showing distinction, in his attempt at spelling out what Wittgenstein might have thought the unutterable content of the poem to amount to. Taking up Engelmann's remark that the poem manages to give "a picture of a life," he expresses his conviction that it "*models* a way of life that Wittgenstein admired and aspired to." And he then goes on to connect this idea of a certain way of life with other ethically relevant hints he finds in the *Tractatus*.[39]

But these are exegetical issues I do not want to explore in this context. What I think has a bearing on the subject of our discussion is Wittgenstein's saying that an inexpressible aspect is *contained* in what has been expressed in the poem. And this remark makes no sense unless people are believed to be capable of noticing this content and making something of it. What poetry can do is to put the expressible in such a way that something not expressible by ordinary uses of words is suggested to those readers who are alive to its allusions and can grasp and perhaps reproduce them in a fashion that makes the signs come alive. I am afraid, however, that in the context of the *Tractatus* as well as in much of the philosophy of the early 1930s the content alluded to does not really gain life in the sense of acquiring some shape (which of course would go against the spirit of an unflinching reading of the saying–showing distinction). But Wittgenstein's investigations into the concepts of noticing aspects, experiencing aspect changes and suffering from aspect-blindness can show us a way of getting some hold on the idea of an aspect or a meaning (inexpressibly) contained in an utterance. It can do so by pointing out a large number of various connecting links (involving both instinctive behavior and rules or conventions) between our concepts of experience and expression and by showing again and again that a flashing of an aspect gains life not only in the world of experiences of that kind but possibly also in the world of expressive acts and signs, even though it may require a poet to endow those signs with potential life.

Notes

1 The various mottos are discussed in the relevant chapter of the first volume of the *Analytical Commentary* on Wittgenstein's *Philosophical Investigations* (=*PI*) by G. P. Baker and P. M. S. Hacker: *Understanding and Meaning*, Oxford: Blackwell, 1980.

2 See Brian McGuinness, *Wittgenstein: A Life: Young Ludwig (1889–1921)*, London: Duckworth, 1988, for information on Wittgenstein's literary *Kinderstube*.

3 The passage which, according to Dummett, Wittgenstein had in mind here can be found in *Grundgesetze*, vol. II, §91: "It is applicability alone that raises arithmetic from the rank of a game to that of a science. Applicability therefore belongs to it of necessity." See Dummett, *Frege: Philosophy of Mathematics*, London: Duckworth, 1991, p. 60.

JOACHIM SCHULTE

4 Dummett, op. cit., pp. 293–4.
5 Cf. for instance Brian McGuinness (ed.), *Ludwig Wittgenstein and the Vienna Circle: Conversations recorded by Friedrich Waismann* (*WVC*), trans. by Joachim Schulte and Brian McGuinness, Oxford: Blackwell, 1979, pp. 150 ff.
6 *The Blue and Brown Books*, Rush Rhees (ed.), Oxford: Blackwell, 1969, p. 3.
7 This contrast is employed several times in Wittgenstein's writings. A particularly instructive passage can be found in MS 110 (*Band* VI), p. 27. Here Wittgenstein discusses the idea that a thought might be seen as consisting of an inorganic part (the sign) and an organic part (e.g. an interpretation, that is, something essentially mental). This remark also occurs in TS 211, pp. 134–5. Another interesting passage is the title of §51 of the "Big Typescript" (=*BT*, TS 213) which consists of three questions: "Is thinking a specific organic process? A mental process specific to human beings? In that case, is it possible to replace it by an inorganic process fulfilling the same purpose, that is, as it were by a prosthesis?" The idea of an organic part of thought is connected with the misleading image of sense as the "soul" of a sentence (cf. e.g. *BT*, p. 268). The numbers of manuscripts and typescripts are those of the catalogue produced by Georg Henrik von Wright ("The Wittgenstein Papers," first publication in: *Philosophical Review* 78 (1969), 483–503, revised and expanded version in von Wright's book *Wittgenstein*, Oxford: Blackwell, 1982; a revised version of the catalogue plus an appendix appeared in: James Klagge and Alfred Nordmann (eds.), *Ludwig Wittgenstein: Philosophical Occasions, 1912–1951*, Indianapolis and Cambridge: Hackett, 1993). The passages quoted or referred to are accessible in the so-called Bergen edition of Wittgenstein's *Nachlass*, Oxford: Oxford University Press, 2000 (6 CD ROMs). Some of the material can also be found in the "Wiener Ausgabe," Vienna: Springer, 1993 ff.
8 *Blue Book*, p. 4. Here and elsewhere the beginning of a new paragraph is signalled by "|".
9 That is, as "merely" physical chess pieces, i.e., without regard for design, workmanship or function.
10 See the essay "Language-games" in Baker and Hacker, *Wittgenstein: Understanding and Meaning*, Oxford: Basil Blackwell, 1980.
11 Typescripts (TS) and manuscripts (MS) from Wittgenstein's *Nachlass* are referred to by the numbers assigned to them in Georg Henrik von Wright's catalogue "The Wittgenstein Papers," the most recent version of which is printed in J. Klagge and A. Nordmann (eds.), *Ludwig Wittgenstein: Philosophical Occasions, 1912–1951*, Indianapolis: Hackett, 1993, pp. 480–510.
12 Wittgenstein, *Philosophical Grammar* (=*PG*), Rush Rhees (ed.), trans. by Anthony Kenny, Oxford: Blackwell, 1974, p. 148, §100. See Kenny, "From the Big Typescript to the *Philosophical Grammar*," Chapter 3 of Kenny's book *The Legacy of Wittgenstein*, Oxford: Blackwell, 1984, pp. 24–37.
13 *PG*, p. 153, §104: "That doesn't mean that it is while we are using a sentence that the system of language makes it into a thought for us, because the system isn't present then and there isn't any need for anything to make the sentence alive for us, since the question of being alive doesn't arise. But if we ask: 'why doesn't a sentence strike us as isolated and dead when we are reflecting on its essence, its sense, the thought etc.' it can be said that we are continuing to move in the system of language."
14 Cf. *PG*, p. 156, §107: "And if we say 'from outside intention cannot be recognised as intention etc.' we don't want to say that meaning is a special experience, but that it isn't anything which happens, or happens to us, but something that we do, otherwise it would be just dead."
15 Cf. *PI* §432. This remark was written in 1945. *PI* §430, which also employs the live–dead contrast, was written at roughly the same time as the above-quoted passages from *PG*, that is, it is contemporaneous with the *Blue Book*.

162

16 I deliberately avoid using Wittgenstein's terminology of "primary" and "secondary" meanings (*PI*, p. 216). For Wittgenstein it is important that a secondary meaning is *not* a metaphorical one: it is characteristic of a secondary meaning that it can be expressed in exactly one way, whereas metaphors can always be reformulated. It would be interesting, however, to explore the question if there are uses of the live–dead contrast where these words cannot be replaced by other ones. If such cases can be discovered, then we should be dealing with secondary uses in Wittgenstein's sense.

17 For more on this point, pp. 159ff.

18 MS 116, p. 316.

19 See e.g. *PI*, p. 215; *Remarks on the Philosophy of Psychology* (=*RPP*), vol. I, G. E. M. Anscombe and G. H. von Wright (eds.), trans. by G. E. M. Anscombe, Oxford: Blackwell, 1980, §77.

20 *RPP* I, §676. Here as well as in other quotations from this book I have tacitly departed from the published translation.

21 Cf. the quotation from *RPP* I, §1059 on p. 155, and my comments on this quotation.

22 It is important that such typical forms of expression can be imitated, often in such ways that the "expression" is grasped immediately. Think of someone savoring the content of a cup of coffee and showing by means of facial expressions that the stuff tasted delightful (or horrible)!

23 *Remarks on the Philosophy of Psychology*, vol. II (=*RPP* II), G. H. von Wright and Heikki Nyman (eds.), trans. by C. G. Luckhardt and M. A. E. Aue, Oxford: Blackwell, 1980, §§464–5.

24 Cf. Wittgenstein, *Culture and Value*, G. H. von Wright (ed.) in collaboration with Heikki Nyman, revised by Alois Pichler, trans. by Peter Winch, Oxford: Blackwell, 1998, p. 71: "Think about how it was said of Labor's playing 'He *is speaking.*'" Josef Labor was a blind organist sponsored by the Wittgenstein family.

25 Cf. the essay on language-games by Baker and Hacker (see footnote 10 above) and my article "Primitive Language Games," in Erich Ammereller and Eugen Fischer (eds.), *Wittgenstein at Work*, London: Routledge, 2004.

26 The importance of the concept "gesture" for much of Wittgenstein's work is explained in my paper "On a Remark by Jucundus," forthcoming in a volume edited by Enzo De Pellegrin and Jaakko Hintikka.

27 To quote an example: "The first 'serious' poetry he [*Auden*] remembered enjoying was *In Memoriam*, which his father used to read aloud, and Poe's 'The Raven' and 'The Bells.' From an early age Wystan learnt to think of poetry as something to be read aloud or recited – an attitude which remained with him for the rest of his life" (Humphrey Carpenter, *W. H. Auden: A Biography*, London: George Allen & Unwin, 1981, p. 9).

28 A much revised version of this remark is printed in *PI*, p. 214.

29 From *RPP* II, §§501–3. "[1]" to "[4]" have been inserted for ease of reference.

30 *PI*, p. 205. Cf. the interesting earlier version of this remark in its original context: *Last Writings on the Philosophy of Psychology* (=*LW*), G. H. von Wright and Heikki Nyman (eds.), trans. by C. G. Luckhardt and M. A. E. Aue, Oxford: Blackwell, 1982, §§682–3, 685.

31 In his manuscripts on the philosophy of psychology Wittgenstein connects his concept of an aspect with the image of "life." Thus on p. 45 of MS 135 he mentions the idea that an aspect will live only as long as it is kept alive.

32 For puzzle-pictures, see *PI*, p. 196 as well as various passages in *RPP* I and II and *LW*. In MS 136, p. 101b, Wittgenstein wonders whether it is possible that of two possible aspects "contained in" a puzzle-picture one is "excluded" while the other is not "alive."

33 Cf. the quotation from *RPP* II, §§464–5, on page 153 above, and *PI*, pp. 213–14; *RPP* I and II, *LW* I, *passim*. See my book *Experience and Expression: Wittgenstein's Philosophy of Psychology*, Oxford: Clarendon Press, 1993, especially Chapter 5, "Experience," with an appendix "Meaning Blindness and Introspection."

34 Wittgenstein, *Lectures and Conversations on Aesthetics, Psychology and Religious Belief*, Cyril Barrett (ed.), Oxford: Blackwell, 1966, §12, pp. 4–5.

35 Here I am in particular thinking of the poem by C. F. Meyer quoted in a letter to Moore (*Ludwig Wittgenstein: Cambridge Letters*, Brian McGuinness and G. H. von Wright (eds.), Oxford: Blackwell, 1995, no. 189, 7.3.41) and the poem "Der Schein trügt" by Gottfried Keller, which Wittgenstein quoted to Elizabeth Anscombe in the 1940s and which she recited in my presence in the course of a conversation in the 1970s (cf. my paper "Ludwig Wittgenstein oder Der ungemessne Schatz," Eckhard Nordhofen (ed.), *Philosophen des 20. Jahrhunderts in Porträts*, Königstein/Ts.: Athenäum, 1980, pp. 15–42).

36 Wittgenstein's letter to Engelmann of 9 April, 1917, in Paul Engelmann, *Letters from Ludwig Wittgenstein: With a Memoir*, Brian McGuinness (ed.), trans. by L. Furtmüller, Oxford: Blackwell, 1967, p. 7. The German original and an English translation of Uhland's poem "Graf Eberhards Weissdorn" can be found on pp. 83–4 of Engelmann's book.

37 McGuinness, *Wittgenstein: A Life*, pp. 110 and 251.

38 P. M. S. Hacker, "Was He Trying to Whistle it?" *The New Wittgenstein*, Alice Crary and Rupert Read (eds.), London: Routledge, 2000, pp. 353–88, pp. 372–3, and in Hacker, *Wittgenstein: Connections and Controversies*, Oxford: Oxford University Press, 2001, pp. 128–9.

39 Michael Kremer, "The Purpose of Tractarian Nonsense," *Noûs* 35 (2001), pp. 39–73, especially pp. 62–4.

9

WITTGENSTEIN AGAINST INTERPRETATION

The meaning of a text does not stop short of its facts

Sonia Sedivy

Rigoletto's voice fills the air: "*No...basto io solo...*" "I will do it myself" the surtitles announce. Sparafucile, Rigoletto's helper – who was about to throw the bagged corpse into the river – stops, waiting to hand his burden to Rigoletto. The music has built to the climax of revelation when Rigoletto will carry the corpse and discover, in the moment of a parent's supreme agony, that it is the corpse of his only daughter rather than that of her defiler. But Rigoletto sits motionless in his wheelchair. More than a thousand pairs of eyes scan urgently back and forth between Rigoletto's surtitled words and actions – or, rather, lack thereof – wondering about the mismatch. Why?

Essays on interpretation usually take their examples from poetry, discussing the nature of the interpretation of distinctively ambiguous texts. But the results thereby obtained do not remain restricted to poetry or to scholarly discussions of interpretation. Rather, the results are picked up and given life in plays or in movies, for example – that is, in productions of texts that lack the hallmark ambiguity of poetry – and come to shape our sense of ourselves as readers and of what it is to read a text. This paper will examine the nature or necessity of literary interpretation and its possible latitude with examples drawn from movies and other performing arts. That is how issues of interpretation are lived – by us, people who like to read and to attend plays, movies, operas. I will argue that a Wittgensteinian understanding of language as an integral dimension of human forms of life speaks against the idea that our relationship to texts is interpretive in nature. A Wittgensteinian approach also undermines the prevailing view that a reader's (interpretive) relationship to a text allows for an unbounded latitude of alternative readings or meanings. Rather, meanings and facts are co-constituted and mutually available within human forms of life, our acculturated forms of life activities in the world. To see how these claims follow we will need to examine the way in which Wittgenstein's re-orientation to language as constituted within forms of life entails that meaning is immediate and that our words don't stop short of the facts; and we will need to examine the nature and extent of the latitude opened up by the notion of forms of life. I will argue that the immediate mutuality of meanings and facts carries over to our textual practices so that our texts make available immediate unities of meanings and narrative facts. My aim is not only to extend Wittgenstein's anti-interpretational understanding of language to literary texts and practices; but I also want to emphasize an aspect of his re-orientation to language that has not been much discussed: his view that meanings don't stop short of the facts. Wittgenstein's work suggests that for an acculturated person, a text presents an immediate meaning just as a face presents an immediate expression. The statements of a text don't stop short of the facts of the text just as the statements of ordinary communicative utterances don't stop short of the facts. Some statements may be unclear just as sometimes a facial expression is not entirely clear. One might be puzzled – by a facial expression or a text – and one might need to seek further information or to think more deeply about the facts that are immediately available. But these are derivative, peripheral cases that can occur insofar as we have the immediate competence from which these fall short. Just as making an error presupposes the ability to perform correctly, so finding something puzzling presupposes the capacity to apprehend things of that sort immediately.

Though the debate on these issues is too extensive to outline in a short space, my proposal can be located efficiently by contrasting it with two key positions that have used Wittgenstein's work: one by Colin Lyas and the other by Stanley Fish. Colin Lyas[1] applied Wittgenstein's work on intentions to argue against the view that an author's intentions are unavailable in a text and hence cannot determine the meaning or interpretation of a text. Lyas's aim was to block the latitude of possible interpretations that seems to open up when the relevance of the author's intentions is denied. Lyas argued that when one finds oneself puzzled by a text, one can arrive at an interpretation (or fix among possible alternatives) by appealing to the author's intentions. Lyas's point is that a Wittgensteinian re-conceptualization of intentions as criterially linked to an agent's (public) actions rather than as private, logically independent mental states gives us a way of understanding how (at least some of) the author's intentions might be manifest in a text. Lyas was responding, of course, to the denial of the relevance of author's intentions by Wimsatt and Beardsley in "The Intentional Fallacy."[2] On the so-called Anglo-American "analytic" side of philosophy, this was the text that unleashed debate about the relevance of the author's intentions in fixing the interpretation of a text.

But Lyas brings Wittgenstein's work into the debate too late. It is understandable that Lyas appealed to Wittgenstein to show that intentions can be manifest in a text since the professional context cast the issue as one about intentions. Following Wimsatt and Beardsley's paper, the debated question was: can the author's intentions determine the meaning of a text so that interpretation is held on the leash of those intentions? But from the perspective of Wittgenstein's work the issue is not in the first instance about the relevance of the author's intentions in fixing interpretation but about the non-interpretational nature of the meaningful phenomena of human life. In the *Philosophical Investigations*,[3] for example, Wittgenstein considers the role of intentions in the context of exploring cases where we are puzzled; where a facial expression, for example, is not immediately clear. He discusses that we need to appeal to intentions when we are puzzled and that we can do so. But by the time he raises questions about intentions in fixing meaning (sections following §433 and following §536), Wittgenstein has already set about trying to re-configure our understanding of language so that questions about intentions are posed against the context of the emerging re-understanding of language. Part of the point of that re-orientation is to show that meaning, like rule-following, is not a matter of interpretation.

Stanley Fish offers a more thorough re-orientation of linguistic meaning along Wittgensteinian lines. His position is pivotal in the debates over interpretation in literary theory and on the so-called "continental" side of philosophy, debates that parallel – yet too rarely intersect with – analytically oriented discussions. In his classic "Is There a Text in This Class?"[4] Fish draws explicitly on the Wittgensteinian idea of forms of life to suggest that one does not arrive at an interpretation of a bit of speech or of a text, but that a meaning is always present to one in one's particular context. His point is two-fold. First, like the question "Is there a text in this class?" a text "does not have a determinate meaning, a meaning that survives the sea change of situations" by virtue of being constituted by "possibilities and norms already encoded in language" and further fixed by the author's intentions. Rather, the hearer or reader's context-governed set of presuppositions determines the meaning she will immediately hear or see. Second, because the institutional practices or forms of life that are constitutive of our presuppositions are necessarily finite, the possible meanings that a reader may find immediate will be similarly circumscribed. Fish's point is that the latitude of possible meanings that seems to be opened, like a Pandora's box, when the author's intentions are eliminated as determinants of meaning is rendered manageably small by the situations and practices or "interpretive communities" within which people find themselves. Fish goes so far as to claim that we can even say which meaning is more normal by virtue of being able to say which context is more "available, and therefore more likely to be the perspective within which the utterance is heard."[5] In other words, while his position opens up the specter of relativism by proposing that meaning is constituted by the reader's situational expectations, this possibility is empty: "while relativism is a position one can entertain, it is not a position one can occupy."[6]

Though Fish brings Wittgenstein into the debate at the right juncture – that is, at the outset in how we conceive meaningfulness rather than further downstream in asking whether and how the author's intentions matter on an interpretational view of language – I want to suggest that he doesn't get it quite right. Yes, it is crucial to stress the immediacy of meaning for acculturated persons. But what is just as crucial in Wittgenstein's thought, yet difficult and elusive to articulate, is that this immediacy is not one-sided, as it were. Meanings are not simply what we hear given our interests and goals, our presuppositions. Wittgenstein's notion of forms of life is not at a level as variable and as "cognitive" as our presuppositions. Hence meanings are not as variable as our presuppositions. Moreover, meanings do not stop short of the facts. The notion of human forms of life suggests totalities or 'packages' in which there is a mutuality of facts and utterances: mutuality of facts and meaningful utterances and texts, of persons and actions and circumstances, of minds and world. Hence I suggest that if we bring Wittgenstein's work to bear on debates of literary interpretation we need to do so right from the outset, like Fish – by re-configuring our understanding of the nature of meaningfulness – yet in a way that includes not only the non-interpretational immediacy of meaning but also the difficult idea that what we say doesn't stop short of the facts. We need to come to terms with the idea that just as if I say "it is raining outside" my words don't stop short of the fact that *it is raining outside*; similarly, if a narrative states that "It rained all morning" its words do not stop short of the fact of the narrative that *it rained all morning*. If we can find a way to grasp this, we will have shown that relativism is not implied, not even as a logical possibility that no single individual can occupy as a matter of fact. This is important because, of course, Fish's reassurance that no single individual can hear a multiplicity of meanings is empty. It is empty because on his view, such a multiplicity can be immediate for a multitude of hearers and readers. This is exactly the latitude of alternative meanings for any text that many find worrisome – the sort of latitude that allowed a recent Canadian Opera Company production to place Rigoletto in a wheelchair so that he couldn't perform the opera's climactic action while singing that he was doing so.

One way to see the upshot of Wittgenstein's approach is that it allows us to maintain a distinction between describing and interpreting a literary work. Putting the point this way might be useful since undermining this distinction is the putative result of a wide range of anti-intentionalist theories – from post-structuralist textualist to philosophical pragmatist approaches. I am proposing that Wittgenstein's re-orientation to meanings and facts as co-constituted within human forms of life allows us to maintain the fact/interpretation distinction, countering the claim that any distinction between describing narrative facts and interpreting them can only be relative and formal. But it is hard to capture the exact nuance of Wittgenstein's understanding of the mutuality of meanings and facts, and it is the exact nuance that we need to bring out to understand the error in holding that

> the descriptive facts are simply whatever we strongly agree upon, while interpretations are simply what commands less consensus and displays (and tolerates) wider divergence.[7]

Moreover, insofar as we maintain a distinction between apprehending the facts of a text and going on to provide further interpretations of those facts, we are posed with the task of explaining the relationship between narrative facts and their interpretation. Thinking about this issue from a Wittgensteinian perspective casts the variability of interpretation in terms of the variability of forms of life:

given both the variability in human forms of life and the immediacy of narrative meanings and facts, what is the scope and role of interpretive practices? Coming to understand the nature of the variability of forms of life will help answer our question.

To help probe this issue, let me introduce a second – more nuanced and problematic – example of textual interpretation for use as our test case, this one from the movies. In the late 1990s movie director Patricia Rozema offered an interpretation of Jane Austen's *Mansfield Park* that turned on situating the events in the novel explicitly in terms of the fact that around 1800 many wealthy English landowners derived a large part of their wealth from plantations in the West Indies that used slave labor. This is noteworthy because it brings external worldly facts into the domestic situations Austen explored, while it is one of the hallmarks of the author's work that she did not bring such facts into her novels. In Rozema's movie the problem of slavery is brought to center stage by the addition of scenes and circumstances and conversations – narrative facts, in short – that are not in the novel. From our perspective, considering Rozema's movie puts pressure on exactly the right point. The claim that a literary work presents an immediate mutuality of meanings and facts seems to be challenged by the possibility of a post-colonial reading of *Mansfield Park*. Yet there is also a sense in which the very identity of *Mansfield Park* requires that such considerations remain extraneous. We are faced with the issue of how much "interpretation" the minimal contextual facts that figure in Jane Austen's novel will support. How can we draw lines between the facts of the novel and extraneous facts added in interpretations made possible by forms of life other than Jane Austen's own? With this example in view, the stage is fully set for our enquiry.

I

...there is a way of grasping a rule which is *not an interpretation*, but which is exhibited in what we call "obeying the rule" and "going against it" in actual cases...

(PI §201)

What is striking in debates over interpretation to a reader of Wittgenstein is the very presupposition of this notion and of the attendant view that meaningfulness is a matter of interpretation. After all, Wittgenstein expends so much effort to disabuse us of patterns in our thinking that issue in the view that rule following, and hence the meaningfulness of concepts, is a matter of interpretation. At the very least, he expends much effort to problematize this view so that – one would think – it would not be simply presupposed. Since space doesn't allow detailed illustration from the many articles collected in volumes with titles such as *Is There a Single Right Interpretation*[8] and *Interpretation and Overinterpretation*,[9] here is one representative example. In the recent *Intention and Interpretation*,[10] Noël Carroll summarizes the debate by stating that "Whereas ordinarily we interpret for intentions, anti-intentionalism maintains that art and literature either cannot or should not be treated in this way."[11] This claim follows upon the opening sentence which makes the apparently uncontroversial assertion that "In the normal course of affairs, when confronted with an utterance, our standard cognitive goal is to figure out what the speaker intends to say."[12]

For a reader of Wittgenstein, this state of the art recalls the rule-following considerations culminating at *PI* §§201 and 202. The middle section of §201 comes to mind at once.

> It can be seen that there is a misunderstanding here from the mere fact that in the course of our argument we give one interpretation after another, as if each one contented us at least for a moment, until we thought of yet another standing behind it. What this shews is that there is a way of grasping a rule which is *not an interpretation*, but which is exhibited in what we call "obeying the rule" and "going against it" in actual cases.

What stands out immediately, given our concerns here, is Wittgenstein's suggestion that it is precisely the latitude of interpretation that shows that we have gone astray in our understanding of rule following as interpretation. This conclusion follows upon his extensive exploration of patterns in our thinking that make it seem that alternative interpretations of the '+' rule are possible. That is, of course, how §201 begins, summarizing Wittgenstein's attempts across many preceding sections.

> This was our paradox: no course of action could be determined by a rule, because every course of action can be made out to accord with the rule. The answer was: if everything can be made out to accord with the rule, then it can also be made out to conflict with it. And so there would be neither accord nor conflict here.
>
> (*PI* §201)

That is, if the meaning of the concept 'plus' or '+' were a matter of interpretation, then any interpretation or course of action, any regular (non-random) way of going on can be claimed to be what the concept specifies. If the rule is '+ n' for '1,' to consider the notorious example, then adding by one up to a thousand but by two over a thousand could be an interpretation of the rule. But if this were the case, then the notion that a way of going on were in conflict with the way of going on specified by the concept would not genuinely apply. Rules and concepts would be indeterminate. As we saw in our first quotation, Wittgenstein clearly states that this paradox results from misunderstanding the nature of rule-following as interpretation and goes on (*pace* Kripke[13]) to gesture to the positive re-orientation to which he is steering us. The beginning of §202 famously asserts that "hence also 'obeying a rule' is a practice." There has been much recent discussion of the normative and communal nature of rule following that is implied by Wittgenstein's claim since practices are norm-governed ways of going on at the level of communities. My point here is that the claim also entails that obeying a rule is immediate since our norm- or rule-governed participation in practices is immediate. Given our concerns in this paper, what stands out most from §§201 and 202 is the way in which they summarize what meaning is not – a matter of interpretation – and gesture to what it is: immediate.

Wittgenstein's investigations of rule following which, as we have seen, support the negative conclusion – that rule following is *not* a matter of interpretation – also include considerations about the role of training that support the positive gesture towards practice. Training is the process by means of which we acquire what we might call a "second nature" of cultural norm-governed ways of being.[14] It is the process of instilling immediate non-interpretive rule following. We acquire our second nature by means of training, by having instilled in us ways of acting and reacting across the multitudinous situations that comprise our forms of life. Wittgenstein suggests that when I understand another's speech or say something myself I am participating in "*customs* (uses, institutions)" (§199). Similarly, when I comport myself politely – or simply as a person – not stepping on other people's toes, not making a mess when I eat, etc. I am automatically following rules and meeting normative standards in ways that have been instilled in me through training. Part of Wittgenstein's point is to see language both as a key dimension yet also as just *one* among the many dimensions of normatively governed human life. We are animals whose first (animal) nature becomes transfigured into a normative cultural second nature through training into norm- or rule-governed ways of acting and reacting. The concept of a second nature is the notion of acquired ways of acting that are instilled through training to the point of seamless automaticity. It is precisely the idea of unreflective, immediate rule following. That is why I suggest that the immediacy of the myriad 'civilized' ways of carrying out our life activities serves as a good example of Wittgenstein's understanding of the way in which linguistic practices figure in and permeate our lives. For a person (an animal with a second nature), the rule-governed immediacy of bodily comportment – that is, the immediacy of one's own bodily comportment as well as one's immediate perceptual grasp of the bodily comportment of others – is not different in kind from the immediacy of one's own linguistic reactions and actions as well as one's immediate grasp of the linguistic activities of others.

> How can he *know* how he is to continue a pattern by himself – whatever instruction you give him? – Well, how do I know? – If that means "Have I reasons?" the answer is: my reasons will soon give out. And then I shall act, without reasons.
>
> (*PI* §211)

"All of the steps are really already taken" means: I no longer have any choice. The rule, once stamped with a particular meaning, traces the lines along which it is to be followed through the whole of space. – But if something of this sort really were the case, how would it help?

No; my description only made sense if it was to be understood symbolically. – I should have said: *This is how it strikes me.*

When I obey a rule, I do not choose.

I obey the rule *blindly*.

(PI §219)

But what is the purpose of that symbolical proposition? It was supposed to bring into prominence a difference between being causally determined and being logically determined.

(PI §220)

The rule can only seem to me to produce all its consequences in advance if I draw them as a *matter of course.*

(PI §238)

But if this is the case, if we follow rules – that transfigure and constitute human life – automatically as a result of our training, then we have the resources for explaining the paradoxically momentary yet also future guaranteeing and past-looking nature of rule-governed action. That is, we can understand how when I say, for example, that "*Mansfield Park* is my least favorite of Jane Austen's novels" all of the following are true. (*i*) I say – and mean– those words at this moment. (*ii*) But insofar as I can say it now, I would mean and understand *the same* by those words on any other occasion. (*iii*) And to mean those words now is for my current linguistic activity to figure properly in a pattern that is extended across time and involves others as crucially as it does the speaker or agent herself. I can say and mean "*Mansfield Park* is my least favorite Jane Austen novel" *now* insofar as my linguistic actions and reactions are part of my second nature, which is to say that I react and act linguistically by virtue of the training I have received (the past looking part of the pattern) and that the automatic yet also intentional and responsible nature of my participation in linguistic community practices vouchsafes that I would mean the same (or follow the rules in the same ways) in the future (the 'future guarantee' or 'logical determination' necessary for rule-following).

In short, second nature is immediate rule-following, and training is what makes it possible (as well as the right potentialities on the part of what Wittgenstein refers to as the "normal learner"). This might mistakenly suggest that the immediacy of second nature rule-following abolishes objectivity.

"So you are saying that human agreement decides what is true and false?"—It is what human beings *say* that is true and false; and they agree in the *language* they use. That is not agreement in opinions but in form of life.

If language is to be a means of communication there must be agreement not only in definitions but also (queer as this may sound) in judgements. This seems to abolish logic, but does not do so.—It is one thing to describe methods of measurement, and another to obtain and state results of measurement. But what we call "measuring" is partly determined by a certain constancy in results of measurement.

(PI §§241f)

The immediacy of second nature rule following is just one half of our "equation," we must not forget the facts. Wittgenstein's suggestion is that just as rule following transfigures human animals into persons (human animals with a second nature), so rule following opens up the domain of objective facts within which human lives take place and with which human beings must deal (by "measuring" and otherwise).

II

When we say, and *mean*, that such-and-such is the case, we – and our meaning – do not stop anywhere short of the fact; but we mean: *this-is-so*.

(PI §95)

Wittgenstein offers this claim as a perfectly ordinary and sound grasp of what we might more ponderously call 'the relation of words to reality' when we stop to reflect and to theorize. Part of his point is that when we stop to theorize, we find ourselves unable to grasp how our words might "not stop anywhere short of the fact." Yet, surely, one can say or write, for instance, that *spring has begun*, and that very same thing, *that spring has begun*, can be the case. One might of course make false statements, but the idea is that when one makes a true statement, then *that* spring has begun is *at once* a fact and the claim I make.

Wittgenstein is not, I think, to be understood as suggesting that there is a "formal identity" between our thoughts and the thinkable world (or aspects thereof). We need to find a way to understand the suggestion that our meanings don't stop short of the facts without hypostasizing, even though what would be hypostasized in this case is only formal structure. Perhaps here is a better way to express what we want to understand.

173

We want to say: "When we mean something, it's like going up to someone, it's not having a dead picture (of any kind)." We go up to the thing we mean.

(*PI* §455)

Yes: meaning something is like going up to someone.

(*PI* §457)

We can approach the idea that our meanings go up to the facts by looking to Wittgenstein's epistemically oriented work in *On Certainty*.[15] Wittgenstein takes pains to show how a holistic system of beliefs is put in place by the way in which we live, by what we do – including what we say – in our various circumstances:

> The child learns to believe a host of things. I.e. it learns to act according to these beliefs. Bit by bit there forms a system of what is believed, and in that system some things stand unshakably fast and some are more or less liable to shift. What stands fast does so, not because it is intrinsically obvious or convincing; it is rather held fast by what lies around it.
>
> (*OC* §144)

Just as when we focus on our ability to follow rules, when we consider our beliefs and judgments "The end is not an ungrounded presupposition; it is an ungrounded way of acting" (*OC* §110). The stress on activity is important because our ways of acting are constrained: both by our environment and by our animal natures, as well as by the cultural forms that have developed over and transfigured those constraints. But it is not only actions that are learned by acting. Judgments are learned by judging. "From a child up I learned to judge like this. *This is* judging" (*OC* §128). "This is how I learned to judge; *this* I got to know *as* judgement" (*OC* §129). "We do not learn the practice of making empirical judgements by learning rules: we are taught *judgements* and their connection with other judgements. *A totality* of judgements is made plausible to us" (*OC* §140). We have considered how Wittgenstein's view that we acquire a second nature through training obviates an explicitly interpretive element in rule-following. Here, in the epistemic context of *On Certainty*, Wittgenstein's point is that ways of acting come together with what those actions involve and concern, and ways of judging come together with what those judgments involve and concern. Our training opens up a mutuality of activity with circumstances and objects of activity just as it makes a mutuality of judging with circumstances and objects of judging immediately available. Wittgenstein indicates this mutuality of the judgments we can make or say and the facts that they concern in passages such as the following: "If you are not certain of any fact, you cannot be certain of the meaning of your words either" (*OC* §114). "The truth of my statements is the test of my understanding of these statements" (*OC* § 80).

This might seem to abolish the objectivity of the facts thus brought into view. After all, "[m]en have judged that a king can make rain; *we* say this contradicts all experience. Today they judge that airplanes and the radio, etc. are means for the closer contact of peoples and the spread of cultures" (*OC* §132). However, John McDowell[16] has tried to show that Wittgenstein is maneuvering towards understanding the objectivity of facts – or towards "realism with a human face," in Putnam's marvelous phrase.[17] McDowell points to our practices of questioning what we believe, checking our evidence as well as our reasons, challenging our assumptions, etc. These practices constitute what McDowell has called "rational answerability" to the world. By becoming trained into these practices – which are integral to our forms of life – we become open to rational demands on our thinking. Openness to such rational demands allows us to revise our empirical concepts and perhaps to develop more adequate ones. But more generally, openness to rational demands infuses our actions and practices and the forms of life in which actions and practices take shape in ever evolving reciprocal relationship. McDowell is suggesting that if we take note of the rational answerability or openness to rational demands that is integral to our practices, then – together with the grounding of our practices in action – openness to rational demands secures the objectivity of the facts that become available in human forms of life. Insofar as the system of activities and beliefs and concepts into which we are trained – by acting and judging like *this* – contains practices of 'rational answerability' to the world, the facts to which we are immediately open are not one-sidedly of our making. Hence, McDowell suggests, these are practices for securing objectivity, for securing that our thoughts become open and responsible to "demands that are there anyway" in a system of empirical concepts. By being open to rational demands, our concepts are of the world; our rational answerability allows us to inhabit the world.

Yes, persons and world come together as aspects of a mutually implicatory package. But that doesn't entail that the facts are simply of our making or up to us – the persons who are co-constituted with the world. There is more in play than our "presuppositions."

> The agreement, the harmony, of thought and reality consists in this: if I say falsely that something is *red*, then, for all that, it isn't *red*. And when I want to explain the word "red" to someone in the sentence "That is not red", I do it by pointing to something red.
>
> (*PI* §429)[18]

III

"He measured him with a hostile glance and said...." The reader of the narrative understands this; he has no doubt in his mind. Now you say: "Very well, he supplies the meaning, he guesses it." – Generally speaking: no. Generally speaking he supplies nothing, guesses nothing. – But it's also possible that the hostile glance and the words later prove to have been pretence, or that the reader is kept in doubt whether they are so or not, and so that he really does guess at a possible interpretation. – But then the main thing he guesses at is a context. He says to himself for example: The two men who are here so hostile to one another are in reality friends, etc. etc....

(*PI* §652)

We are acculturated not only into participating in conversations and thinking about matters on our own. But we are also acculturated into narrative practices wherein narratives present situations and circumstances just as one might discuss situations and circumstances in a conversation or might think about them on one's own.[19] If Wittgenstein is correct that our statements and thoughts do not stop short of the facts, then there is no reason to suppose that the words of a narrative text stop short of the narrative facts. That is, given our background competence in using language to discuss or think about facts, and given the narrative practices into which we are acculturated – indeed, in the wealthy parts of our planet it could not be said that acculturation into actual conversation is more primary than acculturation into narratives since one of our primary forms of interaction with our babies is through books and other narrative forms – a text puts in place a fictional set of facts, just as an ordinary conversation is part of an inseparable package with ordinary worldly facts. As Wittgenstein suggests in *PI* §652 above, the words of a text don't stop short of its facts, making it unnecessary for the reader to supply an interpretation or make any guesses (unless the narrative facts are such as to require him to make some guesses about facts that are not presented). For an acculturated reader, a mutuality of meaning and facts is immediately present.

But insofar as forms of life co-constitute meanings and facts – whether these be worldly or narrative – the question arises how much latitude is involved in the notion of forms of life and hence correlatively for meanings and facts. To bring out the precise nuance of Wittgenstein's approach, it is instructive to compare Fish's use of Wittgenstein's approach to argue for the kind of relativism that Wittgenstein is attempting to displace.

In a later preamble to "Is There a Text in This Class?" Fish indicates that his work is informed by Wittgenstein by invoking the central concept of *form of life*:

the reason that I can speak to someone like Abrams is that I speak to him *from within* a set of interests and concerns, and it is in relation to those interests and concerns that I assume he will hear my words. If what follows is communication or understanding, it will not be because he and I share a language, in the sense of knowing the meanings of individual words and the rules for combining them, but because a way of thinking, *a form of life* [*my emphasis*], shares us, and implicates us in a world of already-in-place objects, purposes, goals, procedures, values, and so on; and it is to the feature of that world that any words we utter will be heard as necessarily referring.[20]

Here are just two examples from the article of Fish's stress on the immediacy of meaning within human forms of life.

> ...the identification of context and the making of sense...occur simultaneously. One does not say "Here I am in a situation; now I can begin to determine what these words mean." To be in a situation is to see the words, these or any other, as already meaningful.[21]

> The argument of the preceding pages can be reduced to the assertion that there is no such first stage [*of "a two stage procedure in which a reader or hearer first scrutinizes an utterance and* then *gives it a meaning"*], that one hears an utterance within, and not as preliminary to determining, a knowledge of its purposes and concerns, and that to so hear it is already to have assigned it a shape and given it a meaning.[22]

But Fish's departure from Wittgenstein is readily apparent. While in the later preamble Fish makes clear that a form of life "implicates us in a world of already-in-place objects, purposes, goals, procedures, values, and so on," the article (which is representative of Fish's approach) focuses one-sidedly on the predetermination of meanings without attention to the co-constitution of facts. Even more importantly, the quotations show that he understands the notion of forms of life narrowly so that a person who has come across reader-centered or New Reader literary theory can be in one interpretive community while someone who has not is in another interpretive community. This narrow understanding of forms of life yields the relativism Fish advocates: meanings may differ widely across interpretive communities (there can be nesting of institutional communities for example) even though they cannot differ widely for any given individual, for whom only certain meanings will be immediate given their (nested) forms of life. Fish's relativism depends on casting the predetermination of meanings (the "*pre*reading" of a text for example) in terms of interests, goals and assumptions as we see in the quotations above. This is key because it casts what "predetermines" meanings as what is clearly variable between us. In other words, it is precisely because the interests and goals and assumptions of different individuals can vary and because Fish casts interests etc., as the predeterminants of meaning that the meanings that are immediate for those individuals might vary as well. But this is not Wittgenstein's view.

> "We're always making presuppositions; if they aren't correct then, of course, everything is different." Do we say this, for example, when we ask someone to go shopping? Are we presupposing that he is human, and that the store is not a Fata Morgana? Presuppositions come to an end.[23]

According to Wittgenstein, meanings are not determined by something that we might characterize as assumptions, interests, or goals, as Fish does, or more generally as presuppositions. We can tell that meanings couldn't be predetermined by anything so variable because if they were so determined, there would be the possibility of precisely that endless succession of alternatives against which Wittgenstein argues in the rule-following considerations. In other words, the rule-following considerations imply not only that (*i*) "obeying a rule is a practice" (*PI* §202), but also that (*ii*) those practices cannot be so variable as to yield a variability of meanings where "each one contented us at least for a moment, until we thought of another standing behind it" (*PI* §201).

Fish latches on to the non-interpretive immediacy of meaning that is a matter of practice – the explicitly declared result of the investigations of rule following. He thinks that he can do so while retaining the thought that different meanings can be immediate for any one person insofar as she can change or expand her presuppositions and that meanings can vary for individuals whose presuppositions differ. But one of the key lessons that stands out from Wittgenstein's *On Certainty* is that the notion of mistake (rather than merely random difference) requires a background of shared judgment. "In order to make a mistake, a man must already judge in conformity with mankind" (*OC* §156). Yet this point holds as well for the variability in our goals, interests and assumptions. We might say: in order to vary in his goals, interests and assumptions, a man must already judge in conformity with mankind.

> No one ever taught me that my hands don't disappear when I am not paying attention to them. Nor can I be said to presuppose the truth of this proposition in my assertions etc. (as if they rested on it) while it only gets sense from the rest of our procedure of asserting.
>
> (*OC* §153)[24]

Hence we can contrast what we might call the logic of Fish's position with Wittgenstein's. Fish holds that meanings can vary insofar as they are "predetermined" by something variable: meanings can change for an individual to the extent that they are determined by something that a person can variably entertain – like interests, goals, assumptions, or "presuppositions" – and meanings can vary between people insofar as their subworlds are differentiated by distinctive interests, goals and assumptions. But we have seen – both in our examination of Wittgenstein's notion of judgments and meanings as part of our second nature and in the above quotations about presuppositions – that Wittgenstein strives to show that our interests, goals and assumptions overlay something that isn't so variable. What is not so variable for Wittgenstein is a level of practice – one might say fundamental practice, though this is a dangerous metaphor – a level at which 'presuppositions' come to an end. It is at this level of practice, at which "presuppositions" come to an end, that human life – with its mutuality of meanings and facts – opens up. Hence, the precise juncture at which Fish needs to depart from Wittgenstein in order to arrive at his relativism of meaning is clear. From a Wittgensteinian perspective, Fish makes the related errors of (*i*) casting forms of life at too superficial and too variable a level; (*ii*) a level that can be articulated in "presuppositions" – interests, goals and assumptions – that would be correspondingly variable; and hence (*iii*) would make immediately available a corresponding variety of 'meanings.' Insofar as Wittgenstein helps us to see these as errors, such Fishian or reader-centered relativism is avoided.[25]

But if forms of life are not as variable as Fish suggests, how variable are they? And if meanings are co-constituted with facts at a practical level "beneath" our presuppositions, what does this suggest for our practices of interpretation? Insofar as there is variation in forms of life, as there surely is, does this variation allow us to maintain a distinction between describing (or simply apprehending) the narrative facts and interpreting them?

One point is readily apparent, the co-constitution of meanings and facts does not foreclose interpretive practices but allocates them to their proper sphere – as practices that we may wish to undertake in order to go beyond the initial immediate openness of the world of a text. Insofar as these are practices that we choose to undertake, we can discuss, challenge, and argue about them, refining or changing them. We might also choose not to undertake them. The ordinary relationship to a text is not interpretive. Establishing this claim was the primary aim of this essay.

IV

In closing, let's consider the variability of human forms of life and how this affects the range of our immediate openness to texts and our interpretive practices by turning to our example of a post-colonial interpretation of Jane Austen's *Mansfield Park* in a popular movie. Here are the only sentences in which Jane Austen indicates the larger socio-economic context for the domestic events the novel details:

> Sir Thomas found it expedient to go to Antigua himself, for the better management of his affairs, and he took his eldest son with him in the hope of detaching him from some bad connections at home.[26]

> Fanny Price tells her cousin: "But I do talk to him [*Sir Bertram*] more than I used. I am sure I do. Did you not hear me ask him about the slave trade last night?" Her cousin answers: "I did – and was in hopes the question would be followed up by others. It would have pleased your uncle to be enquired of further."[27]

Here is an abbreviated list of the ways in which Patricia Rozema realizes her post-colonial interpretation on film: several conversations about slavery; a journal, complete with drawings kept by the eldest son of vicious sexual debauchery committed upon the slaves by his father, the decorous Sir Thomas Bertram; intimations that the son's witnessing of the debauchery and his guilt lead to his own debauched lifestyle in England.

For another example of the movie's interpretive practice, we could also consider the depiction of the central character, Fanny Price. In the range of Jane Austen's heroines, Fanny Price stands out as almost an anti-heroine. She is meek, modest, retiring, painfully shy, virtually unable to speak out loud among her elders. To be sure, Jane Austen makes clear the reasons for her repressed personality. But the movie presents a pert and perky, self-possessed, quick-witted young woman capable of quick repartee – even with Sir Bertram. Surely, one wants to respond, this is to present someone else in Fanny Price's place. The facts of the novel are that Fanny Price is completely self-effacing. Hence it is someone else in Rozema's movie who is self-assured, someone who seems to be missing her own name.

But the additional facts of slavery in the movie change the events and relationships – the facts – of the original text just as much. No alteration in our forms of life, post-colonial, feminist or otherwise, can change facts, worldly or narrative. This is the response to Rozema's "interpretation" that Wittgenstein's work suggests. What is at issue here and in similar cases is not interpretation (or overinterpretation) but modification of narrative facts. To make this response is to claim that we can distinguish between: apprehending or being immediately open to the narrative facts; interpreting them; adding to them; changing them. I suggest that we can do so if we understand Wittgenstein's notion of forms of life as a family resemblance concept. This allows us to understand both the variation in Wittgenstein's notion of forms of life and how this variation brings with it a distinction between apprehending and interpreting facts.

Wittgenstein suggests that some concepts – like the concept of a game, or "all that we call language" – are best understood in terms of family resemblances.[28] I think that he would include the concept of forms of life amongst such concepts. Rather than being specified by necessary and sufficient conditions, forms of life stand in overlapping, criss-crossing patterns of similarities and differences of the sort that are evident amongst the members of families, among games and tools, and among "all that we call language." While they might not all share necessary and sufficient features or some traits of a prototype, members that are near and far are nevertheless conjoined by at least some criss-crossing threads of similarities amongst their differences. In highly diverging cases – such as rugby and solitaire perhaps – what makes both games is not that they share some features in common but that they are connected by overlapping, criss-crossing similarities among games that are like the overlapping threads running between the far ends of a rope. (If one insisted that there is always some common feature, such as that we do both solitaire and rugby for amusement or according to rules, Wittgenstein would respond that such attempts at definition are so general as to "gain" us nothing, just as if one insists that "All tools serve to modify something..." *PI* §14)[29]. Hence, what forms of life would share for the most part would be some overlapping similarities (not common to all members or specifiable in advance for all members) that would be discernible among the differences (where the allowable differences could again not be specified in advance or in principle, "a priori"). Highly diverging forms of life might only be connected by overlapping similarities without sharing any. It might perhaps be possible for forms of life to diverge so much that they would only be bound by the criss-crossing similarities of the forms of life between them – just as when a rope is long enough its ends share no fibers while being connected by the overlapping threads in between. But, whether near or far, because of the overlapping threads of similarity, all would count as 'our' forms of life without sharing anything like a clearly discernible core.

If such complex patterns of 'familial' similarities and divergences obtain among forms of life, then readers of *Mansfield Park* across time and across the globe are bound by overlapping, criss-crossing threads of similarity as well as difference to each other and to Jane Austen herself. Just as I can grasp a game when I come across one, without there having to be any features common to that game and all others, so I can relate to another form of life without there having to be some specifiable range of features that that form of life must share with mine or any others. But, like the strength of a rope, the strength of the connection between forms of life, "does not reside in the fact that some one fibre runs through its whole length, but in the overlapping of many fibres" (*PI* §67). When it comes to forms of life, the "strength" of their connectedness is the immediacy of meanings and facts they open. The overlapping threads of similarity that connect readers to the form of life of *Mansfield Park* make immediate its meanings and narrative facts. And the divergences between readers from different eras and cultures will make different meanings and facts with different connotations stand out from among what is common and immediate. In short, criss-crossing threads of divergences in our forms of life bring variation in what stands out as interesting, problematic or calling for further reflection from the mutually implicatory set of meanings and facts that a novel opens.

Hence, for a reader with what we might call a post-colonial sensibility, Jane Austen's two mentions – of Antigua and the slave trade – might very well stand out, locating the "internal" concerns of the novel explicitly within the "external" socio-economic context, as they wouldn't for a reader contemporary to Jane Austen herself. Such a reader of the post-colonial era might find that the wider context in which the novel's concerns are located alienates her from the novel's concerns, perhaps even blocking enjoyment. While such a reader would presumably not actually imagine the sorts of extraneous facts that Rozema visualizes in her *Mansfield Park*, she might nevertheless be unable to care about the characters and their circumstances because of their historical, socio-economic situation. Alternatively, a reader might find her engagement unaffected by her understanding of the broader facts of empire. Or a reader might feel puzzled and the text might not be quite open to her. Her engagement might be interrupted by wondering about Austen's mentions of Antigua and the slave trade. After all,

Austen moves the action of *Pride and Prejudice* by stationing a garrison in town during the Napoleonic era without any mention of why a garrison would be stationed. So, in *Mansfield Park*, is the mention of Sir Bertram's plantations in Antigua "casual" because she "seems only vaguely aware of the details of these activities"?[30] Or is it anything but "casual," serving to locate Sir Bertram's source of wealth explicitly by an author who otherwise never makes such worldly specifications? At this point, the reader might wonder about Austen's intentions – just as she might wonder when looking at Austen's puzzling smile in our one surviving portrait. She might then set about analyzing the novel with the explicit aim of arriving at an interpretation. (She might seek our professional interpretations to help her resolve the tensions.)[31]

Wittgenstein rehabilitates our sense that readers sometimes pass, as some do in our example, from immediate engagement in the world of a text to interpretation of it. So far, I have cast Wittgenstein's work as helping us regain our sense that the meanings and facts of a text are immediately present to us – for the most part, depending on the forms of life that "grow" the text and the reader of course. But this is to say, in somewhat different terms, that Wittgenstein helps us understand that the "sensuous surface of a work of art"[32] includes meaning – the sensuous surface is immediately meaningful. Just as the sensuous surfaces of the world in which we live are never *not* factual and meaningful, so the sensuous surface of a text is never *any less* immediately meaningful and factual. Simply, the sensuous surfaces of the world and of our texts are immediately meaningful and factual. This is the understanding that we have lost as a result of factors whose investigation lies beyond the scope of this essay. Without stopping to diagnose the reasons for our loss, my concern here has been to examine whether Wittgenstein's approach allows us to reclaim the immediate mutuality of facts and meanings present in the world's sensuous surfaces.

Let me summarize our examination and its results by connecting these ideas. The presupposition that meaning is interpretive in nature is the conviction that the sensuously immediate is distinct from the meaningful and the factual. This was the problem we addressed. What Wittgenstein's work helps us appreciate is that it is *because* the sensuous surfaces of the world and of our texts are immediately meaningful and factual that we can choose to take it "slower" (in Edward Said's phrase), to set out to interpret from what is immediately, sensuously present. The point of this essay has been to show how Wittgenstein's many interweaving considerations make this liberation – the re-affirmation of the sensuous immediacy of meanings and facts – available for us in our engagement with texts, literary and otherwise.

Notes

1   Colin Lyas, "Wittgensteinian Intentions," Gary Iseminger (ed.), *Intention and Interpretation*, Philadelphia: Temple University Press, 1992, pp. 132–51.
2   William K. Wimsatt Jr. and Monroe C. Beardsley, "The Intentional Fallacy," *Sewanee Review* 54 (1946), 468–88.

3 Ludwig Wittgenstein, *Philosophical Investigations*, trans. G. E. M. Anscombe, New York: Macmillan, 1953. Quotations will be indicated by section number in the text.

4 Stanley Fish, "Is There a Text in This Class?" *Is There a Text in This Class?* Cambridge: Harvard University Press, 1980, pp. 303–21.

5 Stanley Fish, "Is There a Text in This Class?" p. 308.

6 Stanley Fish, "Is There a Text in This Class?" p. 319.

7 Richard Schusterman, "Interpretation, Intention, and Truth," Gary Iseminger (ed.), *Intention and Interpretation*, Philadelphia: Temple University Press, 1992, pp. 65–75, p. 72.

8 Michael Krausz, *Is There a Single Right Interpretation?* University Park: Penn State Press, 2002.

9 Umberto Eco, *Interpretation and Overinterpretation*, Stefan Collini (ed.), Cambridge: Cambridge University Press, 1992.

10 Gary Iseminger (ed.), *Intention and Interpretation*, Philadelphia: Temple University Press, 1992.

11 Noël Carroll, "Art, Intention, and Conversation," Gary Iseminger (ed.), *Intention and Interpretation*, Philadelphia: Temple University Press, 1992, pp. 97–131, pp. 97–8.

12 Ibid., p. 97.

13 Saul A. Kripke, *Wittgenstein on Rules and Private Language*, Oxford: Basil Blackwell, 1982.

14 John McDowell has recently re-opened thinking about ourselves in terms of the notion of second nature in his *Mind and World*, Cambridge, Mass.: Harvard University Press, 1994. We owe the development of this notion to Aristotle of course; see *The Nicomachean Ethics of Aristotle*, Oxford: Oxford University Press, 1954. I try to put all these sources together to address issues in contemporary theorizing in philosophy of mind in "Understanding Thought Non-Reductively: As Aristotelian Second Nature," MS.

15 Ludwig Wittgenstein, *On Certainty*, G. E. M. Anscombe and G. H. von Wright (eds.), New York: Harper & Row, 1969. Hereafter cited in the text as *OC*.

16 John McDowell, *Mind and World*, op.cit.

17 Hilary Putnam, *Realism with a Human Face*, James Conant (ed.), Cambridge: Harvard University Press, 1990.

18 *PI* §429 is set up by its companion §428, which discusses how we lead ourselves astray into apparently metaphysical waters when we stop to think and to theorize about the ability of our meanings or our thoughts to reach out to the facts.

> "This queer thing, thought" – but it does not strike us as queer when we are thinking. Thought does not strike us as mysterious while we are thinking, but only when we say, as it were retrospectively: "How was that possible?" How was it possible for thought to deal with the very object *itself*? We feel as if by means of it we had caught reality in our net.
>
> (*PI* §428)

19 Here one might recall the birth of the modern novel in the West from the epistolary form. This form relied at first almost exclusively and progressively less and less on letters in which one person informed another of what transpired, and of what they thought and felt in the circumstances. What stands out – when we think in terms of forms of life and practices – is the painstaking self-consciousness with which narrative conventions that we now take for granted were initially put in place.

20 Stanley Fish, "Is There a Text in This Class?" pp. 303f.

21 Ibid., p. 313.

22 Ibid., p. 310. Fish is exactly and importantly right in denying a two-stage procedure in a way that Richard Rorty seems to have forgotten. It is interesting to contrast Fish's Wittgensteinian outlook here with Rorty's claims in his recent "Pragmatist's Progress"

(in the *Interpretation and Overinterpretation* volume consisting of Umberto Eco's lectures of that title and some critical responses). Rorty casts himself as a "Fishian" while arguing that: "[*A text's coherence*] is no more than the fact that somebody found something interesting to say about a group of marks or noises – some way of describing those marks and noises which relates them to some of the other things we are interested in talking about. (For example, we may describe a given set of marks as words of the English language, as very hard to read, as a Joyce manuscript, as worth a million dollars, as an early version of *Ulysses*, and so on.)" While space constraints don't allow us to consider Rorty's position, it is important to note that Wittgenstein's work implies that no sensible pragmatism (or theory of any other stripe) can embrace the two-stage view that Fish clear-sightedly eschews and Rorty fails to recognize.

23 *Last Writings on the Philosophy of Psychology*, Volume I Preliminary Studies for Part II of *Philosophical Investigations*, Oxford: Basil Blackwell, 1982, §354; Midway Reprint edition 1990. Wittgenstein continues in the next section to specify that a presupposition might be in place only insofar as doubt can be as well:

> But although it might not be a 'presupposition' in this case might it be one in a different case? Doesn't presupposition imply a *doubt*? And doubt may be entirely lacking; or it may be present, from the smallest to the greatest degree.
>
> (*LW* §355)

24 The section that accompanies §153 makes the further point that:

> I do not explicitly learn the propositions that stand fast for me. I can *discover* them subsequently like the axis around which a body rotates. This axis is not fixed in the sense that anything holds it fast, but the movement around it determines its immobility.
>
> (*OC* §152)

25 We can be certain that these are errors from Wittgenstein's perspective because insofar as his notion of forms of life strives to capture what is co-constitutive for meanings as well as facts, Fish's understanding would yield not only a possible plurality of meanings but also a possible plurality of facts. Fish says as much when he indicates the sorts of views with which his is congenial (and which support the "Fishian" hearing of "Is there a text in this class?"). Here is his list: "those psychologists who argue for the constitutive power of perception, or with Gombrich's theory of the beholder's share, or with that philosophical tradition in which the stability of objects has always been a matter of dispute" (op. cit., p. 315). The last item on the list – the purportedly disputable stability of ordinary objects – is precisely one of the principal targets that Wittgenstein's realism aims to help us diagnose.

26 Jane Austen, *Mansfield Park*, New York: Bantam Classic Edition, 1983, p. 24.

27 Jane Austen, *Mansfield Park*, p. 159.

28 See *PI* §65 and following.

> And the result of this examination is: we see a complicated network of similarities overlapping and criss-crossing: sometimes overall similarities, sometimes similarities of detail.
>
> (*PI* §66)

> I can think of no better expression to characterize these similarities than "family resemblance"; for the various resemblances between members of a family: build, features, colour of eyes, gait, temperament, etc. etc. overlap and criss-cross in the same way. – And I shall say: 'games' forms a family.

And for instance the kinds of number form a family in the same way. Why do we call something a "number"? Well, perhaps because it has a – direct – relationship with several things that have hitherto been called number; and this can be said to give it an indirect relationship to other things we call the same name. And we extend our concept of number as in spinning a thread we twist fibre on fibre. And the strength of the thread does not reside in the fact that some one fibre runs through its whole length, but in the overlapping of many fibres....

(*PI* §67)

29 Similarly, if one wanted to insist that "'There is something common to all these [*numerical*] constructions – namely the disjunction of all their common properties' – I should reply: Now you are only playing with words. One might as well say: 'Something runs through the whole thread – namely the continuous overlapping of those fibres'" (*PI* §67).

30 Edward Said, "Jane Austen and Empire," Mustafa Bayoumi and Andrew Rubin (eds.), *The Edward Said Reader*, New York: Vintage Books, 2000, pp. 347–67.

31 Edward Said offers such an interpretation. Intricate and detailed, Said's "Jane Austen and Empire" (op. cit.) allocates a "crucial" and "defining" yet also "casual" "function" to "Austen's few references to Antigua" in *Mansfield Park*. Working from a post-colonial understanding of the British empire, Said focuses on the novel's spatial and geographical facts, highlighting the "small and large dislocations and relocations in space" (p. 353). Said's interpretive procedure is interesting and significant from our perspective in this paper because (*i*) it insists that certain details can stand out for readers acculturated after the empire from a common core that should stand fast; and because (*ii*) it is alert to the tension or even "paradox" of using extraneous facts about empire to interpret these details, facts that far outstrip *Mansfield Park's* minimal allusions to Britain's colonial practices.

32 The phrase "sensuous surface of a work of art" figures in Susan Sontag's attack "Against Interpretation." (In *Against Interpretation and Other Essays*, New York: Farrar, Strauss & Giroux, Inc., 1964, pp. 3–14.) It would muddy the waters to contrast Wittgenstein's work on the non-interpretive immediacy of meaning with Sontag's charge that in our culture interpretation (or focus on content) always distorts our engagement with art (or sensuously immediate form). But we can register the dissonance by reworking her wonderfully suggestive phrase as I do in the concluding paragraph above: Wittgenstein's point is precisely that "the sensuous surface of a work of art" – no less than the sensuous "surfaces" of the world – is immediately factual and meaningful.

10

ON THE OLD SAW, "EVERY READING OF A TEXT IS AN INTERPRETATION"

Some remarks

Martin Stone

And one has to say this in many cases where the question arises "Is this an appropriate description or not?" The answer is: "Yes, it is appropriate, but only for this narrowly circumscribed region, not for the whole of what you were claiming to describe."

(Ludwig Wittgenstein, PI §3)

Fish and Wittgenstein

In literary theory, discussion of Wittgenstein and Stanley Fish often occurs in the same breath, and it is often said that Fish is "Wittgensteinian" in his views. I think this statement is a good indication of Wittgenstein's "unavailability" (to borrow a term of Stanley Cavell's)[1] in some regions of literary theory. Fish is preoccupied with a question concerning the basis of our entitlement, in various domains of discourse, to notions of correctness and objectivity in judgment. Literary criticism and the law supply his main examples. In virtue of what, he asks, is one reading of a literary text or one application of a legal rule correct, and not another? Fish's answer – "the authority of interpretive communities" – bears an obvious resemblance to a thesis Wittgenstein is supposed to put forward in Kripke's much-disputed reading of him. For Fish, as for Kripke's Wittgenstein, "interpretation" appears as a general condition of the possibility of anything meaning anything.

At least two things, I think, ought to be getting in the way of Wittgenstein's reception in literary theory in these terms. First, and most directly, the doctrine of ubiquitous interpretation conflicts outright with Wittgenstein's own discussion of "following a rule." One upshot of that discussion might be put like this: If interpretation is to be possible at all, then the meaning of some texts must be available without interpretation; if everything must be interpreted, then nothing can be. Second, such a reception of Wittgenstein leaves out Wittgenstein's sense of the peculiarity, from what might be called our everyday or ordinary perspective, of the general question Fish is asking; and that, I think, is to leave out Wittgenstein entirely.

In this essay, I want to focus mainly on the second of these two issues – on the nature of the question Fish brings to literary theory.[2] I want to ask: What has this question to do with literary theory? And – assuming this can be explained – would literary-theoretical inquiry change directions if Wittgenstein's thought became available here?

Presumably, most critics haven't considered Fish's question at all. They express views about what this or that work means, but rarely about what its meaning what it does consists in, or about how it is so much as *possible* for someone to get the meaning right. Notice how general the question is. It is not: What makes this or that reading of *Hamlet* (or this or that application of the Negligence Rule) correct? Critics and lawyers do have answers to these questions, answers which refer to features of *Hamlet*, or to the purpose of the rules, or the case to which they are applied. Fish's question is of a different order: How are correct attributions of meaning possible just *as such*? Whatever answer this question is looking for, it must apply as well to any meaning-involving items which the critic or lawyer is apt to cite in his answer. Indeed, any instance of linguistic meaning falls within the ambit of the question. "What makes the sign-post point in the direction of the arrow and not in the opposite one?" (cf. *PI* §§85, 454).

I imagine that a reader of Wittgenstein will want to ask: Is this a real question, admitting of fruitful and substantially correct answers? Is there such a thing as a general explanation of the possibility of a text's meaning one thing rather than another?

> Thought does not strike us as mysterious while we are thinking, but only when we say, as it were retrospectively: "How was that possible?" How was it possible for thought to deal with the very object *itself*?
>
> (*PI* §428)

I take it that if such expressions of Wittgenstein's interest in the origins of philosophy's "how possible" questions mean anything, it is that Wittgenstein does not take the mere existence of such questions to express self-standing problems which give philosophy its subject matter, and which the philosopher is therefore naturally obliged to address. To the contrary, Wittgenstein often suggests that our real need is to discover what happens in our thinking to make the relevant phenomena – e.g., "thought about the object itself" – seem *impossible*, and hence to make philosophical investigation seem urgent and compelling. His treatment of the normativity of meaning – "how is 'accord with a rule' possible" – follows this pattern. The sense of impossibility here comes out in the thought that there is always a gap between a rule and its application in particular circumstances. If someone simply accepted the question as it stands, they would feel compelled – as Fish does – to find some item (a universal, a mental act, an interpretation, etc.) which bridges this gap. One of Wittgenstein's aims, I assume, is to bring his readers to see that the doubt which defines this putative gap is not fully natural

187

or intelligible by our ordinary lights; and, alternatively, that where doubt *is* fully natural, it ceases to be generalizable, and so presents nothing of philosophical interest.[3] Hence Wittgenstein imagines an end to this particular dialectic which consists not in any gap-filling measure, but in a reminder of the everyday perspective from which doubt makes perfect sense *on occasion*, but no quite general gap appears that needs to be filled:

> So I can say, the sign-post does after all leave no room for doubt. Or rather: it sometimes leaves room for doubt and sometimes not. And now this is no longer a philosophical proposition, but an empirical one.
>
> (*PI* §85)

Is Wittgenstein purporting, as is sometimes said, to bring philosophy to an end? This seems inaccurate, at least without serious qualification. Wittgenstein does depict the investigation of particular philosophical problems as ending *non-philosophically*, in a return to the everyday. This is part of his originality: "What *we* do is to bring words back from their metaphysical to their everyday use" (*PI* §116, original emphasis). But precisely because no "philosophical proposition" comes into such returns or endings, Wittgenstein cannot imagine (as, say, Kant could) how *philosophy* could end. That is, philosophy, as Wittgenstein conceives it, can make no warrant that it is terminable, that philosophical problems won't reappear and trouble us out of our everydayness again tomorrow.[4] ("The real discovery is the one…that gives philosophy peace.…Instead, we now demonstrate a method, by examples; and the series of examples can be broken off" (*PI* §133).)

In contrast to this, if Fish has any interest in questions about how philosophy begins and ends, he has kept it a secret. For all one can tell, the question "how is it possible for a text to mean one thing rather than another?" is, for him, no more peculiar than, say, "why does it rain so much in the Pacific north-west?" He simply takes it for granted that the question admits of substantial answers, some of which are right and others wrong. He takes it for granted that a philosophical investigation of meaning must end in a philosophical proposition.

Of course, this puts Fish in a lot of academic company. His remoteness from Wittgenstein, in this respect, would in fact be unremarkable were it not for a different strand of his work, which invites the comparison in the first place. For Fish is also well known for making statements about "theory" like this: "Theory's project – the attempt to get above practice and lay bare the grounds of its possibility – is an impossible one."[5] The declaration that it is "impossible" to "get above practice" is of course a different gesture than any to be found in Wittgenstein. I imagine a Wittgensteinian response would be: "What does 'impossible' mean here – is no one smart enough?" Or perhaps: "Insofar as the expression 'getting above practice' has a *sense*, it is indeed possible to get above practice." But I want to focus on something else here. How is the general account sought by Fish to be described if not as an attempt to give "grounds of the possibility" of our concourse with texts and their meaning? Isn't that just what is on offer when a question like "What makes it the case that *this* action is what the order requires?" meets with an answer like "some community-informed interpretation," as opposed to the sort of answers which actually figure in our practices: answers which attend to features of the text in question or to the situation in which it was uttered (he said *diet* Coke; he was ordering a drink, not discussing a famous English jurist)? If the "interpretive community" answer is a good one, isn't that getting above practice?

Along the same lines, Fish says that he aspires to a "severe [*theoretical*] minimalism," and that "this parsimony of ambition distinguishes [*his*] from almost any other argument in theory."[6] But "so much for parsimony," I feel inclined to say, when Fish nominates "interpretation" as a general condition of the possibility of a text's determinately meaning one thing rather than another. Such "interpretivism" (as I shall call it) looks like nothing less than metaphysics in the classic sense: an attempt to lay bare the conditions of intelligibility of the world as a whole, of everything. The "implications [*of the ubiquitous need for interpretation*] are almost boundless" – Fish says – "for they extend to the very underpinnings of the universe."[7] Are we really supposed to regard this as a bit of hard-won pragmatism, fashioned to combat other suspiciously metaphysical pictures of meaning? Pragmatic sensitivity to everyday settings in which the term "interpretation" finds employment would have located cases in which there is some real uncertainty to be resolved, against a background of cases in which things are clear and there is no call for interpretation. That is, brought back to its ordinary use (cf. *PI* §116), "interpretation" appears as a species of explanation. It is called for when explanations or elucidations are called for, e.g., in the face of real doubt, not the mere notional *possibility* of doubt.[8] In Fish's argument, by contrast, "interpretation" begins to look like another name for – an occupant of the same explanatory place as – divinity: it is the terminus of all other explanations of meaning, the condition on which they depend.[9] (It is not wrong to explain or justify one's action by saying "the fact is he was ordering a beverage" – so long, apparently, as one is prepared to attach the rider that this is so only by way of some interpretation.) Rather than "parsimony," this looks like "theory's project" more or less as Fish describes it: the attempt to get above practice and exhibit its grounds of possibility.

It were as if Fish could imagine no other way to embody his pragmatic instincts than another *theory*; or as if he saw no difference between (1) the "interpretive practice" theory of how determinate meaning is possible, and (2) the reminder – which one finds in Wittgenstein – that, from the point of view of practice, the doubts which inspire such a theory do not arise.

I'm inclined to think there is a conflict between two strands in Fish's work. One strand demands a general account of meaning – an answer to the "how possible" question – and it discounts any answer which itself relies on the sorts of explanations of meaning which actually appear in our everyday practices. The theoretically ambitious nature of this strand is seen in the fact that any such familiar explanations of meaning (e.g., "because he was ordering a beverage," "because the purpose of the statute is to promote quiet") only re-provoke the general question: what makes the attribution of *that* intention to him, or *that* purpose to the text, correct? To me this redoubling of the question means: What the question seeks is an explanation of the possibility of determinate meaning from *outside* our everyday concourse with meanings, one that is not dependent on the kinds of explanations we give, or the kinds of uptake we rely on, in our actual meaning-involving activities. What is demanded is the ground of our practice, its condition of possibility.

The other strand in Fish's work says that any such general ground-giving is "impossible," a fruitless attempt to look at ourselves "from sideways-on" or to get beneath the bedrock of practice.[10] But this strand appears to be cut short. For from the *straight-on* perspective – to continue the metaphor – "an interpretation" sometimes appears to be needed in carrying out an order – when there is some doubt about what is meant – and sometimes not.

Critical pluralism and the exemplarity of literature

If today Wittgenstein's remarks concerning meaning and understanding appear in anthologies of literary theory, part of the explanation, I assume, is that literary theorists have come to take a question like Fish's as relevant to their subject. I have already indicated that I don't find the reason for this to be exactly transparent. Is it an answer to point to the centrality of such a question in Derrida's development of the notion of "deconstruction"? Without more, that only postpones the question: Why is Derrida's criticism of (what he finds to be) a metaphysical or platonistic notion of meaning in Husserl supposed to be relevant to literary theory? The weight of certain historical-institutional facts – the friendly reception of "deconstruction" in literature departments – can perhaps make it hard to see room for a question here: "The study of literature is the study of the meaning of literary texts; so what could be more to the point than an investigation of the concept of meaning?" But if anyone is tempted to take this short way with the question, they might recall that psychology, cooking, politics, economics, and so on, also traffic in "meanings," without thereby making the question of how meaning is possible, or central to theoretical investigation in these fields.

The answer, in the case of literary theory, I think, lies in a certain conception of the "literary" as in some way exemplary of our concourse with meaning, or our dealings with "texts" (or "discourse," "*écriture*," "representation," "signs," etc.) in general.[11] (The presence of these terms in literary theory is often a sign that the relevant conception is at hand.)

I suspect that this conception may even be the predominant one today. One reason for this is that, historically, the alternative has seemed to be a view of literature as having its own unique "literary language," distinct from the language of criticism – a view expressed, for example, in William Wimsatt's proposal that a poem is a "verbal icon," or in Wolfgang Iser's contrast between "literary language" and "everyday pragmatic language," the former opening up a "multiplicity of possible meanings."[12] The general approach here is identified by Monroe Beardsley as a "language concept of literature": "the problem is to discover the marks by which literary discourses are distinguished from nonliterary discourses."[13] Beardsley himself is persuaded that "a case can be made for regarding the possession of an above-normal proportion of implicit meaning as a sufficient condition of being a literary discourse," though he thinks that "imitating" a series of speech acts using sentences which themselves lack illocutionary force may also be a mark of the literary. Both of these – semantic richness and lack of illocutionary force – "are forms of verbal play that set a discourse notably apart from pragmatic functions."[14] Such semantic or ontological contrasts between literary and ordinary discourse have come into critical disfavor, of course.

But do these New Critical views and the view of literature as generic "text" exhaust the alternatives? That seems doubtful. I suspect, rather, that both views share a common feature, which blinds them to another main alternative. I might put it like this: Both expect to be able to identify the object of literary study without having to take account first of the kind of interest we take in literature, what literature means to us, and why we value it. It is as if these theories wanted to explain our responses to literary works (our ways of talking about them, engaging with them, valuing them, etc.) on the basis of materials which would be there anyway, independently of those responses, engagements and valuings. "Textuality," "lack of illocutionary force," "implicit meaning," etc., seem made-to-order in light of such a requirement. What goes missing is the possibility that the specialness of literature might consist in nothing more – but also nothing less – than the special sort of interest we take in texts we call literary.[15] Or perhaps one might say: in the use we make of them. (Wittgenstein: "But if we had to name anything which is the life of the sign we should have to say that it was its *use*."[16] I take this to mean: "We should have to say that it was *our* life (our concourse) with signs" – not something that appears independently of this as its ground or explanation.)

To pursue this, I want to turn now to a commonplace about literature. The commonplace is just that literature has something to do with a practice of critical interpretation, or that there is some important connection between the notions of "literature" and "interpretation." (This commonplace is apparently one of the things that "language views" like Beardsley's are trying to explain.) The connection between literature and interpretation is exhibited in such banal statements as, say, that what literary critics do is interpret works of literature, or that the critic's engagement with the meaning of a literary text is necessarily an interpretive one.

Someone might be tempted to think that these statements are mere platitudes, amounting to nothing more than the trivial reminder that if there are to be literary texts there must also be readers of them, or that the existence of literary meaning requires a reader who construes that meaning. But against this, consider the possible case of a cooking school. The faculty of the school train the students by writing recipes which the students carry out. The students prepare a dish according to the recipe and present the product to the teachers. It might be said that there would be no recipes or culinary meanings without readers of them who use them in cooking, but it would be odd, I assume, to say that what the cooking students do is essentially to interpret the recipes, or that every act of preparing a dish is an interpretation. Naturally, there may be special cases in which the recipe is ambiguous or otherwise defective, and then the students may need to make an interpretation. But if the teachers are good ones and write good recipes, this will not generally be the case. One wants to say: when cooking recipes function as they should, they allow their users to cook without recourse to interpretation. Unlike a work of literature, it would be a criticism of the latest *Better Homes and Gardens Cookbook* to say that it required its readers to engage in extensive *interpretatio*; it would be a reason not to buy it.

My example here is admittedly somewhat fanciful, but what it suggests is clear enough: the statement that the critical response to a work of literature is an interpretive one is not trivial, and does not follow merely from the fact that literary texts demand to be read. I think that the notion of interpretation which appears in this statement has the following features:

1 Interpretations are explanations of the meaning of a text – they are attempts to clarify or elucidate something that is not fully transparent in the text.
2 There can be different, equally good, but incompatible interpretations of a text.
3 Interpretation has an active or creative aspect: it does not merely tease out a meaning that is already there, but shows us something new – and not just in the sense of a meaning that was previously undiscovered, but rather one that the text has only in virtue of the interpretation in question. Meaning, one might also say, is sometimes constructed by acts of reading or interpretation.[17]

If this is right, then a clearer understanding of the commonplace concerning literature and interpretation will need to address a number of outstanding questions. How can an interpretation be both an explanation of what a text means and innovative at the same time? We think of explanations as inert – they do not change their objects, but bring to light what is already there. So it would seem that if an interpretation is innovative, it cannot be explanatory, and *vice versa*. Another difficulty is how to give content to the notion that two interpretations are "incompatible." Are a Marxist and psychoanalytic interpretation of a literary text incompatible, if they do not present any contradiction? Or do they just pertain to different aspects of the text, or take a different sort of interest in it? Still another set of questions concerns the scope of the present concept of interpretation. It seems doubtful that it is proprietary to literary criticism. "Performing interpretations" – e.g., Branagh's interpretation of *Henry V* – would also seem to lend themselves to interpretive pluralism. But does this concept of interpretation actually embrace, as some writers have suggested, what are loosely called the humanities, including the interpretation of law, social structures, history and so on?

These questions cannot be addressed here. I shall assume that interpretive pluralism is indeed an integral part of our engagement with literature, and that, as such, it must enter into an account of what literature is. The question I want to pursue is just whether it is plausible to think that literature's evident openness to interpretation makes it an exemplary instance of discourse in general. Here the two strands I have distinguished in Fish's work point in different directions. On one conception – which Fish seems to favor – the connection between literature and interpretation is something derivable from, or expressive of, a more general requirement of interpretation which conditions the availability of textual meaning *tout court*. On the other conception, the interpretability of literature is just a fact about literature or literary practice, as it has come to pass; it reflects the kind of interest we take in literary texts, and (therefore) the most general sort of intention with which literature is written. On this conception, someone encountering the thought quoted in the title of this essay might do well to borrow the form of one of Wittgenstein's remarks and answer: "You seem to be thinking of literary texts, but there are others. You can make your statement correct by expressly restricting it to those texts." (Cf. *PI* §3.)

The first of these conceptions emerges in deconstructive literary theory. Literature – it is said – is not any sort of special case; rather, "other discourses can be seen as cases of a generalized literature, or archi-literature."[18] Paul de Man's work proceeds from a conviction of this sort. "What is meant," de Man asks, "when we assert that the study of literary texts is necessarily dependent on an act of reading?"[19] "Reading" is a heavy-weather word for de Man: "Prior to any generalization about literature, literary texts have to be read."[20] Naturally they do, you might say: the only alternatives to reading any written text would be having someone else read it to you or learning about it by hearsay. But it is clear that common usage is not what is wanted for de Man's purposes. – That "reading" is unavoidable in the engagement with literature, de Man says, "implies...two things...that literature is not a transparent message...and, more problematically, it implies that the grammatical decoding of a text leaves a residue of indetermination that has to be, but cannot be, resolved by grammatical means, however extensively conceived."[21] Literary meaning – I take this in part to say – is available only by way of application of the pluralistic notion of interpretation I sketched above (p. 192). Starting from his early essays, de Man connects the necessity of reading in this sense with the distinctiveness of literature.[22] But, indeed, not just its distinctiveness, but its exemplarity as well: "Although it would perhaps be somewhat...remote from common usage, I would not hesitate to equate the rhetorical, figural potentiality of language with literature itself."[23] In the background here is of course the New Critical thesis that literary language is exceptionally figural. De Man opposes this thesis by general-izing and incorporating it: Figurality – hence "literariness" as the New Critics understood it – is a "potentiality" of all language. So literature is "privileged" – as de Man sometimes says – to make especially perspicuous or explicit the condi-tions of any use of language.[24] The relation between generalized literature (literature as the figural potentiality of language) and specialized literature ("literature" in common usage) appears to be the relation between a general concept and a type of case which provides the central, focal or paradigmatic realization of it, and thereby exhibits the concept most perspicuously.

But why "equate" literature with anything? Why would anyone want to? De Man's motivation, one might suspect, is the wish to be able to ground a view of the "literariness" of literature in some general property of language, some-thing which – though literature is privileged to bring it to light – could, in principle, be identified even if literature were not yet in view. The same struc-ture of "equation" can be found in Beardsley's "language conception"; only the relevant linguistic property is different. (Since the deconstructive view precisely inverts the "language conception," it is not surprising that they should bear this similarity.) In de Man's case, the relevant linguistic property, it appears, is just that any sign carrying meaning must always be interpreted, in a sense of the word implying creativity or productivity. De Man says as much in an approving gloss on Peirce, which is meant to explain the idea of the "rhetorical" or "figural" in terms of a contrast between "reading" and "unproblematic meaning":

> [*Peirce*] insists...on the necessary presence of a third element, called the interpretant, within any relationship that the sign entertains with its object. The sign is to be interpreted if we are to understand the idea it is to convey. ...The interpretation of the sign is not, for Peirce, a meaning but another sign; it is a reading, not a decodage, and this reading has, in its turn, to be interpreted into another sign, and so on *ad infinitum*. Peirce calls this process by means of which "one sign gives birth to another" pure rhetoric, as distinguished from pure grammar, which postulates the possibility of unproblematic...meaning.[25]

The path from the premise that "the sign is to be interpreted if we are to understand the idea it is to convey" to the exemplarity of literature seems almost a straight shot. To say that some interpretation is required if we are to grasp the meaning of a sign is to say that it is always possible for the sign to mean different things. So if it is in literature where this potential plurality becomes transparent, it is the privilege of literature to reveal the condition of linguistic discourse in general: "Whenever this autonomous potential of language can be revealed by analysis, we are dealing with literariness and, in fact, with literature as the place where this negative knowledge about the reliability of linguistic utterance is made available."[26]

194

Must plain cases be "read" too?

Clearly, a self-styled pragmatist like Fish will have little patience for such decon-structive formulas as that all special discourses are cases of generalized "literature." Yet Fish's message too is that our everyday discourses are blind to the interpretive conditions of their possibility. So there is little here to challenge the deconstructive view. "Literature" would seem to be exemplary among the discourses, insofar as it recognizes its own dependence on interpretation. But what shall we do, on this view, with the *Better Homes and Gardens Cookbook*? Clearly, anyone who accepts the deconstructive conception will need to re-describe things in ways which reveal our everyday, practical view of it to be theoretically naive. Despite his talk about the unsurpassability of "practice," that is just what Fish encourages us to do.

Suppose we ask: Why don't plain or unproblematic cases get in Fish's way? Why don't they lead deconstructive critics like de Man or Culler to abandon the view that it is illuminating to see everything as "literature" in some generalized sense of the term? I know some people are inclined to think that deconstruction must come to wreck once it is remembered that, after all, one can order "steak poivre" at a restaurant and get – of all things! – steak poivre. Of course this is but another version of kicking Dr. Johnson's stone. What is missing here, and what needs to be considered, if "deconstruction" is to be met at the right level of depth, is just the point that separates Wittgenstein and Fish: *viz.*, the unquestion-ingness with which Fish accepts the idea of a philosophical perspective on meaning, an "account" of its possibility. Once this idea is in place as a norm of explanation, the response to all the "steak poivre" examples in the world is easy: The deconstructive thesis is not about whether the phenomenon of plain meaning exists – only a madman would try to deny that – but about the "condi-tions of possibility" of such phenomena.[27] What is contested is not that there *are* plain meanings, but only a certain conception – alleged to be naive or metaphys-ically suspect or both – of how they are possible. (Provisionally, we might say that on the suspect conception, plain meaning is apt to be regarded "as inherently plain, plain in and of itself,"[28] or as invulnerable to misunderstanding.)

But *must* you, if you are to get free of a metaphysically suspect notion of plain meaning, substitute an alternative account of how such a thing is possible? Couldn't you just drop the suspect conception (and drop the bit about "plain in and of itself" and invulnerability) and go on describing plain meanings in an everyday sort of way? For the deconstructivist, the answer is apparently "no." Derrida is perhaps the most explicit about this – about the necessity of a philosophical "account." The mark of the suspect conception, for Derrida, is just that the structural or "essential" possi-bility of misunderstanding (mistake, error, deviance, accident) is left *unaccounted* for:

> We must account for the essential possibility of deviant cases....The essen-tial and irreducible *possibility* of *mis*-understanding...must be taken into account in the description of those values said to be positive....[*This*] possibility cannot be treated as if it were a simple accident.[29]

195

This says, in effect, that either you give the required sort of account, or you are still unwittingly ensnared in the suspiciously metaphysical one – the possibility of an everyday conception of meaning which is neither of these simply doesn't appear here. Given these options, the deconstructive critic will thus feel compelled to say something like this: "Plain cases only *seem* to require no interpretation, because people are in agreement about how things are to be taken and no doubts arise. Nonetheless, doubts are always possible. It is always possible for someone to engage a point of view that calls naturally for a different construction. If this doesn't occur, that only shows the power of interpretive assumptions held in common: it is an 'effect' of interpretation." Such a philosophical use of the term "interpretation" (i.e., as a condition of the possibility of any meaning) is precisely in the service of giving an account of the possibility of meaning which exhibits misunderstandings and deviance as "essential possibilities."

Fish's criticism of H. L. A. Hart's *The Concept of Law* provides a good illustration of this pattern. Central to that work – and in particular to Hart's answer to a figure he calls "the rule skeptic" is a distinction between adjudicatively easy and hard cases: i.e., cases where a legal rule is apparently clear and no interpretation is needed, and cases where judges must exercise "some discretion," as Hart puts it, in order to apply the law. This is grist for Fish's interpretivist mill:

> While there will always be paradigmatically plain cases – Hart is absolutely right to put them at the center of the adjudicative process – far from providing a stay against the force of interpretation, they will be precisely the result of interpretation's force; for they will have been written and rewritten by interpretive efforts.[30]

Adding some context: Hart's general endeavor is to clarify the concept of law by distinguishing the way legal systems can make a course of conduct obligatory from the way this can occur through mere coercive threats, on the one hand, or through moral reasoning, on the other. The central notion needed for this, according to Hart, is that of a social rule. Hart's "rule skeptic" – a figure drawn from some of the American legal realists – finds such a conceptual project to be flawed. His objection is that rules speak only in general terms and thus determine what is to be done in the particular case only by way of some interpretation. It is always possible to apply a rule in different ways, the skeptic reasons, so considerations or morality or policy (if not simply the judge's own ungrounded will) must always be operating at the point of the law's application. Hart has a number of responses to this, but one of them is just to point out that the need for applicative judgment which subsumes particulars under general categories is not a special feature of legal rules: it is a feature of concept-use in general, and so pertains to any sort of linguistic communication. Insofar as communication is possible at all, Hart suggests, people must share a general capacity to recognize particular objects, acts and circumstances as instances of general classifications – there must, in other words, be plain cases, where there is agreement in judgments, as opposed to cases which call for a choice of some kind.[31] The burden of Fish's remark, however, is to suggest that this distinction lacks the substance Hart is inclined to credit it with. Hart is mistaken, according to Fish, to suppose that the apparent compellingness of judgment in plain cases stands opposed to, or to the side of, the "interpretive" work which is felt to be required in other, more problematic cases.[32] Rather, we should see here a distinction within interpretive activity itself: the phenomenon of the plain case testifies to the success or hegemony of a particular interpretation, not the absence or superfluousness of interpretation as such. Thus, just as ordinary discourse, for the deconstructivist, is a special case of "literature," so, here, plain meanings appear as special cases of "interpretation."[33]

But it is worth asking: Why does Fish think this should matter to Hart? Wouldn't it serve Hart's purpose just as well if it were granted that there is a distinction between plain and hard cases under a rule, *however* the notion of a plain case is to be conceived? On Fish's reading, Hart ends up peddling a suspect conception of plain cases – the plain case as "inherently plain, plain in and of itself."[34] But it is hard to see the necessity of this reading. Why suppose that Hart has – or needs – *any* account of how plain cases are possible, or of what makes them plain? I'm inclined to think that Fish's discovery of such an account in Hart tells us more about Fish than Hart: it expresses a blindness to the possibility of a perspective on meaning from which a philosophical explanation of our agreements in judgment simply wasn't felt to be needed. Thus, Hart's complicity with the suspect conception of plain cases seems really to be an inference, for Fish, from two bases: first, the fact that Hart speaks of plain cases (without *any* "account" of them), and, second, the thought that everyone must – willy nilly – have such an account, if not the interpretivist account, then the suspect one. The assumption here is that all talk of plain meanings is implicitly embroiled in one or another philosophical view.[35]

The illusion of possibility

I indicated earlier that Wittgenstein sees an illusion of possibility here. Consider the following statements:

1   2+2=4. That is a fact.
2   2+2=4. That is a "fact," given our shared interpretive framework.
1   The law does not recognize marriage between a person and a goat. That is a fact.
2   The law does not recognize marriage between a person and a goat. That is a "fact," given our shared interpretive framework.

Someone suspicious of the notion of "fact" in (1) of each pair might be tempted by some things Wittgenstein says to embrace (2) instead. But (2) implies that we can make sense of a counter-factual possibility: If our interpretive assumptions were different, then 2 plus 2 might equal 5, or it might be false that the law does not recognize human–goat marriages. When we start to explore these things, however, we find that we can't make sense of them as genuine possibilities. We find that we can't coherently imagine what it would be not to have the "interpretive assumptions" we have.[36] So, in a movement characteristic of Wittgenstein's thought, we return to (1) as the better option, albeit perhaps without the haunting sense that there must be something metaphysically "queer" about it.[37] We remove the quotation marks from "fact." The illusion of possibility here is the illusion that we could view our "interpretive framework" as just one among others. Once we realize that this is an illusion, we realize that the very notion of an "interpretive framework" is an illusion too. For if that notion means anything, it should be possible to make sense of our having a different framework.

Now the intuition that even the plainest meaning is always a determination within a space of possibilities seems essential to sustaining a sense of the accuracy of the interpretivist thesis. It may even seem that the requirement of interpretation has just the same weight as the intuition that a doubt or disagreement about a text's meaning is "always possible." And the same intuition is bound to come into play, I take it, in any explanation of what it is to conceive plain meanings as "inherently plain." If we ask, "Well, isn't it a plain fact that he ordered a diet Coke?" (in a situation where, to all appearances, he ordered a diet Coke), the interpretivist will answer that there is a suspect philosophical conception of what this means, according to which the notion of "a fact" is absolutely hard in a way that would preclude the *possibility* of doubt and disagreement.

It isn't a surprise, therefore, to see that the invocation of "possibility" – or its cousin, the "absence of necessity" – is ubiquitous in Fish's work: it is carried by such terms in his prose as "always possible," "not inescapably," "not immune to," "never invulnerable to," "always open to," "always subject to," "never unchallengable":

> As yet two plus two equals four has not become such a flash point of disagreement, but it could....Until two plus two equals four crosses someone's ambition, it is a fact agreed on by all parties, but this doesn't mean that there are truths above ideology but that there are (at least by current convention) truths below ideology.[38]
>
> While the distinction between core and penumbra [*of a legal rule*] can always be made at a particular moment, at another moment the *interpretive* conditions within which the distinction is perspicuous can be challenged and dislodged.[39]

What ought to strike us here, I think, is how anemic the relevant notion of "possibility" must be.[40] "*Could* be challenged" and "*can* be dislodged" had better not mean that anyone now challenges or doubts in these cases, or even that we could make intelligible to ourselves what it would be for someone to challenge or doubt (cf. *PI* §84). Unless this just means that it is intelligible to suppose we might meet someone who we found we couldn't talk to at all. (Of course, that is not what is wanted here: if we can't talk to someone, there is no basis for supposing that they are challenging or doubting anything we believe.) But if this is right, it might be asked: In what sense is a doubt (as Fish and Derrida say) 'always possible'? In what sense is doubt an 'essential possibility'? Should we accept this? Turning the question around slightly, we might also ask: From what notional perspective does it appear that there is always room for an intelligible challenge? God's? It must be a perspective that is somehow able to survey "all the possibilities" and to locate our own way of seeing things among them.

These questions are meant to elicit a sense of the intimacy between Fish's interpretivism and the sort of "foundationalism" which Fish thinks he is combating. Both involve the fantasy of a theoretical perspective from which we could locate our "own perspective" as merely one among some indefinite range of alternatives. Interpretivism, one might say, is the negative image of foundationalism. And a general moral here is that one does not get rid of philosophical foundations by merely denying that there are any. That is merely a way of preserving the structure of the question which foundational views take themselves to be answering.

Literary interest

Let me now state some of the implications of the preceding discussion in summary form.

1   *Interpretation – everyday and philosophical.* A reader of Wittgenstein will want to bring the word "interpretation" back from its philosophical to its everyday use.[41] Given the nearly intractable history of the word – its institutionalization in theology and law, its appropriation in rhetoric, its investment by philosophy (in, say, the line from Dilthey to Gadamer), and its use in such varied contexts as psychoanalysis, history, art, and personal relationships – this is bound to be difficult. For it is no doubt the various associations which "interpretation" carries with it from these different contexts – and our failure to command a "perspicuous view" of them (cf. *PI* §122) – which partly accounts for our philosophical attraction to such sayings as "every reading of a text is an interpretation" or "there are no facts, only interpretations" – i.e., for our sense that these words say something significant but too deep for everyday inspection.

"Bringing 'interpretation' back..." need not mean restricting "the term 'interpretation' to the substitution of one expression...for another," as Wittgenstein at one point proposes (*PI* §201); performing interpretations, for example, do not involve linguistic substitution.[42] I suspect it would mean, however, locating the general idea of interpretation as a species of explanation. Interpretations are called for where explanations are called for: *viz.*, to clear up or avert some misunderstanding or doubt, or to elucidate a meaning which is not fully apparent. This points to two asymmetries between the philosophical and the everyday use of the term. (1) In the philosophical use, interpretation is ubiquitous, so the need for interpretation no longer contrasts with cases of plain meaning, but with a suspect conception of plain meaning as "inherently plain" or "plain in itself." And when called upon to explain these expressions, the philosopher is apt to say that, on this suspect conception, plain meanings are not only unchallenged or undoubted, but somehow immune to the possibility of doubt or challenge. But (2) interpretation in the everyday sense was directed at actual doubt, not the mere notional possibility of doubt.

2   *The basis of critical pluralism.* Having located interpretation as a species of explanation, we shall not be able to ground the "literariness" of literature in some general linguistic property which makes interpretation a condition of any understanding. At the same time, the commonplace concerning critical pluralism should seem freshly puzzling. Why should it be that there are many good, but incompatible, interpretations of a literary text, in contrast to other texts (e.g., cooking recipes, legal statutes) or to natural phenomena (about which we are apt to say, there cannot be true, but incompatible, explanations)? How can an interpretation be both explanatory and innovative at the same time? As it appears in literary practice, "interpretation" seems to challenge this traditional distinction[43] – that is part of what makes it interesting. But there is no cause to suppose, because the explanation/innovation distinction may not always get a clear grip in the context of literature (and of course not just there), that the distinction lacks the substance we are apt to credit it with in our dealings with texts quite generally.

Critical pluralism, to put this another way, need not stand or fall with the deconstructive conception of it. There is some tendency today to think that to reject literary "deconstruction" must be to incur a commitment to some form of monism, at least as a regulative ideal: the critic is to think of himself as pursuing an ideal interpretation, something determined, it is usually said, by what its author – conceived either historically or as an explanatory construct – intended.[44] But quite apart from the usual deconstructive objections (i.e., intention, like any semantic notion, is itself subject to interpretive construction), there is a difficulty for any "intention-based" monism about literature. An author might understand one of his characters in some specific way. But, described more generally, his intention might also be to create a work of *literature*, hence a work subject to whatever norms of reading and understanding literature is subject to. It begs the question to say that those norms cannot be pluralistic ones.[45]

The unattractiveness of the view that there is an ontologically or semantically special "literary language" is one source of the deconstructive conception of critical pluralism. But the theses that pluralism is a consequence of "literary language," and that it is a consequence of the general "unreliability" of language (which comes to self-consciousness in literature), are not the only options. In fact, both views appear to share a wish to ground aspects of our engagement with literature from outside the domain of the literary. Another possibility is that the openness of literature to interpretation reflects something about the distinctive kind of interest we take in the texts that are called "literary," about the kind of value they have for us, and, generally speaking, about the role they play in our lives. Literary interest would of course enter into the sort of communicative intention with which literature is written, so even literary "intentionalism" should be hospitable to critical pluralism. It seems implausible to suppose that a literary author's intention must, in principle, be just like the intention involved in sending someone shopping to buy apples – only somehow much more difficult to grasp![46]

3   *Types of reading, types of texts.* On the account that emerges here, the old saw "every reading of a text is an interpretation" expresses a norm of literary practice (as we have it) – or perhaps better, a norm for the description of literary phenomena. This would be so in the way that, say, "The judge must always interpret the law" expresses a norm of adjudication. It is worth noticing that these two familiar statements about interpretation in fact say very different things. In the literary case, what is meant is that the critic's job is partly a creative one: she endeavors to reveal something new in the text, or at least to show us something that was not already apparent. Whereas in the legal case, the thought is that the judge must *not* create the law; his role, in contrast to the legislator, is merely to retrieve or specify the meaning of the law in the present case. So conceived, the necessity of literary interpretation would informatively contrast with our dealings with texts like cooking recipes or legal statutes. Three asymmetries seem immediately apparent:

A. The non-applicative aspect of literature. The point or value of recipes or legal statutes is to guide action or to be followed in particular cases. Not every interpretation of a legal rule involves an application of it, but there would be no point in interpreting legal rules apart from the endeavor to follow the law in particular cases. This means that the need to "interpret" is going to be merely occasional or remedial. It arises in relation to indeterminacy concerning how the text is to be followed – i.e., what Hart calls "hard cases." In contrast, it seems partly constitutive of our very notion of a "literary text" that there is no such thing as following it or applying it in a particular case. This is not to say that one *couldn't* endeavor to follow a text that was considered "literature," or that one *couldn't* read a cooking recipe "as literature." The distinction here is not an ontological one between types of texts, or their semantic properties, but between different uses, forms of interest, and values.

B. The indeterminacy-revealing aspect of literary interpretation. From this contrast, it follows that the notion of "indeterminacy" has a different sense, and plays a different role, in the two cases. In the legal case, it may be said that a text is "determinate" just if it functions as a guide to correct action in normal circumstances. Contrariwise, it might be generally "indeterminate" if it is a poor guide, or "indeterminate" with respect to a particular (e.g., an unusual or unforeseen) case. As lawyers know, interpretation helps to resolve indeterminacy – that is its point. Clearly, where the notion of "following" finds no application, "indeterminacy" cannot be identified in this way. What does it mean to say – as de Man does[47] – that a literary text, or a work of art, is "indeterminate"? Apart from such cases as editorial uncertainty about what marks belong on the page, it is hardly clear what contrast this draws. Perhaps it merely expresses the thought that different interpretations of the text are possible, or that there are different interpretations of the text. But then the relation between indeterminacy and interpretation is different in the literary case than in that of the law. In the legal case, interpretation resolves indeterminacy; in the literary case, it exposes or expresses it. In the legal case, indeterminacy is an occasional reason for engaging in interpretation; in the literary case, the text as such is a standing reason for interpreting, and without interpretation, indeterminacy would not be present at all. In the legal case, there are interpretive authorities in a special sense: their judgments are treated as determining what the law requires even when one disagrees with those judgments on the merits; but no one purports to be a literary "authority" in this sense – no one claims that her reading of, say, *Paradise Lost* determines what it means, even apart from what may be said for or against that reading.

C. The value of indeterminacy. These asymmetries correspond to different values which indeterminacy and interpretation have in the two cases. Generally speaking, indeterminacy in a cooking recipe is of negative value; interpretation is to be avoided, if possible. The same is true in a range of legal contexts, though indeterminacy may also sometimes have instrumental value, as, say, when it is deliberately used to confer a larger decision-making authority on a subordinate agency which will then apply a relatively open-ended standard (e.g., "reasonably safe") in particular cases. Also, as lawyers know, it may not be possible to codify notions of justice in ways that provide a decision procedure for every particular case, without the mediation of judgments about what is important in the circumstances giving rise to the case.[48] But the "indeterminacy" which is the correlate of critical pluralism in literature is not – *pace* de Man – any sort of defect or failure. To the contrary, that literature lends itself to multiple and divergent readings is apparently one of the things we celebrate and value about it. And the reason for interpreting a work of literature is not, of course, finally to establish "the meaning" so as to obviate the need for any further reading or interpretation. (Contrast a court's interpretation of a contract in a case where the parties dispute what it requires.)

A brief comment on this last point: Deconstructive critics often speak as if, in the face of multiple interpretations, understanding has broken down. Hence, given their view of "textuality" as the source of pluralism, they speak of the inevitability of "misreading" and "misunderstanding."[49] Here is de Man, after a characteristically virtuostic reading of the different meanings in the title of Keats's "The Fall of Hyperion":

> Faced with the ineluctable necessity to come to a decision, no grammatical or logical analysis can help us out. Just as Keats had to break off his narrative, the reader has to break off his understanding at the very moment when he is most directly engaged and summoned by the text.[50]

But whence "the ineluctable necessity to come to a decision"? Are we trying to decipher a shopping list before the store closes at 5:00 p.m.? Shelley might have said that "poets are the unacknowledged legislators of the world," but must we be so literal-minded as to suppose that literary criticism is therefore a form of judicial review? Why, indeed, shouldn't a critic read in a way which preserves the indeterminacy of a text, just as de Man has done here? In the law, that would be objectionable, for our idea – which rests on a number of considerations – is that a court should reach a non-arbitrary decision for one of the parties. If de Man extends the idea of literary "reading" in questionable ways to non-literary discourses, it would seem he also applies the legal-hermeneutical model where it does not belong. Supposing that we are convinced by de Man's gloss on Keats's poem, why should we not conclude – given that it is a *poem* – that he (and now we) understand the text rather well?

A similar question emerges in relation to Stanley Corngold's account of the variety of readings of Kafka's *Metamorphosis*:

> The negativity of the vermin has to be seen as rooted…in the literary enterprise itself.…The creature…is…language itself (*parole*) – a word broken loose from the context of language (*langage*), fallen into a void of meaning which it cannot signify, near others who cannot understand it.[51]

There is a paradox here, as Alexander Nehamas has seen. If Corngold is right that Kafka has created an allegory of the literary enterprise (as the inevitability of misunderstanding), then the literary enterprise here succeeds, for Corngold has understood the story very well. Hence what Corngold says must be wrong. On the other hand, if Corngold's reading is wrong, then literary communication has failed, so Corngold is right after all! Nehamas takes such a paradox to cast doubt on the coherence of critical pluralism. I'm inclined to think that it shows merely that the deconstructive theorist – by treating literary interest indifferently, as if it were just that interest involved in any "communication" – has inaccurately described literary pluralism's significance. Leave out the thought that where there are multiple readings, understanding has broken down, and the paradox vanishes.

4   *Reasons for interpreting.* I have been suggesting that differences between kinds of texts (legal, literary, etc.) can be expressed partly in terms of different norms, or different necessities, of reading. Suitably restricted to literary texts, the old saw "Every reading of a text is an interpretation" is, in Wittgenstein's sense, a grammatical remark – it "tells us what kind of object" a literary text is (cf. *PI* §§373, 371). The existence of such domain-specific necessities should hardly surprise us. For it must be remembered that we interpret for a reason; interpretation is not something that happens, as it were by a kind of chemical reaction, when readers and texts (or objects which bear meaning) come into proximity. And the reasons why we are interested in interpreting, e.g., history, literature,

neurotic behavior, everyday intentional actions, cooking recipes, and the common law are – needless to say – both overlapping and different. Why should these differences not be reflected in differences in the nature and role of interpretation?

Given what I have called the "pragmatic" strand in his work, it is not surprising that Fish can be found agreeing with this up to a point. For example, respecting the difference between law and literature he says:

> One might contrast the law, where interpretive practice is such that it demands a single reading (verdict), with the practice of literary criticism, where the pressure is for multiple readings (so much so that a text for which only one reading seemed available would be in danger of losing the designation "literary").
>
> The situation is exactly the reverse in literary studies [*as in law*], at least in the context of a modernist aesthetic where the rule is that a critic must learn to read in a way that *multiplies* crises, and must never give a remedy in the sense of a single and unequivocal answer to the question, "What does this poem or novel or play mean?"[52]

One might quibble about the accuracy of the contrast drawn here: what the law requires, it might be said, isn't so much unanimity of reading as authoritative judgment; the law is often happy to brook divergent interpretations of its central concepts;[53] and *heteroglossia*, as Fish himself suggests, is perhaps only the mark of one school of literary aesthetics. Still, Fish's more general point is well taken: what kind of text something is (law, literature, etc.) is internally related to the norms of description and explanation which apply to it. But Fish never allows this sound point to raise doubts about his general interpretivism. For him, the differences that appear here are to be described, not as differences between cases where interpretation is ubiquitous and cases where it is merely occasional and remedial, but as differences in "interpretive practice."[54] This is the theoretical strand in his work. It implies that we are always dealing, in the end, with generic textual stuff under one or another interpretive construction. And if one accepts this bit of philosophy, one is bound to feel that the literary case is really exemplary, for it is in literature that the putative "interpretive" conditions of discourse seem to be most explicit and self-conscious.

5   How is the concept of interpretation that appears in connection with literature like or unlike that which appears in law, psychoanalysis, history, everyday action, or artistic performance? This too emerges as a *question* once we abandon the deconstructive conception of critical pluralism. Rather than assuming there is a unified idea of "interpretation" here, we shall want, in Wittgenstein's words, to look and see.

Notes

Thanks to Richard Moran for a conversation about this paper, and to Won Kyung Chang for valuable research assistance.

1 See Stanley Cavell, "The Availability of Wittgenstein's Later Philosophy," *Must We Mean What We Say?*, 2nd edn., Cambridge: Cambridge University Press, 2002, pp. 1–43.

2 A discussion of the first issue, i.e., Wittgenstein's discussion of rule-following and certain "deconstructive" misunderstandings of it, can be found in my "Wittgenstein on Deconstruction," Alice Crary and Rupert Read (eds.), *The New Wittgenstein*, London: Routledge, 2000, pp. 83–117, as well as my "Theory, Practice and Ubiquitous Interpretation: The Basics," Gary Olson (ed.), *Postmodernism and Sophistry: Stanley Fish and The Critical Enterprise*, SUNY Press, forthcoming.

3 On what it means for an expression to be "not fully natural," see Stanley Cavell, *The Claim of Reason: Wittgenstein, Skepticism, Morality and Tragedy*, Oxford: Oxford University Press, 1979, ch. VIII.

4 One might say: If philosophy comes to an end for Wittgenstein, it does so everyday – for here and now – until next time. Cavell is instructive on this point. See, e.g., "Declining Decline: Wittgenstein as a Philosopher of Culture," *This New Yet Unapproachable America*, Albuquerque: Living Batch Press, 1989, pp. 29–76, pp. 73–4.

5 Stanley Fish, "Change," *Doing What Comes Naturally: Change, Rhetoric, and the Practice of Theory in Literary and Legal Studies*, Durham: Duke University Press, 1989, p. 156.

6 Stanley Fish, "Theory Minimalism," *San Diego Law Review* 37, 2000, 761–76, p. 775.

7 Fish, "Introduction: Going Down the Anti-Formalist Road," *Doing What Comes Naturally*, op. cit., p. 4.

8 This is true even of "performing interpretations" – e.g., Gould's interpretation of the *Goldberg Variations*. This doesn't at first look like an "explanation"; but here too our notion is that interpretation reveals something in the work which would otherwise not be fully perspicuous.

9 Of course, Fish is not alone today in wishing to make the term "interpretation" bear such philosophical weight. One finds a similar inclination in Jacques Derrida. See, e.g., Derrida, "Force of Law: The 'Mystical Foundation of Authority,'" D. Cornell, M. Rosenfeld and D. Carlson (eds.), *Deconstruction and the Possibility of Justice*, New York: Routledge, 1992, pp. 3–67, p. 23; Derrida, *Limited Inc*, trans. S. Weber, Evanston: Northwestern University Press, 1988, p. 148; Derrida, "*Differance*," *Speech and Phenomena and Other Essays on Husserl's Theory of Signs*, trans. D. Allison, Evanston: Northwestern University Press, 1973, p. 149. Unlike Fish, however, Derrida is prepared to consider it a problem that in passages like these he appears to be putting "interpretation" in place of other traditional metaphysical names for "grounds of possibility."

10 Fish, "Theory Minimalism," op. cit., p. 772; see also Fish, *The Trouble with Principle*, Cambridge: Harvard University Press, 1999, pp. 305–6.

11 Cf. Derrida, *Positions*, trans. Alan Bass, Chicago: University of Chicago Press, 1981, p. 11: "If we had the time, we could...ask ourselves too, why the irreducibiltiy of writing and, let us say, the subversion of logocentrism are announced better than elsewhere, today, in a certain sector and certain determined form of 'literary' practice."

12 W. K. Wimsatt, *The Verbal Icon: Studies in the Meaning of Poetry*, Lexington: University of Kentucky Press, 1954, pp. 21–39; Wolfgang Iser, *The Act of Reading: A Theory of Aesthetic Response*, Baltimore: Johns Hopkins University Press, 1978, pp. 24, 184.

13 Monroe Beardsley, "The Concept of Literature," *Literary Theory and Structure: Essays in Honor of William K. Wimsatt*, Frank Brady, John Palmer and Martin Price (eds.), New Haven: Yale University Press, 1973, pp. 23–39, p. 24.

14 Beardsley, "The Concept of Literature," op. cit., pp. 30, 37, 38.

15 Steven Knapp seems to me on the right general track when, against "claims for the cognitive and/or semantic uniqueness of literary language," he proposes "to call 'literary' any linguistically embodied representation that tends to attract a certain kind of interest to itself." *Literary Interest: The Limits of Anti-Formalism*, Cambridge: Harvard University Press, 1993, pp. 2–3.

16 Ludwig Wittgenstein, *The Blue and Brown Books: Preliminary Studies for the* Philosophical Investigations, 2nd edn., New York: Harper & Row, 1960, p. 4.

17 I'm indebted to Joseph Raz's discussion of a concept of interpretation along these lines (and his discussion of the tension between the explanatory and innovative aspects of interpretation) in a paper presented at the Analytic Legal Philosophy Conference in Oxford, 2003.

18 Jonathan Culler, *On Deconstruction: Theory and Criticism after Structuralism*, Ithaca, NY: Cornell University Press, 1982, p.181. See also Derek Attridge, "Introduction: Derrida and the Questioning of Literature," Jacques Derrida, *Acts of Literature*, New York: Routledge, 1992, p. 16: "[T]he re-mark is a permanent possibility in all texts, all signs, but literature has the capacity to stage its operations with unusual forcefulness and to produce unusual pleasure in doing so....That which marks out the specific literary text is also a property of the general text."

19 Paul de Man, "The Resistance to Theory," *The Resistance to Theory*, Minneapolis University of Minnesota Press, 1986, pp. 3–20, p. 15.

20 Paul de Man, "The Rhetoric of Blindness: Jacques Derrida's Reading of Rousseau," *Blindness and Insight: Essays in the Rhetoric of Contemporary Criticism*, 2nd edn., Minneapolis: University of Minnesota Press, 1983, pp. 102–41, p. 107.

21 De Man, "Resistance to Theory," op. cit., p. 15.

22 "[T]he specificity of literary language resides in the possibility of misreading and misinterpretation." de Man, "Literature and Language: A Commentary," *Blindness and Insight*. 2nd edn., Minneapolis: University of Minnesota Press, 1983, pp. 277–90, p. 280.

23 Paul de Man, "Semiology and Rhetoric," *Allegories of Reading: Figural Language in Rousseau, Nietzsche, Rilke, and Proust*, New Haven: Yale University Press, 1979, pp. 3–19, p. 10.

24 See de Man, "Semiology and Rhetoric," op. cit., pp. 19, 17; see also "Criticism and Crises," *Blindness and Insight*, op. cit., pp. 3–19, p. 17.

25 De Man, "Semiology and Rhetoric," op. cit., pp. 8f.

26 De Man, "Resistance to Theory," op. cit., pp. 10, 17; see also "Criticism and Crises," op. cit., p. 17: literature "is the only form of expression free from the fallacy of unmediated expression"; it begins "on the far side of [*the*] knowledge" that "sign and meaning can never coincide."

27 As Fish puts it, "The question is not whether there are in fact plain cases – there surely are – but, rather, of what is their plainness a condition and a property?" "Force," *Doing What Comes Naturally*, op. cit., pp. 503–24, p. 513; see also p. 101.

28 Fish, "Force," op. cit., p. 513.

29 Jacques Derrida, *Limited Inc*, trans. S. Weber, Evanston: Northwestern University Press, 1988, pp. 126, 147, 133; see also pp. 47, 48, 57, 118, 127, 157.

30 Fish, "Force," op. cit., p. 513.

31 H. L. A. Hart, *The Concept of Law*, 2nd edn., Oxford: Oxford University Press, 1994, pp.124–6. The point echoes Wittgenstein, *PI* §242. Hart's appeal to standard instances of classifying terms has sometimes been taken as a part of a particular normative theory of adjudication, a theory of how judges *should* decide cases. This seems to me to be a misunderstanding which arises from a failure to keep in view the argumentative context of his remarks – namely, the skeptical challenge described in the present paragraph. The general point here about Fish, however, does not depend on resolving this point about Hart.

"EVERY READING OF A TEXT IS AN INTERPRETATION"

32 Cf. Fish, "Working on the Chain Gang: Interpretation in Law and Literature," *Doing What Comes Naturally*, op. cit., p. 101. To be clear: what is "compelling" in the sort of cases Hart has in mind is *applicative* judgment – judgment about what the rule requires. Such legally plain cases may nonetheless be adjudicatively hard ones because what the rule requires is felt to be undesirable.

33 For a version of this claim specifically in the context of literature, see J. Hillis Miller, "The Critic as Host," Harold Bloom (ed.), *Deconstruction and Criticism*, New York: Seabury Press, 1979, pp. 217–53, p. 226.

34 Fish, "Force," op. cit., p. 513.

35 A careful reading of *The Concept of Law* should have given Fish pause, for it shows Hart at one point to be flirting – though not exactly endorsing – just the sort of interpretivist view Fish would correct him with: "The plain case," Hart writes, "where the general terms *seem* to need no interpretation and where the recognition of instances *seems* unproblematic or 'automatic', are only the familiar ones…where there is general agreement in judgments as to the applicability of the classifying terms." *Concept of Law*, op. cit., p. 126 (my emphasis). However, I suspect that if Hart had thought about it, he would have followed this by saying: "and what *seems* to be true here really *is* true – no interpretation is required" – the reason being that much of Hart's book is an attempt to give voice to the straight-on view of things, the viewpoint of the engaged participant which Hart calls "the internal perspective."

36 We find, as Jonathan Lear puts it, that "the possibility of there being persons who are minded in any way at all is the possibility of their being minded as we are." "Transcendental Anthropology," *Open Minded: Working Out the Logic of the Soul*, Cambridge: Harvard University Press, 1998, pp. 247–81, p. 250. The present paragraph follows Lear.

37 Cf. Wittgenstein, *PI* §§195, 197.

38 Fish, *The Trouble With Principle*, op. cit., p. 271.

39 Fish, "Force," op. cit, p. 512.

40 See also Fish, "Don't Know Much About the Middle Ages: Posner on Law and Literature," *Doing What Comes Naturally*, op. cit., pp. 294–311, p. 296: "In the example of 'Can you pass the salt?' it is *always possible* that someone at a dinner table may hear the question as one about his abilities…" (my emphasis). This is evidently meant to illustrate the familiar thesis that the meaning of a sentence is sensitive to the context of its utterance. But, for Fish, "there is…no context so perspicuous that its interpretive cues can be read off by anyone no matter what his position; no context that precludes interpretation because it wears its meaning on its face." "With the Compliments of the Author: Reflections on Austin and Derrida," *Doing What Comes Naturally*, op. cit., pp. 37–67, p. 51. So Fish's point must be that it is "always possible" to hear "Can you pass the salt?" as a question about someone's abilities *no matter what came (or didn't come) before or after*. Clearly, if the context was one in which the dinner conversation had ranged over, say, the progress of a particular guest in recovering from surgery, then the observation that "Can you pass the salt?" is open to different readings would illustrate only that an utterance can be, in its context, ambiguous – not (as Fish thinks) that there is a quite general space of interpretive possibility surrounding any utterance.

41 Cf. *PI* §116. If it seems contentious here to speak of an "everyday use" of "interpretation" which isn't philosophical, one might also say: its use in contexts where a question about the very *possibility* of meaning is not in play. Or, if it seems contentious to think that there are everyday contexts which escape the "play" of this question, one might even just say: contexts in which people are going about other business, and have other purposes, than that of giving an answer to such a question.

42 That proposal needs to be understood in its specific argumentative context. I attempt this in my "Wittgenstein on Deconstruction," op. cit.

43 I owe a debt to Joseph Raz here. See note 17.

44 See, e.g., Alexander Nehamas, "The Postulated Author: Critical Monism as a Regulative Ideal," *Critical Inquiry* 8 (1981), 133–49.

45 Ronald Dworkin (who favors interpretive monism on other grounds) has advanced a similar point in the context of both literature and law. See "How Law is Like Literature," *A Matter of Principle*, Cambridge: Harvard University Press, 1985, pp. 146–66, esp. pp. 157–8.

46 Someone might object: "The interest we take in a literary work must surely attach to features of that work. Further, an author's general intention makes for a work of literature only if that intention succeeds. But then it ought to be possible to say what it is for literary intention to succeed, or for a work to be capable of attracting literary interest, independently of the fact that it does attract such interest." The premise here may be granted: a work attracts literary interest in virtue of some properties it has. It doesn't follow, however, that the relationship between such properties and our literary interest must be transparent to us, so that it would be possible to identify what makes something "literature" independently of our experience of the work being what it is. As an analogy, consider that while some remarks are "funny" (and some aren't) it would be natural to be suspicious of the thought that we might come to understand which are the funny ones on the basis of independent-standing properties which might then enter into an explanation of why we have the responses we do. No one, in other words, expects to be able to "equate" funniness with anything (cf. de Man at note 23 above). Literariness is like funniness in this respect. But one important difference, I suspect, is that while comedy engages, but does not in general seek to challenge, our sense of the funny, literature, at least in certain periods, also aims to inform and alter the interest we take in it. This should be remembered when considering specifications of literary interest like Knapp's, note 15 above.

47 See note 21 above.

48 The idea of "reasonable care" in tort law is an example of this.

49 "The specificity of literary language resides in the possibility of misreading and misinterpretation." de Man, "Literature and Language: A Commentary," op. cit., p. 280; see also Miller, "The Critic as Host," op. cit., p. 226.

50 de Man, "Resistance to Theory," op. cit., pp. 16f.

51 Stanley Corngold, *The Commentator's Despair: The Interpretation of Kafka's Metamorphosis*; quoted in Nehamas, op. cit., p. 134.

52 Fish, "With the Compliments of the Author: Reflections on Austin and Derrida," op. cit., p. 54, "Fish v. Fiss," *Doing What Comes Naturally*, op. cit., pp. 120–40, p. 137.

53 As happens, for example, when some say that negligence liability aims to further economic efficiency, while others say that it expresses a distinct idea of justice.

54 Fish, "With the Compliments of the Author," op. cit., p. 54.

Part III

LITERATURE AND THE BOUNDARIES OF SELF AND SENSE

11

ROTATING THE AXIS OF
OUR INVESTIGATION

Wittgenstein's investigations and
Hölderlin's poetology

Richard Eldridge

I

It is evident that the nature of conceptual consciousness is a central topic of *Philosophical Investigations*. The protagonist of the text investigates knowing how to go on (to follow a rule, to determine the next term in a series) in an effort to become clearer about how he or anyone is so much as able to think conceptually at all. Beyond sensory awareness and apt differential responsiveness to our environments, how do we come to predicate concepts of objects and to be aware of ourselves as doing so? What is it or would it be to do so correctly, with 'full justification' before oneself and others – if, indeed, such full justification can reasonably be pursued?

Notoriously a number of answers to these questions are considered and rejected. It is neither necessary nor sufficient for applying a concept correctly that one have an image in mind, that one be simply disposed to apply it in a certain way, or that one apply it as a mechanism does in fact. The criteria for applying a concept are connected 'more tightly' with correct applications than images, dispositions, or actual mechanical workings are; correct applications are rather 'internal' to the content of a concept and to mastery of it. And they are also connected 'more loosely,' in that concepts can change to some extent over time: criteria and applications can shift together as conceptual practice changes in certain regions. The only thing, it seems, that can be said to summarize and elucidate the application of concepts is that "'obeying a rule' is a practice.…There is a way of grasping a rule which is *not* an *interpretation*, but which is exhibited in what we call 'obeying the rule' and 'going against it' in actual cases" (§§202, 201).[1]

Is this more or less negative result the whole story about concept application and about the interest of the text? There are a number of reasons to think that it is not. Focusing on this result alone fails to account for why Wittgenstein begins the text by considering a passage from St. Augustine, with whom, it seems, Wittgenstein identifies deeply, as a figure in whom a conversion into meaningfulness is accomplished.[2] It fails also to account for the presence in the text of striking remarks about continuing temptations, difficulties, and anxieties that this negative result seems not to still. For example, the problems that trouble us are "deep disquietudes; their roots are as deep in us as the forms of language and their significance is as great as the importance of our language" (§111). We *do* "predicate of the thing what lies in the method of representing it" (§104), as though we could not help fantasizing about some perfect justification for concept application that lies in the essence of the object itself, deeper than our practice seems to 'happen to be.' We have trouble paying attention to what we should pay attention to – the varieties and subtleties of actual usage; instead we find ourselves feeling clumsy and doing something else. "Here it is difficult to keep our heads up...; we feel as if we had to repair a torn spider's web with our fingers" (§106). We want, or something in us makes us want, the wrong thing, so that "the axis of our investigation must be rotated, but about the fixed point of our real need" (§108). These remarks suggest that what is needed is a kind of turning around of the soul or a conversion of attention and interest that we have trouble accomplishing fully, so that the text becomes – whatever its teaching or doctrine about concept application – also a narrative or parable of the disquietudes of the human. Above all, focusing on the negative result about concept application fails to account for the structure of the text as an internal dialogue. As we read, it becomes clear, as Cavell puts it, "that each of the voices, and silences, of the *Investigations* are the philosopher's, call him Wittgenstein, and they are meant as ours."[3]

In order to account for these things – Wittgenstein's interest in Augustine, the remarks about temptation and difficulty, and above all the structure of the text as internal dialogue or self-interrogation – it is natural then to take the text as an essentially dramatic record in which successive temptations and overcomings of them, without clear end, are foregrounded over the achievement of definite results. *Philosophical Investigations* then seems to be not a body of doctrine so much as a continuous 'working through' of the plights of the self in the service of what Wittgenstein in the *Big Typescript* calls "the transparency of arguments. Justice."[4] Cavell takes the text this way in noting what he describes as "a struggle with the contrary depths of oneself"[5] in it. I have similarly focused on the text of *Philosophical Investigations* as a dramatic display and acknowledgment of fundamental conditions of human life, according to which "our powers of arbitrary choice...must be accepted...as being open to continuous re-information by...norms of rational willing and expression, against and within changing cultural backgrounds."[6]

But now the worry arises that such a working through and dramatic display could not be *philosophically* significant. No theses seem to be quite established. Arguments appear at best as moves within an ongoing self-interrogation, not as routes to definite results. It seems too 'optional' whether anyone responds to the protagonist's worries and to the drama of the text. Is philosophy here, within this reading, being vaporized into bad literature, as some of my colleagues sometimes ask?

There is no immediate and conclusive reply to these worries about the fate of philosophy once we focus on dramas of self-interrogation. Wittgenstein himself evidently felt worries like these in the course of his investigations, as he wondered, "Where does our investigation get its importance from, since it seems only to destroy everything interesting, that is, all that is great and important? (As it were all the buildings, leaving behind only bits of stone and rubble)" (§118). If the answer to this question is that nothing is destroyed but "houses of cards [*Luftgebäude*: buildings in the air]," then that answer itself seems to fail to return us to what we might have hoped for from philosophy: say, a characterization of the mind and its place in nature, or an account of exactly what it is to apply concepts and to be governed by (nothing more – and nothing less – than our) criteria of correctness in doing so.

Perhaps, then, it will help to address worries about the fate of philosophy (even if not quite to allay them) to compare Wittgenstein's sense of being a person – possessed of judgmental power one knows not how – with a similar sense of the human person that emerges in Friedrich Hölderlin's response to the transcendental philosophies of Kant and Fichte. Hölderlin's philosophical and poetic career begins with his engagement with the Kantian–Fichtean project of establishing the logically necessary conditions of distinctively human judgmental awareness and apperceptively unified consciousness. Like Fichte, Hölderlin hopes initially to revise and 'complete' Kant's transcendental deduction of the objective validity of the categories, in order to show both how we can be at home in nature in knowing it and how we can live freely – both as independent shapers of our lives and in harmony with nature and one another. Unlike Fichte, Hölderlin soon comes to despair of carrying out this showing on the basis of anything like an argument or a philosophical theory. But instead of either simply stopping philosophy or abandoning hopes to live in self-conscious freedom and in attunement with nature and other beings, Hölderlin develops a poetology, an account of the kind of responsiveness to subject matter that should figure in a successful poem that will trace possibilities of life from within human life rather than from a master theoretical standpoint outside it. The central idea of Hölderlin's poetology is that the successful poem will embody *transitions* or *modulations* among experiences and moods of independence and attunement, thereby showing that these experiences and moods can be coherently integrated with one another within a life. Against this background Wittgenstein can be seen to offer in his own itinerary similar transitions or modulations between independence and attunement and so likewise to offer us, through identification with his voices, the possibility for us to acknowledge fundamental conditions of human life. But in order to see this – and to see how and why it might matter – we will need to have some of the details of Hölderlin's poetology before us.

II

As is well known, Kant undertakes in the transcendental deduction of the *Critique of Pure Reason* to establish that the categories or pure concepts of the understanding (especially causality and substance) apply to empirical objects or objects as we can be aware of them through the use of the senses. It is worth a moment, however, to consider just how unusual Kant's argument procedure actually is. He begins, in a move that defines transcendental philosophy, by investigating the necessary conditions of judgmentally structured experience. My consciousness [*Erfahrung*] consists not simply of buzzes, tingles, color patches, and sounds. It is rather an awareness the content of which can be reported in a claim or judgment, for example, a conscious taking of *a* to be *F*.

How do I do this thing? Where do such judgmental takings of things to be thus and so 'come from'? Notoriously, Kant does *not* offer any empirical or scientific psychological answer to this question. Instead he argues that I can have judgmental awareness only if my consciousness is apperceptively unified. That is, I must be implicitly aware (and able if the occasion arises to become explicitly aware) that all my representations (my concepts and intuitions) are mine. Without any relation to a continuing apperceptively unified consciousness, mere quasi-representations (buzzes, tingles, color patches, sounds) would merely 'float by' in awareness, without being combined to form judgments. Quasi-representations would suffice for apt differential response to certain features of an environment, but not for judgment. Judgments, in contrast, are composed of full-blooded representations, and these representations must be one and all mine.

> The manifold representations [*for example, of the color, shape, and position of, say, a cup*] that are given in a certain intuition [*of the cup*] would not all together be *my* representations if they did not all together belong to a single consciousness; i.e. as my representations (even if I am not [*explicitly*] conscious of them as such) they must yet necessarily be in accord with the condition under which alone they can stand together in a universal self-consciousness, because otherwise they would throughout not belong to me. From this original combination much may be inferred.[7]

So genuine representations (concepts and intuitions) can 'fit together' (like the words of a grammatically well-formed sentence that 'fit together' in virtue of being nouns, verbs, determiners, etc.). I do fit them together to form judgments. This is possible only on the condition that these representations are all mine. But what, then, is the further condition under which they can 'stand together' as one and all mine? What does Kant mean by their 'original combination' in one consciousness? – Very roughly, and without rehearsing and assessing the entire argument, Kant claims that my representations (concepts and intuitions) are my products, things I make. In particular, I *use* the pure or non-empirical concepts of the understanding – the categories – to form part of the conceptual content of any first-order, empirical concept I have. For example, *cup* is a *substance-concept*; *breaks* is a *causative relation*. These pure or non-empirical concepts cannot (as Hume saw) be derived from experience. They are rather presupposed by and put to use within all judgmental experience. My having of genuine first-order concepts and intuitions-of-objects requires the use of the categories within them. Through concepts so structured and so used, experience (*Erfahrung*) comes to have the judgmental structure that it does.

Crucially, the categories or pure concepts that are thus put to use in any (judgmental) experience are themselves synthesized *by me*, not derived from passive responsiveness to experience. That we have or form the categories, and so have genuinely judgmental experience, is, Kant argues, the result of "an act of the spontaneity of the power of representation [*or of*] an action of the understanding."[8] Without such *acts* through which the categories are non-empirically formed and embedded within first-order concepts as part of their content, there would not be judgmental experience. Particular judgments then result from further acts of putting together concepts and intuitions (with their necessary, implicit categorical substructural content) to form, for example, predications of the possession of properties by objects.

Kant goes on to argue, notoriously, that although original acts of spontaneity in the formation of the categories are required for judgmental awareness, in the end the categories that are thus formed and used must 'answer to' real, objective, mind-independent features of the objects we are able to experience. In his own formulations of the First and Second Analogies of Experience: "In all change of appearances substance persists, and its quantum is neither increased nor diminished in nature....All alterations occur in accordance with the law of cause and effect."[9] The underlying ideas throughout the argument for these conclusions are (1) that I would not be able to form judgments, understood as aiming at correct representation of something external to me (bracketing the question of whether they in fact hit their targets), if I did not possess the *concept* of an objective (mind- and act-independent) succession of representations; without this concept, I could not so much as take myself to be forming judgments *about objects* (whether reliably or not); and (2) that I can possess the concept of an objective succession of representations only if there are in fact objectively determined (mind- and act-independent) successions of events and arrangements of matter into objects-with-properties in all of the objects external to me that I experience. This difficult argument is as it may be. The argument for these further conclusions has, to put it mildly, occasioned considerable discussion.

What is less often noticed, however, is that Kant goes on from this account of the active role of the subject in the formation of judgmental experience to argue that we are *intelligible beings* capable of free action or of action resulting from "causality through freedom."

> In the case of lifeless nature and nature having merely animal life, we find no ground for thinking of any faculty which is other than sensibly conditioned. Yet the human being, who is otherwise acquainted with the whole of nature solely through sense, knows himself also through pure apperception, and indeed in actions and inner determinations

which cannot be accounted at all among the impressions of sense; he obviously is in one part phenomenon, but in another part, namely in regard to certain faculties, he is a merely intelligible object, because the actions of this object [*viz. in forming the categories and using them to form judgments, as part of the substructural content of first-order concepts*] cannot at all be ascribed to the receptivity of sensibility. We call these faculties understanding and reason; chiefly the latter is distinguished quite properly and preeminently from all empirically conditioned powers....[10]

Or, as Kant puts it in the *Foundations*, "in the final analysis there can be but one and the same reason which must be differentiated only in application [*i.e. in theory and judgment, on the one hand, and in intending and acting, on the other*]."[11]

While we thus ineliminably recognize ourselves as free in both judgment and action, we can nonetheless not investigate empirically *how* we are free. "We do not indeed comprehend the practical unconditional necessity of the moral imperative; yet we do comprehend its incomprehensibility, which is all that can fairly be demanded of a philosophy which in its principles strives to reach the limit of human reason."[12]

III

Kant's immediate successors were not slow to find his conception of the human subject and its powers of judgment and action both tantalizing and obscure. Kant promised to establish both that we are entitled to claim knowledge of an order of empirical nature and that the will is free and bound by moral law, all without dogmatic reversion to putative knowledge of ultimate reality, God's will, or principles of being as such. But is this promise clearly fulfilled? Salomon Maimon remarks in a letter to Kant that he has "made [*his*] peace with the *Critique* very nicely" by "grant[*ing*] what you propound as at least problematical" and constructing "a psychological deduction of the categories."[13] Maimon's reaction is telling. To put forward a psychological deduction of the categories – a scientific psychological account of how they are caused to be formed in the mind – is to intimate that Kant's own deduction of 'transcendental–logical' necessary conditions of experience – of conditions 'under which alone' experience is possible – is unsound, or at least unsatisfying. One wants to know exactly why and how 'spontaneity' operates in us as it does. Failing an explanation of this, Kant's remarks about what we 'must' be doing in contributing to our judgmental experience seem speculative, at least to many readers. So too, then, do his remarks about the freedom of the will and our possession of a power in action of causality through freedom. To grant what Kant propounds as "at least problematical" seems emptily voluntaristic and seems not to offer us the account of the human subject in the world that we want.

And so begins the host of efforts to revise and complete Kant's deduction and demonstration of the reality of freedom, including Reinhold's philosophy of representation, Fichte's *Wissenschaftslehre*, and Hegel's *Phenomenology*, among many others. As Fichte remarks, skepticism (urged by Schulze in his *"Aenesidemus Review"* of Reinhold's system) "has shaken my own system to its foundations, and, since one cannot very well live under the open sky, I have been forced to construct a new system."[14] The effort is to explain how constraint from the world of empirical objects combines with structures of synthesis that are spontaneously produced within the subject so as to yield judgmental experience – all while remaining within the strictures of the transcendental standpoint, eschewing empirical investigations in favor of tracing necessary presuppositions. As Fichte puts it, "Philosophy...must...furnish the ground of all experience,"[15] thereby grounding Kant's system in a way that is more than merely problematical.

It may well be that these efforts are misguided. Notoriously Fichte seems to equivocate on whether he is supplying a causal account of experience or a reason why experience must have the underlying structures that it has. If the former, then we seem to need a better empirical psychology than anything Fichte supplies; if the latter (as Fichte generally intends), then his account of reasons that have to do with necessities of subject activity seems no better grounded than Kant's own account. Kant himself sharply criticized Fichte's efforts to move beyond his own determination of the (transcendentally) logically necessary conditions of experience. "I hereby declare," Kant wrote in his "Open Letter on Fichte's *Wissenschaftslehre*,"

> that I regard Fichte's *Theory of Science* [*Wissenschaftslehre*] as a totally indefensible system. For the pure theory of science is nothing more or less than mere logic, and the principles of logic cannot lead to any material knowledge. Since logic, that is to say, *pure logic*, abstracts from the content of knowledge, the attempt to cull a real object out of logic is a vain effort and therefore a thing that no one has ever done. If the transcendental philosophy is correct, such a task would involve metaphysics rather than logic. But I am so opposed to metaphysics, as defined according to Fichtean principles, that I have advised him, in a letter, to turn his fine literary gifts to the problem of applying the *Critique of Pure Reason* rather than squander them in cultivating fruitless sophistries.[16]

Instead, then, of attempting to discern how experience is "determined" by some impersonal, rational subject activity (Fichte's stance) or substance (Schelling and neo-Spinozism) that is "beyond" or "before" the subject, the right tack is, as J. S. Beck puts it, to "try to get the reader right into this [*subject*] activity itself, *as it discloses itself* originally in...representation."[17] Tracing the 'rules' for subject activity from "within" it, without grounding in the operations of any substance, may well be the path of prudence and insight in philosophy.[18]

IV

But what is it to be "right in the activity" of a subject? How can one persist in this activity well, without guiding assurance about the substantial determination and meaning of this activity? How within subject activity can the independence, autonomy, and dignity of self-conscious selfhood be expressed, together with the maintenance of genuine receptivity toward the world and acceptance of others in a stance of love and openness? Without independence, selfhood is compromised; without love and openness, independent selfhood is empty, nihilistic, and vengefully world-denying. But how can independent selfhood and loving openness be blended? These are the questions that are foundational for Hölderlin's receptions of Kant and Fichte and for his consequent conception of the human subject.

Hölderlin's mature career begins with the 1795 essay fragment "Judgment and Being." Rejecting any Fichtean effort to show how finite subject activity is 'determined' by either absolute Being or impersonal rational subject activity as such, Hölderlin argues that "judgment is...that separation through which alone object and subject become possible, the arche-separation."[19] That is to say, a finite subject as a bearer of judgmental consciousness emerges out of Being. Before there is finite subjecthood proper, there is the condition in which implicit, unactualized "subject and object are united altogether and not only in part;...there and nowhere else can be spoken of *Being proper.*"[20] But this primordial Being as such is, contra Fichte, not subject-like, and finite subjecthood emerges only in separation from it. "This Being must not be confused with identity."[21] When there is subject identity – when, as Hölderlin puts it (alluding to the apperceptive unity of judgmental consciousness), "I say: I am I"[22] – then "the I is only possible by means of this separation of the I from the I."[23] That is to say, finite subjecthood and apperceptively unified judgmental consciousness is essentially displayed in focusing conceptually structured attention on this or that successively: for example, now on a cup, now on a chair. When I do thus focus my conceptually structured attention, then my experience is mine and judgmentally structured, and I am aware of my judgments and representations as mine over time, as I focus on this or that. But this means that in achieving and exercising judgmental awareness I am "opposing myself to myself, separating myself from myself" albeit while "recognizing myself as the same in the opposed."[24] Finite subject identity then requires separation and self-recognition across different moments of conceptual awareness or judgment. And this in turn means that subject identity is not simply given within Being or nature, but instead that it 'stands out' from Being through its own conceptual activity. But in this standing out, immersion in Being proper is lost. "Identity is not a union of subject and object which simply occurred, hence identity is not = absolute Being."[25] It is true that "in the concept of separation [*of the finite subject from absolute Being*] there lies already the concept of the reciprocity of object and subject and the necessary presupposition of a whole [*absolute Being*] of which object and subject form the parts."[26] But unity with absolute Being is lost through the arche-separation through which finite subjecthood comes to be, and the nature of its emergence cannot be traced back across this arche-separation by a finite subject, who remains always within already emerged subject activity. As Hölderlin puts it in the original Preface to *Hyperion*, "the blessed unity, being, in the unique sense of the word, is lost to us."[27] As Dieter Henrich comments, "Hölderlin defines being as the undivided unity of what [*subsequently*] emerges from division in the form of subject and object. Anyone could have seen that it would be circular to derive subject and object from being, so conceived,"[28] which is to say that there can be no theoretical explanation of just how subjectivity emerges from absolute Being: all that can be said is that it emerges via arche-separation from original unity. Any time we as finite subjects undertake to look to see how subjectivity emerges we see only finite empirical objects as they can be seen or otherwise sensed by finite subjects, not absolute Being itself. (In his late hymns Hölderlin thematizes what has been called the self-occlusion of God from us.)

As a result, then, absolute Being – including absolute Being as it presents itself in nature (especially beautiful nature) and in other people (especially in intimate friends and lovers) – remains for Hölderlin not an object of theoretical knowledge, but instead an object of love to be received and accepted and also an object against and through which selfhood must be independently asserted. For Hölderlin, according to Henrich, "as much as love and selfhood tend to be mutually exclusive, they nonetheless belong together, and only then constitute a life in its totality....Yet it is not easy to bring them together in freedom, nor even to conceive of the unity in virtue of which they belong together."[29] There is no possibility of knowing absolute Being and one's route of emergence from it, in such a way that one could be guided by this knowledge securely toward the achievement of both love and selfhood. To this extent, Hölderlin remains opposed to dogmatism and closer to the spirit of Kant's critical philosophy than does Fichte, who in contrast continues to seek orienting explanations of the emergence, nature, and destiny of finite subjectivity.[30] In contrast to that of Fichte, Hölderlin's thought remains dominated by "the truth of skepticism,"[31] the thought that absolute Being demands always that we both assert our independence from it and accept and love it: it cannot be simply known, in such a way that our path is made secure. Unity with oneself as an independent being and with nature and others as objects of love remains always to be achieved. For Hölderlin, as Richard Velkley puts it, "subjectivity entails that disharmony and conflict are intrinsic to the human situation; conflict in turn makes necessary the human quest for resolution in unity."[32] Hence (in Henrich's formulation) "in the conflict of love and selfhood [*the human subject*] runs [*its*] course, either errantly or with self-understanding."[33]

V

"The path of life," then, "does not lead back into the origin."[34] Instead, the best that we can achieve, in life and in art, is

an ordered *modulation* of acts in which each of the tendencies of life [*especially love–fusion vs. selfhood–independence*] is momentarily released

> ....Art, like the consummate life, will but repeat harmoniously the *processes* of the actual, and deliver its oppositions from their conflict through completeness and order.[35]

Hölderlin develops his famous *Wechseltonlehre* – his doctrine of the modulation or exchange of poetic moods – precisely in order to characterize how order or modulated succession may be achieved in a poem in repetition of "the processes of the actual" in life. Order or modulated succession in poetry and in life then stands in place of impossible master theoretical knowledge of the place of finite subjecthood in relation to absolute being as process through which the composition and composure of the self may be achieved. As James H. Donelan usefully characterizes this move,

> self-positing through opposition *to* the material [*as in Fichte's effort to know the ground of finite subjecthood in absolute Being/subject activity*] has given way in poetry and music to self-positing through opposition *in* the material [*as the finite subject moves coherently through opposed moments of attention and mood*]. [*In this way there is*] a material existence for self-positing activity.[36]

Finite subjecthood maintains its existence in and through successive acts of attention and interfused moods, and it maintains its existence well when these acts and moods are ordered, modulated, in their succession of one another.

Donelan argues cogently that Hölderlin developed his *Wechseltonlehre* under the inspiration of the theory of harmonic modulation in musical composition, as expounded in Christian Gottfried Körner's 1795 essay "Über Charakterdarstellung in der Musik," published in Schiller's journal *Die Horen*.[37] In the essay fragment "Wechsel der Töne" [*"The Modulation of Tones"*] Hölderlin offers a specific theory of the proper developments or actions of epic poetry, lyric poetry, and tragic poetry as they should move from their various beginnings into opposites and finally into resolutions. The complexes of subject matter, diction, and mood through which poems properly move are analogized to key centers, and they are characterized by Hölderlin in terms such as "naïve, heroic, idealistic, naïve–heroic, ideal–heroic," etc.[38]

Of more interest, however, for Hölderlin's understanding of the life of a finite subject and of its possibilities of development is his longer essay "On the Operations of the Poetic Spirit" [*"Verfahrungsweise des poetischen Geistes"*] (1800?).[39] In this essay, Hölderlin develops his theory of modulation specifically as an account of the processes of the actual through which finite subjecthood exists and through which its composure may be achieved, when modulation is smooth and natural.

The essay begins with a series of reminders of things of which the poet must be aware. Chief among these is the thought that "a conflict is necessary between [*1*] the most original postulate of the spirit which aims at [*the*] communality and unified simultaneity of all parts, and [*2*] the other postulate which commands the spirit to move beyond itself and reproduce itself" (62) as apperceptively unified, independent selfhood, sustaining itself across opposed acts of attention. This conflict can in turn be understood as resulting from the demands that the work have both spiritual content or a presentation of "the interrelation of all parts" of nature and spiritual form or an "alternation of parts" as they are variously attended to by a finite subject (62). This conflict can be partially, but only partially, resolved in that across successive acts of attention "harmonious alternation" can "replace as much as was lost of the original relation and unity of the parts" (63) in absolute being, from which finite subjecthood has emerged. Such harmonious alternations can "satisfy the demands of the spirit" (63) to some degree, even though the opposition of "spiritual tranquil content" (the wholeness of nature) and "spiritual alternating form" (a finite subject with its specific acts of successive attention) remains "irreconcilable" (64). "Material identical striving" (or a self-identical, specific finite subjectivity) and "material alternation" (or the actual scenes, events, or thoughts that successively occupy attention) are also irreconcilable, but when there is harmonious alternation of subject matter, mood, and tone, then each "renders tangible" (64) the other.

Any poem will be composed of either (a) sequences of events, perspectives, and realities, (b) sequences of desires, representations, thoughts, and passions, or (c) sequences of fictions and possibilities, and in each case the sequence can be treated either objectively (as a matter of things that happen independently of any subject's attention) or subjectively (as sequences of a subject's acts of attention) (64). The harmonious development of a sequence requires, however, that it have an "authentic cause" (64) which serves as the "foundation of the poem" (65) in forming or controlling "transition between the expression, that which is presented, the sensuous subject matter, that which is actually pronounced in the poem, and…the spirit, the idealistic treatment" (65) or the moods, attitudes, thoughts, and feelings of the self responding to the sensuous subject matter. "Between the expression (the presentation) and the free idealistic treatment, there lies the foundation and significance of the poem" (66). A successful poem, that is to say, presents sensuous subject matter (sequences of events, thoughts, or possibilities) as infused with appropriately responsive thoughts, feelings, moods, and attitudes on the part of a responding, composing subject, and vice versa. When an authentic cause or foundation controls the transitions within a poem, then "does the poet provide the idealistic [*the finite, striving, self-opposed, self-identical human subject*] with a beginning, a direction, a significance" (10). The poet's modulated attention, thoughts, feelings, attitudes, and moods model or show, that is to say, how any human subject might appropriately respond to this sensuous subject matter. "At this point the spirit, which appeared as finite by virtue of the [*subject/object*] opposition [*and the opposition of itself to itself in successive acts of attention*], is tangible in its infinity" (69). Through modulated transitions the poet as finite human subject can feel himself to be – although independent and apart from absolute Being as such – also harmoniously related to it, to share an underlying life with things. Through identification with and even participation in

221

the poet's subjectivity (especially in lyric), readers too can balance a felt sense of independent selfhood with a sense of belonging to a whole in love.

But this felt sense of independence and connection remains aesthetic and not an object of theoretical knowledge. The poetic self cannot "become its own object" (71). Were it to undertake to do so – to reflect directly on itself rather than via attention to sensuous subject matter – then it would find only "a dead and deadly unity," "an infinite stagnation," a vengeful, world-denying, empty ego.

Nor does this felt sense of independence and belonging altogether resolve contradictions that attach inherently to the life of any finite subject. The poetic and human subject remains always entangled in a triangular relation among the sensuous subject matter cognized or attended to, the actual content of the cognition (the subject's thoughts, feelings, attitudes, and moods), and the self-opposing, self-identical I that is doing the cognizing (71). The subject

> has to remain inevitably in contradiction with himself, within the necessary conflict (1) of the striving for pure selfhood and identity, (2) of the striving for significance [*Bedeutenheit*] and differentiation, (3) of the striving for harmony....
>
> (74)

Nonetheless, if the human subject is neither "too selfless, that is, devoted to...object[*s*] in a too self-forgetful manner,...nor too selfish, that is, hovering between its inner foundation and its object in a too undecided, empty, and indetermined manner" (78), then it can manage – to an extent, and for a time, within certain scenes and moments of relationship – to be more or less 'at home' with itself, with empirical objects, and with other human subjects, all somehow within a whole whose essence we cannot know.

VI

In the Preface to *Philosophical Investigations*, Wittgenstein comments on the structure of his writing. He felt, he tells us, compelled "to travel over a wide field of thought criss-cross in every direction" and compelled not by mere idiosyncrasy or personal compulsion but by "the very nature of the investigation" (p. ix). There is no single originating insight or intellectual intuition in virtue of which the place of the finite subject in the world can be conclusively established. Instead there are sequences of thoughts about subjectivity and conceptual consciousness, themselves prompted by phenomena of human life and language as, one might say, their 'authentic causes.' The criss-cross travel through thoughts about the human – a progress, not an exposition of a theory – remains controlled, however, by the "natural inclination" of "my thoughts" (p. ixe). Despite their lack of control by any guiding insight that governs their place in a systematic exposition, these thoughts are here portrayed by Wittgenstein as falling into chains of natural inclination, transition, or modulation one into another.

Everywhere the course of thoughts remains surrounded by awareness of the materiality of human being in the world, an awareness announced first in §1 in the thought that the shopkeeper "*acts*" with words, as he identifies and distributes apples, and then deepened in §2, as we are introduced to the builder and his assistant who call for and pass blocks, pillars, slabs, and beams. It is pronounced that there is, to adapt Donelan's phrase, here "a material existence for self-positing activity," for subjects doing things with words in the form of calls and responses.

Despite the emphasis on the material existence of human subjects with one another in their doings, it is also repeatedly emphasized that we are unlike other animals: sapient, not merely sentient.[40] Other animals "simply do not talk" (§25). It is undeniable, primitive, that we have a life of thought with other human subjects:

> What gives us *so much as the idea* that living beings, things, can feel?

> Is it that my education has led me to it by drawing my attention to feelings in myself, and now I transfer the idea to objects outside myself? That I can recognize that there is something there (in me) which I can call "pain" without getting into conflict with the way other people use this word? – I do not transfer my idea to stones, plants, etc.
>
> (§283)

> We *see* the life of other subjects as subjects immediately in their bearing and action.

> The human body is the best picture of the human soul.
>
> (p. 178e)

> My attitude toward him is an attitude towards a soul. I am not of the *opinion* that he has a soul.
>
> (p. 178e)

> "I believe that he is not an automaton", just like that, so far makes no sense.
>
> (p. 178e)

It is for us unavoidable, immediate, that we share with other subjects a life as self-conscious subjects, able to talk, to follow rules, and to think. This life of subjects with one another happens in and through material practices; we should not be 'taken in' by a picture of human conceptual consciousness according to which "the world is dark. But one day man opens his seeing eye, and there is light" (p. 184e). Coming to thought and finite subjectivity is more a matter of halting emergence in and through material practice with others than *that* picture suggests. Within material practice with others, we are present to ourselves and to one another as subjects.

Yet this presence is also mysterious to us. We want to know, theoretically, how and why we are minded as we are as finite subjects. It feels to us as though we were, somehow, cast out into finite subjectivity from original immersion in nature, and we want to know how this is so. We ask ourselves questions such as, "What makes this utterance into an utterance about *him* [*a person whom I see vividly before me*]?" (p. 177e). Where does my–our thought, my–our conceptually structured awareness *come from*? Is it a matter of my having images or dispositions in mind or mechanisms at work within me? No; these routes of explanation are one and all nonsense. What accompanies images or dispositions or what comes about via a mechanism fails to 'match up' with how criteria of correctness control the application of a word. Yet we continue to want an explanation.

> We should like to hypostatize feelings where there are none. They serve to explain our thoughts to us.

> '*Here* explanation of our thinking demands a feeling!' It is as if our conviction were simply consequent upon this requirement.
>
> (§598)

In the grip of this desire for an explanation, we *do* "predicate of the thing what lies in the method of representing it. Impressed by the possibility of a comparison, we think we are perceiving a state of affairs of the highest generality" (§104). Yet we remain present to ourselves and to one another as subjects only within ordinary material practices of language use and thought rather than constituted as self-sufficient observer–conceptualizers apart from them. Always "the *deep* aspect of this matter readily eludes us" (§387).

Instead, then, of discovering once and for all who or what we are as thinking, concept-mongering subjects *apart* from material practices, the only thing we can do is live out our conflicting tendencies *within* ordinary, material, linguisticconceptual practice, as we variously assert our selfhood in partial independence of it (we can invent new terms, modify conceptual schemes, and take to myth and metaphor) and accept, acknowledge, and even love the ordinary as the only possible vehicle of the life of a finite subject.

We can set up "*objects of comparison* which are meant to throw light on the facts of our language by way not only of similarities, but also of dissimilarities" (§130). For example, "a cry is not a description. But there are transitions [*Übergänge*]. And the words 'I am afraid' may approximate more, or less, to being a cry. They may come quite close to this and also be *far* removed from it" (p. 189e). In seeking to find "my way about" (§123), "finding and inventing intermediate cases" (§122) that modulate into one another will be important, always, rather than 'determining' the nature of our being in the world once and for all, as somehow a function of either 'soul substance' or 'bodily substance' (the brain) that we can observe theoretically from without, so as to track the emergence of subjectivity.

What is one to make of this 'philosophy' of the human subject, a philosophy that – like Hölderlin's 'philosophy,' poetology, and poetry – insists everywhere on the impossibility of theoretical explanation of subjectivity and on the importance of transitions, modulations, of thought, attention, attitude, mood, and feeling, with other beings, as crucial to the life of any finite subject? Answers that we give to this question will depend on what we hope for from philosophy – 'anthropologico–poetic' 'elucidation' or theoretical explanation. If we cannot quite give up wishes for theory and for absolute mastery of and within our practices, it is, perhaps, nonetheless the course of wisdom to recognize these wishes as wishes, within the texture of our ongoing lives as finite subjects with others within nature, and then to try to live with these wishes gracefully, within genuine modulations between selfhood–independence and love–attunement. Or so, at any rate, both Hölderlin and Wittgenstein undertake to teach themselves, and us, in and through their exploratory writing about the human.

Notes

1 Ludwig Wittgenstein, *Philosophical Investigations*, 3rd edn., trans. G. E. M. Anscombe, New York: The Macmillan Company, 1958, §§ 202, 201, p. 81e. All subsequent references will be given in the text by section number or by page number for the Preface and for Part II.
2 See my discussion of why Wittgenstein cares about Augustine in my *Leading a Human Life: Wittgenstein, Intentionality, and Romanticism*, Chicago: University of Chicago Press, 1997, pp. 121–32.
3 Stanley Cavell, *Conditions Handsome and Unhandsome: The Constitution of Emersonian Perfectionism*, Chicago: University of Chicago Press, 1990, p. 83.
4 Wittgenstein, "Philosophy: Sections 86–93 of the So-Called 'Big Typescript' (Catalog Number 213)," James Klagge and Alfred Nordmann (eds.), *Philosophical Occasion 1912–1951*, Indianapolis: Hackett Publishing Company, 1993, p. 171.
5 Cavell, *This New Yet Unapproachable America*, Albuquerque: Living Batch Press, 1989, p. 37.
6 *Leading a Human Life*, p. 7.
7 Immanuel Kant, *Critique of Pure Reason*, trans. Paul Guyer and Allen W. Wood, Cambridge: Cambridge University Press, 1997, B132, p. 247.
8 Ibid., B130, p. 245.
9 Ibid., B224, p. 299; B232, p. 304.
10 Ibid., A546–7/B575–5, p. 540. Cf. also Kant, *Foundations of the Metaphysics of Morals*, trans. Lewis White Beck, Indianapolis: The Bobbs–Merrill Company, 1959, "How is a Categorical Imperative Possible?" [453–6], pp. 72–74, especially "I recognize myself qua intelligence as subject to the law of the world of understanding and to the autonomy of the will" [453–4], pp. 72–3.
11 Kant, *Foundations*, [391], p. 8.
12 Kant, *Foundations*, [463], p. 83.
13 Salomon Maimon, "Letter to Kant, September 20, 1791," Kant, *Philosophical Correspondence*, ed. and trans. Arnulf Zweig, Chicago: The University of Chicago Press, 1967, p. 175.
14 J. G. Fichte, "Letter to J. F. Flatt, November or December 1793," cited in Daniel Breazeale, "Fichte's *Aenesidemus* Review and the Transformation of German

Idealism," *The Review of Metaphysics* XXXIV (1981), p. 548. For further surveys of the reception and revision of Kant at the hands of Fichte, Reinhold, *et al.*, see Frederick C. Beiser, *The Fate of Reason: German Philosophy from Kant to Fichte*, Cambridge, MA: Harvard University Press, 1987, esp. Chapters 8–10 on Reinhold, Schulze, and Maimon.

15 J. G. Fichte, *The Science of Knowledge*, ed. and trans. Peter Heath and John Lachs, Cambridge: Cambridge University Press, 1982, p. 9.

16 Kant, "Open Letter on Fichte's *Wissenschaftslehre*, August 7, 1799," *Philosophical Correspondence*, p. 253.

17 J. S. Beck, "Letter to Kant, June 17, 1794," *Philosophical Correspondence*, p. 215; emphasis added.

18 Onora O'Neill has been the most eloquent defender in recent Kant studies of this critical standpoint, arguing that principles of subject activity, theoretical and practical alike, can be *vindicated* as principles to which we are always already implicitly committed in our already existent subject activity, though they cannot be *validated* by reference to any substantial reality apart from that activity. See O'Neill, "Vindicating Reason," Paul Guyer (ed.), *The Cambridge Companion to Kant*, Cambridge: Cambridge University Press, 1992, and O'Neill, "Reason and Autonomy in *Grundlegung III*," O'Neill, *Constructions of Reason*, Cambridge: Cambridge University Press, 1989. Reason together with its principles is for us, as she puts it, an always present *factum* of our lives as subjects, not a *datum* to be explained from without. ("Reason and Autonomy," p. 65.)

19 Friedrich Hölderlin, "Judgment and Being," *Essays and Letters on Theory*, ed. and trans. Thomas Pfau, Albany: State University of New York Press, 1988, p. 37.

20 Ibid.

21 Ibid.

22 Ibid.

23 Ibid., p. 38.

24 Ibid.

25 Ibid.

26 Ibid., p. 37.

27 Hölderlin, "Preface to *Hyperion*," cited in Dieter Henrich, "Hölderlin on Judgment and Being," trans. Abraham Anderson, *The Course of Remembrance and Other Essays on Hölderlin*, Stanford: Stanford University Press, 1997, p. 84.

28 Henrich, "Hölderlin in Jena," trans. Taylor Carman, *The Course of Remembrance*, p. 107.

29 Henrich, "Hegel and Hölderlin," trans. Taylor Carman, *The Course of Remembrance*, p. 124.

30 Note, however, that Fichte's explanation is peculiarly crossed by doubt and that Fichte himself falls into revision after revision of his system, never settling on any single explanation. See Eldridge, *Leading a Human Life*, pp. 63–71 on the succession of continual cycles of procession (fall) and epistrophe (return) in Fichte's writing.

31 Henrich, "Hölderlin on Judgment and Being," p. 82.

32 Richard Velkley, "Introduction," Henrich, *The Unity of Reason: Essays on Kant's Philosophy*, Cambridge, MA: Harvard University Press, 1994, p. 2.

33 Henrich, "Hegel and Hölderlin," p. 128.

34 Ibid., p. 134.

35 Ibid.

36 James H. Donelan, "Hölderlin's Poetic Self-Consciousness," *Philosophy and Literature* 26 (2002), 140.

37 Ibid., pp. 136 ff.

38 Ibid., pp. 138–9; see also Hölderlin, "On the Difference of Poetic Modes," *Essays and Letters on Theory*, pp. 82–88, where Hölderlin presents a large table (p. 87) of succes-

sions of basic tones, languages or dictions, and effects for each of naïve poetry, energetic poetry, and idealistic poetry.

39 All references to this essay will be to the version of it in *Essays and Letters on Theory*, pp. 62–82, and will be given by page number in the text.

40 See Robert Brandom's discussion of sapience vs. sentience in his *Making It Explicit: Reasoning, Representing, and Discursive Commitment*, Cambridge, MA: Harvard University Press, 1994, pp. 4–8.

12

AUTOBIOGRAPHICAL CONSCIOUSNESS

Wittgenstein, private experience, and the "inner picture"

Garry L. Hagberg

I

Positioned on the edge of solipsism, it was Schopenhauer who famously asserted that the world is my representation. We know that Schopenhauer's philosophy exerted a strong influence on the early Wittgenstein, whose equally famous – and equally metaphysical – claim in his *Tractatus* that the world is all that is the case, resoundingly announced his early entanglement with grand metaphysics (if in linguistic, rather than ontological, form).[1] Schopenhauer's claim makes the world a mental, or individualistically interior, representation that is, indeed, private to the mind of the individual whose representation it is, a representation that constitutes at once the contents and the boundaries of private consciousness. It is thus, to borrow Thomas Nagel's phrase, not only a claim concerning the necessity of entering that individual's consciousness (where this possibility is denied by the solipsist and debated by others) to know *what it is like* to be that individual; it is, for Schopenhauer, a far stronger claim. The world is not a larger, realist place within which that individual consciousness is contingently situated, but rather the very *idea* of the world is unintelligible without *first* positing the existence of an individual consciousness that constructs it as, indeed, its *own* representation.

This powerful claim was not far from the articulated view of the young and early Wittgenstein in his *Notebooks, 1914–16* and the *Tractatus* – with which he was, in his far deeper reflections in his rapidly maturing remarks in the *Blue Book* and then his fully mature remarks of *Philosophical Investigations*, to wage a kind of reverse-Oedipal battle with his former self (the first skirmishes with that twenty-five- to twenty-seven-year-old self breaking out in his lectures of 1932). In the *Notebooks* entry of June 11, 1916, Wittgenstein, having already said that he knows that this world exists – and one might reasonably load a good deal of metaphysical freight into his word "this," i.e., he means it in the proprietary sense of Schopenhauer's "my" – observes that he is placed in it just as an eye is placed in its visual field. Rather like an analytical commentary on Schopenhauer's grand claim, this striking way of putting how it is we are positioned in this world is a precise analogy to the visual field understood as the content and the boundary of our experience. Giving the claim a chiseled precision, he adds the potent sentence "That life is the world," i.e., the world, its substance and its extension, is given within the mental, or interior experiential analogue to the visual field of the eye, that is the private, individual consciousness. Returning to the theme on July 24, 1916, he writes simply "The World and Life are one" (which became *Tractatus* 5.621), but then adds three sentences: the first, "Physiological life is of course not 'Life'," defies any physicalistic reductionism and emphasizes by the exclusion of the physiological the mental, the psychological interior. But then the second sentence – as though anticipating his much later undercutting of the entire behaviorism-versus-Cartesianism dichotomy – quickly rejects the polar opposite: "And neither is psychological life." Having evaded these twin reductive exclusions, he states the more encompassing, and more Schopenhauerian, claim: "Life is the world." And the Schopenhauerian character of this pronouncement is further brought out in his entry of August 7: "The I is not an object," that is, to put it one way that seems consistent with at least the spirit if not the letter of his remarks in those years, the referent of the first-person pronoun is not one among many other particulars in the world that exist autonomously from their names, in this case the "I," but rather is itself the necessary condition of that world. That referent, like the referent of Schopenhauer's "my" in "my world," is, like the visual field of the eye, not *itself* encountered, not *itself* seen.[2]

Thus Wittgenstein adds four days later "I objectively confront every object. But not the I." And then closing, in a drop of grammar, whatever small gap there might remain between the early Wittgensteinian and the Schopenhauerian senses of these claims, on August 12, 1916 writes "The I makes its appearance in philosophy through the world's being *my* world."

This conception of the self as an interior consciousness whose boundary we do not perceive and whose nonencountered existence is the precondition for the world – for that consciousness, a world that is *mine* without remainder – takes a central place in the *Tractatus*. In 5.633, Wittgenstein encapsulates, and advances, the Schopenhauerian points above: "Where *in* the world is a metaphysical subject to be found?"; his italicized "*in*" now calling attention to the notion that the I, the self, is *not* an object like others in the world that we come across, identify, describe, confirm-as-existing, and so forth. He continues (anticipating his debate with an interlocutor who consistently voices philosophical positions showing the grip of philosophical pictures): "You will say that this is exactly like the case of the eye and the visual field." Saying just that, however, implicitly leaves open the possibility of encountering the eye itself as an object in, or – differently – the limit of, that visual field, and so Wittgenstein adds: "But really you do *not* see the eye." And then, advancing the argument in favor of this conception, makes the point that the role the eye plays in the visual experience is, as it were, *offstage*: there is nothing observable "*in the visual field* [*that*] allows you to infer that it is seen by an eye," the consciousness of selfhood, on this model or picture, functioning analogously as (to cast the matter in terms reminiscent of Kant) nonperceived precondition for experience. And he had prepared the way for these observations with 5.632: "The subject does not belong to the world: rather, it is a limit of the world," where that was in turn prepared for by his famous remark in 5.62 concerning what he there identified as the element of truth in solipsism: "The world is *my* world: this is manifest in the fact that the limits of *language*" – now adding a densely compressed articulation of the picture of exclusively inward, or private, language with which he will also do battle in *Philosophical Investigations* and change the course of modern philosophy as a result – "(of that language which alone I understand) mean the limits of *my* world." Thus the Schopenhauerian metaphysics is transmuted from an ontological to a linguistic thesis, and it reaches its culmination in 5.641: "The philosophical self is...the metaphysical subject, the limit of the world—not a part of it." And, as a limit, the self is, indeed, the *only* limit: in 6.431, we find "So too at death the world does not alter, but comes to an end," thus reaffirming the Schopenhauerian–Wittgensteinian claim that any intelligible talk of an existent world will be, ipso facto, of a mind-dependent one; and then, in 6.4311, "Death is not an event in life: we do not live to experience death," and a sentence later, linking this to the deep analogy of the philosophical self and the eye and its visual world: "Our life has no end in just the way in which our visual field has no limits."

All of this, to this point, casts light on the metaphysical picture that rests beneath all of these self-defining utterances; this conceptual model, or picture, is expressed with the very greatest linguistic density in 5.63: "I am my world." The philosophical intuitions concerning the nature of the self that are formed and fueled by the conceptual picture Wittgenstein has adumbrated in his early writings in fact account for a good deal of our attraction to autobiographical writing. To the extent that we all-too-naturally think of the self and its place in its world in a fashion consistent with Wittgenstein's early position, we then all-too-easily construe autobiographical writing as a special *kind* of writing: a kind that promises not only a glimpse of the world as seen through other eyes (which would be interesting or magnetic enough), but rather a glimpse – or indeed a sustained, long look – into *another* world, a world that is, in the foregoing metaphysical and consciousness-dependent sense, "*my*" world, i.e., the world of the autobiographer's. And as such, we thus think of autobiographical writing as a kind of literary antidote to the true element of solipsism to which Wittgenstein referred within the larger context of his Tractarian metaphysics, and we – if only in a sense that could never attain true or complete entry into the mind of the other but still holds out the promise of other-mind understanding – expect a view not merely of what it is like for another to live in our world, but rather the far more personally and philosophically compelling view *into another's world*. But every component of this picture, this way of intuitively modeling the conscious self in its autonomous world and then subsequently longing to cross the skeptical divide into the mind-world of the other, Wittgenstein battled against in his mature philosophy. Bewitching forms of language, lodging conceptual confusion deep in the intuitive substrate, inculcate in us not metaphysical truths of self-consciousness, but rather misleading pictures that shape all of our subsequent thinking on the subject. And it would be bewitching linguistic forms that Wittgenstein came to identify as the enemy – the enemy of conceptual clarity – during, and increasingly strongly after, his 1932 lectures. And the following of this struggle against these earlier, and seemingly natural, ways of thinking – ways of seeing consciousness and selfhood – should prove of immediate relevance to an increasingly full and increasingly clear account of the position of the self investigating itself, i.e., of autobiographical consciousness.

Consider the striking difference in method, tone, and what one might call *way of seeing* the issue, in the *Blue Book* (dictated to his Cambridge pupils in 1933–34):

> The difficulty which we express by saying "I can't know what he sees when he (truthfully) says that he sees a blue patch" arises from the idea that "knowing what he sees" means: "seeing that which he also sees"; not, however, in the sense in which we do so when we both have the same object before our eyes: but in the sense in which the object seen would be an object, say, in his head, or in *him*. The idea is that the same object may be before his eyes and mine, but that I can't stick my head into his (or my mind into his, which comes to the same) so that the *real* and *immediate* object of his vision becomes the real and immediate object of my vision too. By "I don't know what he sees" we really mean "I don't know what he looks at," where "what he looks at" is hidden and he can't show it to me; it is *before his mind's eye*. Therefore, in order to get rid of this puzzle, examine the grammatical difference between the statements "I don't know what he sees" and "I don't know what he looks at," as they are actually used in our language.
>
> (p. 61)[3]

Wittgenstein, now in a different voice from that of his former Tractarian self, is not stating a metaphysical limit of experience and showing something of the solipsism that cannot within the limits of our world, the limits of our language, be said ("what the solipsist *means* is right"[4]). He is, rather, asking if the very formulation of the problem (now demoted to a "puzzle") can make *sense*, and the tribunal that judges that question will not be Schopenhauerian metaphysics of selfhood, but ordinary linguistic usage. Looking to see how such phrases *are* used in our language will break the hold of the picture, which it does by calling into question the very sense of the various articulations of that picture. Now Wittgenstein is placing that picture-driven and conceptually bewitching language up against the standards of our *usage*, and he will go on to conclude that there indeed can be, and are, contexts of human discourse within which we intelligibly speak of not knowing what someone sees, but these will prove soberingly unlike the problem that other-minds skepticism and mind-enclosed solipsism see here: they do not reduce to the problem of not being able to get access to the inner content – the putative *immediate* content – of his experience. And similarly, he observes in the subsequent discussion that, in regard to the concept "person," we are at liberty to choose from multifarious, context-sensitive usages that, as he tellingly suggests, amount to choosing "between many different kinds of analogy" (p. 62).[5] Analogies for personhood, for the self, for consciousness, exert great power on our thinking, and to think of consciousness as a locked chamber, to think of the contents of that chamber as perception that will thus seem ineluctably private, to think of our experiencing of the world as hidden, but hidden inwardly, all conspire in favor of the Schopenhauerian – early-Wittgensteinian conception of the self and its world, and that way of picturing the positioning of consciousness in turn fuels the kind of fascination with autobiographical revelation mentioned above. The breaking of that spell is accomplished in language, and thus Wittgenstein, in the final pages of the *Blue Book*, turns to the instructive particularities of linguistic usage of the first-person pronoun that loosen the grip of those analogies, those pictures. He is showing, if not quite yet explicitly saying, that understanding the variegated grammar of the "I" is necessary if we are to understand the nature of the consciousness that defines selfhood, in a way unlike that which his former self envisioned.

Both calling a troublemaking group of phrases to the court of usage and picking up a thematic thread from his earlier philosophy – though now addressing it in a transformative manner – he writes:

> What tempted me to say "it is always I who see when anything is seen," I could also have yielded to by saying: "whenever anything is seen, it is *this* which is seen," accompanying the word "this" by a gesture embracing my visual field (but not meaning by "this" the particular objects which I happen to see at the moment). One might say, "I am pointing at the visual field as such, not at anything in it." And this only serves to bring out the senselessness of the former expression.
>
> (p. 64)

Wittgenstein then articulates directly and forcefully the way in which we are all-too-easily misled into thinking that the foregoing metaphysical utterances possess meaning just as do nonmetaphysical expressions, "for we wrongly compare our case with one in which the other person can't understand what we say because he lacks a certain information" (p. 65), and then adds, as if writing an abbreviated recipe for the sustained labors of *Philosophical Investigations* to follow, "(This remark can only become clear if we understand the connection between grammar and sense and nonsense)." The grammars of the self, of the "I," of consciousness, do not behave, on inspection, at all like the way we expected under the influence of misleading analogies, bewitching language, and conceptual pictures, and indeed we will be enabled to see those grammars as exhibited in usage clearly, nonprismatically, *only* if we therapeutically free ourselves of their domination. (That therapeutic project we will examine below, in his remarks on consciousness in *Philosophical Investigations*.[6]) And he is writing in

self-defense, against an anticipated interlocutor who will insist that, wholly independently of any tribunal of usage, he knows he means something intelligible
and profound by his Schopenhauerian utterances on self and world. Against this
expected reply – and very plausibly a reply made by his own former, Tractarian
self, in the early 1930s – he writes: "The meaning of a phrase is not a mental
accompaniment to the expression. Therefore the phrase 'I think I mean something by it' or 'I'm sure I mean something by it,' which we so often hear in
philosophical discussions to justify the use of an expression is for us no justification at all. We ask: '*What* do you mean?,' i.e., 'How do you use this expression?'"
(p. 65). And that test, using the measure of intelligible usage, is one that the
metaphysical utterances concerning the "I" cannot pass, which the final part of
the *Blue Book* sets out to demonstrate on the level of grammatical detail. The
work he undertakes in those pages of the *Blue Book* is far too intricate to recount
fully here, but a few passages may stand for the whole.

Exposing the influence of misleading analogies, Wittgenstein observes that
when we use the word "I" as a subject in a sentence, we can far too easily believe
the illusion, created by the empirical fact that we do not use it because we recognize a given person by his bodily characteristics, that we really use the word to
refer to a bodiless something, an inner, metaphysically hidden ego that has its
seat in our body, but is of a different ontological kind from it (p. 59). And *that*
conception of selfhood is, of course, foundational to the Schopenhauerian meta-
physic and the correlative conception of autobiographical revelation; it is
fundamental to the entire conception of the reading of an autobiography as a
philosophical event, i.e., looking – to the extent that we can use language – into
the mind of another with the pre-later-Wittgensteinian metaphysics. And of the
sense of metaphysical privacy endemic to that way of thinking, he writes "When
I say 'Only this is seen,' I forget that a sentence may come ever so natural to us
without having any use in our calculus of language" (pp. 65–6).

But the conception of the self – and thus the subject of autobiography – as an
inner point of consciousness whose seat is, contingently, the body, is a picture that
dies hard. It is, as we now know, preserved, even against our better judgment,[7] by
the illusions of grammar. He writes "Now the idea that the real I lives in my body
is connected with the peculiar grammar of the word 'I,' and the misunderstandings this grammar is liable to give rise to" (p. 66). At this stage of his development
Wittgenstein draws a contrast (one to be made with much greater subtlety in
Philosophical Investigations and his mature writings on the philosophy of psychology)
between categories of cases where "I" is used as an object and those where it is
used as a subject. If I refer to my broken arm, the bump on my forehead, or the
fact that I have grown six inches (p. 66), I am using the first-person pronoun in the
I-as-object sense; conversely, if I say that I think it will rain, or I see an elephant, or
I hear a distant flute, or I have a toothache, I am using the first-person pronoun in
the "I-as-subject" sense. The distinguishing mark of the former category of usage is
that it involves the recognition of a person, where, Wittgenstein pointedly adds,
there is (however remote) a possibility of error, e.g., in an automobile accident I may

feel a pain in my arm, in disoriented confusion see my neighbor's broken arm, and mistakenly (probably very briefly) think it mine, or I could look into the rear-view mirror, see a bumped head, and take it (momentarily) as mine. There is, importantly, no such possibility of even the most fleeting error in the "subjective" cases of having a toothache, hearing a flute, seeing an elephant.

That the pseudosentences formed by the words "But are you sure it is you who sees the elephant?," "But are you sure it is you who has the toothache?," are nonsensical linguistic curiosities is self-evident – and that they convey a hint of metaphysical depth is telling. Such linguistic curiosities transgress the boundaries of sense; they are, Wittgenstein observes, not only bad moves, but "no move of the game at all" (p. 67).[8] It is, indeed, impossible to "moan with pain by mistake, having mistaken someone else for me" (p. 67). Thus, he encapsulates the point here, to make a statement about one's pain using the first-person pronoun is no more a statement *about* that person than is the moaning of that person.[9] The conflation of these twin categories of cases – indeed very close to what Ryle famously termed a "category mistake"[10] – yields strong and deeply misleading support for the conception of metaphysical privacy that is at the heart of the Schopenhauerian–early-Wittgensteinian way of thinking that so quickly generates the correlated picture of autobiographical consciousness. If we can be wrong about the arm or the bump, perhaps we can be wrong about the pain, thus driving a wedge between ourselves and our embodied experience, making that embodiment seem contingent and, in a metaphysical sense, superfluous to who we truly are – which in turn makes a Cartesian interior seem to be precisely what we want autobiographical writing to report on[11] and the "walled garden"[12] to which we want, as readers, entry. Or, to take the grammatical conflation the other way (and thus cause different metaphysical trouble), we might all too easily think that because there exists no logical room for error in the "subjective" cases, that there similarly exists none in the objective, and we respond to any imagined counterexamples (of the automobile-accident kind above) by saying that we never make errors about what we *seem* to see or experience, thus driving a wedge between ourselves and the world we inhabit and with which we interact.[13] And this in turn, through an appeal to a variant of the sense-data picture of human experience, makes our experience seem incorrigible within the Cartesian interior, and thus when we turn to autobiography it will be again – and here the two kinds of conflations, the subjective category of I-usages assimilated to the objective and vice versa, converge – the truthful presentation of that interior content that we will want and that we will think of as autobiographical truth. And if we, or some parts of us, insist that regardless of the disentangling of grammatical conflations that might preserve categorical clarity with regard to usages of the first-person pronoun, the word "I" still must mean one determinate thing, Wittgenstein reminds us that the first-person pronoun is a tool, an instrument in our language, with a variety of context-sensitive employments: "The word 'I' does not mean the same as 'L.W.' even if I am L.W., nor does it mean the same as the expression 'the person who is now speaking'" (p. 67). The mistake to make at precisely this juncture would be to thus believe that "L.W." and "I" in this case mean *different* things – that would be to cling to a fixed-referent conception of meaning-determination, where each word functions as, or like, a name. So he adds: "But that doesn't mean: that 'L.W.' and 'I' mean different things. All it means is that these words are different instruments in our language" (p. 67).

Such observations do not, of course, *replace* one philosophical picture with another: they, by contrast, loosen the grip of the picture and the way of seeing the problem that is enforced by that picture. This deeper philosophical process brings a kind of light, or a new way of seeing, not accessible when, more superficially and conventionally, the picture in question is merely supplanted by another. And such transformations of our ways of seeing problems, invariably within particularized contexts of inquiry, just is the process and progress of the later philosophy in its full maturation. Emphasizing that the meaning of a term or an expression depends entirely on our use of it, Wittgenstein, in the closing passages of the *Blue Book*, writes – against a way of seeing codified in his early writings – "Let's not imagine the meaning as an occult connection the mind makes between a word and a thing, and that this connection *contains* the whole usage of a word as the seed might be said to contain the tree" (pp. 73–4). Transmuted to the understanding of autobiography, the meaning determined by the occult connection would constitute something of a holy grail of other-understanding: not only knowledge of the other's Cartesian interior, but, in a grander metaphysical Schopenhauerian manner, the world as represented in that other's inner-meaning-laden consciousness. But that conception, that picture, of the interior self and its meaning-determining occult processes, if only a myth born of misleading analogies and grammatical conflations, must be intricately removed in order to rightly grasp the nature of the self and its contents as revealed in our autobiographical practices. With that thought, we turn – having seen both Wittgenstein's starting point on these issues and his middle-period reaction against his own former way of thinking – to the intricate removal of misconceptions of consciousness of his late, mature work. Only this kind of removal will allow a clarified view of the richly human autobiographical endeavors in which we engage.

II

In *Philosophical Investigations* §416, Wittgenstein's imagined interlocutor suggests that, because we humans agree in saying that we see, hear, feel, and so forth, we must thus be our own witnesses that we have *consciousness*. Mindful of the snares of language, of misleading analogies, and of the necessity of context for making intelligible, sense-bearing moves within a language-game, Wittgenstein replies "But how strange this is! Whom do I really inform if I say 'I have consciousness'?" And then turning the focus from communicating the fact of our consciousness to others to self-reporting, asks "What is the purpose of saying this to myself...?" And he reminds us that there *are* cases, contexts, in which we might tell someone who witnesses our fainting spell, "I am conscious again," but the implicit warning is that such cases are, on the level of grammatical appearance, similar to the interlocutor's philosophical utterances, but in truth nothing like them at all. Pursuing this contrast between grammatically disguised nonsense and the intelligible, he begins §417 with the question "Do I observe myself, then, and perceive that I am seeing or conscious?" He dismantles the apparent but deeply misleading sense of obviousness about this in layers. First, we find the concept of *observation* called into question. Wittgenstein does not fully undertake such an investigation here (he did describe his book as "a machine to think with" and does characteristically leave a good deal of work to the reader), but if we were extensively to consider cases in which we readily and unproblematically speak of *observing* a thing or situation, we would see that the case of self-consciousness is *nothing* like that – indeed to the point where we would feel disoriented in trying to apply the term "observation" to the situation at all. And the close reading of autobiographical self-investigation shows precisely this, as a number of cases considered below will suggest.

But then Wittgenstein, at the next layer, asks "Why not simply say 'I perceive I am conscious'?" This would, however, constitute a kind of thinly disguised conceptual recidivism, since the concept of *perception*, on a similar investigation, would seem equally remote, equally detached from the real language-games of self-investigation. Thus he asks, again in a kind of analytical shorthand, "But what are the words 'I perceive' for here?" This phrase, as an instrument in our language, would show *not* the true underlying nature of the ordinary case of consciousness, but rather, if applicable at all, only that our attention is disposed in a particular way. One might say (Wittgenstein does not, but a thorough investigation of the ground he is rapidly moving over would suggest it) that the phrase "I perceive I am conscious" is a kind of pleonasm of self-reportage for the cleaner "I am conscious." But these statements do not capture the ordinary case of a person's consciousness either, for in what cases do we *report*[14] on our states, and in what contexts do we *say* "I am conscious"? In the fainting case in which the *question* of consciousness has come to the fore, perhaps; in the stream of conscious life, never. This is a sentence grammatically similar to "I am hungry," "I am cold," "I am delighted," and, by slight extension, "we are not amused." And the sense of these remarks lends illegitimate support to their grammatically similar self-report of consciousness, one that can deliver only a false promise of intelligibility.

But how then should we characterize the evident fact that most of us go through life conscious most of the time (and *that* – the particularities and nuances of that experience that is for each of us distinctive to us – is again how we think of the subject matter of autobiographical writing)? In §418, Wittgenstein asks "Is my having consciousness a fact of experience?" And he assembles some stray thoughts that seem to endorse, indeed to necessitate, such a general claim: don't we say that persons have consciousness while trees and stones do not? And (in §419) if we speak of a tribe with a chief, must not that chief have *consciousness*? "Surely," he continues the voicing of this grammatically misled line of thinking, "we can't have a chief without consciousness!" There are contexts in which we speak of consciousness as an attribute or as a state of a person, including ourselves, but there is a deep logical difference (disguised by grammatical similarity) between saying that green or hot are properties some things possess and others don't and that consciousness is a property some things have and others don't, and so it is a property *of that kind*. Some chairs are green, others are not, so we can ask how many chairs in a room are green, how many not. It would transgress conceptual-logical limits to inquire in turn, however, into the nature of greenness itself – the disorienting generality of this question (a question of a metaphysical kind logically *very* different from either a physicist's question about the wave-behavior of green color, or the neurophysiologist's question concerning the ocular system that allows us to differentiate green from blue) is a symptom of our having lost our link to legitimate moves in the language-game. Similarly, various kinds of things come into, and pass out of, existence in all kinds of contexts; such particularized contexts are, again, *very* remote from the generalized question concerning not, say, when the self-reflective awareness of a kind evinced in Petrarch's sonnets or the hyperromanticized, nervously over-wrought self-image epitomized by Goethe's *Werther* came into existence, but rather – although grammatically similar but logically different in the extreme – what the nature of existence, or indeed of Being, *itself*[15] might be. If some chairs are green, and some exist, is then existence not a property? If some entities are conscious, and others not, is not consciousness a property? And here again, the word "as," versus "is," condenses a cloud of philosophy into a drop of grammatical difference.

Wittgenstein asks if we cannot imagine that the people around us are automata, that they lack consciousness, and that, e.g., the liveliness of a group of children is the result only of automatism (§420). He predicts that we will, in one reaction to this suggestion, find the words, the sentences, expressing this "automata view" of persons becoming quite meaningless when they are, as it were, held up against the reality of the persons. Or as a second reaction to the suggestion, we might momentarily provoke an uncanny feeling in ourselves. He then speaks of this in terms of "seeing a living human being as an automaton…," and therein lies the grammatical cue (which relates directly to his important remarks on aspect-perception and the phenomena of "seeing-as" in Part II, §xi) that calls for more elucidation than Wittgenstein gives it in this passage of his "machine." That we can try to see persons as automata (and if slightly successful, experience the sense of the uncanny) suggests, erroneously, that if we aren't seeing them as automata, then we must, in the ordinary case, be seeing them as something else – which in this context would obviously be characterized as beings-with-consciousness. This is a grammatically parallel construction that leads us astray precisely because, in the ordinary case, we don't see persons *as* anything; we see that it *is* a person, or group of children, etc., before us. And those we see, not on an additive model (which the misapplication of the seeing-as construction would here strongly suggest) where the perception of the person is analyzable into its constituent parts with the separable property of consciousness being added to an isolated body or a humanoid mechanism, but in terms of the irreducible, unanalyzable, "attitude towards a soul," *Eine Einstellung zur Seele*, of which Wittgenstein writes.[16] That this distinctive attitude is *basic* to human beings, i.e., fundamental to *any* understanding of who, what, and how we are, is what gives the strength to the ordinary nature of our person-perception sufficient to make the first reaction Wittgenstein articulates common, where the words and sentences expressing the automata-view quickly seem meaningless. This, to express it in a drop of grammatical difference, is the triumph of "is" over "as." The picturing of the consciousness of the person as ontologically distinct from, and only contingently *related* to, what we will then call *embodiment*, is fueled, in part, by the notion that we see persons as entities-with-the-property-of-consciousness, and it is not then long until we are, in keeping with this dualistic picture of selfhood, asking how we can – or, solipsistically, *if* we can – gain access to that inner realm, and we then look to autobiography in that light, with those philosophical motivations and their correlated expectations. In short, this is yet another juncture of thought at which a misconstrual of the self, as a kind of grammatical–optical illusion, makes us inquire into the nature of consciousness *itself*, i.e., in isolation from the human practices, engagements, and interactions that assure the intelligibility of the concept of consciousness in the first place, and this in turn causes us to deeply miscast the nature of autobiography and, particularly, autobiographical truth.

In *Philosophical Investigations* §426, Wittgenstein contrasts the chiseled precision and seeming clarity of the pictures, the conceptual models, we employ in philosophical thinking about sense and meaning with the actual diverse uses we make of the concepts under scrutiny, saying that the latter invariably seem, by contrast with the former, "something muddied." He likens this to our conceptual tendencies in thinking about set theory, where "the form of expression we use seems to have been designed for a god," i.e., the way we tend to speak of such issues *in the abstract* sounds like what he now, in his mature philosophy, understands to be the falsifying neatness – indeed, a false rigor – of the way of thinking given articulation in the *Tractatus* (where the true rigor is now to acknowledge, comprehend, and painstakingly earn an overview of the particularities of the concept in question). That imagined godlike view in set theory, or in the philosophy of language in determining sense and meaning, is perfectly parallel to the case of picture-driven autobiographical thinking: that godlike perspective – precisely the position we desire to occupy in understanding the mind of another and which, on the model in question, we hope autobiography might provide or approximate – is possessed, he writes, only by one "who knows what we cannot know," and then adding a phrase that renders the connection we are now considering between a conception of sense and meaning and a conception of autobiographical content explicit, "he sees the whole of each of those infinite series and he sees into human consciousness."

But Wittgenstein as quickly places his mature thought against that reiteration of his old way of thinking, saying that those icy pictures where everything would be fixed *"unambiguously,"* high and remote from any genuine use in human contexts, are like pontifical vestments we might don but nevertheless can do nothing with, since we lack what would give such vestments meaning and purpose. In the actual use of expressions, he adds, "we make detours, we go by side-roads." Autobiographical writing is similarly a process of taking detours and following up side roads; the autobiographer is, rightly if more messily understood, not in the position of the god with regard to himself, nor do we, as readers, ascend to that Olympian position. But those pictures, again, die hard; we might well say to ourselves in such contexts of person-interpretation (or any biographical project, broadly construed) that "while I was speaking to him I did not know what was going on in his head" (§427). But Wittgenstein adds, diffusing the misleading power of the picture and thus showing the great importance a seemingly small grammatical restructuring can assume, that, in saying this, "we only mean what elsewhere we should mean by saying: we should like to know what he is thinking." And thinking is an activity that we can *make* seem occult and ineluctably private in accordance with the dualistic picture of the self that underlies the presently disputed way of construing autobiography – but it *need* not seem so.[17]

Thus §428 begins with the interlocutor's sentence "This queer thing, thought," and that misled remark only heightens the sense of mystery of first-person content and the sense that such thought is the private maker of the hidden Schopenhauerian world of the other. But the mature Wittgenstein of *Philosophical Investigations* counterposes "—but it does not strike us as queer when we are thinking. Thought does not strike us as mysterious while we are thinking, but only when we say, as it were retrospectively: 'How was that possible?'" In accordance with the picture, the genuine understanding of another person's thinking, another person's thought, would be a metaphysical impossibility; in accordance with a far less neat reality, such understandings, sometimes characterized as genuine in contexts where that word marks an important contrast, will come in a thousand different forms (it is perhaps literature that best provides the vast catalogue of cases of other- and self-understanding of precisely the kind Wittgenstein repeatedly suggested we assemble) – reminders of what we *actually*, contra the picture, say and do – in order to change our way of seeing, to loosen the grip of the falsely unifying picture. Returning to a theme from the *Blue Book*, where he reconsidered the question of a word as a sign, the "life" of that sign, and the dichotomy this terminology insinuates, in §432 Wittgenstein, having said that every sign *by itself* seems dead (having said what he did in the *Blue Book*, of course he is wary of this sign-versus-life distinction, although he does not record this wariness here), he states that the life comes from its *use*. No godlike speaker, as sole owner of inward meanings, breathes life into them. And if that is true, then we, as readers of autobiography, ought to be given our freedom from the false prison[18] of two deep misconstruals, in which we attempt to break out of ourselves and gain entry into the meaning-determining, or linguistically "life-breathing," mind of another. The position – of us, and of the autobiographer – is *wholly* different. It is the *use* in our language of self-descriptive, or self-investigative, terms that gives them their "life"; free of a misleading picture of autobiographical consciousness, we can begin to see the varied examples of autobiographical writing for what they are – instructive reminders, against the deceptions of generalizing theory, of what we do.

The sense that the *content* of lived experience, whatever else one says (or whatever Wittgenstein has said), is, as a brute fact of life, metaphysically private, is one that seems to want to survive Wittgenstein's reflections to this point, and there is good reason to think that this sense, however incompatible with all the ground Wittgenstein has covered and however clearly picture-driven in all the ways heretofore considered, was felt by Wittgenstein himself. For after finishing Part I of *Philosophical Investigations* in 1945, he turned (in 1946) to problems exclusively in the philosophy of psychology, to which he devoted the following three years almost without interruption. And it is not too long before the question of the content of experience comes up. In *Remarks on the Philosophy of Psychology*,[19] Volume 1, §109, Wittgenstein asks "Where do we get the concept of the 'content' of an experience from?" This idea, of course, co-conspires with those guilty conceptions and pictures, and in giving us a dualistic conceptual model for the content of experience, at the same time gives us a conceptual model for the content of autobiography. At this stage of his reflections the answer to his question is clear, and he wastes no time in answering it. He writes – giving voice to his early way of thinking even now, only a few years before his last writings in *On Certainty*[20] – "Well, the content of an experience is the private object, the sense-datum, the 'object' that I grasp immediately with the mental eye, ear, etc." That private object[21] would be the inner object upon which the private diarist introspects, and (for our present concerns) it would be the inner representation of world-constituting Schopenhauerian significance, knowable only to the autobiographer, and upon which that self-describing, self's-world-defining author introspects in order to capture the inner content for which the autobiographical writing serves as external descriptive–narrative counterpart. Thus Wittgenstein adds the phrase, "The inner picture." Reminding himself, and us, once again of the gulf that separates this picture from the particularities of our practices, he then asks "But where does one find one needs this concept?"

The notion of the private content of experience, its attendant conceptual confusions, and the misleading analogies that give rise to the notion in the first place (i.e., the concept of the inspection of an object as it shapes our parallel notion of introspection and inner object; the concept of a description of an outward object generating the deeply misled notion of expressive utterances,[22] or avowals, as inward-directed descriptions, and so forth) submerge and resurface recurrently throughout the remarks of this period, but it comes to the surface explicitly as late as §896, indicating that this is indeed, as a problem that first appeared in his earliest writings, never very far from Wittgenstein's concerns. He begins by announcing the topic, and then proceeds to articulate the impulse one feels to speak in ways dictated by the underlying picture:

> The *content* of experience. One would like to say "I see red *thus*," "I hear the note that you strike *thus*," "I feel pleasure *thus*," "I feel sorrow *thus*," or even "*This* is what one feels when one is sad, *this*, when one is glad," etc. One would like to people a world, analogous to the physical one, with these *thus*es and *this*es. But this makes sense only where there is a picture of *what* is *experienced*, to which one can point as one makes these statements.

"One would like," meaning to feel impelled in the grip of a picture, to people such a world with these "thuses and thises," and that is precisely what we do undertake if we regard autobiographical, or any kind of self-descriptive (dangerously put) or self-investigative writing, as the narrative externalization of that content. The *use* of such sentences is, again, very much unlike that suggested by the picture, and real introspection,[23] or self-reflection, as it *actually* occurs in contexts of human inquiry is the kind of thing we can see for what it is, without dualistic-prismatic distortions, only when free of the picture that would falsely give the "thuses and thises" a sense. And if we *cannot* point inwardly to the inner "what," how then should we proceed? Not by attempting to capture the essence of consciousness in the act of Cartesian introspection – where the content of experience is knowable only unto itself, and, in grander terms, where the world is made of those representations – but rather by *turning to cases*.

III

It was Plato who first wrote of the tripartite self, introducing near the beginning of our tradition a conceptual model of the self that, by its very structure, secured the possibility of both inner harmony, and if that is possible, inner disharmony. (He himself established this inner divisibility with an example of a person who, on seeing a fallen soldier in a ditch, feels arising in himself a morbid curiosity to more closely inspect the corpse but at the same time a higher inner voice instructing him to rise above this low impulse; he gives in, saying to himself "Go ahead, damn you, and feast your eyes on this banquet for sordid appetites!"[24]) Rousseau, in his *Confessions*,[25] describes himself in accordance with the conceptual model of an internally divided self, and one would initially think of this as a case that quite clearly suggests that the human phenomenon in which we are interested here is hermetically sealed within the Cartesian interior – we are after all speaking of *inner* disharmony. Rousseau writes, "Thus there began to form in me...a heart at once proud and affectionate, and a character effeminate and inflexible, which by always wavering between weakness and courage, between self-indulgence and virtue, has throughout my life set me in conflict with myself, to such an effect that abstinence and enjoyment, pleasure and prudence have alike eluded me."[26] It is all too easy to bring to this everything Wittgenstein encapsulated as "the inner picture." But then where indeed do we have a *need* for this concept? In understanding the sentences Rousseau employed to describe this characterological double-tendency, we need to *contextualize* Rousseau's remarks (as he himself does in the pages from which the passage is taken), considering cases of his deeds, his words, and combinations thereof in which one can see sometimes pride, sometimes a sentimental affection that seems incompatible with that proud heart, or inflexibility and courage manifest in one strand of his engagements with life, and weakness and self-indulgence manifest through another. And in understanding the result he describes, i.e., a person who is as a consequence at once enduringly anhedonic and chronically imprudent, we need, not access to a ghostly realm, but access to those multiple engagements in life, and a grasp of the way those many and diverse cases of human action and interaction do plausibly divide into each of the two strands. Moreover, it is a grasp of such cases, such particulars, that will give us an understanding of the person sufficient to see that this self-description is an exaggeration made in the interest of dramatic flair as well as neat conformity to, indeed, a philosophical picture.[27] Importantly, it is a grasp of those lived particulars that allows us to judge (or if "judge" is too harsh a word, to develop a sense of the veracity or the plausibility of) the self-description. We do *not* make this judgment by holding the sentence of self-description up against the inward psychic state to determine its correspondence to inner states of affairs. Where, as Wittgenstein inquires, *do* we need this picture?

When Jill Ker Conway describes Frederick Douglass as "the most articulate chronicler of the male American runaway slave's experience,"[28] the articulateness to which she refers is not Douglass's ability to describe an inner state in outward terms as the picture would suggest. And she puts the word "inner" to work in the way that we, in ordinary language, understand it: she writes that Douglass "begins the account of his life by showing the reader an inner world of emotional and physical suffering, and grief at betrayal, which is charged with romantic passion."[29] The depiction of the inner world is accomplished by showing him being torn from the security of his grandmother's cabin as a youth, teaching himself to read against all odds, his rejection of and disgust with the slaveholders, a life-defining fight with a particularly brutal slave driver, and the growing anger, disgust and unrelenting moral horror that led to that violent confrontation. It is formative experience, followed by a long strand of increasingly interconnected thought, speech, and action, that makes what we call his inner struggle intelligible, and the interconnections of that strand are strengthened in the retrospective writing. These are events, with an increasing sense of moral teleology, in a person's life that we would only call "external" or "outward" when thinking of them in relation to the inner picture. Thus it would be wrong, if in a sense a corrective (somewhat indeed like a ladder to be climbed and then kicked away), to say that we understand the inner through a grasp of the external, the outer. That way of putting the matter would lead us (i.e., grammatically mislead us) to see what we know of the person's life as *evidence* for the inner life – but the concept "inner," as Wittgenstein is showing, does not *work* like that. We understand the coincidence, deeply meaningful for Douglass, that during the speaking tours of his later years he found himself speaking in the courthouse just beside the very jail in which he had been incarcerated for his failed first break for freedom, not in terms of ontologically hidden deep inwardly knowable meanings, but in terms of the particularities of his experience and the context, or in Wittgenstein's sense, the form of life, within which those particularities assume significance.

Conway, noting an outburst of memoir-writing among women of the Progressive Era, turns to Jane Addams, and Conway observes that the "extensive use of conditional tenses and the passive voice"[30] gives rise to questions concerning what we might call the transparent sincerity of the memoir. Conway herself reaches the exaggerated conclusion – too general to be convincing – that, "We can be sure that whenever women autobiographers are hiding behind the passive voice and the conditional tense, they are depicting events in which they acted forthrightly upon a preconceived, rational plan."[31] Conway is surely right to say that the emergent patterns of such grammatical details in any autobiography are worth scrutiny, and that, at least in some cases, we thus arrive at a question concerning that autobiographical writing as describing or as *making* the character of that life; she goes wrong in asserting that we will invariably know the conclusion to reach in the face of such grammatical patterns. This is not at all to endorse a generic skepticism in such matters – we *can* know, but not in any way that does not arise from a nuanced, detailed grasp of the particulars of the life in question.[32] And in cases where we find autobiographical dissimulation of any one of countless kinds, we will judge the truth of what is written in relation to what we can and do sensibly call the inner life, but where that inner life is assessed in the manner of the Douglass case above, and not in terms of Wittgenstein's inner picture. The intentions of a person, against which we would judge the dissimulation, are not ontologically kept secrets.[33]

But there are, of course, secrets. Ellen Glasgow (insightfully discussed by Conway), writer of an autobiography depicting her life in the aristocratic South in late nineteenth- and early twentieth-century America, describes the moment of falling in love in a way that reminds us that Wittgenstein's "attitude towards a soul" runs along a continuum, from barely noticing the presence of a person (but still, most significantly, *barely*; i.e., the attitude is ineliminably present as constitutive of person-perception) to being acutely aware of one person's presence in a large crowded room – where one's attention is, seemingly beyond volition, magnetized to a single human focal point despite where one is visually looking. Glasgow writes "I felt my gaze drawn back to him by some invisible thread of self-consciousness,"[34] and she adds a passage later "What I knew, through some vivid perception, was that the awareness was not on my side

alone, that he was following my words and my gestures, that a circle of attraction divided us from those around us...." Her articulation of this vivid
perception provides an equally vivid description of the *Einstellung* in its height-
ened form, and she goes on to tell the tale of her seven-year secret affair with
the man in question (who was married). Looking back on that part of her life
and the way she lived it, she wrote "Only on the surface of things have I ever
trod the beaten path. So long as I could keep from hurting anyone else, I have
lived, as completely as it were possible, the life of my choice. I have been
free."[35] But secretly free: as Conway describes it, hers was "a private world
behind the mask of conformity."[36] There is indeed a secret here, and it is
perfectly sensible to speak of the mask of conformity behind which is lived the
real life. But when we see this kind of language at *work*, we see that the mask is
not one that conforms in any way to the philosophical picture of the inner
versus the outer; it is not a hidden truth *in that sense.*

Continuing his writings in late 1948 and early 1949 (that appeared as *Remarks
on the Philosophy of Psychology*), Wittgenstein wrote near the last of those
manuscripts some remarks of central relevance to the gaining of a non-picture-
driven, clarified overview of the hidden, or the secretive, against its
misconceptualizations. In them (published as *Last Writings on the Philosophy of
Psychology*, Volume 1, §974), he writes: "Nothing is hidden here; and if I were to
assume that there is something hidden the knowledge of this hidden thing would
be of no interest. But I can hide my thoughts from someone by hiding my diary.
And in this case I'm hiding something that might interest him." Glasgow's secret,
what one might term the ontological nature of her hiding, should be placed on a
continuum of cases next to the hiding of a diary and not at all next to the imagined metaphysical "hiding" (where indeed the inner is modeled on the outer and
the grammar of hiding objects generates the picture of hiding inner, private
objects) within a Cartesian interior. The life of her secret affair is *lived* by a
human being, not by a hermetically sealed point of inward consciousness, as is
what we will intelligibly call her public life that masks what we similarly understand – *in* the larger stream of life – as her private life. And if the
analogy-influenced direction of our thoughts turns back once again to the
notion that the mental, whatever else one may say about the real-versus-the-
metaphysical understanding of the hidden, is *always*, despite these usages, still
hidden in a special way, Wittgenstein writes in §976: "What I say to myself
silently he doesn't know: but again this isn't a matter of a 'mental process,'
although there may be a physical process taking place here which might do
instead of words spoken out loud if the other did know it. So also a physical
process here might be called 'hidden'." If we do make sense of the word
"hidden" here, it does not, against the inner picture, refer exclusively to the
mental – just as Glasgow lived both a public and a private life, but, if we contex-
tually render intelligible the words "public" and "private," we grasp them in a
way that speaks against the grammatically misled way of construing the meanings of those words.

Siegfried Sassoon's war memoir offers a description of events that yields a sense of what it means to find oneself in a position where one can only guess at another's private thoughts. He writes that his company had been issued orders to expand a newly captured German trench, but that just as they arrived he was handed new overriding orders to go back. He writes (with an honesty concerning the unclarity of motive that itself unsettles the privacy picture) "Just as we got there a second runner overtook us to say that my bombers were to go back again. I sent them back. I cannot say why I went on myself; but I did, and Kindle [his Lance Corporal] stayed with me."[37] He continues to describe a scene of increasing confusion in battle, where he comes upon the body of a just-killed German officer, and he writes of "an impulse" that made him "lift him up from the miserable ditch,"[38] propping the fallen enemy officer against a small embankment and wiping mud from the officer's eyes and mouth with his coat-sleeve. One might do worse than to characterize this as a momentary triumph of "an attitude towards a soul" over the competing conception of a dehumanized enemy, and what Wittgenstein describes as "discerning the humanity in a person" Sassoon illustrates very well. He writes "Hoisting him a little higher, I thought what a gentle face he had…," and he goes on to give voice to what he describes as his "dim" – but as is clear to any reader, rapidly strengthening – "sense of the futility which had put an end to this good-looking youth." (Here again, his *speculation* on that dim sense – his words are "Perhaps I had some dim sense…" – itself repudiates any residual notion to which we might at this late point cling of inward retrospective transparency.) Sassoon shortly reports that Kindle, for whom he felt a special responsibility owing both to his youth and his staying with Sassoon while the others retreated (no doubt only exacerbated because he himself did not feel sure he knew why he stayed when ordered to retreat), was killed, immediately provoking in him an extremely dangerous rage-fueled attack on the German sniper who found Kindle in his sights. Later, he returns to headquarters, passing the bodies of Kindle, the German, and very many others en route, and he was overcome by the dismayed sense of utter pointlessness of losing thousands of lives over a few hundred yards of bombed-out land in rural France. Here we will not say that we can only guess at his private thoughts: he has expressed them forcefully – and the only one we would *call* private is the last sense of dismay at irrational and wholesale slaughter, where privacy is brought into the language-game in order to mark the contrast between what he could and could not say to his superiors at headquarters. But of what follows, we may well say this: back in London, he and his fellow survivors, many of whom were now amputees, blinded by shrapnel, or shell-shocked (i.e., clearly men who would never see battle again), were, incredibly, required to attend lectures on the nature of trench warfare given by a young staff officer who had never been in the field. *There* we say, subsequent to the distinction between the private and the public having been put into play to mark the particular contrast that it does, that we can only imagine his private thoughts at that moment.

Wittgenstein, continuing his remarks, writes in §977: "'What I think silently to myself is hidden from him' can only mean that he cannot guess it, for this or that reason; but it does not mean that he cannot perceive it because it is in my soul." It is likely that the young lecturing staff officer could not guess much of Sassoon's private thoughts, for the particular reason that he knew nothing of the experience that preceded Sassoon's arrival in that room along with the more general reason that he had not seen battle himself. Knowing more of Sassoon's experience, we can do somewhat better at guessing; his thoughts, or rather the kinds of thoughts he might have had, are less hidden to us, and we say we can only guess at what he might have been thinking not as a marker of any metaphysically enforced epistemic limit, but because this is a way of expressing our comprehension of the experiential preconditions of outraged indignation. Such a sentence is not used to identify an object that is unperceivable because it is hidden within a soul.

Glasgow, as we saw, lived both a public and a private life, with the private, mostly, hidden; Sassoon had both public and private thoughts, where for reasons of military authority he had – in that context – to keep his private thoughts private. And indeed, some of them would have likely been beyond the understanding of, e.g., the inexperienced lecturer. But these forms of intelligible privacy and publicity are not for metaphysical reasons beyond the lecturer's reach – it is not that *kind* of question of "reach." One might have said, looking at Glasgow's life, "I wonder what's going on behind that public persona," and one might have said, of Sassoon in those lectures, "I wonder what's going on behind that face." Wittgenstein wrote, as his next remark late in those inquiries of 1949, "You look at a face and say 'I wonder what's going on behind that face?' – But you don't have to say that. The external does not have to be seen as a facade behind which the mental powers are at work." And in a variant of this passage, even better for our purposes, he wrote " – But you don't have to think that way. And if someone talks to me quite obviously holding nothing back then I'm not even tempted to think that way." We do not read "external" facial or bodily "signs" as evidence for inner events; these sentences do not function in that way. And we ought not to think that because in some suitably particularized circumstances we can and do ask what is going on behind the public display that thus all person-perception should be modeled on guessing, or collecting outward evidence for, the hidden interior: the human experience of sensing that someone is holding something back can put such sentences to work; such a sense is hardly, as Wittgenstein is observing, the key to the universal nature of all human interaction. We think in accordance with those phrases, those wonderings, *when*, and only when, we have occasion to do so.

In another war memoir, by Peter Ryan,[39] we are presented with a story of an eighteen-year-old Warrant Officer in New Guinea, recently occupied by the Japanese, whose troop movements he is sent (with hopelessly inadequate provisions) to monitor and report on. After extensive and truly extraordinary, unrelenting life-threatening difficulty behind Japanese lines, he was finally ordered back to the base, but just short of safety his group was attacked on what had been until recently fairly safe ground. He submerged himself under the slime of a disgusting swamp with only nostrils protruding as he felt in his ears the pressure caused by the boots of the Japanese soldiers as they squeezed through the adjacent mud. Later, having developed malaria, he was evacuated, and while walking down the jungle airstrip to the evacuation plane he passed a Japanese soldier, very obviously mortally wounded, under severe interrogation by Australian intelligence officers. Ryan wrote: "As I looked at his face, wasted with fever and suffering, I suddenly felt more akin to him than to the Australians who would not let him die in peace. His eyes, wonderfully large and soft, met mine. In that brief second I hoped he could read the message in my face." It is not only that Ryan discerned the humanity of the dying soldier and, here too *in extremis*, again showed the insuppressible presence of the *Einstellung*. It is more that in this fleeting moment of reflection upon a human face he wondered if what was going on in *him* was readable in his face. Such questions, in such contexts, do have meaning, and they can prove definitive of a person's subsequent character and allegiances; Ryan concludes his memoir with the rejection of his nationality and a newly cast and deeply felt sympathy for the sufferings of all soldiers in war. To understand this, and to comprehend the significance of his own question concerning the fundamental human solidarity the dying enemy may or may not have been able to read in his face, we need nothing of the "hidden" – whatever that might be – in the sense to which Wittgenstein is objecting, nothing private *in that sense*. We do, however, need something private in the intelligible, contextualized sense that we have seen in Glasgow and Sassoon. Ryan wrote that, well beyond his initial naive enthusiasm for what he expected to be the high adventure of war, that just before looking at the dying enemy soldier in that way, he had come to recognize "how useless your whole mission was, how futile and purposeless your death would have been, and, above all, when your sober but aching eye discerns that nobody whose business it might have been took the least trouble to see that you got at least a reasonable chance of living."[40] Where we wonder what is going on behind a face, or where we wonder if someone can see what is going on behind ours, what we need is at least a sense of, and ideally an intimate knowledge of, the *lived* life that stands behind the utterance, the gesture, or the facial expression in question. *That* is the true substance of biography and, self-reflectively, autobiography. And, as Wittgenstein is arguing, none of that is hidden in the metaphysical sense. Were it not for misleading grammatical analogies to hidden objects and the bewitchments of language that generate what Wittgenstein so compactly labeled "the inner picture," we would not, as he wrote in the variant to his remark 978 of March 1948, even be tempted to think that way.

Notes

1 Schopenhauer, *The Word as Will and Representation*, trans. E. F. J. Payne, vol. 1, §§ 1 and 10; vol. 2, chap. 1, New York: Dover, 1966; Wittgenstein, *Tractatus Logico-Philosophicus*, trans. D. F. Pears and B. F. McGuinness, London: Routledge & Kegan Paul, 1961. See, in this connection, the entry "Consciousness" in Hans-Johann Glock, *A Wittgenstein Dictionary*, Oxford: Blackwell, 1996, pp. 84–6, which I have found very helpful. The Schopenhauerian influence does not wane quickly: Glock notes that as late as Wittgenstein's lectures in 1930–33 (as recorded by G. E. Moore), he said "All that is real is the experience of the present moment" (p. 85).

2 Thomas Nagel, "What Is It Like To Be a Bat?" *Philosophical Review* 83 (1974), 435–50.

3 See Wittgenstein, *Notebooks, 1914–1916*, ed. and trans. G. E. M. Anscombe, Oxford: Blackwell, 1961, entry on Aug. 4, 1916 (p. 80).

4 Wittgenstein, *The Blue and Brown Books*, Oxford: Blackwell, 1958, p. 61.

5 See Glock, *A Wittgenstein Dictionary*, "Solipsism," pp. 348–52 for a succinct discussion and a helpful set of references throughout Wittgenstein's published and unpublished writings on this topic; the Schopenhauerian influences are helpfully brought out by Glock.

6 *The Blue Book*, p. 62. At this point Wittgenstein writes into his discussion an implicit justification of his own method. He observes that the word "personality" has no one legitimate heir any more than does the word "philosophy."

7 I discuss this more fully in "Davidson, Self-Knowledge, and Autobiographical Writing," *Philosophy and Literature* 26 (2002), 354–68.

8 I offer a fuller discussion of the language-game (and its significance for aesthetic understanding) in *Meaning and Interpretation: Wittgenstein, Henry James, and Literary Knowledge*, Ithaca: Cornell University Press, 1994, chap. 1, "Language Games and Artistic Styles," pp. 9–44.

9 I discuss some of these nuances of self-description in Wittgenstein's philosophy in "The Self, Speaking: Wittgenstein, Introspective Utterances, and the Arts of Self-Representation," *Revue Internationale de Philosophie* 219 (2002), 9–47.

10 Gilbert Ryle, *The Concept of Mind*, London: Hutchinson, 1949; see esp. "The Origin of the Category Mistake," pp. 18–23.

11 See my "Wittgenstein and the Question of True Self-Interpretation," Michael Krausz (ed.), *Is There a Single Right Interpretation?* University Park: Penn State Press, 2002, pp. 381–406.

12 For insightful (and instructively discordant) discussions of the picture of privacy and its attendant problems of self-knowledge in recent Wittgenstein-inspired philosophy, see Crispin Wright, *Rails to Infinity: Essays on Themes from Wittgenstein's* Philosophical Investigations, Cambridge, Mass.: Harvard University Press, 2001, sec. 3, "Privacy and Self-Knowledge," pp. 215–374; and John McDowell, *Mind, Value, and Reality*, Cambridge, Mass.: Harvard University Press, 1998, sec. 3, "Issues in Wittgenstein," pp. 221–321. See esp. McDowell's "Intentionality and Interiority in Wittgenstein," pp. 297–321, where his intricate diagnosis of the grip of a conceptual picture (what he here usefully calls "the framework") indeed shows how deeply such pictures are lodged in our language and how persistent they continue to be not only in contemporary Anglophone philosophy of language and mind but also in work that is allegedly Wittgensteinian in nature.

13 See Donald Davidson's remarks in "Knowing One's Own Mind," *Self-Knowledge*, Q. Cassam (ed.), Oxford: Oxford University Press, 1994, pp. 43–64; see esp. pp. 60–4 on the difficulties of overcoming a pernicious picture of the mind enforcing the belief that thoughts require (external-world-mediating) mental objects.

14 I offer a discussion of Wittgenstein's particularly relevant passages in "The Self, Speaking," in part II, "First-Person Avowals," pp. 19–27, and in "The Self, Reflected: Wittgenstein, Cavell, and the Autobiographical Situation," K. Dauber and W. Jost

(eds.), *Ordinary Language Criticism: Literary Thinking after Cavell after Wittgenstein*, Evanston: Northwestern University Press, 2003, pp. 171–198.

15 For an exceptionally lucid, compact review of what one might call the etiology of this kind of intellectual quandary, see P. M. S. Hacker, *Wittgenstein: On Human Nature*, New York: Routledge, 1999, pp. 5–14.

16 For a more detailed discussion of this irreducible attitude, see my *Meaning and Interpretation*, "Against Reductionism," pp. 129–38. I think one can see a good deal of directly relevant philosophical detail (on person-perception in relation to the irreducible attitude) in Mozart and Da Ponte's *Don Giovanni*: see my "Leporello's Question: *Don Giovanni* as a Tragedy of the Unexamined Life," in a collection on the aesthetic issues in that opera edited by L. Goehr and D. Herwitz, Princeton: Princeton University Press, forthcoming.

17 I offer a much fuller account of this particular matter in "The Self, Thinking: Wittgenstein, Augustine, and the Autobiographical Situation," P. Lewis (ed.), *Wittgenstein, Aesthetics, and Philosophy*, Aldershot: Ashgate, 2004.

18 I borrow this telling phrase from Anthony Kenny, *The False Prison: A Study of the Development of Wittgenstein's Philosophy*, vols. 1–2, Oxford: Clarendon Press, 1987.

19 Wittgenstein, *Remarks on the Philosophy of Psychology*, vol. 1, ed. G. E. M. Anscombe and G. H. von Wright, vol. 2, ed. G. H. von Wright and Heikki Nyman, Oxford: Blackwell, 1980.

20 Wittgenstein, *On Certainty*, G. E. M. Anscombe and G. H. von Wright (eds.), Oxford: Blackwell, 1969.

21 In *Philosophical Investigations*, 3rd edn., trans. G. E. M. Anscombe, Oxford: Blackwell, 1958, §§243–363 (but not only here; these remarks trace back to the lectures on private experience given in 1934–36). I offer a sketch of the significance this holds for an understanding of artistic creativity in *Art as Language: Wittgenstein, Meaning, and Aesthetic Theory*, Ithaca: Cornell University Press, 1995, chap. 6, "The Silence of Aesthetic Solipsism," pp. 118–35.

22 See, for a fuller discussion, my "The Mind Shown: Wittgenstein, Goethe, and the Question of Person-Perception," *Goethe and Wittgenstein: Seeing the World's Unity in Its Variety*, F. Breithaupt, R. Raatzsch, and B. Kremberg (eds.), *Wittgenstein Studien*, Band 5, Frankfurt am Main: Peter Lang, 2003, pp. 111–26.

23 See "The Self Speaking," §3: "Real Introspection," pp. 27–47.

24 Plato, *Republic*, trans. R. W. Sterling and W. C. Scott, New York: W. W. Norton, 1985, p. 134.

25 Rousseau, *Confessions*, trans. J. M. Cohen, New York: Penguin, 1953.

26 Ibid., p. 23.

27 This is hardly the only time Rousseau wrote in correspondence to philosophical–conceptual pictures of selfhood (thus showing, if it needs to be shown, that cases of autobiographical writing are not ipso facto antidotes to misleading philosophical pictures). He wrote, to take one example, "the first, the greatest, the strongest, the most inextinguishable of all my needs was entirely one of heart. It was the need for intimate companionship, for a companionship as intimate as possible, which was the chief reason I needed a woman rather than a man....This singular need was such that the most intimate physical union could not fulfill it; only two souls in the same body would have sufficed. Failing that I always felt a void" (*Confessions*, p. 386, quoted and helpfully discussed in Jill Ker Conway, *When Memory Speaks: Reflections on Autobiography*, New York: Alfred A. Knopf, 1998, p. 23). This enduring, emotionally sensed void is one consequence of picturing the self in terms of a metaphysical dualism that engenders the problems of other-minds skepticism and, in its most virulent form, solipsistic privacy. The conceptually therapeutic methods articulated by Wittgenstein in his later philosophy are intended to dislodge such conceptual pictures or heuristic models by effecting a change in one's way of seeing, not only the

problem before us, but also the conceptual substructure, the framework upon which that problem is built. I discuss this therapeutic conception of philosophical work in "On Philosophy as Therapy: Wittgenstein, Cavell, Autobiographical Writing," *Philosophy and Literature* 27 (2003), 196–211.

28 Conway, *When Memory Speaks*, p. 23. As will be clear in what follows, I am deeply indebted to Conway's discerning work of assembling highly instructive cases (although she does not mention Wittgenstein, her collection of cases is reminiscent of Wittgenstein's notion of "assembling reminders for a particular purpose"). Admittedly, the purposes to which I put the cases differ greatly from hers, but the indebtedness remains (indeed, I would never have encountered many of the more obscure cases she presents and discusses), as will be clear in the following.

29 Conway, *When Memory Speaks*, p. 23.

30 Ibid., p. 49.

31 Ibid., pp. 49–50.

32 It is noteworthy in connection with *some* autobiographical writing serving as antidotes to simplifying metaphysical pictures of selfhood, that Margaret Sanger (in *Margaret Sanger: An Autobiography*, New York: W. W. Norton, 1938, pp. 86–7, quoted in Conway, p. 53), describing her life's work, argues for just such a particularized understanding – and one that implicitly combats, not only the Cartesian picture, but also a kind of reductive-behaviorist picture of selfhood as well. She writes "A woman in childbirth was not merely a woman in childbirth. My expanded outlook included a view of her background, her potentialities as a human being, the kind of children she was bearing and what was going to happen to them."

33 See the foundational monograph by G. E. M. Anscombe, *Intention*, Oxford: Blackwell, 1957, for a broadly Wittgensteinian treatment of the subject.

34 Conway, *When Memory Speaks*, p. 55.

35 Ibid.

36 Ibid.

37 Ibid., p. 77.

38 Ibid. (and following quotations), pp. 77–8.

39 Ibid., p. 79.

40 Ibid., p. 82.

13

MONOLOGIC AND DIALOGIC: WITTGENSTEIN, *HEART OF DARKNESS*, AND LINGUISTIC SKEPTICISM

James Guetti

Any connection between Wittgenstein and Conrad may at first seem suspect. Wittgenstein was an infant when Conrad was achieving what his narrator Marlow calls "my farthest point of navigation"[1] in the Congo, and he was still a child when *Heart of Darkness* was published. So far as I have been able to determine, Wittgenstein never read Conrad. And the only work of Wittgenstein's to which Conrad before he died could have had access, the *Tractatus*, would scarcely have interested him. But these and other particular separations might amount to unnecessary evidence for what might seem obvious to any reader of both of these writers: the novelist and the philosopher were worlds apart.[2]

Thus it is all the more interesting to consider – for what I shall try to show are good reasons – that with regard to their estimations of what language can and cannot do, and of what language must do in order to *be* language, they were of much the same mind. One of Wittgenstein's most insistent and admonitory distinctions – between working "meaning" and merely idling "sense," or "logic" – may fit perfectly with Conrad's own linguistic apprehensions and commitments. Reciprocally, the conception of language and linguistic behavior displayed most strikingly in *Heart of Darkness* and extended throughout Conrad's subsequent fiction may shed light upon certain philosophical problems that have occupied many of Wittgenstein's commentators.

The proposition that in *Heart of Darkness* something is amiss with language is nothing new in literary studies, of course. But still we may note briefly how the narrative conditions here compel the inference that the "problem" of this story is linguistic before it is anything else. What in many other narratives a reader is able to *presume* – a certain way of saying and telling – is in this story puzzlingly exposed, right from the start:

> The yarns of seamen have a direct simplicity, the whole meaning of
> which lies within the shell of a cracked nut. But Marlow was not typical
> (if his propensity to spin yarns be excepted), and to him the meaning of
> an episode was not inside like a kernel but outside, enveloping the tale

which brought it out only as a glow brings out a haze, in the likeness of one of these misty halos that sometimes are made visible by the spectral illumination of moonshine.

(48)

Not a reassuring introduction; and its most disturbing aspect may be its simplest one: the idea that "the meaning of an episode" is somehow outside rather than inside it, and rather a matter of surfaces than depths, is perhaps for us – in part precisely because of Conrad – no longer so startling as it may have been for his contemporary readers. But still we may often seem just to assume, especially in cases that most interest us, that the most preferred meaning, even the "truth," must be something inward, and central, and deep.

Even more important, however, and contrary to what that other, "frame" narrator has said about his story-telling, for much of the "progress" of his narrative, this is Marlow's own assumption. His journey toward Kurtz is "inward" in every imaginable sense, an effort at both physical and metaphysical penetration that is punctuated continually with impatient rejections of outward appearances, of "surfaces" of all sorts.

Yet such rejections may be seen to be as far as Marlow gets; for his attempts at penetration, from his journey's outset, are exposed only in their frustrations. These continual and often metaphorical signs of imaginative retardation, however, are more sharply focused when, at one stage or another, the claim that the "light" of his narrative is superficial, and reflected, and spectral, is *dramatized* in its failure to yield anything of substance: as when, on his way to Kurtz, even after the grisly death of his native helmsman, whom he had admired, he appears to throw overboard – along with his blood-soaked shoes – all expectation of any *extra*-linguistic discovery:

> There was a sense of extreme disappointment, as though I had found out I had been striving after something altogether without a substance. I couldn't have been more disgusted if I had traveled all this way for the sole purpose of talking with Mr. Kurtz. Talking with…I flung one shoe overboard, and became aware that that was exactly what I had been looking forward to – a talk with Kurtz….The man presented himself as a voice. Not of course that I did not connect him with some sort of action. Hadn't I been told in all the tones of jealousy and admiration that he had collected, bartered, swindled, or stolen more ivory than all of the other agents together? That was not the point. The point was in his being a gifted creature, and that of all his gifts the one that stood out preeminently, that carried with it a sense of real presence, was his ability to talk, his words…

(113–14)

We may understand more clearly why "action" of any sort seems "not the point," and how the language of *Heart of Darkness* seems devoted to remaining both exposed to a reader and occupied only with itself, by considering a moment in the story that surely ought to be more outwardly focused. Upon reaching the Inner Station, Marlow proceeds to examine, through his spy-glass, Kurtz's ruined house, along with what appear to be a few fence posts topped with ornamental knobs:

> And then I made a brusque movement, and one of the remaining posts of that vanished fence leaped up in the field of my glass. You remember I told you I had been struck at the distance by certain attempts at ornamentation, rather remarkable in the ruinous aspect of the place. Now I had suddenly a nearer view, and its first result was to make me throw my head back as if before a blow. Then I went carefully from post to post with my glass, and I saw my mistake. These round knobs were not ornamental but symbolic; they were expressive and puzzling, striking and disturbing – food for thought and also for the vultures if there had been any looking down from the sky; but at all events for such ants as were industrious enough to ascend the pole. They would have been even more impressive, those heads on the stakes, if their faces had not been turned to the house. Only one, the first I had made out, was facing my way. I was not so shocked as you may think. The start back I had given was really nothing but a movement of surprise. I had expected to see a knob of wood there, you know.
>
> I returned deliberately to the first I had seen – and there it was, black, dried, sunken, with closed eyelids – a head that seemed to sleep at the top of that pole, and, with the shrunken dry lips showing a narrow white line of the teeth, was smiling, too, smiling continuously at some endless and jocose dream of that eternal slumber.
>
> (130f)

Some particular narrative techniques that function in this story for the suppression of "action" and even of the "objective" parts of any action are in evidence here. Marlow's personal and unexplained reaction of throwing back his head is immediately followed by an obscure reflection upon what remains to a reader unseen, and by a joke that might be horribly callous – "food for thought and also...for such ants as were industrious enough to ascend the pole" – if one *did* know what Marlow was looking at. And that is revealed at last only in an aside, when he imagines what is *not* the actual case in the story: "They would have been even more impressive, those heads on the stakes, if their faces had not been turned to the house."

By virtue of this musing, delaying reflection upon not only the observable facts but also their logical possibilities, the first clear "image" that a reader has of one of those heads is altogether after the fact – "I returned deliberately" – and thus "food" for nothing *but* "thought"; so that the actual "shrunken dry lips" and the fanciful "endless and jocose dream of that eternal slumber" seem to exist on the same logical plane: as if the visual details of this narrative were no more and no less apprehensible than Marlow's arbitrary speculations; or, more simply, as if the narrative "matter" of *Heart of Darkness* impartially might always include what was observable in the world of the story and what was not: those non-existent vultures, for example.

This one-dimensional "linguisticness" of *Heart of Darkness* – and Marlow's apparent determination, at least on this side of his mind, to transform every-thing into the same condition of unrestricted and unsecured logical possibility – is in one respect just a matter of habitual narrative timing. That is, a more grammatical explanation of a reader's impression that the language of this story continually fails to penetrate to or connect with "reality" is simply that its syntax constantly fails, or refuses, to achieve ordinary – which is to say, *temporal* – development.

We may understand what sort of syntactic timing is absent here if we imagine for a moment that Marlow, like the heroes of Conan Doyle or Sax Rohmer, were accompanied by a straight man less complex or reflective than himself, to whom, when Marlow threw back his head, he might pass that spy-glass, and who might then exclaim, "Great Scott, Marlow! They're human heads!" This more climactic syntactic rhythm would be much more "penetrating." It might seem even a more "referential" grammar, as if someone in the scene or sequence were looking directly at something. And such language would *seem* to "point" here, I suggest, simply, and crucially, by *stopping*. Indeed, as multidirectional as Marlow's own grammar is, even it would be shaped into a syntactic progression just by such a period. The straight man's exclamation, by putting a stop to the narrative line, would establish it *as a line*.

Thus we may appreciate more fully that first narrator's early misgivings about Marlow's way of talking: "we knew we were fated, before the ebb began to run, to hear about one of Marlow's inconclusive experiences" (51). For syntactic conclusion or completion seems necessary to the apprehension that words *can* point beyond themselves. Various reasons for this may be worked out,[3] but they may be, somewhat figuratively, summarized by the proposition that narrative "stops" characteristically have the effect of projecting a reader on past them – on to where, at least for the moment, there are no further words – and achieve a sort of descriptive efficiency just by appearing to establish certain, although temporary, limits to what might otherwise remain merely verbal, or logical.

But just as this story of a journey on a river is itself told on a river, while waiting for a turn of the tide that eventually is missed, Marlow's narrative sequences characteristically do not achieve the syntactic completion that would generate at least the illusion of something beyond them. Both the consecutive-ness and the periods of his grammar are continually retarded and suppressed by grammatical disparities: between adjective and noun, among adjectives for the same noun, between subject and verb, among the clauses of sentences, among sentences. Thus narrative advance is suspended, logical space condensed, and any apprehension of an imagined world beyond the words of this story impaired.

But now we should ask, why? For all the "describing" that Marlow appears to attempt in *Heart of Darkness* and upon which Conrad seems to insist throughout his work – as in his famous, or notorious, preface to *The Nigger of the "Narcissus"*, for example – why do both gravitate so consistently to grammatical forms that conspicuously and continually weaken language's descriptive capacities?

> He was silent for a while.
> "… No, it is impossible; it is impossible to convey the life-sensation of any given epoch of one's existence – that which makes its truth, its meaning – its subtle and penetrating essence. It is impossible. We live, as we dream – alone …"
>
> (82)

And if the linguistic straits are this dire, then why is Marlow so meditative and even complacent about them and their reciprocity with human isolation? More crudely, and suspiciously: what other cards – other than those incommunicable "life-sensations" and "essences" – does he have up his sleeve?

For, as I have already implied, there is another side to Marlow's mind. Or at least he from time to time declares a set of values which seem exempt from his displays and explicit recognitions of language's descriptive and communicative incapacities. From the moment of his arrival in the Congo, Marlow insists upon the worth of simple, practical human activity – of *work* – even though, as might by now be expected, this insistence is expressed upon occasions when the efficiency of work is questioned, when "work" doesn't seem to work:

> "A horn tooted to the right, and I saw the black people run. A heavy and dull detonation shook the ground, a puff of smoke came out of the cliff, and that was all. No change appeared on the face of the rock. They were building a railway. The cliff was not in the way or anything; but this objectless blasting was all the work going on."
>
> (64)

As *Heart of Darkness* develops, it appears that "all the work going on" anywhere is as aimless, undirected, and "objectless" as this "blasting." Yet against this current Marlow continues to maintain his allegiance to purposeful activity. And it is most interesting that he seems much less disturbed by the epistemological difficulties I have noted than he is by the physical or practical inefficiencies that he encounters. Indeed, it seems only for its practical consequences that the thorough disconnection in this narrative between words and their "objects" or applications is distressing to him at all, even when the moral ramifications of such a predicament may seem to a reader, at the very least, unpleasant. Marlow is "horror-struck," to be sure, by the spectacle of the "grove of death," where the natives wait to die: "not enemies…not criminals…nothing earthly now – nothing but black shadows of disease and starvation, lying confusedly in the greenish gloom" (66). And yet this same reaction seems to occur, once again, on the same logical plane, or to be of the same narrative weight, with observations of much less moral significance: with the "wanton smash-up" of "a lot of imported drainage pipes," with "a boiler wallowing in the grass" (63), and with all the "pieces of decaying machinery" that he encounters. Thus it would seem that Marlow is affected rather by the condition of "lying confusedly" than by what in particular occupies this condition. The dying natives and the scattered and abandoned tools and machines are equally distressing, in that both are unorganized and unemployed.

If such an attitude seems callous, then we should consider the purposes that "employment" serves for Marlow:

> "You wonder I didn't go ashore for a howl and a dance? Well no – I didn't. Fine sentiments, you say? Fine sentiments, be hanged! I had no time. I had to mess about with white-lead and strips of woolen blanket helping to put bandages on those leaky steam-pipes – I tell you. I had to watch the steering, and circumvent those snags, and get the tin-pot along by hook or by crook. There was surface-truth enough in these things to save a wiser man."
>
> (95)

The name for what might "save" Marlow here – this "surface-truth" – seems as patched together and jury-rigged as his "tin-pot" steamboat itself, which emphasizes its amoral or aphilosophical status: no "fine sentiments" here. Of course what he is saved from at this moment is merely some sensual depravity, whose appeal is crudely minimized as "a howl and a dance," and this is only a small part, or result, of the "reality" he remarked a few moments before, some "inner truth" to this strange world and narrative that could be somehow "felt" but, of course, not specified.

Yet, as we have seen, the principal source in *Heart of Darkness* for this larger threat, this "reality" that is reciprocal, and even identical, with forms of language that cannot attain to it, is – at least until he and a reader encounter the story's central character – Marlow himself. And so what his "work" so luckily saves him from is himself; or it saves "one side of his mind," as I put it earlier, from the other; or it saves him from his own inconclusive and limitless talk. And this brings him, and us, to Kurtz.

Although neither Marlow nor a reader may recognize this until the later stages of *Heart of Darkness*, there is no doubt that Marlow and Kurtz are similar sorts of talker. The latter's journalist colleague reports that Kurtz "'had faith – don't you see? – he had the faith. He could get himself to believe anything – anything. He would have been a splendid leader of an extreme party.' 'What party?' I asked. 'Any party,' answered the other" (154).

But Marlow himself, at one or another moment in his story, seems just as able to "get himself to believe anything." The "hollowness" that proves fatal to Kurtz is built into this narrative; and the main character of *Heart of Darkness* degenerates and dies because he embraces the epistemological conditions that its narrator seems most to favor, even while that narrator appears to recognize the danger of these conditions for his own identity:

> "I have wrestled with death....It takes place in an impalpable grayness, with nothing underfoot, and nothing around, without spectators, without clamour, without glory, without the great fear of defeat, in a sickly atmosphere of tepid skepticism....If such is the form of ultimate wisdom, then life is a greater riddle than some of us think it to be. I was within a hair's-breadth of the last opportunity for pronouncement, and I found with humiliation that probably I would have nothing to say. This is the reason why I affirm that Kurtz was a remarkable man. He had something to say. He said it."
>
> (150–1)

It would seem, of course, that Kurtz had rather too much to say. Still Marlow maintains that he committed himself at last, and "judged," as if Kurtz were ultimately less "hollow" than Marlow himself:

> "Since I had peeped over the edge myself, I understand better the meaning of his stare, that could not see the flame of the candle, but was wide enough to embrace the whole universe, piercing enough to penetrate all the hearts that beat in the darkness. He had summed up – he had judged. 'The horror! The horror!' He was a remarkable man....It is his extremity that I seem to have lived through. True, he had made that last stride, while I had been permitted to draw back my hesitating foot."
>
> (151)

Yet surely Kurtz's "judgment" – "The horror! The horror!" – is among the most opaque pronouncements in literary history. It may seem to Marlow that Kurtz has at last achieved "some sort of belief," but this phrase resonates ironically with the proposition that Kurtz was always capable of *some* sort of belief. And Marlow's description of Kurtz's final incisiveness is, as usual, so polyglot as to generate doubt not merely about whether it was indeed "penetrating" but even about whether it was anything at all.

Still we have to acknowledge here Marlow's two dominating claims: that he "understands" Kurtz's situation, since he himself "had peeped over the edge," and that he himself did not make "that last stride." Of course the latter might be as little to say that Kurtz died, in which case the former alludes to Marlow's almost dying of fever himself before getting out of the Congo. But, once more,

257

no such physical inference ever seems appropriate in this narrative, just because its syntax always says more, always continues on past such a firm implication. More generally and more important, however – and because of this same syntactical continuousness – a reader may infer that the "edge" in question has little to do with physical death, or even with any moral or ideological limit. For the very limitlessness of Kurtz's language would seem to require that any "glimpsed truth" be only more of the same. "The horror! The horror!" would thus appear to be Kurtz's response to the utter and solitary vacancy of all that he has said and could say.[4]

Marlow appears explicitly to justify such an estimation in his account of his own "position" in an earlier confrontation with Kurtz:

> "There was nothing either above or below him, and I knew it. He had kicked himself loose of the earth. Confound the man! He had kicked the very earth to pieces. He was alone, and I before him did not know whether I stood on the ground or floated in the air. I've been telling you what we said – repeating the phrases we pronounced – but what's the good?…They had behind them, to my mind, the terrific suggestiveness of words heard in dreams, of phrases spoken in nightmares."
>
> (144)

Marlow's recognition here of a linguistic transformation – rather than of any merely moral one – of course echoes his previous description of his own verbal capacities: "It seems to me I am trying to tell you a dream …" (82). But the "terrific suggestiveness" of words in both cases more importantly implies that this "dream" or "nightmare" language is characterized by unrestrictable logical possibility. So Kurtz is "loose of the earth" because his language is; and his ultimate "judgment" would thus only be that any judgment is possible.

This "horror" – this dramatized deterioration of linguistic probability, with its consequent detachment of language from any purchase upon the world – would seem to assign to *Heart of Darkness* text-book status as a skeptical document, whose implications were quite similar to the claims of certain contemporary philosophers: language is so vulnerable to its own logical possibilities that it is only rendered meaningful by our memberships in some "linguistic community," whose conventional behaviors may restrict and regulate logic.[5] In such a view, one's thorough separation from "kind neighbours ready to cheer you or to fall on you" (116), from "a butcher round one corner, a policeman round the other" (114), would be followed inevitably by linguistic mutation.[6]

The linguistic disease that follows upon such isolation, furthermore, seems as contagious in *Heart of Darkness* as the most ardent skeptic would want it to be. For in his confrontation with Kurtz Marlow seems to share the other's condition: "He was alone, and I before him did not know whether I stood on the ground or floated in the air." And yet he, as we have noted, is "permitted to draw back [*his*] hesitating foot" and, apparently, to avoid Kurtz's unequivocal recognition of the epistemological "horror." So his own skepticism at last, as he says, is only "tepid." But here we should recall that this is not because of the strength of Marlow's counter-skeptical principles but because he has been too preoccupied and distracted by his work – simply too busy – to see what Kurtz may have seen.

This consideration, too, fits nicely into a skeptical attitude: what is unstable or unreliable about language – the allotropicness of its logic – is *necessary*. And what stands against this permanent threat is just some accidental way of acting. But this philosophical extension from *Heart of Darkness*, I want now to suggest, would be inaccurate. For as contingent and "lucky" as Marlow's defense against linguistic insecurity might appear, it may be shown – after Wittgenstein – to be even more "necessary" to language than the shifty logic it stands against. Marlow's allegiance to *work* – however accidental his access to such activity – may be taken to be a crucial ingredient in a quite anti-skeptical estimation of linguistic behavior.

The "communitarian solution" to linguistic skepticism – once again that the meaningfulness of our ways of speaking depends upon our continuing participation in a society of speakers – has been attributed to Wittgenstein himself, though not, as I see it, successfully. But it has perhaps been more persuasively held to solve *problems* that he discovered in his treatments of linguistic rule-following, problems that may be summarized as follows: the meaningfulness of what we say might seem determined solely by linguistic rules, but is not; for a rule, of itself, does not tell us how to follow it; and imagining some further rule for such instruction only involves us in an infinite regress. Thus it is inferred that, in Wittgenstein's view, nothing within the logic of language terminally arbitrates how to use that logic, and such governance must therefore come from language's "outside," for which "social" or "communal" situations and interactions, once more, have seemed the likeliest candidates.

Now this reading of Wittgenstein seems to me only partly correct. I think it quite accurate to his thinking to maintain that logic cannot govern the use of logic, but inaccurate therefore to claim that language in its entirety is always at risk. For throughout his work after the *Tractatus* he was at pains to show that *logic* should not be taken for *language*, nor the rules of the game for the game itself:

> It is a rule of grammar dealing with symbols alone, it is a rule of a game. Its importance lies in its application; we use it in our language. When we talk about propositions following from each other, we are talking of a game. Propositions do not follow from one another as such; they simply are what they are. We can only prepare language for its usage; we can only describe it as long as we do not regard it as language. The rules prepare for the game which may afterwards be used as language.[7]

These remarks cast an entirely different light on the logical multiplicity and instability that the linguistic skeptic considers so telling: *it is just a matter of logic* that propositions "do not follow from one another as such," for they can do so only in a "game" in which they are put to use. And thus what the logician might *describe* as a "language" we do not so far even *regard* as one until it is in use.

It should be noted here as well that this abstraction of "rule" from "game" – if one supposes that such "analysis" has any *descriptive* bearing on a language-game as it actually plays out – is, by the measure of Wittgenstein's conceptions of rule following in the *Philosophical Investigations*, entirely misguided.[8] The logician or grammarian may to be sure describe logic as if it were separate from the language in which it functions; indeed such separation would seem just the result of such description. Thence to conceive, however, that this division is indigenous to language as it is used would be fantastic. For the anti-skeptical point here is that doubt about language's actual capacities can be neither started nor stopped by merely logical considerations or fascinations.

The fundamental, and most important, difference between the skeptical position and Wittgenstein's own, then, is a difference concerning what may be counted as language. For the former, the rules of language are what so count, and these must therefore be themselves regulated, if they are going to work, somehow from somewhere presumably else. But for Wittgenstein, as I have begun to suggest, what should be counted as language is much more than its abstractable rules. And on this point, as I remarked earlier – even though Marlow's narrative mode in *Heart of Darkness* seems itself so logically disposed, and so unworking and unworkable – Wittgenstein and Conrad were of quite the same mind.

That claim may be articulated by considering the only moment in *Heart of Darkness* when Marlow clearly connects his conception of and allegiance to work with a sort of language, though not, just as clearly, his language. On his way to Kurtz, and oppressed by the atmosphere of uselessness that surrounds him, Marlow – accidentally, of course – comes upon an abandoned book, *An Inquiry into Some Points of Seamanship*:

> Not a very enthralling book; but at first glance you could see there a singleness of intention, an honest concern for the right way of going to work, which made these humble pages, thought out so many years ago, luminous with another than a professional light. The simple old sailor, with his talk of chains and purchases, made me forget the jungle and the pilgrims in a delicious sensation of having come upon something unmistakably real.
>
> (99)

Characteristically, *Heart of Darkness* does not allow us direct access to this book, so we cannot see how this "honest concern for the right way of going to work" is actually manifested in its syntaxes. But we can make some likely guesses: this book – with its "talk of chains and purchases" and presumable descriptions of various other "points of seamanship" – was evidently written to be useful to someone, to make a difference in what someone might do, to be *practically* mean-ingful. And it is important that such intentions may fit even though the book has been itself abandoned, and thus isolated from any actual work, or even though Marlow himself has, when he finds it, no immediate use for it. For the principle that the meaning of a great many varieties of expression is indicated in their use does not require that any such expression be actually and presently at work, but only that it have the capacity for use, that its "work," or at least its "workable-ness," is somehow embodied in it.

That is not so mysterious a proposition as it may sound. For it may be shown that the potential for making "differences" that meaningful expressions possess is at least in part a function of differences that occur within these expressions themselves. I have tried on other occasions to demonstrate how this may be so, but it is not necessary to reproduce those arguments here.[9] For we already have indications, from an earlier part of this discussion, of how certain syntaxes need to be composed in order to make a difference in what one next says or does. These are verbal forms that seem "linear" by appearing to progress in time, that are constructed as sequences on the way to some completion. And we should recall that the readiest way for putting at least a temporary stop to Marlow's own excessive fluencies was to imagine another speaker in the situation, and thus to transform his unsequential and reflexive monologue into a *dialogue*.

Perhaps that last conception may seem too obvious to bear emphasis; but that, I suggest, is because the dialogic "figure" or "structure" is so built-in to what language is as to be *presumable*, especially with regard to the business of terminating syntaxes. In the sequence involving "those heads on the stakes," the result of such terminations seemed to be a "referential" pointing, toward some-thing real. But syntactic terminations might allow for all sorts of actions other than such basic "perceptions." The periods of any set of expressions may be generally practical because they incline one to continue beyond these expres-sions, as if beyond the language itself, in all sorts of ways. Thus one might say that a language-game is useful at least in part by virtue of the "spaces" or "gaps" among its periods, and, especially, after its last period.[10] And the most effective way of establishing such periods – the most effective way of organizing syntaxes into sequences – is the dialogic figure.

But now it may again appear that Kurtz's difficulty has been just that he has had no company, no one to whom to talk, so that by the time Marlow reaches him he has apparently forgotten how to stop talking. And once more his situation – and to some extent Marlow's own – might appear a problem for the "commu-nitarian solution" to linguistic skepticism to answer. The absence of community deprives one not only of various sorts of "logical regulation" from local customs and institutions but also – and more to my point in this discussion – of the more vital and actual regulation generated by dialogue with other human beings. So again it might seem that language cannot take care of itself, and that the only cure for its hereditary disease has to come from somewhere else.

But if my reading of Wittgenstein is accurate here then there is and need be nowhere else. If language is always the employment of language-games, then our ways of speaking are entwined not only particularly, with temporary ways of acting and talking, but also, more generally, with human "forms of life"; and I suggest that the "dialogic figure" of linguistic behavior that I have been describing is a perfect example of the latter, and therefore may be available to us even when the former are not.

So the actual presence of a linguistic community may be dispensable. And in this connection we should remember that no present company seems necessary to Marlow at those moments when he is able to insist at least upon the *idea* of working language. More important, his "delicious sensation of having come upon something unmistakably real" does not issue from any dialogic encounter with any actual human being, but simply from finding a book. It is not another person that is discovered at this moment, but another language, a set of syntaxes different from those he himself is disposed to use. And thus it would seem that all the linguistic isolato requires is access to ways of speaking other than his own presently insistent vocabularies. The dialogic motive in language is independent of either company or solitude: it requires only another imaginable mode of language with which to talk.

But how could Kurtz in his isolation have been deprived of this requisite minimum to meaningful language? If the motive to dialogue is as fundamental to language as I am suggesting, why should the absence of community weaken it? The crude answer to that question is that the language is not the language-user, and that under certain circumstances one individual or another may lose his grasp on the whole of what language, in its operations, *is*. That, of course, is hardly a skeptical proposition; though it may be descriptive of the skeptic's own exceptional posture.

This is to say that certain circumstances – and social isolation is only one of these – *may* affect a speaker's grammatical habits, and incline him to speak some-thing other than a "whole language." But this means that the crucial "isolation" here is not any mere absence of human community. It is the isolation of a gram-matical track which ordinarily is just one part of language as it naturally functions, but which, when separated from that "whole language," comes only to resist what before it both resisted and required, and to take strange dominion. Whether or not Marlow's inconclusiveness and Kurtz's madness are more likely for the absence of actual human community, these are *surely* the results of an absence in their speech of certain, ordinary grammatical modes. More simply, they speak always and only – and this is true even when Kurtz is talking at Marlow, or Marlow at his listeners on the *Nellie* – in the first person.

But why should the perpetuation of first person grammar result in the entire deactivation of one's language, in its thorough transformation, in Wittgenstein's terms, from "working" to "idling"? It may be that this has something to do with linguistic criteria:

What is the criterion for the sameness of two images? – What is the criterion for the redness of an image? For me, when it is someone else's image: what he says and does. For myself, when it is my image: nothing. And what goes for "red" also goes for "same."[11]

This remark is perhaps the most concise and pointed formulation of a line of argument that runs throughout Wittgenstein's later work: if we can be said to know what others do and say, and even what they imagine or think or feel, by observation, then we cannot be said similarly to "know" about our first person experience, just because our relation to the latter is not the relation of observation that "knowledge" requires. It might therefore seem that first person expressions – "I am tired," "I have a headache," "I am thinking" – are either more or less "certain" than "knowledge." But really a different kind of certainty is involved here, since, *for the person who employs them*, such expressions are not subject to empirical testing.

This general inclination of the first person mode to "non-criterialness," when sustained as it is in *Heart of Darkness*, may seem a linguistic nightmare, where one's expressions were always static, and idle. These expressions would not be nonsense, but something worse. For there would be no "sense" to stand against them. In the same way, the perpetual first person would not amount to the domination of or the insistence upon the self. For there would be nothing there but the self. The continuous expression of the "self" thus can yield no self.

But to recognize such a catastrophe may make it even more difficult to understand why one might incline toward it. This is not just a question, once more, of any circumstantial lack of resistance, in the form of other speakers or grammars; because even if the former were absent, the latter need never be. Thus what *Heart of Darkness* may show is how much has to be done to, and even against, language, how much language as we use it needs to be re-formed, to establish such inert and hyper-logical conditions. And even if actual, social isolation may be considered catalytic for such reformations, it is only that. For, once more, it is a *linguistic* isolation – an isolation of a kind of grammar, a part of grammar – that counts here. But to understand more fully what this isolation amounts to, and especially to understand the temptation toward it, we should explore a connection that has been implicit in my arguments here: between the exclusive first person grammatical mode and solipsism.

That Kurtz is a sort of solipsist is dramatized so often as to require no belaboring: his insistences on "I" and "my" – "my Intended, my station, my career, my ideas" (147) – and so on. But the following passage is especially effective in establishing that this is not mere "selfishness":

> "And I wasn't arguing with a lunatic either. Believe me or not, his intelligence was perfectly clear – concentrated, it is true, upon himself with horrible intensity, yet clear....But his soul was mad. Being alone in the wilderness, it had looked within itself, and, by heavens! I tell you, it had gone mad."
>
> (145)

Such "intelligence" of oneself, I believe, in accord with Wittgenstein's later philosophy, would amount to a contradiction in terms. How would one go about retrieving it? How would he "observe" himself? What would be his criteria for the truth about himself? And what difference would this all make? But it nonetheless may be interesting, in relation to Kurtz's example of exclusive first person grammar, to consider an earlier remark of Wittgenstein's concerning solipsism:

> For what the solipsist *means* is quite correct; only it cannot be *said*, but makes itself manifest. The world is *my* world: this is manifest in the fact that the limits of *language* (of that language which alone I understand) mean the limits of *my* world.[12]

This conception, I believe, becomes less difficult – and also less apparently contradictory to Wittgenstein's later philosophy – if we consider how much it has to do with first person grammar. That the world, when I speak in that grammar, is my world means that I thus include the world, and surround it: that the limits of my language are its limits, that my view of the world is from those limits, and that my position "in" this world is at those limits.

> But if I in the first person am the limits of the world, then I am not in the world.

> The subject does not belong to the world: rather, it is a limit of the world.

> Where *in* the world is a metaphysical subject to be found? You will say that this is exactly like the case of the eye and the visual field. But really you do *not* see the eye.
>
> (5.632, 5.633)

This, I think, is to say that, from this grammatical vantage, I *cannot* "look into myself," as neither could Kurtz, for I am not there to be seen. Thus my existence *in* the world is dependent upon and only expressible in other modes, in the grammars of the second and third persons. And now it should be even clearer how Kurtz has "kicked himself loose of the earth," and how necessary to linguistic sanity is what I have called the "dialogic figure."

Therefore, though we may entertain for a while the notion of a permanent first person and the power of its logical seductiveness, in the end we must return to dialogue. Which is to say that there must *be* an end to this story, even though it strains to establish its own endlessness, if it will be a story: Kurtz – maddened already beyond the world – must die, but Marlow, as physically and linguistically exhausted as he has become, must return to tell. And even if he later only talks *at* his listeners on the *Nellie*, with no apparent expectation of or even concern for being understood, what I have called the "dialogic figure" of language is nonetheless eventually reaffirmed. For in his ultimate dialogue in the narrative, with Kurtz's "Intended" – even though immersed "in the triumphant darkness from which I could not have defended her – from which I could not even defend myself"(159) – he says, "The last word he pronounced was – your name"(161). As a lie, this may not appear to be any considerable retrieval or redemption. But while it defends both her and him it also defends the language; for in skepticism there are of course no lies.

What then about poor Kurtz? Bad luck, one might say, if he considered that Marlow was just "lucky" to maintain his grasp upon the necessity of work and working language, upon the necessity of dialogue. Yet Marlow's luck consists only in his finding occasion for what he already and undeniably has the inclination. And evidently it was this very inclination to imagine other languages that Kurtz lacked. To recognize, once again, that a person's understanding of what he has to *do* with language may be deficient, or that in certain circumstances he might gravitate catastrophically to one mode of language to the exclusion of all others, may be saddening; but it is not a justification for linguistic skepticism.

Thus it would seem that Conrad and Wittgenstein, despite their lack of obvious association, shared a doubled view of language. What the poet reveled in, to paraphrase O. K. Bouwsma, gave the philosopher many bad nights. But both were occupied, in their different ways, with the fascinating prospect of language idling, language as mysteriously suggestive and delusive, and as paradoxically "existing" and substantial, as a dream, and occupied as well with what must be seen to stand against that dream in daylight.[13]

Notes

1   Joseph Conrad, *Youth, Heart of Darkness, The End of the Tether*, New York: Oxford, 1984. Further references to *Heart of Darkness* are to this edition and are given in the text.

2   Except for their mutual interest in Schopenhauer, whose influence upon both the novelist and the philosopher has been well documented. It may not have been the same sort of "influence": Conrad seems to have drawn attitudes – general conceptions about the world such as certain kinds of "pessimism" – from Schopenhauer; whereas Wittgenstein's adoptions were surprisingly specific conceptions – and even particular phrases – that became technically important to his way of addressing language. But still this "triangular" relation may be worth pursuing, though that would require, at least, another essay.

3   As I have tried to do in the "Afterword" of *Wittgenstein and the Grammar of Literary Experience*, Athens, Ga.: University of Georgia Press, 1993.

4   The solitariness of this "vacancy," as I shall try to show more fully, is fundamental to Kurtz's linguistic predicament. And thus the simplest, and by no means disregardable, reading of "The horror! The horror!" – that it indicates an apprehension of the ultimate aloneness of *dying* – becomes all the more powerful: as the final confirmation of a life of aloneness.

5   For example, Saul Kripke, *Wittgenstein on Rules and Private Language*, Cambridge, Mass.: Harvard University Press, 1982.

6   Such a development from such a situation was always of intense interest to Conrad. Kurtz's "aloneness" and consequent degeneration is perhaps just the most striking

and extravagant dramatization of a predicament that occupied his author more and more explicitly throughout his career after *Heart of Darkness*, and which he even – in *Under Western Eyes* – came to identify as "moral isolation," a conception that some readers have since considered crucial to the understanding of his fiction. But it may now be clear that this figure of "isolation," here at its inception in Conrad's work, is in the first place a matter of *language*, and radically problematic because it allows not merely for any particularly immoral "howl" or "dance," but for *any* expression or behavior whatsoever.

7 Desmond Lee (ed.), *Wittgenstein's Lectures, 1930–32*, Chicago: University of Chicago Press, 1982 p. 57. These remarks may seem difficult, and to be sure are only Lee's version of what Wittgenstein actually said. And yet I think that the conception of the relation of logic to language that they indicate is borne out and supported throughout Wittgentein's own writing.

8 One might ask, what after all *is* a "rule" without a game in which it is employed? And the two most immediate answers to this question, I believe – and as I have tried to show in "Idling Rules," *Philosophical Investigations* 16 (1993), 179–97 – are either "nothing" or "an idling *concept*."

9 They may be found in *Wittgenstein and the Grammar of Literary Experience*, in "Meaningful Consequences," *The Philosophical Forum* 30 (1999), 289–315, and in "Acting From Rules," *International Studies in Philosophy* XXVIII (1996), 43–62, the latter two essays co-authored with Rupert Read.

10 "Acting From Rules" contains an account of how rule-following behavior may be considered to occur within such "gaps."

11 Ludwig Wittgenstein, *Philosophical Investigations*, trans. G. E. M. Anscombe, New York: Macmillan, 1968, §377. Further references will be given in my text by paragraph number.

12 Ludwig Wittgenstein, *Tractatus Logico-Philosophicus*, trans. D. F. Pears and B. F. McGuinness, London: Routledge & Kegan Paul, 1961, 5.62. Further references will be given in my text by paragraph number.

13 Some parts of this paper draw on my "Wittgenstein, Conrad and the Darkness," *Symploke* 2 (1994).

14

WITTGENSTEIN AND FAULKNER'S BENJY

Reflections on and of derangement[1]

Rupert Read

> Ben sat in the chair, his big soft hands dangling between his knees, moaning faintly. Suddenly he wept, a slow bellowing sound, meaningless and sustained....Then Ben wailed again, hopeless and prolonged. It was nothing. Just sound. It might have been all time and injustice and sorrow become vocal for an instant by a conjunction of planets.
>
> (William Faulkner, *The Sound and the Fury*)[2]

I want in this paper to conjoin Wittgenstein's (and Wittgensteinian) thinking to a particular piece of prose by one of the greatest writers of the twentieth century: William Faulkner. I am interested in Wittgenstein's possible utility as a virtual literary critic. And especially, in using properly Wittgensteinian thinking in order to understand the *philosophical* lessons that I think great literature can yield for us.

This might beg the following question: *How ought we* to think of the impact of Wittgenstein's philosophizing upon literature? I suggest that one responds with considerable indirection to such a question, a question probably close to the mind of anyone reading the essays in this volume; for, as Wittgenstein so often maintained and practiced, one ought not to be too quick to assume that a question which 'intuitively' suggests itself is in fact the right question to ask. In this case: we should not be too quick to assume that one could in the first place comfortably divide questions concerning aesthetics and concerning the meaning of literature from questions concerning philosophy of mind, or (more specifically) philosophy of mental health/illness. Wittgenstein very frequently moved seamlessly from philosophy of mind to philosophy of maths,[3] or from aesthetics to 'meta-philosophy' to philosophy of psychology.[4] Fundamentally, he rejected *the* division of philosophy into separate 'subject areas.' If we are to follow him in thinking about literature, we should consider doing the same.

I aim below to explore a direct connection between literature and what is nowadays often called 'the philosophy of psychopathology.' I expound a literary critic – James Guetti – putting Wittgenstein to work in thinking about the work of Faulkner. I then extrapolate from this treatment some morals concerning the philosophy of mental health/illness. If my extrapolation is effective, I will have presented to the reader a way of seeing Faulkner *as* Wittgensteinian, a way which yields a distinctive and novel set of doubts concerning whether severe mental illnesses (e.g. 'hard cases' of schizophrenia) can be unproblematically said to be understood/understandable (at all).[5]

There have been various efforts in recent years to apply 'Wittgensteinian' methods to the understanding of various severe mental illnesses, especially schizophrenia. The most notable is that of the clinical psychologist, Louis Sass. Sass has written two major books[6] and a wealth of papers since the late 1980s, which to an unprecedented extent[7] develop a serious Wittgensteinian philosophy of psychopathology. The greatest single novelty of that philosophy of psychopathology is that it proceeds by means of a detailed and quasi-literary examination of 'deranged language': especially, autobiographies of schizoid persons, and great (and obscure) works of literary Modernism. Sass's argument, in a nutshell, is that the nature of the most intriguing and impenetrable psychopathologies can be understood by means of analogy to the character of Modernist writing (and of Modernist 'characters,' with their (often) excessive or self-destructive introspectiveness). In producing his philosophical readings in turn of Modernist texts (e.g. those of Dostoevsky, Kafka, Artaud) in which the characters or narrators are 'symptomatic' of serious cultural and (perhaps relatedly) mental maladies, Sass draws explicitly on Heidegger, Foucault and, above all, Wittgenstein. He thinks that these philosophers enable us to diagnostically understand what is going on in such texts – and in the texts of those philosophers (e.g. Kant, Fichte, Derrida) who Sass believes embody, preview and reflect, in a 'purified' form, the absurd hyper-reflexive and alienated logic – in short, the derangement – of both schizophrenia and (more 'lucidly') of literary Modernism.

Whereas 'schizophrenia' is almost invariably seen these days as a disease or disorder or phenomenon of functional or cognitive deficit, Sass reads it instead as centrally involving cognitive excess, hyper-reflexivity, even 'hyper-rationality.'[8] Sass severely questions whether anyone has as yet developed an adequate account of the character of schizophrenic delusions. He proposes his own account, on which such delusions are like those suffered by a philosopher (e.g. 'the solipsist,' or 'the private linguist') drawn into conceptual absurdities. In sum, Sass argues that we can understand the key features of schizophrenia by analogy to the character of highly-inward-looking Modernism…and then by analogy to how Wittgenstein diagnostically offers an account of solipsism.

I do not intend to discuss Sass's work in detail here.[9] I follow him in very largely rejecting scientific or quasi-scientific *explanations* of schizophrenia, primarily because – even if effective within their own terms (e.g. predictively) – such explanations fail to deliver any improved *understanding* of schizophrenia. They fail, for example, to give us a handle on its phenomenology. Understanding some of the causes behind schizophrenia, as we probably increasingly do, is not then, in my sense, understanding schizophrenia, understanding the people who suffer from it.

I find Sass's critique of existing accounts of schizophrenia to be very stimulating and very effective; but I do not believe that his efforts to offer a positive alternative 'Wittgensteinian' understanding of schizophrenia, even via literature, are likely to be altogether successful.

The most serious strictly philosophical difficulties for Sass's project are those raised (indirectly) by Cora Diamond's work:[10] If Wittgenstein has a resolute conception of nonsense and of philosophical writing, and it follows that would-be philosophical 'positions' such as solipsism are in fact completely unstable, are in fact nothing, are just invitations to nonsense, then it appears also to follow that any attempt to extract a nugget of something understandable from – to expand our conceptual knowledge *via*[11] the relevant Modernist texts, let alone from schizophrenic narratives themselves – is in one important respect doomed to failure. It doesn't help us to *understand* Schreber, if the concept via which we could apparently be led to understand his text (i.e. 'solipsism') *merely appears* to have any solidity or stability, but is actually…nothing at all.

Rather, after Diamond, a *properly* Wittgensteinian approach would show that, except in a rather remote sense of the word 'understanding,' there probably cannot be any such thing as understanding the totality of the words, actions, and experiences of the very severely 'mentally ill,' of persons who are perhaps truly worth calling deeply different from ourselves in the way they now think.[12] I aim to argue below that sophisticated appreciation of Wittgenstein and of Modern Literature tends toward a somewhat more 'pessimistic' conclusion than Sass's. To the deflationary conclusion, that is, that we are ill-advised to claim that serious cases of schizophrenia can in the end be successfully understood or interpreted, *via* Wittgenstein, or *via* literature (or by any other means).

In a way, I am 'extending' Sass's line of argument: I want to say that the logical conclusion of Sass's line of thought, paradoxically enough, is that consistently 'hyper-rational' thought may ultimately become, in an interesting sense, unrecognisable as thought at all. I suggest that we have not been given good reason to think that there can be any such thing as understanding an actual person who is thoroughly in the grip of such absurdities as Sass describes. To do so, to be able truly to understand a lived solipsism, would in the end be somewhat like understanding 'logically alien thought' – but the point, as Wittgenstein was the first to argue, is that it is of no use (or more crudely, no meaning) to us to think that there is any such thing as 'logically alien *thought*.' (*A fortiori*, there can't be any such thing as understanding 'it.')[13]

I intend to begin arguing this in detail by discussing briefly how one ought perhaps to understand Wittgenstein's important remarks on dreams and altered states of consciousness in *On Certainty*, and drawing a *partial* analogy to hard cases of schizophrenia.[14] I will then use Guetti's reading of Faulkner (specifically, of Faulkner's Benjy, the 'speaker' of the first quarter of *The Sound and the Fury*) to rebut an obvious objection to my conclusion drawn from *On Certainty*.[15]

For Wittgenstein, it is very important to note that veridical accounts[16] of dreams can only be given from outside the dream context. (This is a conceptual point, not an empirical one.) This is what renders the whole procedure of Cartesian doubt so pointless and logically awry.

This is how Wittgenstein put the point, in the closing sections of *OC*, in his great last words:

> If someone believes that he has flown from America to England in the last few days, then, I believe, he cannot be making a *mistake*. [For that would be 'too big' to be a mistake.] // And just the same if someone says that he is at this moment sitting at a table and writing.
>
> "But even if in such cases I can't be mistaken, isn't it possible that I am drugged?" If I am and if the drug has taken away my consciousness, then I am not now really talking and thinking. I cannot seriously suppose that I am at this moment dreaming. Someone who, dreaming, says "I am dreaming", even if he speaks audibly in doing so, is no more right than if he said in his dream "It is raining" while it was in fact raining. Even if his dream were actually connected with the noise of the rain.
>
> (*OC* §§675–6)

One might try putting Wittgenstein's point here thus: Cartesian scepticism is pragmatically self-refuting. If one allegedly supposes that one is dreaming, then it follows from the supposition that one is not engaged in normal potentially-public talk or thought. One's 'quasi-thought' in such circumstances – in this case, the mental occurrence of "I am dreaming" – is not a serious candidate for truth-evaluation, etc. One is not correctly placed to make a *claim*. So any 'quasi-claim' one makes need not be taken seriously. For there is nothing that it is to take such a pseudo-claim seriously.

Put in this way, we see that Wittgenstein is traduced (hereabouts) if one takes 'pragmatic self-refutation' to be somehow inferior to 'real' or 'semantic self-refutation.'[17] Wittgenstein's point is that Cartesian scepticism cannot even get off the ground: it makes no truth-claims or truth-denials to evaluate. We have here, then, a whole epistemological tradition condensed into a drop of grammar. Now, this does not imply that we have here, already, an effective response to or diagnosis of scepticism. That takes a lot longer, and must, I believe, have the kind of character indicated in Stanley Cavell's work. Most 'Wittgensteinians' are under an illusion, if they think that Wittgenstein provides a handy, correct way of silencing or refuting 'the sceptic.' Nor does the above imply that there cannot be any such thing as someone enjoying or enduring the mental occurrence, "I am dreaming," or that such occurent quasi-thoughts do not, by means of an apparently quite logical process, eventuate perhaps in a real mental confusion or paralysis, which can take on a Cartesian mode of presentation. If we think of schizoid intellectuals in certain moods, or indeed of sufferers from schizophrenia

– for example, of the famous cases of Daniel Schreber or Adolf Wölfli – in the light of Wittgenstein's remarks, then ought we to say simply that they are confused? That they made clear mistakes, errors? Are they, as the influential 'cognitive deficit' accounts of schizophrenia would suggest, simply the victims of frequent or permanent mistakenness?

Following Sass, I suggest not. *But,* and this is the important point, nor does that imply that we can actually succeed in genuinely understanding, in having as any kind of live or even intelligible option for ourselves, the 'hypothesis' of the sceptic (or of the schizoid individual).[18] A genuinely Wittgensteinian view, if we are to work with the vital passage from *OC* just quoted, would rather involve not just a questioning (as in Sass's work) of the crude mainstream picture of schizophrenics as poor 'reality-testers,' and a remarking (as in Sass's work) of the analogies between their 'testimonies' concerning themselves and (say) solipsistical philosophic moments (which involve not error by a 'mythology' of language), but also a clear noticing of the limited degree to which we can take seriously – or even comprehend – what they (that is, sufferers from severe schizophrenic delusion) say, *at all*. Someone who says "I am dreaming" while they are asleep is making no claim. Is someone who says the same while they are awake – and that is roughly what Schreber said, when he said that he thought he was dreaming up all around him continually, from the insects that buzzed before his eyes to the 'fleeting-improvised men' (the people, in reality) that he met on his travels – any *better* off?

I am suggesting that the peculiar, 'autistic' hyper-thinking – the hyper-rational thinking, as Sass would have it – of a Schreber might be best 'understood' as yielding nothing that we can succeed in recognising as (a) thought, as such. We might call what Schreber comes up with under such circumstances, 'quasithought.' 'Quasi-thought,' 'thought' or 'talk' in the nowhere 'beyond' the limits of thought, consisting of quasi-thoughts which are, roughly, 'logically alien,' which can only be mentally compassed through an overly hopeful and presumptuous process of analogy, or through imaginative mental projection of quite dubious status, is, strictly speaking, not to be regarded as comprehensible. As Wittgenstein once remarked, in discussing the related problem of 'private language': "I cannot accept his testimony because it is not *testimony*. It only tells me what he is *inclined* to say" (*PI* §386). We must be wary of taking seriously – of thinking that we can *interpret* or otherwise understand – what there are no clear criteria for (the evaluation of). One cannot evaluate mere *inclinations* for their epistemic reliability. One can only evaluate the likes of *testimony*.

An account of a dream can be given only from outside a dream, and 'inside' the ordinary. But with severe schizophrenia, one might say, *there* is *no outside*. There is no such thing experientially (for the sufferer) as an outside to psychosis, or at least to the kind of continual oscillation between systemic quasi-solipsistic delusion and everyday reality which we find in much of the case-history of, for example, Schreber.[19] While outside (ordinary) thought there is arguably nothing but the nothing that is (for example) psychosis. An experience, naturally, but probably not one that can be rendered in terms making sense. After a certain point, 'moments of lucidity' cannot count for much – where all would-be 'testimony' is only more mere inclination to speak,[20] where *the sufferers themselves* are no more confident of their so-called 'testimony' than of their so-called 'delusions.' If Sass is roughly right about the analogy between schizophrenia and solipsism, and if Wittgenstein (on my reading) is right, then it follows that badly-off schizophrenics are *not in the reality-testing game*.[21] But this negative remark is about *as close as we can get* to an accurate or apposite positive characterization of what game it is that they *are* playing.

For to be outside delusions (outside the 'fly-bottle,' 'inside' ordinary life) is *ipso facto* no longer to be a first-personal 'authority' on this condition. A retrospective account – one prescinding from the form of the condition, of the delusions – is not authoritative. But an 'internal'[22] account is an account without authority either: arguably, it's *at best* what someone is *inclined* to say, rather than a *testimony* as to what their experience is. The 'accounts' given by the very severely mentally ill of their experiences are in this respect precisely like the 'account' Wittgenstein's dreamer gives of what is happening to him while he is dreaming. They do *not* constitute testimony. To rely upon such 'accounts' is to be victim to a deep philosophical illusion.

Ergo, there can be *no* authoritative first-personal account of what severe schizophrenic experience is like. (We can comprehend a great deal of what those afflicted with schizoid conditions say and do, and *some* of what goes on in the more rarefied 'worlds' of schizophrenic delusions (of, e.g., thought-insertion, or of continual framing and re-framing and the overlap of frames), but not, I strongly suspect, all.) And so, strictly speaking, any such accounts, if they try to hang together, cannot themselves be anything more than nonsense, at least in significant part. For, even if you succeed in stabilizing one part of the account, another part will inevitably be(-come) unstable.

The situation is not so much like that of trying to make sense of a sentence such as, [A] "Chairman Mao is rare," which with ingenuity can be done, but more like that of trying to make sense of a long string of words such as, [B] "I hope that your to go to work is my day at the office unfortunately dry person that he is is well."[23] One can only make sense of some of the particles or phrases here at the *expense* of others, and I suggest that one is therefore best-advised to say that there is no such thing as succeeding in making sense of this 'sentence' as a whole. Thus, strictly speaking, there is no satisfactory logico-semantical separation of the sentence into meaningful parts, either.[24]

Thus purely empathetic understanding of sufferers from chronic schizophrenia is (also) ruled out. We had better say: There is no such thing as my understanding what it is like to be you, if there is no such thing as you understanding what it is like to be you. 'What it is like to be you' is just undefined, we might most usefully say, in such cases.[25]

Now, where we *cannot genuinely learn* from asking the person themself, or from an autobiography, I submit that ultimately we have *no* adequate means of evaluating or testing the reliability of any account that *we* should like to give. There is not enough of a 'check' on the account we might choose to give. We have recourse then only to purely external, scientistic accounts – and, as already remarked, I do not believe that *those* accounts can ever enable us genuinely to understand a human being.

That is the guts of my suggestion, paradoxical and uncomfortable though it might seem. I claim that the kinds of resources we humans have for under-standing one another – for understanding one another's *actions*, and being – resources drawn upon in literature and elaborated and stylized in the human/social sciences, are largely not sufficiently present in hard cases of schizophrenia, *including* in those who (like Schreber) seem shot through with thinking and introspection.

But if one accepts Wittgenstein's line of thought in *OC* and *PI*, then – without immediately retreating to a scientistic and simplistic 'cognitive deficit' account of schizophrenia – it may yet appear that a plausible and natural route of objection to my claim remains open. That objection would run roughly as follows:

'Perhaps you still have in mind too narrow a model of what "understanding" must be; perhaps the language of schizophrenics might safely be said to give us a way of speaking about the nature of schizophrenic experience in *something* like the way that the language of the stream-of-consciousness novel gave us a way of understanding / representing / speaking about the nature of thinking. (A way which has since become popular in for instance English and Composition classes (e.g. 'intensive writing,' perhaps some 'brainstorming'), as well as, of course, in certain forms of psychoanalysis and therapy.) Why shouldn't this give us a way / *be* a way of understanding schizophrenic experience?'

Well, this 'way' may well be of considerable use; and we can call it "under-standing" if we want to. I am going to try to make it unattractive to do so. I will suggest that we oughtn't to assimilate what it is that the objection recommends to "understanding." Because I think that it would constitute a serious philosophical mistake (or myth) to say that stream-of-consciousness writing (or for that matter psychoanalytic free association), even when efficaciously popularized beyond the *avant-garde*, gave us a way of capturing the *form* of thinking, or of saying what thinking is truly like. We should be careful to avoid making similar 'mistakes' in difficult cases of 'schizophrenic language.'

I wish then to question the idea that one can validly attain an interpretation of a pre-existing psychological phenomenon by means of finding a new 'appo-site' way of 'describing' – of verbally 'depicting' – it. Let me illustrate my contentions here: by reference to William Faulkner's superb use of a 'stream of consciousness' method in the opening part of *The Sound and the Fury*. It is an example peculiarly appropriate for our present purposes, as will shortly become plain, in virtue of the strictly limited (and not to be over-estimated) but neverthe-less intriguing affinities between Faulkner's protagonist, Benjy, and (say) Schreber. At this point let me begin, by quoting extensively from James Guetti:

I want to take a case…[*of recognizing a text as "another language"*]…in which it may seem self-evident that a way of speaking is…"psychologi-cally" identifiable, and therefore apparently controlled by its connections with a reader's own intelligible vocabularies from beyond the text, when in fact as a language it takes much more dominion than that. The best single example I can give…is from Faulkner's *The Sound and the Fury*, Benjy's narrative:

"…I went out the door and I couldn't hear them, and I went down to the gate, where the girls passed with their booksatchels. They looked at me, walking fast, with their heads turned. I tried to say, but they went on, and I went along the fence, trying to say, and they went faster. Then they were running and I came to the corner of the fence … and I held to the fence, looking after them and trying to say."

What Benjy is "trying to say" … is that he thinks he sees, or expects to see, or, more certainly, that he wants to see his sister Caddy, whom he used to meet on her way home from school; and he is trying as well to do something that he can never do, to talk to another human being. But what his "trying to say" amounts to, we also know, is a continuous loud and horrible bellowing. And … we know as well that Benjy now, at the age of thirty-three, is large, shambling, fat, drooling, and an "idiot."[26]

One is inclined to assume that we have a way of 'psychologically' identifying Benjy, and that that controls our understanding of Faulkner's text, but Guetti wishes to contest (and, roughly, reverse) that assumption. For, as Guetti goes on to observe of this "idiot," Benjy, who "bellows," and who yet seems somehow in Faulkner's hands to be the centre of a somewhat solipsistic intelligence:

[*W*]hat seems most interesting is the way that Benjy's comparative inca-pacity…becomes his individual capacity and power.…[*H*]is inability to conceive of causal sequences enables him to notice a very great deal as it happens.…And his failures at "trying to say"…become his "saying" to a reader.

This effect depends…on Benjy's continuousness to a reader over a time.…[*W*]hat I am suggesting is that, sooner or later, a reader ceases to [*regard*] Benjy's words as the language of an "idiot":…"Father…looked at us again. Then the dark came back, and he stood black in the door, and then the door turned black again. Caddy held me and I could hear us all, and the darkness, and some-thing I could smell.…Then the dark began to go in smooth, bright shapes, like it always does, even when Caddy says that I have been asleep."

…[*T*]o understand the emotional force of Benjy's language, is to say that it somehow generalizes his case, and that his appeal is the appeal, and his language the words, of a "child." His vulnerability, which is equivalent to the fact that his wonderful imaginings must remain frustrated and potential, his perpetual innocence that will be hurt again and again...all underwrite his image as a child. And so one might say that Benjy's text...moves us...by connecting with what we already know about children.

Or by connecting with what we *think* we know. For what in fact do we know about such childhood? How do we know that experiences for children are so beautifully discrete and yet so synchronizable..., or that – when a child slept – "the dark began to go in smooth, bright shapes"?... I would suggest, then, that we do not recognize that Benjy is a "child" by extension from what we know about other children. If there is such a "recognition" here, it probably goes in the other direction: we know about other children by Benjy; he sets a standard; he is the child. Indeed, he so moves us because probably he is somehow more a "child" than any particular child could be.[27]

The last two sentences are crucial. Benjy is perhaps a 'paradigm,' a 'prototype.'[28] In his language something is exemplified more perhaps than it is ever found in the real world; and it is described in such a way that we now *have* a way for describing 'better' that real world (or so, at any rate, we feel).

What happens as Benjy's narrative develops, I think, is rather like what Wittgenstein describes...when he says that "the same proposition may get treated at one time as something to test by experience, at another as a rule of testing" (*OC*, 15). Benjy's language ceases to be dominated by the rules of the grammars we bring to it; it becomes, for its duration, itself the dominating language. And the reason why this seems so remarkable is that it amounts, again, to a reversal of what we think we are doing with such narratives. For we at least begin by feeling that we "understand" them by placing them in some sort of comparative relation with rules and vocabularies of which we are assured; and yet, sooner or later, these narratives come to exceed such presumptions and to achieve a different kind of status. The character...becomes "right" to say what he says not because we can explain his speech "psychologically,"...but because through the appeal of its sustained presence his language is transformed from a sort of "dialect" or merely local grammar into the only way of talking, into a [*'language'*] a reader must speak as he reads.[29]

As with Benjy, so with Schreber *et al.*: Do we really understand them, by analogy or extension from things we do understand? Or is it that eventually we hear what they are saying as 'sufficient unto itself'? Like with much strong 'Modernist' literature (e.g. later Gertrude Stein, some 'L.A.N.G.U.A.G.E.' poetry[30]). More obviously even than in Benjy's case, we surely don't, I would want to claim, really *understand* extreme Modernist poetry – however good it is.

We must come to 'speak' Benjy's 'language,' rather than to continue to 'translate' it from 'idiot-talk' into our own talk, if we are to be able to get anywhere with this text, to be able to *appreciate* it. *Maybe* this can in some sense be done, at least 'in the imagination,' with schizophrenia (and maybe with other severe mental conditions, such as autism, too – as for instance the high-functioning autist Donna Williams's wonderful books[31] may bring us to think). But it is not clear that such 'imaginability' actually gets us very far (see *PI* §395). If we think of Benjy's 'talk' as *like* 'another language' we must *not* think of it as a fully decodable, interpretable language, even in principle.[32] And that makes all the difference. We may hear or even 'speak' Benjy's 'language' – but we still, I want to suggest, don't *understand* it, in the sense in which we *do* normally (virtually always, in fact) fairly fully understand each other's words, each other's utterances.[33] I am not saying that we must *actually* translate (or interpret) someone's words in order to understand them (as I think Quine (and Davidson) unwisely hold). The deepest problem for us with Benjy's language is not even that we are unable to translate or interpret it without fatally violating it. The problem is that when we try to 'go on' with it sensitively in the imagination, we encounter deep difficulties and disquietudes, because we are required to go on with something we cannot actually succeed in imagining, something it is not at all obvious it has a sense to imagine.

It is important to keep in focus, then, what is principally on the table, in the 'language' of a Benjy. As Guetti holds, it is *imaginations* of sense, and experiences *of language*, that are at issue here, experiences of 'grammatical' effects; not communications, not just meaning or signifying. Our everyday language, and certain linguistic items (e.g. ordinary utterances in foreign languages) that we can translate or paraphrase into it without any worrisome violence or loss, involve sensical significations, whereas Benjy's discourse in the main does not.

Discourse which must remain 'another language' – discourse that, like poetry, is language which exposes to our view its own form, rather than allowing itself to be translated into everyday prose, into its alleged 'meaning' (or 'moral') – discourse such as Benjy's, does *not* involve any ordinary signification (at least, not *centrally*, in terms of the features of it which are distinctive). Contrary to appearances, it does not really make *sense*. And nor, ultimately, does some of Schreber's discourse, *even in context*. This is not in the slightest a criticism; it is simply an orienting device, a reminder of how best to approach the text.

We are led by Faulkner's 'empathy' and erudition – and perhaps by the decoding 'game' he sometimes encourages the reader to engage in, the game of trying to identify 'what Benjy is *actually* talking about' – to believe that we understand now the psychology of someone with a serious mental disturbance, or of "the [*young*] child." But, as Guetti asks: What do we really know of these things? What does it *mean* to know of these things?[34] I am *not* making the point that this is fiction – in fact, I have no doubt that in its way Faulkner's writing is more illuminating about *real human beings' minds* than many an average shelf's load of psychology or psychiatry textbooks. But all we have here is a 'language' which we can now use to 'represent' abnormal – or child – psychology; or, better, to give instances of it. We have a language, for it, then (now); but we do not, I think, have knowledge of it.

It might be objected that it is dangerous to assimilate the case of 'the child' to that of 'the schizophrenic.' This is surely true – finding schizophrenic thinking to be directly analogous to the alleged-mode-of-thinking of children (and of 'primitive' peoples) is a highly dubious legacy of psychoanalytical thinking on schizophrenia, and has rightly been thoroughgoingly critiqued by Sass, among others. If pressed, I should for the sake of my argument here give up any claims I might seem to be making to the non-comprehensibility of the 'world' of the child, and simply suggest that the morals of Guetti's discussion *do* apply to the 'remote' 'world' – the *non-world* – of the chronically schizophrenic person. Strictly, much of that language *is* sound and fury, signifying nothing.[35] One does violence to that language if one renders its sentences into our own, into sentences that successfully signify, sentences that mean, sentences that have a use (as opposed to having various grammatical and psychological and associative effects upon one). Insofar as one 'translates' (say) Benjy's tale – his sentences – into our language, one strips away their 'literariness,' their particularity, transforming them into our own pale reflections (of them), finding ways of making sense of them such that they are no longer nonsensical, alien.

Of course, the objection can be made that surely Benjy's 'talk' is already a translation. Benjy does not actually speak; and we are only 'hearing' such of his stream of thoughts as language can in some sense give expression to. What could possibly constitute a rendition into language of the private thoughts of a mute idiot that *didn't* in some sense amount to a translation? But it is the necessary words "in some sense" to which I think we should attend here. The question is: what sense we can properly make of Faulkner's 'transcription' of Benjy's thought; or in what sense this writing gives us access to an 'alien' mode of thought. And my suggestion has been: that the sense in which Faulkner gives expression to Benjy's mind in *The Sound and the Fury* yields many fine things, but does not yield anything that we will be wise and happy to call *sense*, in the end. In a way, then, the objection under consideration here only strengthens or redoubles the case I am making in this paper. One might say that Faulkner has already "translated" Benjy's thought for us; my suggestion is that it is unwise of us to claim to understand *even the "translation."* We do so, ironically, at the cost of giving up on Benjy's 'alterity,' and thus obscuring from sight (or sound) his nature.[36] To turn Benjy's talk into sense violates it, and loses him and his "experience." Having tried to understand Benjy's words, we must eventually *throw* the quest to make a consistent sense out of them *away*, at the price of otherwise simply turning Benjy back into one of us. Paradoxically, the best understanding of Benjy we can come to have lies in our eventually jettisoning our efforts to understand him, or at least in coming to recognise that we cannot come to understand *him* in *any* of the ways in which we are most reasonably tempted to think we can.

We must try to overcome our desperate wish to try to understand his 'tryings to say.'

Thus my 'reading' of schizophrenic etc. madness is not romantic. I am with Sass in thinking that the 'mad' person does not change into something rich and strange, but into something so poor that it is more deeply strange than Sass has tended to allow. I am not saying that madness is another world(s), or 'another country.' I am saying that, when sufficiently severe, and indeed if and when and as a consequence of bearing a terribly strong patina of rationality ("hyper-rationality" and "hyper-reflexivity," again, are the terms which Sass uses), *it is not a "world" or "country" or "land" at all*, but *only* the mirage of one. The best understanding we can come to have of such a mirage is the full recognition of the continued and repeated and perhaps-inevitable failures of all efforts to understand. For there is perhaps no world there, but only a mirage.

One might then with most profit say, that 'the stream of consciousness novel' actually succeeded in generating a new paradigm for what we would come to regard as or count as *expressing thoughts*.[37] When most successful, it generated the powerful illusion that it was *accurately expressing a previously-existing-but-as-yet-ineffable phenomenon*.[38] That there could in an important sense be no such thing as doing that in this case nor in others like it (for grammar/language *is not responsible to reality*; only (some) *statements* are), we do not see. "Capturing" and turning the forms of our thought[39] into a content – even one "to be gestured at"– is not a possible project.

No more for schizophrenia than for literature, or philosophy.[40]

In conclusion, then, the would-be objection to the lesson I drew from *OC* fails. The least misleading thing to say about certain cases of severe 'mental illness' is probably that there can be no such thing as understanding them. (And then, of course, no such thing as misunderstanding them either. They just aren't *candidates* for understanding.) We have no criteria *via* which cognitively to evaluate them, and so *whatever we attempt to say of them by way of affirmative characterization will be arbitrary*, and in a way quite misleading.[41]

My charge against Sass is that he veers too close to making schizophrenic delusions *make sense*, or *have content*. He makes it sound like they do after all have a sense, only it is an ineffable or senseless or confused sense (cf. *PI* §500). This latter is philosophically incoherent.[42]

My critique of Sass remains however a deeply sympathetic one. For while what I say in this paper is probably "the least misleading thing" there is to say, hereabouts, as opposed to *any* attempt positively to characterize the nature of severe 'mental illness,' which will be *in a way* quite misleading, this nevertheless leaves open that such attempts will in a way *not* be that misleading. And, as importantly, this leaves quite open, further, (1) that my remarks too are not necessarily unmisleading, and also (2) that things that others have said about these matters may be at their best roughly as unmisleading as what I have said. I would put most of Sass's work in category (2); and I am aware (*à la* (1)) that my own remarks run several risks: specifically, that it will appear that I am *saying* something (uttering a controversial thesis), in this paper;[43] and that I may, faultily, lead readers to think that I have undermined Sass's 'hyper-rationalist' reading of schizophrenia, etc. I have not. I *have not challenged* Sass's hyper-rationalist construal of schizophrenia and the 'Apollonian disorders.' I believe, negatively, as he does, that 'cognitivist' and 'psychoanalytical' readings of schizophrenia etc., different as they are, fail in a roughly shared – and in both cases, drastic – fashion to understand the humanity, the rationality, of the patient. And I would go so far as to say that I believe, affirmatively, as he does (I think), that virtually all of psychopathology consists in the suffering human being trying to find safety,[44] trying to understand their condition, trying to understand the world, trying to make sense of what seems to them nonsensical.

I only suggest that the end product of all this, in severe cases, still leaves the sufferer terribly far from us: that, for instance, the degree of withdrawal from the world involved in the desperate attempt to find safety, to find certainty, of genuinely psychotic persons is in general too great for us to comprehend. We can 'understand' it at most only in the kind of way we can 'imaginatively enter into' solipsism, or into Benjy's 'world.' In other words, we cannot understand it, in any ordinary sense of those words, without doing serious violence to it, without translating it into something it is not.

My remarks here do not undermine Sass's account, then. They only press the point that (we should at least seriously consider the possibility that) no account can be given which stabilizes (e.g.) severe cases of schizophrenia into something that we can unmisleadingly be said to understand, without falsifying them. If we were to broaden the sense of what it is to give an 'account' of serious mental disorder to include thoroughgoingly *processual* 'accounts,' 'accounts' which are aware that the forms of words they use cannot be successfully stabilized by us without the point of employing them being lost, 'accounts' where the words that feature in them can in a very important sense only be mentioned (not used) by us, then we could still allow that Sass gives such an 'account' (and we might want to say the same of Faulkner).[45] If giving an 'account' is allowed to be only 'taking part in' such a process, without any kind of propositional or sensical claim-making stopping point, then so be it.

Sass would presumably say that this is enough. That the fundamental phenomenon hereabouts must surely be that we are doing what we must: trying any which way we can to speak (trying to say… Our own position, in doing the philosophy of psychopathology, is not so different from Benjy's…) of *people*, who are having *experiences*. Yes, of course. And yet…no. Because what appears to happen under extremis is that any more or less Kantian conditions of experience are left behind. Not, I have suggested, for 'another' conceptual scheme – but for a nothing, for a chaos of crossed language-games, or of schemata continually collapsing under their own weight. It may even be necessary for the purposes of understanding ourselves and not projecting our experiences onto others to consider the possibility of saying that (hyper-)rational human beings can cease to have what are untendentiously called *experiences*.

I only differ from Sass, then, in the following regard: in taking his thoughts about severe psychopathology *to their logical conclusion*, I draw the inference that the states of mind of sufferers from such pathologies are only arbitrarily identified in ways that we can be untendentiously said to understand.

Is this not an anti-Wittgensteinian conclusion? Am I, for example, being overly narrow still, failing to treat 'understanding' sufficiently as a 'family-resemblance concept' with a variety of different cases? Mustn't there be a sense in which a 'respectful,' hermeneutic-ish, Wittgensteinian approach to this matter would involve us finding a way, perhaps some kind of 'indirect' way, of describing correctly the experience of the sufferer from schizophrenia?

Not really, as Wittgenstein himself makes clear. I would invite those who feel inclined still to disagree with me and to answer the above questions in the affirmative, to offer their rival interpretation of the following remark of Wittgenstein's, a remark precisely consonant, it seems to me, with the line of argument which I have pursued in this paper: "Suppose you say of the schizophrenic: he does not love, he cannot love, he refuses to love – what is the difference?!"[46]

The difference between saying these things of the ordinary person is weighty. That a person refuses to love potentially implies a criticism not present in their being unable to love, for example. But Wittgenstein specifically rejects such discrimination, in the case of "the schizophrenic."[47] It does not matter which of these we say: there can be no such thing as getting (hard cases of) schizophrenia right. *You* can call being able to say everything and nothing – being able to say whatever you like – "understanding," if you wish! *I* would prefer to restrict the use of that term to contexts in which there is a tolerably clear distinction between understanding and *not* understanding someone. What we can be intelligibly said to understand in another – in the sense of understanding what their actions are, or understanding their motives for action, or empathetically understanding them, etc. – is (most of) the hurly-burly and variety of ordinary life. But most serious schizophrenia does not fall under that heading. It is better seen as the persistent *semblance* of another language – very much like the semblance of another language that we find in Wittgenstein's 'private linguist,' a philosopher subject to an illusion of sense, an illusion that his words, in the way he finds himself wishing to employ them, mean anything at all.

Getting Faulkner right involves seeing that his novel displays to us language which, ironically, cannot be translated or interpreted into sense…without irreducible "loss" or "garbling." An odd kind of "garbling," admittedly: a garbling which inadvisedly turns nonsense into sense.…We need to see Faulkner's language "clearly," as a language of paradox, of indeed nonsense masquerading beautifully as sense. Faulkner's art – his artifice – is the brilliant creation of a self-deconstructing illusion of meaning, an illusion of sense. The illusion perhaps that we can make sense of the 'life-world' of a young child, or of an 'idiot' – or, I have argued, by extension, of some sufferers from 'chronic schizophrenia.' If I am right, we can see Faulkner as an artist whose art bears among other things a very particular aspect: an exemplification of deflationary Wittgensteinian 'philosophy of psychopathology.'

In sum, I urge upon the reader that s/he at least *consider* an *option* – that the most impenetrable cases of 'schizophrenia' are best described not as cases of a different form of life, but, despite appearances, of no form of life at all. This is an option which has not to date been even considered in 'the literature' of/on psychopathology. What this option frees us from are the tyrannies of Scientistic or Humanistic Rationalisms; and from the mirror-image tyranny of Post-Modernism, and its love-affair with alterity. The tyranny, that is, of the neo-romantic insistence that not to be indefinitely open to others is necessarily unethical.

When our everyday criteria really do run out, I want to insist that the following option be available: the possibility that we will *pragmatically* (we are finite creatures; we cannot always try to understand forever, if we want to do anything else with our lives) and even *justly* conclude that probably we are not missing anything, by giving up (on understanding someone). There can of course be real encounters with otherness: one thinks of successful and celebrated philosophical cases such as Wittgenstein and Frazer's 'savages,' Winch and the Azande, Kuhn and Aristotle, McIntyre and Homer, *and* latterly Sass and *some* of those whose writings etc. he writes of. But *not necessarily all.*

A sufferer from severe schizophrenia remains a human being, of course, and indeed a thinker; and we can get somewhere with them, moreover, by taking them as a 'hyper-thinker.' But their thinking takes them to 'somewhere' deeply strange, strange such that we cannot find our feet with them without losing pretty much all sense of *their* having lost pretty much all their footing. They live something that we can at best enter imaginatively into entertaining[48] (i.e. the thoughts of metaphysical philosophers; i.e. in the end, nothing). That is my suggestion.

I do not of course remotely claim to have exhaustively established the truth of this suggestion. I claim only that *it is an option* for 'reading-as' the brilliant 'deranged' writings of Faulkner and (by extension) of Schreber, 'Renée,' etc.; and that it deserves fairly serious consideration. *Not* for *scientistic* reasons, but for (roughly) *literary* reasons.[49]

Notes

1   Thanks to David Rudrum for help with the title of this paper.
2   William Faulkner, *The Sound and the Fury* (corrected text), New York: Vintage, 1984, 1929, p. 288.
3   See e.g. *Philosophical Investigations*, 3rd edn., London: Macmillan, 1958, p. 232; henceforth *PI*.
4   See e.g. pp. 14–8 of *Lectures and Conversations on Aesthetics, Psychology and Religion*, Oxford: Blackwell, 1966.
5   In the following paragraphs, I draw on my "Recent Work: The Philosophy of Literature" (jointly written with Jon Cook), *Philosophical Books* XLIII (2001), 118–31.

6 *Madness and Modernism: Insanity in the Light of Modern Art, Literature and Thought*, New York: Basic Books, 1992; *The Paradoxes of Delusion: Wittgenstein, Schreber, and the Schizophrenic Mind*, Ithaca: Cornell University Press, 1994; henceforth 'Paradoxes.'

7 Stanley Cavell is an important predecessor of Sass: in that Cavell (especially perhaps in his *The Claim of Reason: Wittgenstein, Skepticism, Morality and Tragedy*, Oxford: Oxford University Press, 1979) not only details the philosophical inter-involvement of scepticism and madness, but does so in significant part *by means of* readings of great literary works (especially in his readings of Shakespeare's tragedies (see *Disowning Knowledge: In Six Plays of Shakespeare*, Cambridge: Cambridge University Press, 1987, and also "The Avoidance of Love: A Reading of *King Lear*," *Must We Mean What We Say?*, New York: Charles Scribner's, 1969, pp. 267–353, and "Macbeth Appalled," *Raritan* 12:2 (1992), 1–15; and *Raritan* 12:3 (1993), 1–15)).

8 Consult Sass, "The Consciousness Machine: Self and Subjectivity in Schizophrenia and Modern Culture," Neisser and Jopling (eds.), *The Conceptual Self in Context*, Cambridge: Cambridge University Press, 1997; and the books referenced above.

9 I have done so in my "On Approaching Schizophrenia Through Wittgenstein," *Philosophical Psychology*, 14 (2001), 449–75. That paper takes the line of thought indicated in the present paper more robustly and single-mindedly than I now would. That is: I am now less unsympathetic to Sass than I was two years ago. The interested reader might wish to *compare* the two papers with that in mind.

10 These serious difficulties that Diamond raises for Sass are the central topic of my 2001 paper (ibid.), and are discussed also in my "The Philosophy of Literature," op. cit.

11 S. Olsen and P. Lamarque published their influential (humanist and anti-literary-theoretic) book, *Truth, Fiction, and Literature*, Oxford: Oxford University Press, in the same year as Sass published his *Paradoxes of Delusion* – 1994. Olsen and Lamarque argue a *general* case that literature *qua* literature is not a source of conceptual knowledge, and that literature's literary/aesthetic qualities are falsified by claims and readings to the contrary – a claim that, if true, would buttress the more specific Diamondian (and Guettian) suspicions of Sass's project given here. However, this *general* case would be opposed by, for instance, Cavellians or Diamondians who believe that literature can *sometimes* function *as* philosophy (e.g. as ethics). It remains to be seen, in other words, whether Olsen and Lamarque can stand up to 'literary Wittgensteinian' scrutiny.

12 When I speak of "the very severely mentally ill," I may be using that term in a more restrictive way than is at first apparent to the ear. I mean to speak of those on whom, I suggest, all our efforts to understand founder. Not a case of (say) auditory hallucination where we can reach agreement with the voice hearer on what they take themselves to be hearing, but a case where our every effort fails either by our own lights or by theirs. A case, perhaps, such as those of Schreber or of "Renée." (Both of whom consistently reject the understandings offered by others – and even by themselves – of their experiences. For detail, and consideration of some further "clinical material," see again my "On Approaching Schizophrenia Through Wittgenstein.") In short, I am concerned here with cases which seem to require for their possible comprehension a whole "new mode of representation" (as in Faulkner – see below).

13 For argument to these conclusions, see Jim Conant's "The Search for Logically Alien Thought," *Philosophical Topics* 20 (1991), 115–80; and the papers by Crary and Cerbone in *The New Wittgenstein*, Crary and Read (eds.), London: Routledge, 2000. Extending the line of thinking in these authors, I am suggesting (at *least*, for the sake of argument) that we consider that seriously-felt solipsism may take to such a pathological extreme our rational modes of thinking that, inadvertently falling thereby into being a fantasy of a wholly other way of thinking, "it" fails to be any kind of (way of) thinking at all. We can enter into "it" only in the specific and peculiar "imaginative"

sense set out in Diamond's paper in Crary and Read, *The New Wittgenstein* (op. cit.), *and* in Guetti's work on imagination (see also n.19 and n.20, below).

14 There are of course very serious limits to the analogy. First, because 'schizophrenics' *speak*, unlike Faulkner's Benjy, and unlike two-year-olds. Second, because (after Sass), I do *not* want to gainsay how (pathologically) constant, quasi-scientific and *rational* much of the thinking and speaking of most 'schizophrenics' is (whereas Benjy's thinking is (for instance) deeply marked by non-rational breaks). Nevertheless, I urge the reader not to be overawed by these fairly massive *dis*-analogies; for I think that the analogy will still prove of philosophical use, if the reader risks following it through.

15 *On Certainty*, Oxford: Blackwell, 1969. Henceforth *OC*. (For a fuller picture of the way I read *OC*, with special reference to the important question (in the present context) of "the ineffable" in Wittgenstein, see my essay in Daniele Moyal-Sharrock and William Brenner (eds.), *Investigating* 'On Certainty', London: Routledge, 2004.)

16 Towards the end of this paper, I will consider a challenge to my argument here which I think there is *something* to be said for: that there is a danger that we beg the question against Sass if we demand *a stable account*.

17 I.e. for Wittgenstein, "pragmatic self-refutation" is never "mere." For Wittgensteinians do not believe that there is a separate and superior realm of "semantics." One might risk putting it this way: for Wittgenstein, language is pragmatics 'all the way down.'

18 See notes 27 28, 32 and 33, below.

19 See Sass's *Paradoxes, passim*; and Schreber's *Memoirs of my Nervous Illness*, trans. Ida Macalpine and Richard Hunter, Cambridge: Harvard University Press, 1988/1903.

20 Like the inclinations to speak in certain ways of metaphysically inclined philosophers, which is exactly what Wittgenstein is referring to in *PI* §386. (Cf. Cora Diamond's "Ethics, Imagination and the Method of the *Tractatus*," *The New Wittgenstein*, op. cit. 149–74, for a vital discussion on the process and limits of attempting to grasp (or effectively imagine) those inclinations (and those speakings).)

21 I differ slightly here from Ivan Leudar, who in his wonderful book, *Voices of Reason, Voices of Insanity: Studies of Verbal Hallucinations* (jointly written with Philip Thomas, London: Routledge, 2000), argues that voice hearers such as Schreber are continually engaged in mundane processes of "reality-testing," and are pragmatically dealing with their (bizarre) world. But the difference can be partly accounted for by pointing out that I aim to be dealing with some of the most extreme cases, moments and aspects of schizophreniform delusions (by analogy to dream-worlds and the world of the child/"idiot"), cases where I believe that Leudar's and Thomas's otherwise powerful account reaches a limit, and gives out.

22 It is important to note that the scare-quotes around words such as "internal," "inside" and "limits" here are essential. They indicate that there is no proper contrast-class to these terms as used in these philosophic contexts. E.g. there is no such thing as an "outside" to the ordinary, only the fantasy of metaphysics and the reality of delusion or interminable confusion.

23 A great (and more extended) fictional example of what I am talking about here, I would suggest, is Lucky's speech in Beckett's *Waiting for Godot*.

24 I am not here falling into a scientistic "word salad" account of "schizophrenic language." See below for why not; a preliminary indication as to why not can be found in the reminder that I am only making an *analogy* to the difficulties one inevitably has in making sense of [B], above.

25 It might be objected here that, while there can be no *testimony* in such cases, nevertheless a cry or a flinch (or a nonsense-sentence) can be expressive of how things are with the subject. A two- or three-year-old child – or a cat – cannot *report* on their experience but can still give a degree of *expression* to it, and thus give us some access to the character of it. So, it might be reasoned, the character, the form, of first-person accounts – or rather, expressions – at least *expresses* the subject's experience (the expe-

rience of a "schizophrenic," or of an idiot, or of a child). My response to this objection is the meat of my account of Faulkner's Benjy, below. To anticipate: I accept the objection only as long as one does not try to retain a sense of there being an effable (or, for that matter, "ineffable") *content* to the "expression."

26 *Wittgenstein and the Grammar of Literary Experience*, Athens: University of Georgia Press, 1993, p. 86. Cf. *The Sound and the Fury*, op. cit., particularly the segments early on in the novel wherein some of the black characters explicitly recognize the patternedness and in a way deep "intelligence" of Benjy's particular sensitivities (to names, *etc.*), as well as of *his confusions*. Somewhat like some "people with schizophrenia," Benjy at times manifests deep and even otherwise-unavailable insights. In a fuller presentation, we should explore these matters; but in this paper, I am focussing upon the respects in which Benjy *lacks* what we should ordinarily and properly call "comprehensibility," and in which accounts of him, as of people with serious schizophrenia, are therefore arbitrary.

27 Ibid., pp. 87f. The turning of the direction of understanding "in the other direction" here is somewhat reminiscent of Kripke's (somewhat more extreme) strategy *vis-à-vis* rule-following, which he attributes to Hume, under the name of "inversion" or "reversal." See e.g. pp. 93ff. of Kripke's *Wittgenstein on Rules and Private Language*, Cambridge, MA: Harvard University Press, 1993.

28 And one might with profit here compare the function of "paradigms" in science according to Thomas Kuhn. A thoroughgoing scientific revolution, such as the Chemical Revolution, yields radically new paradigms of thinking, and thus produces a *deep* difficulty for scientists in understanding even their own past views. I am suggesting that a *more extreme* version of the same process is at work in cases of radical literary innovation and artifice, of "literary revolution" – and afflicts the severely psychopathological, similarly. (For detailed discussion, including of the connection between incommensurability in science and in literature, see my *Kuhn*, Oxford: Polity, 2002, jointly written with Wes Sharrock.)

29 Guetti, pp. 88–9 (my italics).

30 A fine example is the opening of J. H. Prynne's *Word Order*, Kenilworth: Prest Roots Press, 1989.

31 Her extraordinary first person "account" of autism, in *Nobody Nowhere*, London: Doubleday, 1992 and in *Somebody Somewhere*, London: Doubleday, 1994.

32 Cf. the very opening of *The Sound and the Fury* (just as marvellous and strange as the closing of Benjy's narrative, where Guetti focusses his attention, as above): "Through the fence, between the curling flower spaces, I could see them hitting....They took the flag out, and they were hitting. Then they put the flag back and they went to the table, and he hit and the other hit....// They were hitting little, across the pasture. I went back along the fence to where the flag was. It flapped on the bright grass and the trees." If one insists on "translating" Faulkner's / Benjy's extraordinary turns of phrase such as "curling flower spaces" (not to mention the intransitive use of "hitting," the ungrammatical expression, "hitting little," the impossible 'action' of the flag, etc.) into ordinary English, the power of this "language" is lost. We should think of its metaphoricity as *strong*, as live, as *untranslatable* – unparaphrasable – except at the cost of losing its "grammatical" or "representational" *effect(s)*. The same is true *of many of the "metaphors" of schizophrenic language*. And yet it is in those "metaphors" that all that is most important to an understanding of schizophreniform experiences etc. seems to reside.

33 In a fuller presentation, we should consider more closely different senses of the word "understanding." See my *Kuhn*, op. cit., especially pp. 161–6, or my "On Understanding Kuhnian Incommensurability: Some Unexpected Analogies from Wittgenstein," *Wittgenstein Jahrbuch*, 2001/2, Frankfurt: Peter Lang, 2003 (pp. 151–72).

34 Now, one should not overdo the otherness of the very young. We are not very often *consciously baffled* by young children (though it is important that we are perhaps much more often baffled by them than by our contemporaries). Our being baffled perhaps more still by the mentally disabled or 'ill' may be in part a function of their lesser numbers and greater variety. And I think we should note, along with that, that a lack of conscious bafflement at some beings does not in any case imply an understanding of their world. I think that Guetti is right to at least ask what it even *means* to claim to understand the world of a two or three year old.

35 Or, more accurately still: just meaning nothing, in the sense in which the word 'meaning' is intimately tied to *use*. For detail on why the word "signify" may tend to lead one astray hereabouts, see my "What Does 'Signify' Signify?" *Philosophical Psychology* 14 (2001), 499–514.

36 This reminds one of Peter Winch on the Azande, stressing that to understand them it is necessary first to take seriously their difference, and place them further from us than has been usual. But Benjy, unlike the Azande according to Winch, does not return, on my view, from the placement at a distance. He *remains* deeply strange. (However, I think that, just as Winch believes we can crucially learn something about ourselves by learning about the Azande, so one can learn a good deal about oneself by "learning" – or consistently failing to learn – "about" (or "from"?) Benjy (or Schreber). As David Rudrum (in conversation) puts it: it's not just that I'll teach you differences. It's also that differences teach you "I.")

37 My thought here is akin to that of Ian Hacking (both his important writings on regimes of truth-and-falsity and his work on the emergence of new possibilities for human being – e.g. being a 'multiple,' a person with M. P. D., on which see his *Rewriting the Soul: Multiple personality and the sciences of memory*, Princeton: Princeton University Press, 1995), and of Kuhn (on there being no criteria beyond the paradigm). "But doesn't something become a new paradigm *because* we feel that it gets things right?" Maybe, but so what? Because a brave new metaphor "gets it right" somehow, does it follow that metaphors are always translatable, or that they are in any interesting way *discovered* to be *correspondent to reality*? In suggesting "No" for an answer, I follow Guetti (and, on this issue, Donald Davidson).

38 Very approximately, *à la* Roland Barthes's "reality effect," which concerns the generation of an effective appearance of "realism," of expressing a pre-existent reality, by means of subtle textual techniques. See pp. 141ff. of his *The Rustle of Language*, Oxford: Blackwell, 1986. See also Joseph Reed's *Faulkner's Narrative*, London: Yale, 1973, which partially anticipates Guetti in arguing for a non-realist rendering of Faulkner's language. (One might ask whether my argument has the result that there can be no such thing as understanding *literature*. This will follow only for literature with "a strong grammar," with a serious "difference." I am not committed to implausible claims such as that there can be no such thing as understanding *Pride and Prejudice*, or *War and Peace*.)

39 And likewise, it follows from the above, the forms of *reality* too. The reason why capturing the form of *language* or of *thought* is likely to strike us as a more exciting project is just that it is a newer one.

40 It might be objected here that, in allowing that one can come successfully to represent schizophreniform etc. thought, I have conceded to Sass all that he needs. In answer to this objection, I would say: First, that it is true that what I am saying is in a way distinct from what Sass wants hereabouts only by a hair's-breadth; but yet, seeing that there is a hair here and getting the breadth of this hair right is important. And second, that a lot hangs on what one understands by "successfully" – I have allowed that one can do something(s) that is (are) worth calling perspicuously representing schizophreniform etc. thought, but not that in doing so one becomes able to state the form or nature of such thought truly. The whole point of this paper is (a) that coming

to see a kind of writing as adequate to a form of thought (or for that matter to a dimension of reality) is only little like coming to an understanding of that form of thought, and (b) that there is a further wrinkle in this case: the 'form of thought' in question here may in the end be so very remote that we should pause before continuing to regard what we have done as coming up with a mode of representation of a form of *thought*.

41 These conclusions buttress those of my "On Approaching Schizophrenia Through Wittgenstein" (op.cit.), a companion paper to the present paper in this regard. (See also n.9, above.)

42 Care is needed, as intimated below, not to use this point to rule out of order the very project of comprehending confusions or failures-to-make-sense. A resolute ruling out of the very idea of a senseless sense must not bring with it a ruling out of the reality of people finding themselves in the position of striving to utter something like a proposition with a senseless sense – as perhaps Sass and Schreber alike (and Benjy too, unconsciously?) find themselves striving.

43 When all I mean to be doing, after Wittgenstein, is perspicuously presenting 'something,' and trying to avoid misunderstandings that we (including I) are prone to, hereabouts.

44 A point I hope to pursue more fully in future work is this: I think Sass under-estimates the crucial motivating role of *fear* and sheer *terror* (fear of letting one's guard down, of things becoming unbearable, of death, of torture, of insanity, of the power over one of other people, of "God," etc.) throughout "the Apollonian disorders."

45 Again, the part of Faulkner's "account" manifested in Benjy's narrative is of course particularly paradoxical in being an account given by one...who doesn't talk. But again, Benjy still acts and "expresses himself"; and, as Wittgenstein always urged, what is most important about language is language in action or as action, not language as something radically separate from or "above" action. What we are about in this paper is understanding or accounting for (linguistic and non-linguistic action) – and understanding where that project of understanding gives out.

46 *Culture and Value*, Chicago: University of Chicago Press, 1980, p.77.

47 *Benjy* does seem to love, deeply. He hangs out at a golf course just to hear random strangers utter a word that echoes his sister's name. He can't express his "love" in any (other) way. But it still very much seems to be love....But perhaps that in turn is a temptation which we need to overcome, in the course of our reading Faulkner's masterly novel. I would suggest that we are likely to overcome it, by the very end of the novel, if we take seriously the other "views" of Benjy (other than "his own") which Faulkner offers us. We must not give up prematurely on our wish to find love in Benjy, or in "the schizophrenic"; but we may eventually decide, albeit reluctantly, to withdraw the word from our account of them, much as we may decide to withdraw the word "language" from our account of what Wittgenstein's "builders" are uttering, or to withdraw the word "proposition" from our account of what most of the strings of words encountered in the *Tractatus* are.

48 Again, we are here in the territory of the extremely difficult issues explored by Diamond in her "Ethics, Imagination..." (op.cit.); and again, we run the risk of intimating a greater gulf than there is between such 'imagination' on the one hand and 'understanding' another subject's 'world' on the other. All I can do is reiterate that I think the refusal to entertain such a conception of imagination as, following Diamond, I have tentatively urged in this paper, results in *either* a kind of scientistic begging of the question against 'the schizophrenic' *or* a pre-judgment in favour of something like the metaphysics of post-modern "alteritistic" humanism.

49 Many thanks to James Guetti, Louis Sass, David Rudrum, Angus Ross, James Conant, Kathleen Stock, Cora Diamond, Lyndsey Stonebridge, Richard Allen, Malcolm Turvey, Ivan Leudar, Emma Willmer, and Nadine Cipa. Portions of this paper draw on (and expand, adapt and update) my "Literature as Philosophy of Psychopathology," forthcoming in *Philosophy, Psychology, Psychiatry*.

Part IV

FICTION AND
THE *TRACTATUS*

15

FACTS AND FICTION

Reflections on the *Tractatus*

Alex Burri

Introduction

In this paper I shall investigate what theory of fiction can be constructed on the basis of the *Tractatus* in general and Wittgenstein's picture theory of language in particular. Although Wittgenstein has not commented on the problem of fictional discourse in his early writings, it is perfectly possible to make observations about it from a Tractarian perspective. In doing so I shall simply presuppose Wittgenstein's early ontology and philosophy of language (or a particular interpretation thereof) and then try to find out what conclusions relevant to the theory of fiction may be drawn from these presuppositions. Especially, I shall try to answer two clusters of questions. First: what is the subject matter of a fictional text? what is a novel, for example, speaking about? what ontological status do so-called fictional entities have? And second: does fictional discourse have cognitive value besides, say, aesthetic or entertainment value? can we gain genuine knowledge from fiction?

Alternative views on the ontology of fiction

The question of what fictional texts are really about invites quite different answers. This is due to the fact that we can ask a series of subordinate questions whose respective answers lead to a plethora of possible positions with regard to the ontology of fiction. The first and most general of these subordinate questions is whether fictional texts are about anything at all. Is there really something fictional statements refer to – or is it, quite to the contrary, characteristic of fictional texts that they do not speak about anything?

In my view, the radical thesis that fictional texts are not about anything at all would only be tenable if the statements they consist of were either senseless or subject to a purely instrumental interpretation in the spirit of van Fraassen. However, fictional statements are obviously not senseless. In fact, not only do we *understand* a sentence like "Sherlock Holmes lived in Baker Street" without a second thought but we even regard it as *true or false* (at least in the context of Arthur Conan Doyle's stories). *Prima facie* this is strong evidence for the claim that fictional statements have some sort of truth-makers and are, therefore, about something.

Now van Fraassen has argued to the effect that theoretical statements occurring in scientific theories such as "Neutrinos have non-zero rest mass" cannot, positivist and operationalist claims to the contrary, be regarded as disguised reports on observables or measurement procedures and must, therefore, be understood literally, i.e. non-metaphorically. Nevertheless, theoretical statements do not, according to van Fraassen, have a truth value. In consequence, there is no need to believe that the entities they postulate are real.[1] One way to interpret this contention, which is not exactly van Fraassen's, is to say that theoretical statements merely are a convenient instrument we use in order to "save the phenomena." To put it in Quine's words: "the conceptual scheme of science [is] a tool, ultimately, for predicting future experience in the light of past experience."[2]

However, such an instrumentalist interpretation of a certain class of statements presupposes that their context provides us with a second, quite different class of statements which really have a truth-value and with regard to which the former class can be used as a tool. In the case of scientific theories this is the class of observational statements. But fictional contexts preclude any instrumentalist interpretation because they contain *nothing but* fictional statements. Therefore, they lack the indispensable counterpart to the observational statements in science.

I conclude that fictional statements have truth-makers and are about something. This does not commit us to a liberal ontology or even a kind of Meinongianism, however. For we are not forced to claim that a fictional statement like "Sherlock Holmes lived in Baker Street" must be understood literally and is about Sherlock Holmes or Baker Street, respectively. On the basis of philosophical analysis it may well turn out that such a fictional statement refers to something quite different from what its surface grammar suggests. The statement does not have to be taken at face value in order to have a truth-maker. One may, that is to say, very well regard "Sherlock Holmes lived in Baker Street" as true (in the context of Conan Doyle's detective stories) without having to concede the existence of Sherlock Holmes. In order to do so one merely has to produce a suitable *paraphrase* of the original statement – a paraphrase that can or should be taken at face value. According to this proposal, it is the literally understood paraphrase, then, that places before our view the actual truth-maker and actual referent of the original statement.

For the sake of simplicity I am going to call the things fictional statements are about "fictional entities." As the above considerations have already shown, fictional entities need not be the things fictional statements, taken at face value, pretend to be about. If fictional statements must at first be paraphrased in order to display their real truth-makers, then fictional entities will turn out to be *ersatz* entities. Hence, Sherlock Holmes could, in principle, be anything whatsoever – a real person, a psychological state, a prime number or what have you. That just depends on the feasibility and appropriateness of the paraphrase in question.

As arithmetic is about numbers, fictional texts are about fictional entities. Although there can hardly be an objection to that mode of expression, in itself it is uninformative. For as long as we have not specified what fictional entities are, we learn nothing by being told that fictional texts are about fictional entities. Moreover, in the case of fictional entities, as opposed to, say, physical or biological entities, we lack a reasonably clear preconception of their nature.[3] And this makes for a considerable difference between science and fiction. That is why the need for philosophical clarification is much stronger in the case of the latter. At the same time, however, the range of possible answers will grow with it.

The second subordinate question is whether fictional entities are abstract or concrete. Anyone who opts for the first alternative will typically align the ontology of fiction with Platonist accounts in the philosophy of mathematics,[4] while proponents of the second alternative will usually bring fictional and ordinary discourse as much into line with each other as possible.

Apparently, the latter view is primarily motivated by an urge to save the alleged cognitive value of fictional discourse. For if fictional entities were abstract, it would be far from clear how the reading of a novel, for example, could possibly impart worldly knowledge to us.[5] And in contrast to mathematics, we are unable to run an indispensability argument in order to account for the cognitive value of fiction. Whereas mathematical statements are indispensable for the formulation of scientific theories and, in consequence, an essential part of our "web of belief," fictional statements are not. An overall theory of the world can do without them.

It is not my aim, however, to compare these two options with respect to their mutual advantages and disadvantages. I am merely interested in examining them from a Tractarian perspective. After having answered the question of whether fictional statements are about anything at all in the affirmative (for completely general reasons), we must, that is to say, ask ourselves whether fictional entities have to be considered abstract or concrete according to Wittgenstein's early philosophy. This question can very well be answered because Wittgenstein has put forward in the *Tractatus* some overarching ontological theses which exclude one of the alternatives.

Wittgenstein's Kantianism

Within the framework of the *Tractatus*, fictional entities must be concrete because there are no such things as abstract entities according to Wittgenstein's early philosophy. The reason for this is rooted in what I call "Wittgenstein's Kantianism." That the *Tractatus* can be read as a piece of Kantian philosophy is, of course, not a new thesis. Erik Stenius has devoted a whole chapter of his introductory book to it.[6] But he relates the Kantian motifs apparent in the *Tractatus* primarily to its limiting or "transcendental" undercurrent:

The task of (theoretical) philosophy is for Wittgenstein as for Kant to indicate the limits of theoretical discourse. But since what belongs to theoretical discourse is what can be 'said' at all in language, the investigation of this limit is the investigation of the 'logic' of language, which shows the 'logic of the world.'...What Kant's transcendental deductions are intended to perform: this is performed by the logical analysis of language.[7]

This is without doubt the case. But I am interested in another aspect of the *Tractatus* that is connected to the one Stenius is stressing – namely Wittgenstein's Kantianism with respect to ontology. One of the most central claims in the *Critique of Pure Reason* is the thesis that "the conditions of the possibility of experience in general are likewise conditions of the possibility of the objects of experience."[8] It constitutes a cornerstone of Transcendental Idealism, i.e. the view that every object of experience must have (or conform to) certain forms in order to be a possible object of experience at all. The forms of experience are imposed on the objects of experience by the structure of the human mind, i.e. our perceptual and cognitive apparatus. And we can find a modified version of this Kantian thesis in the *Tractatus*: "A speck in the visual field, though it need not be red, must have some colour: it is, so to speak, surrounded by colour-space. Notes must have *some* pitch, objects of the sense of touch *some* degree of hardness, and so on."[9] Having some color or other, that is to say, is a form of visual experience; therefore, it automatically and necessarily transposes to the objects of visual experience.

Now Wittgenstein distinguishes between the form and the material properties of things. The property of being red, which he alludes to in the remark quoted, is a material property while the property of being colored is a (Kantian) form of (visual) objects. A material property is contingent; a thing can have it or not. Therefore, it can only be instantiated by a composite thing (see *TLP* 2.0231), i.e. a so-called "complex" (*TLP* 3.24), "complex of objects" (*TLP* 4.441), or "configuration of objects" (*TLP* 2.0231). In contrast, having a pitch and being colored are properties that are necessarily instantiated by the things that have them – simply by virtue of the fact that these things are objects of (auditory, visual, etc.) experience. A thing we have an experience of must have one (first order) property or another – or else we could not experience it. And the (second order) property of having one (first order) property or another is a necessary property of that thing, i.e. one of its forms.

Wittgenstein adds: "Space, time, and colour (being coloured) are forms of objects" (*TLP* 2.0251). A speck in the visual field, that is to say, of necessity has not only a certain color but also a certain position and period of time at which and during which it is present in the visual field. Apart from these spatio-temporal and phenomenal forms objects also have a logical form. The logical form is a combinatory property of objects: "Just as we are quite unable to imagine spatial objects outside space or temporal objects outside time, so too there is no object that we can imagine excluded from the possibility of combining with others" (*TLP* 2.0121). Since a combination of objects is what Wittgenstein also calls "a state of affairs," this means that "it is essential to things that they should be possible constituents of states of affairs" (*TLP* 2.011).

Now it seems quite obvious that the objects of the sense of touch *need not* have a color and that the objects of the sense of hearing *cannot* have a color – cases of synaesthesia notwithstanding. Therefore, certain forms such as having a pitch, being colored or having a certain degree of hardness are not universally instantiated. But logical form, i.e. the property of potentially relating to other objects (the property of being a possible constituent of states of affairs), is instantiated by all objects whatsoever. That is why Wittgenstein sometimes simply calls it *the* form of an object: "the possibility of its occurring in states of affairs is the form of an object" (*TLP* 2.0141).

If logical form were really the only form that is instantiated by all objects, one could not conclude from Wittgenstein's Kantianism on its own – i.e. from the assumption that every object has at least one non-trivial property essentially[10] – that all Tractarian objects are objects of experience and hence concrete. For even *prima facie* abstract objects have a logical form. The number 17, for example, could neither exist nor be what it is if it would bear no relation to other natural numbers. After all, being the successor of 16 is essential to the number 17.

However, since it is necessary that all objects whatsoever can occur in states of affairs, there would have to be *abstract* states of affairs for abstract objects to exist. And in consequence, we would have to *compare* a mathematical statement (or any other statement allegedly referring to abstract objects) with an abstract state of affairs in order to tell whether it is true or false (cf. *TLP* 2.223). But this is not how we find out about mathematical truth: "the possibility of proving the propositions of mathematics means simply that their correctness can be perceived without its being necessary that what they express should itself be compared with the facts in order to determine its correctness" (*TLP* 6.2321).

The deeper reason for this is that the truth or correctness of a mathematical statement cannot depend on the existence of a state of affairs. For states of affairs are "changing and unstable" (*TLP* 2.0271) and therefore *contingent*. If mathematical statements really were to depict (abstract) states of affairs, there would have to be necessarily existing states of affairs as well as genuinely depicting propositions that are true *a priori*. But "there are no pictures that are true a priori" (*TLP* 2.225), and "whatever we can describe at all could be other than it is" (*TLP* 5.634).

Hence, there are no mathematical or otherwise abstract states of affairs and, as a result of that, no abstract objects either. A natural number like 17 is not an object at all but "the exponent of an operation" (*TLP* 6.021) or, as it were, a rule determining how often an operation has to be applied. In consequence, mathematical statements are "pseudo-propositions" (*TLP* 6.2) that, like the tautologies of logic, "do not represent any possible situations" (*TLP* 4.462).

All Tractarian objects are concrete, i.e. of spatio-temporal form. Like logical form, space and time are universally instantiated. Therefore, fictional entities must be concrete, too.

Ersatz entities

After having established that fictional entities must be concrete according to the Tractarian picture, we are now confronted with the question of what kind of entity they are. Especially, we have to discuss whether fictional entities are *ersatz* entities or not. This coincides with the question of whether a fictional statement like "Sherlock Holmes lived in Baker Street" has to be understood literally. If not, then it must be possible to give an appropriate paraphrase that *can* be taken at face value and thus enables us to read off what the original statement is really about. The entities explicitly mentioned in the paraphrase would then be *ersatz* entities functioning as substitute referents of the fictional names (such as "Sherlock Holmes" and "Baker Street") that occur in the original statement.

Reverting to *ersatz* entities is very popular in all areas of philosophy. For example, second order quantification over properties and relations is typically circumvented by introducing *sets*, a new kind of (abstract) individuals, into the domain of the first order quantifiers. Thereafter, first order quantification over sets – i.e. extensions of predicates – enables us to simulate second order quantification over properties and relations. The former thus become *ersatz* entities for the latter.

In the case of fiction, tokens of linguistic expressions literally present themselves as concrete substitutes for Sherlock Holmes and other fictional entities. David Lewis calls this proposal "substitutionalism" and stresses: "Sub-sti-tutionalists simulate quantification over fictional characters by quantifying for real over fictional names."[11] According to this doctrine, then, it is the *occurrence* (or the tokening) of the sentence "Sherlock Holmes lived in Baker Street" in Conan Doyle's novels[12] that constitutes the truth-maker for the claim that Sherlock Holmes lived in Baker Street (in the context of Conan Doyle's detective stories).

Linguistic expressions, and especially tokens thereof, meet the Tractarian requirement that fictional entities must be concrete. Moreover, substitutionalism fits perfectly into the framework worked out in Wittgenstein's early philosophy. For according to the picture theory of language, a sentence is made true by a fact which corresponds to (or coincides with) the thought expressed by that sentence. In order to be able to do so both the sentence and the thought expressed by it must have the same structure, the same logical form as the corresponding fact. Hence, if the proposition that Sherlock Holmes lived in Baker Street is made true by the tokening of a certain sentence in Conan Doyle's novels, then that very sentence must have the logical structure of a fact. And this is exactly what Wittgenstein says about sentence tokens ("propositional signs") in particular and pictures in general: "What constitutes a propositional sign is that in it its elements (the words) stand in a determinate relation to one another. A propositional sign is a fact" (*TLP* 3.14; see also 2.14 and 2.141).

Thus the *Tractatus* supports the substitutionalist interpretation of fictional discourse. However, there is reason to reject it: if the occurrence of certain sentences really were to ground the truth of fictional statements, then one would have to interpret the *general terms* and the *logical vocabulary* in a substitutionalist manner as well. Combined with the picture theory of language and its built-in doctrine of truth-makers, substitutionalism is an all or nothing matter. But the truly problematic expressions are the proper names and singular terms whereas predicates like "red" and sentential connectives like "or" do not seem to cause particular trouble. According to van Inwagen, for example, a predicate like "fat" retains its ordinary meaning in fictional discourse (although the property of being fat is not really *predicated* of a fictional character such as Mrs. Gamp or Sherlock Holmes but merely *ascribed* to it – in van Inwagen's technical sense of "ascribing").[13] And this is a very natural way to handle the semantics of general terms in fiction. According to the substitutionalist-*cum*-Tractarian view, however, "fat" would no longer stand for the property of being fat but would instead denote certain words occurring in fictional texts.

A substitutionalist might say in response that the interpretation of fictional statements is analogous to Frege's interpretation of direct speech according to which "one's own words ... first designate words of the other speaker, and only the latter have their usual meaning."[14] As in quotation, words occurring in fictional contexts would, that is to say, display a kind of deferred reference or meaning: they stand for linguistic expressions that have their usual meaning; and this, in turn, enables them to *borrow* the standard meaning from the expressions they stand for. Such a solution is inadequate in the case of fiction, however. It is true that one could thereby do justice to van Inwagen's intuition concerning general terms but at the same time one would revive the very problem substitutionalism was intended to solve, i.e. the problem of fictional names. For in contrast to "fat," the linguistic expression "Sherlock Holmes," which serves as the referent of the identical fictional name, does not have a usual meaning or standard reference at all.

Within the framework of the *Tractatus* substitutionalism fails because its semantic analysis of singular terms inevitably affects the semantics of general and logical terms as well. If it were possible to account for the meaning of singular terms used in fiction without thereby touching on the unproblematic rest of the vocabulary, then we would be far better off. And I think that an appropriate treatment can indeed be put forward.

Building block ontology

Apart from spatio-temporal and phenomenal form, Wittgensteinian objects also have a logical form that enables them to combine with each other, thus giving rise to more complex things. What we usually call "objects" in everyday life are nothing but configurations of ultimately simple objects which "make up the substance of the world" and "cannot be composite" (*TLP* 2.021). Here I am going to use "complex" as a generic term for all compound things, comprising both (atomic) states of affairs, i.e. *Sachverhalte*, and (non-atomic) situations, i.e. *Sachlagen*. Since complexes are assembled entities their *possibility* is entirely determined by the logical (read: combinatory) form of the simple objects they are (or could be) composed of. "If all objects are given," Wittgenstein emphasizes, "then at the same time all *possible* states of affairs are also given" (*TLP* 2.0124), adding: "objects contain the possibility of all situations" (*TLP* 2.014).

The totality of all possible states of affairs is called "logical space" (*TLP* 1.13) and we can define a possible world as a maximally consistent subset of logical space. From this and the considerations just made it follows that every possible or "imagined world, however different it may be from the real one, must have something – a form – in common with it" (*TLP* 2.022). The real world differs from merely possible worlds neither in its form nor in the simple objects it is composed of but rather in the way these basic building blocks are combined with each other. In contrast to merely possible worlds, the actual world *exclusively* consists of existing (*bestehenden*) states of affairs (see *TLP* 2.04). In Wittgenstein's usage, existing states of affairs and existing situations are called "facts" (see *TLP* 2 and 2.06).

According to the Tractarian view, fictional entities are neither abstract nor a kind of *ersatz* entity. It is therefore natural to assume that fictional texts such as novels describe (parts of) possible worlds, i.e. (partial) ontological recombinations of the actual world. However, I consider this thesis to be untenable in its general and unrestricted form. For a possible world in the Tractarian sense may very well contain *actual* complexes. On the one hand, of course, there are possible worlds not having any states of affairs or situations in common with the actual world. On the other hand there also are possible worlds that contain at least some *facts*, i.e. complexes simultaneously present in the actual world. That is to say, a possible world can be a mixture of both existing and non-existing states of affairs or situations.

But a fictional world, a world as described by a novel, cannot, it seems to me, contain any complex occurring in the actual world as well. For otherwise we would get insurmountable difficulties with the notion of fictional truth. Let us assume for the sake of the argument that at least the familiar proper names (like "London" or "Baker Street") to be found in Conan Doyle's detective stories refer to actual entities. Then Conan Doyle's statement that Sherlock Holmes lived in 221B Baker Street would turn out to be false since there was no such house in late nineteenth-century London. At that time Baker Street was much shorter than it is today – its house numbers ran from 1 to 85. Therefore, both the city and the street Sherlock Holmes lived in cannot be the actual London and the actual Baker Street, respectively. And such considerations can be generalized. The statements of a novelist are always authoritative as far as fictional truth is concerned. And because fictional truth always outdoes empirical truth, we should, on pain of contradiction, not expect fictional proper names to refer to actual complexes.

In contrast to real things, that is to say, fictional objects are *merely* possible entities. Consequently, fictional worlds are *merely* possible worlds, i.e. worlds that have no complexes in common with the real world. But how can that be? Why should it be impossible to *describe* (as opposed to *name*) an actual complex in a novel? Surely, in addition to the point concerning truth there should also be an *ontological* reason for fictional entities never being actual. And indeed there is. As we shall see, fictional entities, unlike actual ones, have no depth, i.e. they are not completely determinate.

Complete analysis and full clarification

Whether there was, say, a green house at 15A Baker Street in the actual London of 1895 is completely determined even if we may no longer be in a position to figure out the correct answer. But I deny on principle that the question of whether there was a green house at Conan Doyle's fictional Baker Street, number 15A, has an answer at all. For Conan Doyle remains silent about it. Apart from problems due to vagueness it is at least in principle possible to answer all conceivable questions concerning the actual Baker Street. But nothing similar is possible with regard to Conan Doyle's fictional Baker Street. That is what I mean by its "not being completely determined." And it is the in principle underdetermination of fictional entities that precludes their being actual and thus turns them into merely possible things.

Now the notion of in principle underdetermination can be elucidated with the help of the Tractarian concept of complete analysis. According to Wittgenstein, every statement about actual complexes "can be resolved into a statement about their constituents and into the propositions that describe the complexes completely" (*TLP* 2.0201). In other words, every such statement can be expressed in a "completely analysed" (*TLP* 3.201) proposition or propositional sign, respectively. If such an analysis is performed, "the configuration of [*simple*] objects in a situation corresponds to the configuration of simple signs in the propositional sign" (*TLP* 3.21). In a completely analyzed proposition, that is to say, "there must be exactly as many distinguishable parts as in the situation that it represents. The two must possess the same logical (or mathematical) multiplicity" (*TLP* 4.04). By analysis we finally get to "elementary propositions which consist of [*simple*] names in immediate combination" (*TLP* 4.221). Cor-res-pondingly, a completely analyzed proposition is a truth-function of elementary propositions.

The analysis of a statement does not "resolve the sign for a complex in an arbitrary way" (*TLP* 3.3442), and hence "a proposition has one and only one complete analysis" (*TLP* 3.25). Although a completely analyzed sentence (or "propositional sign") specifies both the exact sense and the exact truth condition of the original statement, Wittgenstein conceded in his *Notebooks* that the truth condition of an *ordinary* statement about complexes may not always depend on the exact arrangement of their constituents.[15]

For example, when I claim that the chess pieces are in the box, I do not commit myself to a particular arrangement of the individual pieces within the box. Quite to the contrary, as long as the complete set of chess pieces is in the box, there are countless particular arrangements that could make my claim true. Without opening the box and thereby reverting to experience I cannot, therefore, produce a complete analysis of my statement. Nevertheless, I could, at least in principle, subject it to what Peter Simons calls a "full clarification." Such a clarification would, by means of a very long disjunction, enumerate every possible arrangement of the individual chess pieces that could as a matter of fact make my claim true: "a fully clarified proposition may be thought of as a vast disjunction of fully resolved propositions, only one of which happens to be true."[16] Thus it specifies, right down to the last detail, the *intended* truth condition of the original statement.

The underdetermination of fictional entities finds its expression in the fact that fictional statements cannot be completely analyzed but at best fully clarified. Of course, they share this peculiarity with many ordinary statements about complexes like the claim that the chess pieces are in the box. Nonetheless, there is an important difference: in the case of the latter, we are usually able to verify with the help of experience which particular arrangement of the complex's constituents really obtains and thus accounts for the truth of the statement. In other words, if we are in possession of a full clarification, we can typically find out which part of the vast disjunction happens to be true. But in the case of a fictional statement such as "After Holmes's departure for the concert, I lay down upon the sofa,"[17] this is not so. For example, it is impossible to find out – be it by experience, by testimony or by any other means – whether Dr. Watson lay down to the left or to the right. It remains underdetermined which of these spatial arrangements of the complexes referred to by "I" and "the sofa" really is the truth maker of the statement in question.

Fictional statements cannot be analyzed completely, even by reverting to *a posteriori* experience. For apart from the reading of the fictional texts in question there is no "fictional experience" that could provide us with additional information about the entities and situations described therein. All we can possibly learn of these fictional complexes has to be found in the corresponding texts themselves. And what they pass over in silence we cannot speak about either. In the case of fiction underdetermination is not an epistemological notion but an onto-logical one.

Searching for cognitive value

From a Tractarian point of view fictional entities must be concrete, non-*ersatz*, and merely possible complexes which are underdetermined in principle. Nevertheless, the general and logical terms entering into their descriptions retain their usual meaning. We can now turn to the question of whether a text that is about such entities has cognitive value – whether we can gain genuine knowledge by reading it. Now quite independently of any specific analysis of the fictional entities themselves many people would straightforwardly deny that literature is able to convey any worldly information at all – simply because they consider fiction to be a form of make-believe irrelevant to the way the world really is. But although I have sympathy for that position I think that we should not jump to such a conclusion preemptively. After all, one could not only say in response that literature obviously is educational but also bring a historical argument to bear that has been put forward by Richard von Mises: both the systematic explanations of ancient metaphysics and later day science on the one hand and the make-believe of what we now call "literature" on the other hand have their origin in pre-Socratic cosmogony;[18] and bearing in mind that they go back to the same roots, it would be surprising if they radically differed in cognitive value.

In order to sort things out we should, therefore, better take the ontological status of fictional entities into account. Otherwise the dispute over whether fiction is able to impart genuine knowledge to us will remain sterile and unproductive. Certainly, if fiction has cognitive value, then it can increase our understanding of the actual world. But how, we must now ask ourselves, can that be from a Tractarian point of view?

First, let us have a look at an answer that might seem promising at first glance. One could argue that the information gained by reading fictional texts amounts to a kind of knowledge by testimony. Not all empirical knowledge, that is knowledge about contingent situations or states of affairs, stems from one's own experience. Quite to the contrary, most of it is second hand and came down to us by hearsay, written records, and other kinds of imparting. Hence, one might be tempted to assume that the reading of a fictional text provides us with second-hand knowledge of the author's experience – or at least with a sort of simulated experience enabling us to gain certain insights. Within a Tractarian framework, however, these options are excluded because according to it fictional texts always are about merely possible entities. And in being *merely* possible, a fictional entity cannot be the object of any experience and, in consequence, not an object of the author's experience either. To put it in other words: if fictional texts were about the author's experience, their objects would be fully determined. In consequence, we could, at least in principle, answer the question whether there was a green house at Conan Doyle's fictional Baker Street, number 15A. But this, I have claimed, cannot be done.

However, it is still open to the advocate of cognitive value to adopt something like the following view. Fiction, one may say, provides us with *causal* or *conditional* knowledge about the world. For one could, on the one hand, very well concede that a single fictional statement, taken in isolation, remains strictly uninformative because there is indeed no actual state of affairs or actual situation it could correspond to, i.e. carry information about. On the other hand, one could nonetheless claim that a *sequence* of fictional statements might contain information about causal relations obtaining in the actual world. This view has been put forward by von Mises:

> The logical place of narrative poetry is in the vicinity of the *Gedankenexperiment* (hypothetical experiment) of the physicist. We suppose that a young man traveled in this manner, and we further suppose, ..., and further ...Then it is claimed, in the first place, that the assumptions do not contradict one another according to our experience and, in the second place, that this or that further chain of events follows according to general experience from the assumptions. Thus, what the writer presents is *experiences* about the interconnections of observable phenomena, and primarily of phenomena that belong to human social life.[19]

That is, conceived of as a thought-experiment, a fictional text bears some resemblance to a certain kind of *reductio ad absurdum* proof in which a problematic premise gives rise to a conclusion that stands in contradiction to background knowledge. In such proofs the problematic premise itself is not *asserted*, i.e. acknowledged as true, but functions as a mere assumption. Having derived the conclusion from it (and from unproblematic further premises), however, we can conditionalize the deduction as a whole and make the assertion that *if* the premises are true, *then* the conclusion is true, too. But since the conclusion stands in contradiction to background knowledge, we can then use *modus tollens* in order to both derive and assert the negation of the problematic premise without ever having asserted the premise itself. Similarly one could claim that a fictional text as a whole expresses a certain kind of if–then knowledge even though no fictional statement taken in isolation is ever asserted or ever acknowledged as having a Tractarian truth condition on its own.

Consequently, fictional texts would have cognitive value because they provide us with knowledge of causal relations obtaining between states of affairs, events, worldly states, or what have you. From a Tractarian point of view, however, this answer is not satisfactory either. In a nutshell, the reason for this is that the early Wittgenstein is not a realist with regard to causality but a Humeian. He denies that causality is "an inner necessity like that of logical inference" (*TLP* 5.1362) and stresses that "there is no causal nexus" (*TLP* 5.136). This means that causality is not an intrinsic relation and, therefore, that a singular causal statement of the form "*a* caused *b*" is not made true by an internal property of (or a mechanism inherent in) *a*. Rather, what makes it true according to the Humeian picture is the general fact that states of affairs, events or worldly states of type *A* regularly precede states of affairs, events or worldly states of type *B* (or, alternatively, that the occurrence of an event of type *A* increases the probability of an event of type *B*). Causality, that is to say, is rooted in certain over-arching regularities finding their expression in lawlike statements. And it is the existence of such a general pattern or regularity which justifies our belief in a singular causal proposition of the form "*a* caused *b*."[20]

Now if certain regularities function as both the *ratio essendi* and the *ratio cognoscendi* of all singular causal statements and their corresponding conditionals, then fictional texts cannot provide us with causal knowledge we do not already have. For then the truth of a conditional statement extractable from, say, a novel uniquely depends on the regularities to be found in the actual world. In consequence, fictional texts are unable to broaden our causal knowledge. When Wittgenstein remarks: "the laws of physics...still speak, however indirectly, about the objects of the world" (*TLP* 6.3431), we may well add: the causal conditionals extractable from fiction still speak, however indirectly, about the regularities of the actual world.

A third proposal would consist in characterizing fictional knowledge as *modal* knowledge, that is as knowledge about which complexes, states of affairs or situations are possible and which are not. In mathematics, the most important, though not the only,[21] criterion for the provability of a conjecture is actually *having* a corresponding proof. Analogously, one may say that the most important criterion for the possibility of something (a complex thing or situation) is actually *describing* it (in non-contradictory terms). And this, it seems, is exactly what fiction does. Hence, one may conclude that fiction is able to teach us whether certain things are possible, and thus to provide us with modal knowledge.

From a Tractarian point of view, this position is not viable either, however. For fictional entities have no depth; in contrast to actual ones, that is to say, they admit of no complete analysis and cannot, therefore, be decomposed in a unique and definite way into their fundamental constituents. Of fictional entities we know but their superficial description, and experience is unable to fill in the gaps in our knowledge. A complete description of those fundamental constituents and their arrangement is in principle out of reach. But that means, in turn, that we do not really know whether the entities supposedly described in fictional texts are possible. In order to find this out we would have to check whether their complete description contains a contradiction or not. In other words, we would have to see whether the logical form of the elementary Wittgensteinian objects enables us to combine them in a way that is compatible with the superficial description of the complex they putatively give rise to. Without a complete analysis of fictional entities at hand, however, such retro-engineering is unavailable to us.

In consequence, we must, I think, acknowledge that fiction indeed lacks cognitive value – at least when considered from a Tractarian point of view. This still leaves open whether the reading of fictional texts can impart certain *abilities* to us. But the acquisition of abilities, even if they should turn out to be cognitively valuable, is not the same thing as gaining knowledge.

Notes

1   See Bas C. van Fraassen, *The Scientific Image*, Oxford: Clarendon Press, 1980, pp. 10–12.
2   W. V. Quine, "Two Dogmas of Empiricism," *From a Logical Point of View*, Cambridge, Mass.: Harvard University Press, 1961, pp. 20–46, p. 44.
3   After the decline of the mechanistic worldview, according to which matter (conceived of as solid, inert and sluggish) can only interact through direct contact, this is

arguably no longer true of physics. Whereas one had a reasonably clear preconception of physical entities and their interaction before Newton's theory of gravitation threw first doubts upon it, contemporary physics has completely washed away our antecedent understanding of what material or physical entities are (cf. Noam Chomsky, "Language and Nature," *Mind* 104 (1995), 1–61, 3–6). Apart from understanding physical entities to be whatever physical theories quantify over, there does not seem to be any non-trivial alternative left.

4 This has, for example, been done by Peter van Inwagen in his "Creatures of Fiction," *American Philosophical Quarterly* 14 (1977), 299–308. He claims that fictional entities are abstract in the sense that they do not occupy a certain region of space–time and are intangible (cf. p. 306).

5 Moreover, one would be confronted with an additional problem well known from the philosophy of mathematics: how could we acquire any knowledge of these abstract entities themselves? – Certainly not by perception or any other causal means since abstract entities are causally inert. Cf. Paul Benacerraf, "Mathematical Truth," *The Journal of Philosophy* 70 (1973), 661–79.

6 See Erik Stenius, *Wittgenstein's Tractatus*, Oxford: Blackwell, 1964, pp. 214–26.

7 Ibid., p. 218.

8 Immanuel Kant, *Critique of Pure Reason*, trans. by Norman Kemp Smith, New York: St. Martin's Press, 1965, B 197.

9 Ludwig Wittgenstein, *Tractatus Logico-Philosophicus*, trans. by D. F. Pears and B. F. McGuinness, London: Routledge, 2001, 2.0131. Henceforth referred to as *TLP*.

10 The non-triviality clause is intended to exclude such properties as being self-identical or being an object.

11 David Lewis, "Noneism or Allism?" *Papers in Metaphysics and Epistemology*, Cambridge: Cambridge University Press, 1999, pp. 152–63, p. 159.

12 This condition is probably too strict. It may very well suffice if "Sherlock Holmes lived in Baker Street" can be deduced (according to the logic presupposed by the author) from sentences occurring in Conan Doyle's novels – for example from a paragraph containing a sentence like "More than once during the years I had lived with him in Baker Street I had observed that a small vanity underlay my companion's quiet and didactic manner" (Arthur Conan Doyle, *The Sign of the Four*, Oxford: Oxford University Press, 1993, p. 5).

13 See van Inwagen, op. cit., p. 305.

14 Gottlob Frege, "On Sense and Meaning," trans. by Max Black, in Peter Geach and Max Black (eds.), *Translations from the Philosophical Writings of Gottlob Frege*, Oxford: Blackwell, 1980, pp. 56–78, p. 58.

15 Cf. Peter Simons, "The Old Problem of Complex and Fact," *Teoria* 2 (1985), 205–25, pp. 215–17.

16 Ibid., p. 217.

17 Arthur Conan Doyle, *A Study in Scarlet*, Oxford: Oxford University Press, 1993, p. 41.

18 See Richard von Mises, *Positivism. A Study in Human Understanding*, trans. by Jerry Bernstein and Roger G. Newton, Cambridge, Mass.: Harvard University Press, 1951, pp. 287f.

19 Ibid., p. 292; his emphasis.

20 That Wittgenstein indeed accepts the so-called thesis of the Nomological Character of Causality becomes clear, it seems to me, in *TLP* 6.36.

21 As Peter Simons has pointed out to me, there are theorems whose proof in a standard system of first-order logic cannot be written down but that can be easily demonstrated in any standard axiomatic system of second-order logic. Cf. George Boolos, "A Curious Inference," *Logic, Logic, and Logic*, Cambridge, Mass.: Harvard University Press, 1998, pp. 376–82.

16

WITTGENSTEIN'S *TRACTATUS* AND THE LOGIC OF FICTION

Dale Jacquette

A picture can present relations that do not exist! How is that possible?

(Ludwig Wittgenstein, *Notebooks*)[1]

An analysis of meaning

Wittgenstein was as profoundly influenced by his appreciation of fiction as by his reading of philosophy, mathematics, science, and devotional literature. Wittgenstein reportedly carried with him a copy of Dostoevsky's *The Brothers Karamazov* along with Tolstoy's *The Gospel in Brief* during his tour of duty in the Austrian army in the First World War, and is said to have made a detailed phonetic study of Dostoevsky in Russian while learning the language in preparation for a planned but ultimately abandoned emigration to the Soviet Union.[2] The unique literary style of Wittgenstein's *Tractatus Logico-Philosophicus* owes much to the aphoristic devices of Lichtenberg, Schopenhauer, and Nietzsche, all of whose writings Wittgenstein was deeply familiar with already in the early period of his thought when the *Tractatus* was being composed.[3] There is a kind of avant poetry and music to the clipped sentences of the *Tractatus*, reminiscent of the minimalist works of modern architecture that Wittgenstein admired.

The *Tractatus* explicates a universal theory of meaning. Wittgenstein's early logical atomism, picture theory of meaning, and the doctrine of the general form of proposition are designed to explain the possibility of any logically possible language, any meaningful sign system. A language, according to Wittgenstein, must be capable of describing logically contingent states of affairs in sentences whose underlying transcendent symbolic forms can be completely analyzed as conjunctions of elementary propositions. These represent atomic facts and are in turn constituted by concatenations of names for simple objects in exactly corresponding one to one correlations with logically simple objects, whose forms are distinguished as space, time, and (generic phenomenal) color.[4] The *Tractatus* as a result appears ideally suited to explain the meaning of scientific discourse for the description of facts that Wittgenstein argues constitute the world, expressing the complex occurrences that can be built out of such rudimentary space–time–color states of affairs as red-here-now, or color-c-at-place-p-and-time-t.[5]

Does Wittgenstein's *Tractatus*, in addition to offering a logic and semantics for the languages of natural science, also provide a logic and semantics of fiction? The question is crucial in understanding the full scope and potential applicability of Wittgenstein's early theory of meaning. We cannot avoid the issue if we want to fathom precisely how the *Tractatus* is meant to function as an account of the meaning of language. The expression of thoughts in a novel or other work of fiction is presumably as much a meaningful use of language as the propositions of a scientific treatise. We might therefore say that Wittgenstein's *Tractatus*, if it is to be a universal analysis of the meaning of language, must equally provide both a logic of science and a logic of fiction. Whether the *Tractatus* actually contains at least the basis for an adequate logic of fiction can thus be said in part to determine whether Wittgenstein's early logic, metaphysics, and semantics is philosophically satisfactory as a general theory of meaning. An appraisal of Wittgenstein's semantic project should therefore remain an open question until the adequacy of Wittgenstein's system as a logic of fiction is considered. The problem admits of no simple answer, but depends as we shall see on what we mean by and require from a logic of fiction.

From true science to false science to fiction

To make a case for Wittgenstein's early philosophy as including a logic of fiction, it is appropriate to begin with the semantics of scientific language. The same provisions needed to express true descriptions of existent empirical facts equally make it possible to express false descriptions of nonexistent facts, relative to the actual state of the world. The true/false polarity in meaningful predications of properties to complex objects in science parallels the semantic if not psychological capability of telling deliberate lies that accompanies the possibility of relating truths. We cannot have one without the other, where the possibility of telling the truth presupposes and implies the possibility of lying, and conversely.[6]

As *TLP* 2.1 states, "We make to ourselves pictures of facts." If not all depictable facts exist, then, in addition to making pictures of facts just as they exist in the actual world, we can by the same ability exercised in another way make to ourselves pictures of facts that do not exist in the actual world, but in some other nonactual, merely logically possible world. We make to ourselves true and false pictures of facts. We do true and false science and we engage in sheer yarn-spinning; we tell stories, we make things up, invent fables, plot and write and narrate fictions in the lyrics of songs, poems, short stories and novels. The same linguistic largesse that enables us to make pictures of facts in science and colloquial descriptions of the existent actual world also enables us to create an art of literature. We can choose alternatively to make pictures of existent facts in a true science, or to produce fictional tales and purely imaginative picturings of nonexistent states of affairs that are not intended to correctly portray the facts of the actual world.

Truth-telling in science has its dual in false science, even on the part of sincere honest language users who intend only to describe the existent facts of the world as they actually obtain, but just happen to get things wrong. The history of science is replete with examples of false science, of descriptions and hypotheses that might have been true, had the actual world only been different, but that turned out to be false. We can cite in evidence the description of the solar system as containing only seven planets, accepted by astronomers in the past, or of the sun orbiting the earth, of spontaneous generation, of nonexistent continents and animal species conjectured as existing in remote parts of the world, and the like. The semantic resources by which Wittgenstein proposes to explain the meaning of true sentences in accurate scientific descriptions of existent logically contingent states of affairs, if sufficient, must be competent also to explain the meaning of false sentences when science happens to err. Wittgenstein acknowledges the semantic true/false polarity in the scientific description of states of affairs when he declares:

2.21   The picture agrees with reality or not; it is right or wrong, true or false.
2.221   What the picture represents is its sense.
2.222   In the agreement or disagreement of its sense with reality, its truth or falsity consists.
2.223   In order to discover whether the picture is true or false we must compare it with reality.
3.24   A complex can only be given by its description, and this will either be right or wrong. The proposition in which there is mention of a complex, if this does not exist, becomes not nonsense but simply false.[7]

If there can be true science, there can also be false science. And if there can be false science whose meaning is covered by Wittgenstein's logic and semantics, then it might appear to be but a short step from the logic and semantics of false science to a logic and semantics of fiction. Why not simply construe stories, novels, opera librettos and the like as something like a false description of the world, or a description of another logically possible world, in which the events depicted in a work of fiction nowhere transpire at any time in the actual world?

A false science about complex objects and states of affairs that do not actually exist is not that different from a short story or novel about complex objects and states of affairs that do not actually exist. Within the logical–semantic framework of Wittgenstein's early philosophy, what is needed to bridge the gap between true or false science and fiction? There are similarities and dissimilarities between false science and fiction in Wittgenstein's truth–functional logic and picture theory of meaning, some of which are obvious and others of which require more thoughtful inquiry to discover. Are the similarities between fiction and false scientific descriptions of nonexistent complex objects and nonexistent facts strong enough to support, while the dissimilarities so insignificant that they can be discounted in recognizing, the proposition that Wittgenstein's *Tractatus* contains at least the foundation for if not an implicit logic of fiction?

We have already remarked that false descriptive science and fiction agree in offering depictions of complex objects and states of affairs that do not actually exist. Insofar as Wittgenstein's logic and semantics are adequate to explain the meaning and logical structures of false descriptive science, to that extent and in at least this limited respect the theory should also be adequate to the logic of fiction. Let us avoid the substantial objections that have been and might be raised against Wittgenstein's tripartite doctrine of logical atomism, picture theory of meaning, and doctrine of the general form of proposition, and assume for the sake of argument in spite of powerful counter-considerations that the early Wittgenstein is basically on the right track in the *Tractatus*, in order to ask whether the theory he offers there with respect to scientific discourse could be made to apply straightforwardly also to the language of fiction. If fiction and false science have in common the description of complex objects and states of affairs that do not actually exist, there are also potentially important differences. A false science is ordinarily intended to be a true description of objects and events that fails because in one way or another it gets things wrong, whereas a work of fiction is not intended as a true description, but as an effort to entertain an audience, or in some cases to change attitudes, to offer insights into the human condition, and the like, with what the author from the outset understands to be descriptions of nonexistent complex objects or nonexistent states of affairs.

The author of a false scientific description can but does not usually expect to be factually mistaken, but not so in the case of the author of a work of fiction. The author of a false science errs and should be expected to withdraw a false scientific description if and when the falsehoods are discovered. By contrast, a critic attempting to raise the same kinds of objections to a work of fiction would be said either not to understand the concept of fiction or not to know that a particular document was meant to be a work of fiction. We must also recognize that science sometimes uses fictional entities heuristically to explain its principles and that novels often contain true propositions of history and science. We rightly criticize a scientist but not a novelist for falsely describing as existent a phantom planet that does not actually exist. Wittgenstein can accommodate these differences under the rubric of his primary Fregean principle that we are to look to the use of language in order to understand its meaning. Wittgenstein writes in 3.262: "What does not get expressed in the sign is shown by its application. What the signs conceal, their application declares." The same sentence, "There exists a tenth planet," has a different application in a work of false science than in a work of fiction. Can these distinct uses of the same sentence be correctly interpreted by the *Tractatus* theory of meaning, serving for different uses of language as a logic and semantics of science and fiction?

Criteria for a logic of fiction

We can only make further progress in assessing Wittgenstein's analysis of meaning by identifying what we need and want from an adequate logic of fiction. What shall we say are the essential capabilities of a formal semantics of fictional literature?

Let us take a typical work of fiction as an example and ask what features are needed in order to understand its meaning. It should not matter which we choose, but it might be best to begin with the usual canon, avoiding for the time being radically "experimental" literature that may present special interpretive problems. We might turn to Charles Dickens, let us say, rather than Djuna Barnes or James Joyce or e.e. cummings, or we might select Daniel Defoe, Tobias Smollett, Mark Twain, Saul Bellow, Nathaniel Hawthorne, James Agee, Philip Roth, Ernest Hemingway, or just about any recognized author of fiction. To understand the logical and semantic requirements of fiction we shall consider Herman Melville's classic novel *Moby Dick*, and, indeed, only a single sentence summarizing one aspect of the novel. We shall try to make sense of the assertion that in Melville's fiction, Captain Ahab sought to kill the great white whale, Moby Dick.

What is the language of fiction, and what is its logical form? What are the logical presuppositions and formal semantic requirements for what we could agree to call a logic of fiction? What should we expect to be validly and relevantly entailed by an adequate logic of fiction? We consider the following features as minimally needed for the semantics of fictional discourse, discussing the rationale for and implications of each in turn. We want to be able:

(1) To refer to and describe the properties of objects and states of affairs that do not actually exist.
(2) To interpret the sentences of a work of fiction ostensibly about the properties of objects and states of affairs that do not actually exist as true in at least some cases relative to the nonactual worlds that are partially described in a work of fiction.
(3) To enter into the deductive reasoning of fictional characters and narrators with respect to the situations they are described as experiencing, and nontrivially to derive logically valid inferences from the descriptions of the objects and states of affairs described in a work of fiction.
(4) To understand the personality and character development, and explain the intentional psychological states, beliefs, desires, emotions, and the like, of fictional characters, as they are described in a work of fiction.

If these are the minimal requirements for an adequate logic and semantics of fiction, then we shall see that, with appropriate qualifications, the *Tractatus* satisfactorily explains the meaning of fiction in the sense of satisfying requirements (1)–(3), but does not make sufficient provision for requirement (4). The reasons why Wittgenstein's early theory of meaning does not meet condition (4), moreover, are instructive with respect to broader issues in Wittgenstein's philosophical psychology, and point toward a way of understanding the limitations of his rejection of the existence of psychological subjects and propositional attitudes both in fiction and folk psychology. The purposes of a complete logic of fiction thus have more far-reaching consequences for Wittgenstein's early philosophy.

Our first task is to explain and defend the choice of requirements (1)–(3), after which we will turn to the more problematic condition for Wittgenstein's logic in requirement (4). We want intuitively to be able to make sense of talk about the nonexistent objects and states of affairs ostensibly described in a work of fiction. We expect that the sentences in a story or novel, or those that summarize elements of its plot or storyline, such as the sentence, "Captain Ahab sought to kill Moby Dick," are intelligible, and that in some sense they refer to and predicate properties of the nonexistent objects and states of affairs ostensibly described in a work of fiction, as requirement (1) proposes. Nor is it sufficient to be able merely to refer to and predicate properties of the nonexistent objects and states of affairs ostensibly mentioned in works of fiction. The predications must also be true in or relative to the fictional contexts in which they appear, even if they are not true in or of the actual world. The propositions of a work of fiction should at least conditionally, relatively or qualifiedly, turn out to be true in an adequate logic of fiction, as requirement (2) maintains. If we can refer to Captain Ahab and Moby Dick in Melville's novel as interpreted by a given logic of fiction, but it is not true that Captain Ahab sought to kill Moby Dick, then we cannot make any sound inferences about the action of the novel, for it will be equally false in that case that Captain Ahab bore a grudge against Moby Dick, sailed the *Pequod* in order to hunt down Moby Dick, lost a limb in a prior encounter with the whale, and the like.

We recognize that in the actual world there are no such beings as Captain Ahab or Moby Dick, except in those cases where a work of fiction is based, even loosely, on real life persons, objects, or events. Thus, we also acknowledge that it is false in or relative to the actual-world that Captain Ahab sought to kill Moby Dick, where neither Ahab nor the whale exist. It is another matter to say that it is false in or relative to Melville's story that Captain Ahab sought to kill Moby Dick, and most logics of fiction make provision for truth evaluations relativized either to the actual world or to merely logically possible worlds or fictional story contexts.[8] A logic of fiction that is sensitive to such a requirement preserves logical consistency with the conflicting facts of the actual world by specifying that while it is false-relative-to-the-actual world that Captain Ahab sought to kill Moby Dick, it is true-relative-to-Melville's-story that Captain Ahab sought to kill Moby Dick, even though it is false-relative-to-the-actual-world that Captain Ahab sought to kill Moby Dick. There can also be cases of overlapping facts between the actual world and the story context of a work of fiction, as when we truly say that New Bedford is a nineteenth-century whaling town relative-to-the-actual-world *and* relative-to-Melville's-story.

Story-context truth relativization additionally makes it possible to support inferences according to requirement (3) within story contexts that permit a reader or audience member to enter into the deductive reasoning of characters in a story as part of a fictional world that an author creates or partially describes in constructing a work of fiction. If we relativize the truth of sentences in or relative to the objects and states of affairs in a story, then we can follow the reasoning of the characters by soundly drawing inferences from the information presented as part of the story interpreted semantically as true relative to the story context. Classical deductive logic can then be expected to hold with respect to the truth-relativized sentences in and about a work of fiction in precisely the same way that they do in science and ordinary discourse in order to satisfy requirement (3).

Wittgenstein's logic and the semantics of fiction

If criteria (1)–(3) are accepted as requirements for a logic of fiction, how does Wittgenstein's theory of meaning measure up to these conditions? Does the *Tractatus* provide a logic of fiction at least with respect to the first three conditions?

Wittgenstein's *Tractatus* meets requirement (1) insofar as nonexistent complex objects and states of affairs are concerned. However, the simple objects of the *Tractatus* are an important exception. As the substance of the world, the simple objects must belong to or in a sense be logically available for the constitution of all different logically possible states of affairs.[9] Although Wittgenstein does not speak of logically possible worlds as such, his references to the logically possible different combinations of simple objects in the atomic facts that ultimately constitute the world bear an obvious positive analogy to Leibniz's concept of a logically possible world. If we consider only complex objects (*Komplexe*) rather than simple objects (*einfache Gegenstände*), and ordinary states of affairs (*Tatsachen*) rather than atomic facts (*Sachverhalte*), then Wittgenstein's *Tractatus* unequivocally provides a logic and semantics that is capable of referring to and predicating properties of nonexistent (complex) objects and states of affairs.

When Wittgenstein, in the very first sentence of the *Tractatus*, introduces the concept of "the world," he is evidently speaking not of the actual world but of any (logically possible) world; it is the *idea* of the world that matters to Wittgenstein. He draws inferences about *the* world in the same way that he speaks of *the* object or *the* state of affairs, which is to say in an abstract and general way, to speak of the concept of *any* of these things as related by the metaphysics of logical atomism. *The* world is any world you please, provided only that it is a world. This is clear also from the fact that Wittgenstein identifies what he refers to as the world with the total reality.[10] We could also naturally say the same kind of thing outside the sphere of Wittgenstein's *Tractatus* generally about *the* law (in any society at any time), *the* weather (anywhere in the world at any time of any year), *the* family, and other things besides. We do not always mean a particular thing as analyzed by Russell's (1905) theory of definite descriptions when we refer to *the x* or *y*, as Russell also surely understood, but sometimes to any specimen of the relevant kind.[11] This, in any case, is how Wittgenstein apparently thinks of *the* world in the opening logical atomistic metaphysics passages in the *Tractatus*, as *any* way in which a world might be constituted as a structure of any choice of atomic facts.[12] Wittgenstein's *Tractatus*, by contrast, could not make sense of a work of fiction that took as its premise the existence of a different set of simple objects, except to note that the correct semantic interpretation of such an anti-Wittgensteinian fiction, if Wittgenstein is right, would still presuppose and in that sense revert at the meta-linguistic level to the simple objects of the *Tractatus*, uniformly populating every logically possible world as the transcendent metaphysical ground of all determinately meaningful language.

If we have followed the fragment of Wittgenstein's logic that seems to provide the basis for a logic of fiction, or for the description of nonexistent (complex) objects and states of affairs, then we should be prepared to agree that we can only correctly describe an object if we can provide a *true* description of it. The *Tractatus* explicitly offers at least part of what is expected from a logic of fiction in that it describes nonexistent (complex) objects and states of affairs. To do so, however, the logic must also implicitly permit the true predication of properties to nonexistent (complex) objects and hence true predicational propositions within a work of fiction. The *Tractatus* does not expressly include an obvious syntactical method of disambiguating truth ascriptions to propositions that are to be evaluated as descriptions of existent entities and states of affairs in the actual world as opposed to others about nonexistent objects and nonexistent states of affairs in false sciences or works of fiction. The relativization of truth ascriptions to the actual world, fictional story contexts or nonactual merely logically possible worlds by the hyphenation or indexing device we have described can nevertheless be added to Wittgenstein's logic to serve this end. If such a low-tech way of drawing the necessary distinctions is adopted, then we can reasonably conclude that although Wittgenstein's *Tractatus* in extant form does not provide an adequate logic of fiction in the sense of satisfying both conditions (1) and (2), it readily meets the requirements of condition (1); and with a conservative and arguably implicit distinction between truth ascriptions to propositions, the logic and truth value semantics of Wittgenstein's *Tractatus* can also be extended beyond its official limitations to satisfy condition (2).

A description by which an object can be referred to and its properties considered can only be a true description of the object, even if the description is not true relative to the actual world, but only to a nonactual merely logically possible world or story context. There is no way to describe an object accurately, regardless of its ontic status, by considering only false propositions describing the properties an object does not have. A false description, if we know that it is false, conveys a limited quantity of information, but does not provide enough knowledge about an object to distinguish it from all other objects. A tomato, for example, just like a pike, is neither cubical nor flammable nor prime nor divisible by 2, although a tomato is evidently a very different thing than a pike, whether by this we mean a pointed staff or a freshwater fish. Even if we were to detail all of the properties an object does not have we could not say enough to distinguish an object from all other objects. The inadequacy of negative characterizations of existent objects applies with equal force to nonexistent objects, including the ostensible objects putatively referred to and made the predication subjects of true attributions of constitutive properties in a work of fiction.[13]

Finally, if both logic of fiction requirements (1) and (2) are satisfied by Wittgenstein's *Tractatus*, then presumably requirement (3) should also be satisfied. The interpretation of sentences in and about a work of fiction as true descriptions of or true predications of properties to nonexistent complex fictional objects relative to the actual world, nonactual merely logically possible worlds, such as those partially described by a given story context, also makes it possible to enter into the valid or invalid deductive reasoning of the characters in a story within a Wittgensteinian logic of fiction. These again will be also relativized as needed to the same logically possible worlds or story contexts that make it possible to understand essential movements of plot and the inferences of fictional subjects, narrators and logical relations among the states of affairs and events portrayed in a work of fiction. By allowing relativized true predications of properties to nonexistent complex objects and states of affairs in the *Tractatus*, Wittgenstein satisfies the first three of the four conditions we have considered as requirements for an adequate logic of fiction. The remaining requirement (4), as we shall now see, raises difficulties not only for Wittgenstein's theory as a logic of fiction, but equally for his philosophical psychology and semantics of scientific and everyday discourse.

Character, personality, and propositional attitude in fiction and folk psychology

If the *Tractatus* with adjustments can satisfy the first three requirements of a logic of fiction, there yet remains a recalcitrant feature that might be regarded as necessary for a complete theory of the meaning of fiction. We might still expect a logic of fiction, as condition (4) stipulates, to make intuitively correct sense of the personality, character development, motives, feelings and emotions, beliefs, desires, and other psychological states attributed to the *dramatis personae* of a work of fiction.

Those familiar with Wittgenstein's early semantics can anticipate that there are serious limitations for the *Tractatus* logic of fiction in this category. Similar restrictions on the meaningfulness of certain sentences in fiction can also be found elsewhere in Wittgenstein's semantics. We can, for identical reasons, discount as unavailable to Wittgenstein's picture theory semantics any truth ascriptions to sentences in a work of fiction that would not sustain a truth valuation in the *Tractatus* logic and theory of meaning if they were to appear in scientific or everyday discourse. If a character in a novel, for example, exclaims, "Murder is foul," or "All of Rembrandt's paintings are beautiful," or "Reality is one, all else is illusion," those sentences, and many others like them, must be judged nonsensical by a *Tractatus* logic of fiction as much as in its logic of science and general semantics, without special exception. We cannot get away with nonsense in fiction that we cannot get away with in science and ordinary thought

313

and language according to the *Tractatus*. The same is true of Wittgenstein's assessment of pseudo-propositions ascribing propositional attitudes to real or fictional putative psychological subjects.

Whether or not it is possible to do so within the framework of the *Tractatus*, we might naturally expect it to be true in accord with condition (2), for example, as a description of fictional complex objects and states of affairs, that in the story Melville tells, it is true that Captain Ahab sought to kill Moby Dick. It is hard to imagine how we could understand the events Ishmael narrates in Melville's novel if in a given logic of fiction it does not turn out to be true that Captain Ahab sought to kill the great white whale. As we need in an adequate logic and semantics of fiction to be able to enter into the reasoning of fictional characters in order to understand the author's characterization of motives that determine a story's action and plot, so we also need a foundation by which it can become at least logically possible to grasp the emotions and passions of fictional characters whose situations, backgrounds, and frames of mind are described in a work of fiction.

Wittgenstein dismisses propositional attitudes as non-proposition-building. This means that according to Wittgenstein we cannot produce a new proposition by embedding another proposition in a belief or other propositional attitude context. Thus, if Wittgenstein is right, a new proposition does not result from inserting the proposition 'It is raining' into the context 'I believe that ____,' to yield, as we would otherwise ordinarily expect, 'I believe that it is raining.' Indeed, Wittgenstein must deny that propositional attitudes can ever be used to construct more complex propositions. The reason is obvious when we reflect that the general form of proposition as explained especially in *TLP* 6 involves a purely truth-functional operation of joint negation, and that propositional attitudes are not truth-functionally related to the propositions they appear to qualify. From the fact that it is raining, for example, it does not follow logically that I believe that it is raining nor that I do not believe that it is raining; nor, conversely, does it follow from the fact that I believe (or do not believe) that it is raining that it is true (or false) that it is raining.[14] Whether Wittgenstein's strategy is entirely successful is a question for another occasion. The fact is that Wittgenstein's logic in the *Tractatus* not only fails to make special provision for interpreting the meaning of putative propositional attitude contexts in works of fiction, but does not recognize their meaningfulness, beyond the form of the genuine propositions to which they attach or that are embedded in propositional attitude contexts, even in ordinary descriptions of contingent actual world complex objects and states of affairs. This again is a general limitation of Wittgenstein's picture theory of meaning in the *Tractatus*. It affects not only the logic of fiction, however truncated, in Wittgenstein's analysis of meaning, but also its applications to such ordinary uses of colloquial language for describing the putative psychological states of thinkers, including all so-called folk psychological descriptions of qualia, emotions, and intentional psychological states.

If we *require* an adequate logic of fiction to enable a reader to enter into the beliefs, desires, and emotions as well as the abstract logical, mathematical, and practical reasonings of fictional characters, then the logic and picture theory and truth value semantics of Wittgenstein's *Tractatus* inevitably fall short of providing an adequate logic of fiction, by virtue of failing to satisfy requirement (4). It is surely true that in at least what Wittgenstein refers to in *TLP* 5.5421 as the "psychological subject" as it is spoken of in "contemporary superficial psychology" there is no more *meaning* to the sentence "Subject *S* thinks (doubts, believes, hopes, fears, etc.) that *p*" than there is to "*p*" whether in fiction or in pseudo-scientific discourse.[15] In Wittgenstein's logic, there is no special meaning to be found and understood in the psychological state of Ahab as he seeks to kill the great white whale. All the seething psychological undercurrent of Ahab that motivates his actions in the plot of the novel are invisible to Wittgenstein's picture theory semantics and general form of proposition, just as they are in Wittgenstein's semantics of what we today call folk psychological phenomena.

Arguably, it is as important for a logic of fiction to be sensitive to the "superficial" psychologies of fictional characters as it is in the case of colloquial linguistic descriptions of the folk psychologies of living psychological subjects. Insofar as Wittgenstein's logic and semantics in the *Tractatus* does not do interpretive justice to the superficial psychological intentional, qualitative or emotional states of fictional characters, does not enable us validly and nontrivially to infer that Captain Ahab might try to do certain things because of his psychological attitudes toward Moby Dick, to that extent we might reject Wittgenstein's theory as failing to provide all that is required of a logic of fiction. If we take away all this from the logic and semantics of fiction, then at the very least we take away something irreplaceable from the understanding and enjoyment of literature as a verbal entertainment and source of insight into various aspects of the human condition. Since Wittgenstein's *Tractatus* seems to impose this limitation, on the grounds that there are in fact no existent psychological subjects or propositional attitudes, the logic of fiction that is subsumed by the *Tractatus* logic and semantics to that extent and in that regard does not constitute an adequate logic of fiction, any more than it constitutes an adequate logic of the scientific true or false description of "superficial" subjective psychological attitudes or states of mind.

Wittgenstein is nevertheless free to adopt an anthropological standpoint with respect to the truth conditions of propositions ostensibly about the subjective thoughts and feelings of psychological subjects, whether in real life or in a work of fiction. Wittgenstein can say that it is not only semantically permissible but scientifically necessary to include as part of the complete description of *the* (any logically possible) world the facts of "superficial" psychology, however superficial they may be. Such representational and emotional states are part of the complex facts that constitute the actual world and many other nonactual merely logically possible worlds, including those incompletely described in or otherwise projected by works of fiction. We fail to describe the world of contingent facts completely if we do not also record the fact that Ludwig thought about tennis on Monday

DALE JACQUETTE

and on Tuesday Bertrand wanted to spend the day bicycling. If this much is allowed in the ontology, logic, and semantics of the *Tractatus*, then that should also be all that is needed to explain the fictional thoughts and feelings of fictional characters in works of fiction, in the same superficial anthropological sense of psychology as in folk psychological descriptions of psychological states.[16]

Notes

1 Ludwig Wittgenstein, *Notebooks 1914–1916*, G. H. von Wright and Elizabeth Anscombe (eds.), trans. by Elizabeth Anscombe, Oxford: Basil Blackwell, 1969, 30 September 1914.
2 See Ray Monk, *Ludwig Wittgenstein: The Duty of Genius*, Harmondsworth: Penguin Books, 1991, pp. 115–36, 342–3.
3 Sources for the main literary and philosophical influences on Wittgenstein's style in the *Tractatus* are collected in Dale Jacquette, *Wittgenstein's Thought in Transition*, West Lafayette: Purdue University Press, 1998, especially pp. 4, 13–14. See also Marjorie Perloff, *Wittgenstein's Ladder: Poetic Language and the Strangeness of the Ordinary*, Chicago: University of Chicago Press, 1999.
4 Ludwig Wittgenstein, *Tractatus Logico-Philosophicus*, C. K. Ogden (ed.), London: Routledge & Kegan Paul Ltd., 1922; all references are to this edition. See especially 2.024–2.0271; 2.172–2.18; 4.12; 6.13; 6.421.
5 2.022–2.023: "It is clear that however different from the real one an imagined world may be, it must have something – a form – in common with the real world. This fixed form consists of the objects."
6 I discuss the lying and truth-telling polarity in Jacquette, "Wittgenstein on Lying as a Language Game," *The Third Wittgenstein*, Daniele Moyal Sharrock (ed.), Ashgate Publishing, forthcoming.
7 See also 1.2–1.21; 2.05–2.06; 2.17–2.18; 2.224; 4.023; 4.05–4.06; 4.1–4.11.
8 John Woods, *The Logic of Fiction: A Philosophical Sounding of Deviant Logic*, The Hague: Mouton and Co., Publishers, 1974, pp. 35, 38, 60. Terence Parsons, *Nonexistent Objects*, New Haven: Yale University Press, 1980, pp. 26–27, 59–60, 64–69, 75–77; "A Prolegomenon to Meinongian Semantics," *The Journal of Philosophy* 71 (1974), 561–80, pp. 575–577; and "A Meinongian Analysis of Fictional Objects," *Grazer Philosophische Studien* 1 (1975), 73–86, pp. 83–85. Joseph Margolis, *The Language of Art and Art Criticism: Analytic Questions in Aesthetics*, Detroit: Wayne State University Press, 1965, pp. 153–6. I offer similar proposals for story-contexting in Jacquette, *Meinongian Logic: The Semantics of Existence and Nonexistence*, Berlin: Walter de Gruyter, 1996, especially pp. 256–64. See Jacquette, "Intentional Semantics and the Logic of Fiction," *The British Journal of Aesthetics* 29 (1989), 168–76; Jacquette, "Truth and Fiction in David Lewis's Critique of Meinongian Semantics," *Metaphysica: International Journal for Ontology and Metaphysics* 2 (2001), 73–106; Jacquette, "David Lewis on Meinongian Logic of Fiction," Wolfgang Huemer and Marc-Oliver Schuster (eds.), *Writing the Austrian Traditions: Philosophy and Literature*, Edmonton: Wirth-Institute for Austrian and Central European Studies, 2003, 101-119.
9 2.021–2.0211.
10 2.063.
11 Bertrand Russell, "On Denoting," *Mind* 14 (1905), 479–93.
12 This reading of Wittgenstein's use of the term "the world" agrees with Raymond Bradley's *The Nature of All Being: A Study of Wittgenstein's Modal Atomism*, Oxford: Oxford University Press, 1992, especially pp. 3–65. The interpretation is at variance with Max Black's in his *A Companion to Wittgenstein's Tractatus*, Ithaca: Cornell University

Press, 1964, pp. 29–31. In many instances, Wittgenstein apparently plays on the ambiguity between definite reference to the actual world and the characterization of any world as constituted by any complete structure of facts in logical space.

13 Wittgenstein makes a similar point when he asks rhetorically in 4.062: "Can we not make ourselves understood by means of false propositions as hitherto with true ones, so long as we know that they are meant to be false? No! For a proposition is true, if what we assert by means of it is the case; and if by '*p*' we mean ~*p*, and what we mean is the case, then '*p*' in the new conception is true and not false."

14 5.621–5.6331; 5.641.

15 5.541–5.5422. I discuss these aspects of Wittgenstein's rejection of propositional attitudes and the psychological subject in Jacquette, *Wittgenstein's Thought in Transition*, chapter 4, "Transcendence of the Metaphysical Subject," and Jacquette, "Wittgenstein on Thoughts as Pictures of Facts and the Transcendence of the Metaphysical Subject," *Wittgenstein and the Future of Philosophy: A Reassessment after 50 Years / Wittgenstein und die Zukunft der Philosophie. Eine Neubewertung nach 50 Jahren*, Rudolf Haller und Klaus Puhl (eds.), Vienna: öbv&hpt, 2002, pp. 160–70.

16 5.5421. In 5.631, Wittgenstein writes: "If I wrote a book 'The world as I found it,' I should also have therein to report on my body and say which members obey my will and which do not, etc." Note that the book Wittgenstein describes would *not* be a novel – although there has since come to be written a rather good novel of that name about Wittgenstein and Russell and others in their circle. (Bruce Duffy, *The World as I Found It*, Boston: Houghton Mifflin Company, 1987) – but something more like a folk psychological quasi-scientific report by an average knower checking among other things which body parts do and which do not obey the will. Here Wittgenstein seems to make an unmistakable allowance for the kind of facts we have been following in more contemporary terminology in calling folk psychological, unequivocally intentional, but as such belonging only to superficial empirical psychology, in something like an anthropology of representational facts by one of those representing animals who make to themselves pictures of facts. Wittgenstein significantly writes in a letter to Russell from 19 August 1919, *Letters to Russell, Keynes and Moore*, von Wright and McGuinness (eds.), Oxford: Basil Blackwell, 1974, Letter (R37) to Russell 19 August 1919: "I don't know *what* the constituents of a thought are but I know *that* it must have such constituents which correspond to the words of Language. Again the kind of relation of the constituents of thought and of the pictured fact is irrelevant. It would be a matter of psychology to find out." Wittgenstein adds: "Does a Gedanke consist of words? No! But of psychical constituents that have the same sort of relation to reality as words. What those constituents are I don't know."

Part V

THE LARGER VIEW

17

UNLIKELY PROSPECTS FOR APPLYING WITTGENSTEIN'S "METHOD" TO AESTHETICS AND THE PHILOSOPHY OF ART

Joseph Margolis

I begin lamely – to catch the dithering of any usual effort to get one's bearings in reading Wittgenstein profitably before any genuine clue deigns to present itself. I do finally arrive at a judgment that I find convincing and pursue it among familiar texts in aesthetics and the philosophy of art, persuaded that there cannot be any uniquely correct way to read the "later" Wittgenstein. I also acknowledge that, by favoring a non-standard reading, I have somehow made Wittgenstein out to be a more conventional philosopher than he is usually said to be. I believe he is. He is certainly no Wittgensteinian. Beyond that, I must ask you to be patient with the argument that follows. It's peculiarly true in analyzing Wittgenstein that in order to assess the relevance of his texts for the questions that arise in the philosophy of art – and, for that matter, the philosophy of literature – we must speculate very broadly about the nature of his general "method." That may strike you as an arid way of proceeding. I don't believe it is. But I trust you will find that the argument gathers strength as it continually discards false leads and arrives at long last at a fairly sensible conclusion. Wittgenstein, I venture, is worth the labor.

I

It is indeed difficult though by no means impossible to draw fresh philosophical lessons about the fine arts from Wittgenstein's various writings. The likeliest candidate texts, as you might suppose, are thought to be the *Philosophical Investigations* and allied discussions; but the pickings are distinctly slim. One wants to know, naturally enough, whether there is some systematic reason why this is so, since so much of what Wittgenstein offers seems so promising and perceptive about the human *Lebensform*. I review, with some misgivings that you're bound to catch, a small selection of recent efforts to apply Wittgenstein in aesthetics and the philosophy of art, but I warn you that the record is not impressive. The fact is that where he is at his best, where he may be applied with profit, Wittgenstein is often read in a way that actually reverses his characteristic advice – say, with

regard to mind/body dualism, the privacy of the mental, the analysis of intentions and the intentional; and where he introduces his most distinctive and
powerful innovations – say, with regard to the analysis of a "language game"
[*Sprachspiel*] and a "form of life" [*Lebensform*] – he regularly fails to explore his
own best notions in sufficient detail (or even in the right direction) to yield decisive results in his own name or to guide those who mean to read him with care
(whether as followers or detractors) in explicating the relationship and difference
between cultural and biological (or natural) things.

Wittgenstein is peculiarly inexplicit about such matters and altogether too
easy to read in tendentious ways. Nevertheless, there surely are important and
worthwhile distinctions to be teased out of his abundant texts. I say this with the
nagging worry that the usual readings of the "later" Wittgenstein have probably
misjudged his lesson rather badly – zealously in fact – and that that lesson hardly
yields any reliable sense of a determinate method. Although, of course,
Wittgenstein's own skilled practice is clear and fluent and conveys a distinct air of
being on the edge of a particularly large and compelling discovery about the
nature of cultural life itself.

Wittgenstein typically affords little more than a conversational stream of
conceptual distinctions embedded in ordinary discourse, which, even where illuminating, is too often pressed (by others) well beyond their transient lessons and
assured intent. To the extent that he is philosophically explicit – we know he
avoids academically formulated disputes – he actually does tender (in spite of
what he repeatedly says against philosophy) a number of substantial bits of
philosophical advice about particularly egregious mistakes, to which his usual
piecemeal entries return again and again. It is just here, where we may recover
his philosophical "doctrines" – always terribly elusive – that it may be possible to
craft a modest sense of a "Wittgensteinian" aesthetic. Nevertheless, in spite of
his very attractive improvisations, Wittgenstein almost never pursues his best
examples in ways one might have hoped would yield an important clue or two. A
surprising number of ingenious "applications" (by others) of Wittgenstein's inim-
itable simplicity fail to get beyond the few large lessons he himself ventures to
reveal through his own ephemera; in fact, more often than not, they confirm the
ease with which Wittgenstein's best thoughts mislead us as readily as the endless
false leads he so deftly exposes. And, of course, he warns us repeatedly that that
is bound to be true, without providing a rule beyond the familiar "look and see."
The record of "applying" Wittgenstein to the philosophy of art is, I'm bound to
say, largely the record of a sustained failure. It is, I think, the result of an
entrenched misreading and a misplaced optimism.

I venture to say that, in the *Investigations*, Wittgenstein is obviously drawn to
the flux of language: *not* by any means to linguistic chaos (because of course he
makes meticulous distinctions) but more because of a profound mistrust of
grand generalizations and the familiar philosophical longing for fixed essences.
His teaching "method" is decidedly elenctic, in a way that invites comparison
with the "method" of the early Platonic dialogues (which he seems to have

discounted). But if so, then we begin to understand why it is so difficult to *apply* his "method" specifically in aesthetics: the truth is, there *is* no method, and where we might require "doctrinal" direction, Wittgenstein erases as much as he can of the explicit traces of the doctrines that have guided his own account.

Marjorie Perloff, who has authored a genuinely inventive *use* of Wittgenstein's *Tractatus* and *Investigations*, speaks, understandably, of Wittgenstein's "Heraclitean epigrams" (which, problematically, she draws from the *Tractatus* rather than from the *Investigations*).[1] Her approach is "figuratively" helpful in drawing attention to the transient contexts in which Wittgenstein's "meaning" is perspicuously caught – against considerable odds – but it leaves our philosophical longings unfulfilled. Perloff is perfectly open about the constraints she imposes on reading Wittgenstein:

> My own interest is less in what the *Tractatus* "says" about proposition-ality, tautology, etc., than in what it *is*, especially in its later sections, which break abruptly with the "clarity" of the opening and turn to matters of ethics and religion in a series of gnomic utterances...whose formulations "solve" nothing.[2]

She says the same of the *Investigations*, endorsing Stanley Cavell's interest in the "spiritual struggle" (involving, as Cavell says, "the contrary depths of oneself").[3] In that same sense, she treats Wittgenstein as an exemplary poet of a new kind, in a spirit that encourages her to read a collection of important literary figures as having composed their own work in ways aptly, but improbably, illuminated by Wittgenstein's example.

Nevertheless, however sensibly she applies her reading of Wittgenstein, it invariably leaves the implied philosophical issues largely unexamined, even neglected, unless the intended instruction (Perloff's or Wittgenstein's) is simply that we should abandon the entire search. In particular, nothing that she says about the "poetic" Wittgenstein seems helpful in explicating the Tractarian proposition "Ethics and aesthetics are one and the same [*Eins*]" (*TLP* 6.421).[4] The related proposition, "Ethics is transcendental" – and, therefore, aesthetics – seems vacuously obvious, *if* we understand the severe restrictions Wittgenstein imposes on the *Tractatus*. But how can one make sense of the Tractarian assertion in the context of the *Investigations*? It cannot be that ethics and aesthetics *are* "mystical" or "transcendental" there, in any sense akin to what Wittgenstein means (or may have meant) by the "mystical" in the *Tractatus*; for there is no sense in which *anything* is "beyond" the purview of ordinary discourse examined in the *Investigations*. Certainly, by the time of Wittgenstein's *Lectures and Conversations on Aesthetics* (and related topics), there is no hint of any conceptual restriction of the Tractarian sort. The matter is hardly pursued in any memorable way; in fact, apart from the Tractarian world, it has no recognizable import at all; and, in the *Tractatus*, it is a sort of place marker of what has not been directly addressed – and could not be. (Though Wittgenstein has of course written a "Tractarian" account of ethics.)

We must then look beyond Perloff. I concede that, in her appreciation of what Wittgenstein must have been doing both philosophically and "poetically," Perloff does indeed provide in an oblique way an instructive lesson about how to read Gertrude Stein's and Samuel Beckett's notoriously difficult prose.[5] Here, Cavell is undoubtedly more successful in interpreting Wittgenstein's philosophical contribution. Except that, regarding Part Four of *The Claim of Reason*, which conveys Cavell's most distinctive way of reading Wittgenstein in terms of his own theme of skepticism, he admits:

> I have found the *Investigations*, I suppose more than any other work of this century, to be paradigmatic of philosophy for me, to be a domi-nating present of the history of philosophy for me. This has meant, as these things will, living with the sound of it, subjected to the sound. To find a certain freedom from that sound was therefore necessary if I was to feel I was finding my way in an investigation of my own preoccupa-tion...I should say, accordingly, that as my book moves into the latest strata, and continuously after about the first fourth of Part Four, I no longer regard my citations of the *Investigations* as interpretations of it.[6]

Just so. So perhaps we must move on again. (These examples begin to suggest an unwelcome conclusion.) It is hard to think of an American philosopher more thoroughly "Wittgensteinian" than Cavell; but his final debt seems to be more in the way of inspiration than of shared "doctrine." "Doctrine," I want to suggest, is *needed*, if we are to be able to apply Wittgenstein's "method" to his elenctic specimens. Because, of course, there is no determinate method, though there is indeed instruction!

II

I am reasonably certain of at least two features of the *Investigations* – one bearing on Wittgenstein's "method" (as I shall say), the other on his "doctrine" – that qualify the likeliest advantage of applying Wittgenstein's texts to the problems of aesthetics and the philosophy of art. You may protest, of course, that Wittgenstein never advances any philosophical thesis in the *Investigations* or in allied texts. But that can't be entirely right, as Wittgenstein's objections to the possibility of a private language make perfectly clear.[7] Viewed more systematically, the *Investigations* surely provides a running argument against the atomism of the *Tractatus* (the doctrine of "simples" and "complexes"), which of course *is* a piece of philosophical work in the plainest and most conventional sense.[8] The recent turn towards so-called "therapeutic readings" of both the *Tractatus* and the *Investigations* I take to signify (in a welcome sense) the fact that Wittgenstein's "method" proceeds in a way that is "internal" to "our everyday forms of expression and to the world those forms of expression serve to reveal." To some, *that* needs to be construed as being opposed to, or incompatible with, *any* "metaphysics" at all. But I suggest that, read more carefully, it must make room for a tacit realism embedded at least *in* natural-language practices *and*, with due care, in metaphysical conjectures embedded in the same language – "doctrines," in my lingo – that eschew any "external" point of view, any view that supposes that we can escape the internalist constraint.[9] I warn you that the disjunction of ordinary and metaphysical language harbors that false way of reading Wittgenstein overwhelmingly favored among philosophers – philosophers of art particularly.

In this same sense, to venture an interpretation of Wittgenstein's notion of the human *Lebensform* would be to begin to formulate a "philosophy of culture" – *a fortiori*, part of the ground for a philosophy of art or an aesthetics. But Wittgenstein is very nearly completely silent here: that is, silent about the conceptual ground needed for his own philosophical work and for its application to the arts. Furthermore, despite his obvious contempt for academic philosophy, the internalist stance is *not*, as such, at all opposed to working with metaphysical issues. No one, to my knowledge, has ever formulated a demarcation line between "metaphysical" and "everyday" language; and, of course, the *Tractatus* itself is proof enough that, in Wittgenstein's opinion, metaphysics easily penetrates "everyday use." (I shall come back to the matter of the *Lebensform*.)

In short, I think it impossible to apply Wittgenstein's distinctions and exemplary cases without employing his "method"; *and* I am convinced that his "method" is "therapeutic" primarily (perhaps even solely) in its rejecting any "externalist" standpoint (say, against Bertrand Russell) and by adhering to an "internal" standpoint (partly, at least, by way of an emendation of Frege's notion of logic's being internal to thought).[10] Seen this way, the "method" must be supplemented by "doctrines" capable of articulating what, in respect to any pertinent "philosophical" concern (metaphysical or epistemological, say), could be supported by considerations internal to "our everyday forms of expression and…the world those forms of expression serve to reveal," without being confined to those expressions alone. Anything more restrictive would, I suggest, render Wittgenstein's "method" utterly devoid of determinate meaning. I would not claim, however, that such a practice can always count on being self-consistent. I doubt it could be. In fact, I doubt that the *Investigations* is completely self-consistent. But I daresay, to insist on disjoining metaphysics and "everyday use" is already to violate the "internalist" constraint! If one denies this, I say, so much the worse for philosophical "therapy."

Beyond that, I take note of the fact that there is a tantalizing line of interpreting Wittgenstein's texts that treats both the *Tractatus* and the *Investigations* (said to be continuously caught up with a common, if evolving, method) as distinctly "Kantian," in a sense that continues but "improves" on the purpose of the first *Critique*.[11] I grant the pleasant challenge of such a line of speculation and I emphasize only that to admit its suggestiveness is to begin to see how "method" and "doctrine" are ultimately inseparable, whether drawn in the straightest way from Wittgenstein's own texts or, more adventurously, from a reading of the Western philosophical tradition itself.

Newton Garver suggests that Wittgenstein brings together (in his view of the *Lebensform*) the transcendental "possibility" of language and the "natural history" of human linguistic behavior.[12] But Garver does not tell us how this conjunction of themes functions "doctrinally" – or how it might yield important invariances of language and thought. It seems designed to explain nothing in particular! Garver offers no more than this: "Given the world as it actually is, what determines our form of life is not *how* we use words and sentences, but *that* we use them."[13] Fair enough. But surely *that* confirms that the "method" must be supplemented by philosophical "doctrines" adjusted to one or another sector of inquiry. Wittgenstein himself says little more on the matter: "We want to *understand* something that is already in plain view. For *this* is what we seem in some sense not to understand" (*PI* §89).[14] But what is this *this* exactly? I take the passage to be a piece of public relations hype. What is most characteristic of the *Investigations'* lesson is that very little about language *is*, finally, genuinely clear. What would be the point of worrying about "bewitchment" if that were not so?

Garver characterizes the pertinent Wittgensteinian texts as "meager." He reports Max Black's conclusion that " 'form of life' is a deliberately vague expression, which has no clear and firm implications and for which it would be a mistake to seek a clear and precise understanding." Norman Malcolm (he adds) regards the concept as absolutely central "in Wittgenstein's thought," though Malcolm does not offset Black's judgment[15] and, indeed, the two findings prove to be embarrassingly compatible. It may even be that *our* conjectures about how to apply Wittgenstein to the problems of the philosophy of art may help us understand what the *Lebensform* itself entails rather than the other way around. But then, we are disadvantaged in both directions.

In any event, ever since Hegel (some would say, ever since the third *Critique*, though I would not), it has not been considered self-contradictory to characterize a philosopher as extending the spirit of Kant's transcendentalism, by retiring *its* apriorism and/or its insistence on invariance or universality as a condition *sine qua non* of the intelligibility of change itself. We are asked to believe that Wittgenstein favored the thesis that there must be a necessary or changeless ground for the very "possibility" of the flux of experience or for ensuring that the experienced world constitutes a totally ordered unity. But neither claim can be supported in a detailed way by the actual text of the *Investigations*,[16] and Garver nowhere attempts to construct the argument required. Nor, I should add, is it at all clear what possible grounds might be offered (in accord with the supposed "method" of the *Investigations*) for reclaiming even a relaxed Kantianism.

III

All of the foregoing amounts to a crashing stalemate. I'll have no more of it. There must be a better way of proceeding. I turn, therefore, to actual efforts to *apply* Wittgenstein to standard problems in aesthetics and the philosophy of art. Is a Wittgensteinian critique of aesthetics and the philosophy of art promising at all? Perhaps not. I offer as a stalking horse, for the sake of a better start, the respectable effort of Garry Hagberg's *Art as Language*, possibly the latest and one of the most sustained labors to date to *apply* Wittgenstein's *Investigations* as a running assessment of recent philosophies of art. The book ranges fluently over a wide selection of figures and is clear and crisp and well informed. Treat it as a fair specimen at least. There are, I may say, very few efforts of comparable detail.

Nevertheless, if you concede the thrust of my remarks thus far, you have more than an inkling of the confessedly very weak sense in which Hagberg's critique could possibly be said to "apply" Wittgenstein's "method" in an authoritative or accurate way. I don't say this to fault Hagberg's effort *a priori*, or his conclusions (most of which I would dispute, I admit); but I must draw attention to the fact, first, that Hagberg pretty well guides himself by a free-wheeling reading of "Wittgenstein's famous remark concern[ing] a *constant* battle against the bewitchment of our intelligence"[17] and, second, that he pursues his examples in a way that, on closer study, proves to be essentially unaffected by Wittgenstein's actual practice and "doctrines."

Certainly, Hagberg takes pains not to violate any of Wittgenstein's best-known convictions (his stand on the possibility of a private language, for example). He is Wittgensteinian, however, "in spirit" only, certainly *not* "in method" in any straightforward sense. He fails, for instance, to consider any competing conceptions of how Wittgenstein actually worked; he fails to come to terms with the sort of questions raised by the new "therapeutic reading" or the allegedly "Kantian" cast of Wittgenstein's texts. That means – I think Hagberg's own text bears me out – that he himself is bent on exposing (what *he* takes to be) the metaphysical or epistemological "bewitchment" of a variety of doctrines in aesthetics and the philosophy of art that *his* treatment helps us to escape (if it really does) in a way *he* cannot possibly pin down as capturing and applying Wittgenstein's own method. That is, even if his analyses are brought into accord with one or another of Wittgenstein's leading remarks.

Hagberg never actually supplies a reasoned sense of how we should assess his own Wittgensteinian scruple. More troublingly, we cannot even tell, on his own grounds, whether specific philosophies of art (specific "metaphysics," if you please) are rightly judged defective merely because they *are* versions of metaphysics, or because they happen to violate constraints that Wittgenstein imposes on defensible "descriptions" of a given sector of inquiry (the arts, in the case before us), or because of some considerations that are not even "Wittgensteinian."[18]

To be candid: I cannot see that Hagberg actually uses Wittgenstein in any way that conforms with the sprawling instructions of the *Investigations*. He does indeed address local puzzles that one would hope Wittgenstein would have applied his own procedures to, but his arguments are quite standard in a purely academic sense and owe almost nothing to what might rightly be called

Wittgenstein's own "method" – that is, nothing beyond admiration and respect and a personal preference for one or another piece of Wittgensteiniana. Nevertheless, I salute Hagberg's loyalty to Wittgenstein. I believe there is no other way to proceed. We ourselves are groping for a coherent picture of Wittgenstein's "method" – or at least for assurances that he actually had a determinate and principled "philosophical" practice.

We do certainly see how brilliantly Wittgenstein worked; but, for all that, I confess I have never seen a convincing statement of Wittgenstein's general "method." For example, he cannot rightly be said – as he himself urges – to "bring words back from the metaphysical to their everyday use" (*PI* §116): first, because "everyday use" is often deeply affected by one or another form of mind/body dualism, which he rightly opposes; second, because the seeming correction of such a "mistake" is itself "metaphysical" and thus exceeds whatever counts as "everyday use"; third, because if that is so, then it cannot be true (as he also says) that "where there is sense there must be perfect order" (*PI* §98); and, fourth, because if all this is admitted, then we can no longer construe "bewitchment" as a charge *entirely free of philosophized bias*.

But that means that Hagberg must be relying on his own counter-considerations in appraising his own specimen versions of "art as language" – and, there, *his* findings of "bewitchment" are verdicts of an altogether different kind from Wittgenstein's, whether valid or not. I admit, therefore, that I introduce Hagberg with the expectation of dismissing anything we might claim to be a Wittgensteinian aesthetic, except in the loosest inspirational sense, that is, a sense that would require Wittgenstein (as well as Hagberg) to submit to the alien rigors of a more fully worked-out philosophy! There's a turn you may not have considered.

If I read Wittgenstein aright, the "bewitchment" matter (hence, the "therapeutic" corrective) must invoke (*i*) our adhering to the "internalist" standpoint already mentioned; (*ii*) our respecting the complexities of ordinary discourse (but then how exactly do we fail, in "doing" philosophy?); (*iii*) testing, on specifically philosophical grounds distinct from but congruent with (*i*), any "doctrinal" generalization or proposal, whether drawn from Wittgenstein or from another philosopher, whether in accord with or contrary or neutral to any doctrine of Wittgenstein's choice; and (*iv*) conceding that philosophical proposals are quite capable of being in full accord with (*i*)–(*iii*) despite their taking improvisational liberties in the use of terms or venturing very large generalizations beyond the world our "everyday use" reveals. (Hagberg would not agree.)

Hence, philosophy may legitimately depart from "the everyday forms of expression and the world [*they*] reveal." And if that is so, then Wittgenstein's "method" probably cannot be entirely consistent in invoking (*i*)–(*iv*). It is certainly not true that just any philosophical pronouncement must lead us into the "bewitchment" Hagberg dreads. To hold to that would render Wittgenstein's elucidations as pointless as our own, since we cannot supply a rule for determining what the right scope of a pertinent generalization should be.[19]

No. The truth is, we are not clear at all about how Wittgenstein proceeds: we are not clear about his "method"; and we have no secure sense of how familiar philosophical conjectures or proposals – that mean to abide by the bland constraints I've just collected as (*i*)–(*iv*) – are ever justifiably discarded as Wittgensteinian "bewitchments." Bewitchment is not an operable criterion of anything, and generalization is impossible to avoid. Frankly, Hagberg cannot tell us how, criterially, on Wittgensteinian grounds, acceptable philosophical generalizations may be distinguished from those that are unacceptable. No one can. Our picture of Wittgenstein's way of working can only be an uncertain fragment of his actual "method." If *we* mean to use his method, then *we* must supplement our own instruction by explaining *our* way of incorporating *his* skills. But what are they? Insisting on "context" – Hagberg's caution – sets as many problems as it solves. Hagberg says no more on this account; and *we* are frankly at a loss to supply a demarcation between the "internalist" and "externalist" treatment of "everyday use." We grasp the cautionary lesson, but there is no rule for actually applying it. It is more a badge of honor than a criterion of any kind.

Otherwise, we are forced, as Hagberg is, to challenge particular theories by our own lights *and then* supply, anecdotally, evidence of a measure of textual congruity with selected remarks drawn from Wittgenstein. I am not willing to treat *that* as "a Wittgensteinian aesthetic," and I am not willing to dismiss out of hand just any philosophical "departure" from "everyday use" (a bewitchment) – or, indeed, just any excursion into metaphysics or epistemology, without further ado. Notice that, on Malcolm's and Garver's view, Wittgenstein must have relied in some way on his own "metaphysical" convictions! No one has explained how Wittgenstein's "method" makes room for that or for its denial.

In the vicinity of the bewitchment remark (*PI* §109) – which also contains the line that directs us to proceed with our analyses by excluding "anything hypothetical in our considerations," it being the case that we do not seek "new information" but only arrange "what we have always known" – Wittgenstein confesses, reflecting on the philosopher's penchant [*as in the* Tractatus] for the "essence" [*das Wesen*] of "knowledge," "being" and the like: "A picture [*Bild; that is, a "doctrine"*] held us captive [*that is, Wittgenstein, in the* Tractatus]. And we could not get outside it, for it lay in our language and language seemed to repeat it to us inexorably….What we do [*now*] is to bring words back from metaphysical to their everyday use" (*PI* §§115–116). Yes, but not without metaphysical encumbrances and not with quite the assurance Wittgenstein exhales! Here, his own remarks convey a mixed message: metaphysical confusion is "inexorably" embedded in our routine use of language; yet, we simply bring "words back [*now*] from metaphysical to their everyday use"! How would the Wittgensteinians explain this?

This shows that Wittgenstein acknowledges the way in which "metaphysics" penetrates "everyday use," so that he *cannot* be offering a "method" that separates the two sorts of idiom reliably. The very idea of a disjunction would violate what he actually says. But it also shows that a corrected policy would certainly violate what *Hagberg* believes Wittgenstein's method requires.

Here, Hagberg applies what *he* construes to be Wittgenstein's instruction, *as a way of rejecting philosophers' doctrines that are found to depart from "everyday use"* – either generally or necessarily. Hagberg does this rather skillfully (in *Art as Language*) against a sizable company of philosophers – closing his account with a sustained criticism of Arthur Danto and myself – essentially for these reasons: (*a*) a need to "bring words back from the metaphysical to their everyday use" and (*b*) a need to expose conceptual distinctions that rightly incur the charge of "dualism." I mean this only as a passing summary of Wittgenstein's "method" seen from Hagberg's vantage, which I assure you cannot be consistently defended. (Though it is indeed *Hagberg's* "method.")

For my own part, I think we cannot get much beyond the sparest *sine qua non* of Wittgenstein's "method," which, apart from his own brilliant improvisations, comes to no more than an internalist warning that collects transient "grammars" and plausible "language games" hospitable *at once* to combinations of "everyday use," empirical discovery, *and* "metaphysical" intuitions that, improvisationally, lead or follow linguistic usage and our sense of the world it apparently reveals. That is the whole of what I understand by Wittgenstein's "therapeutic" practice – or the new "internalism." I don't think there can be any single right method, unless in an uninteresting autobiographical sense applicable to Hagberg or Cavell or Richard Allen[20] or Ben Tilghman (whom I shall introduce very shortly). We ardent philosophers are entirely free to improvise (as does Wittgenstein himself) what to count as the fruitful "doctrines" *by which* we mean to guide our running "internalist" comparisons of idioms, grammars, language games, that we first put into play for an occasion or a passing purpose! We cannot do better, but it is actually enough for modest gains. Have patience, please.

IV

All of Hagberg's specimen cases (in *Art as Language*) are occupied with the charge of "dualism" vis-à-vis the very idea of "art as language." They also pose among themselves, though for very different reasons, the same counter-question regarding the bare relevance of actually applying Wittgenstein's "method" to their respective philosophical "doctrines." It may be entirely fair, for example, to submit Susanne Langer's philosophy of art to a Wittgensteinian critique (as Hagberg does), since Langer herself professes to have been influenced by the Tractarian account of propositions – in going beyond the "sayable" (as Hagberg says). She is in fact the first figure to be examined at length in Hagberg's book and (I believe) the only one (of those examined) to have made such an admission. Still, Langer's theory is much closer to Ernst Cassirer's account of "symbolic forms" than to Wittgenstein's atomism; hers is not a "dualist" theory in any sense in which *Wittgenstein* may (in the *Tractatus*) have been Hagberg's principal dualist. Langer's view maintains just the opposite of Wittgenstein's view in the *Tractatus*.[21] This is an especially unpromising start, therefore, in a review of the actual *use* of Wittgenstein in appraising the work of familiar philosophies of art: the misapplication of the dualist charge to a philosopher of art (and culture) who is actually known to oppose dualism – notably, in analyzing the expressive properties of music. One senses a deeper prejudice than the evidence could possibly support.

I admit that Langer's theory of art, the theory of nondiscursive symbolic forms, is badly formulated. Still, when rightly understood, it could not be dualistic in the sense Hagberg features, because of course it is not meant to be psychologistic in any way and because its faults have nothing to do with invoking the need to "bring words back...to their everyday use."[22] Read this way, Wittgenstein's "method" is simply irrelevant to any proper assessment of Langer's thesis, which fails (to the extent that it does) for garden-variety philosophical reasons.[23] Hagberg's argument simply misfires here. Wittgensteinians may protest, but what evidence can they offer to show that there are no "philosophical" questions that escape their "method"?

Danto's theory presents an entirely different difficulty for Hagberg. In fact, it poses a very pretty paradox. Because, unlike Langer, Danto actually invokes Wittgenstein's objection against any principled disjunction between thought and language (or, between perception and language) in the context of supposedly "enlanguaged" thought (or "theory-laden" perception) – *and then takes a philosophical position deliberately opposed to Wittgenstein's!* Danto opts for the *necessity* of finally *separating* perception and the description (or interpretation) of what is said to be perceived; he thereby risks – well, more than risks – a "dualism" of thought and language (despite his Hegelian proclivities).

Nevertheless, though I agree (with Hagberg) that Danto cannot defend his claim convincingly, I don't believe Wittgenstein's insistence on "everyday use" would help us at all, since there is plenty of evidence that Danto's dualism can actually be supported by prevailing habits of ordinary discourse; we would have to pick and choose whatever served our purpose. Is there a Wittgensteinian rule for that? Furthermore, *if* Wittgenstein (or Hagberg) cared to mount an argument against Danto, he would have to turn to a standard philosophical objection, whether cast in terms of a language game or not! I see no other way of proceeding. The picture is becoming rather muddled.

Danto's reading of Wittgenstein is, actually, extremely perceptive – so perceptive in fact that (in my opinion) it does his own theory in. Danto interprets Wittgenstein as having broached a *philosophical* doctrine that *he* (Danto) finds, in an extreme form, in Schopenhauer and Nietzsche and, contemporaneously, in T. S. Kuhn and N. R. Hanson – and (of special interest to philosophers of art) in Nelson Goodman. "Wittgenstein did not [Danto says] draw [the] extreme consequences [these others did, namely,] that in an important respect, observers with different theories do not perceive the same thing."[24] He then summarizes Wittgenstein's view this way:

Wittgenstein's chief thesis [in *Philosophical Investigations*] was that we cannot as easily separate perception and description as had been taken for granted by philosophers, including himself in his great metaphysical work, the *Tractatus Logico-Philosophicus*....By the time he wrote the *Investigations*, Wittgenstein was of the view that we do not have, as it were, the world on the one side and language on the other, but rather that language in some way shapes reality, or at least our experience of the world.[25]

It is hard to see how if, as is plain, Danto is perfectly aware that Wittgenstein was bound to draw attention to the grounds on which he viewed the *Investigations* as rejecting the central thesis of the *Tractatus*, he could fail to see that the same consideration would render his own theory of perception at least as vulnerable. If he had thought of matters in this way, he would have realized that he could not rely (as he does) on a mere *obiter dictum* to clinch his argument regarding "artistic perception." Nevertheless, adopting Danto's point of view, we may ask exactly how a Wittgensteinian can answer Danto's counter-claim, knowing full well that Danto surely grasps *Wittgenstein's* claim and sees how a relevant run of "everyday use" would lend it credence? There's a stalemate there.

Danto seems to think there's room for a third option between admitting the penetration of perception by language or theory (with metaphysical, even relativistic, consequences, as in Kuhn's account, possibly also in Wittgenstein's in the *Investigations*) and a denial of penetration (as, implicitly, in the *Tractatus*): perhaps, he thinks, the pertinent forms of perception *are* penetrated but only "to a degree," so that some *parts* of reportable perception are actually *not* penetrated! That does seem to be Danto's thesis all right; in fact, it's the premise of Danto's well-known theory of the (occasional) perceptual indiscernibility of different artworks and matched artworks and non-artworks (Warhol's *Brillo Box*, Danto's imagined series of painted red squares, Duchamp's readymades). But there's no argument advanced in the paper Hagberg reviews. The result is that Danto's position looks like (and is) a form of metaphysical dualism when seen in a Wittgensteinian light. (Though I'm bound to say it looks like dualism from any standard non-Wittgensteinian point of view as well.)

In any event, Danto sorts the opposing theorists as "internalists" and "externalists":

The internalists want to say we see different things, the externalists that we see the same things but against the background of different sorts of beliefs, so that we may have different expectations, but the phenomenology of perception is otherwise neutral to the beliefs.[26]

Here, one begins to see that the question of "degree" is misleading: the externalists deny that, in the relevant cases, it's perception that is penetrated – it is only belief that is penetrated; whereas the internalists insist that perception's penetrated as well. I don't see how the difference between the two positions could fail to be exclusionary, an issue very different from whether, *within* the internalists' space, the *perceptual* differences that result from "penetration" are likely to be phenomenologically diverse or not.

Danto speaks of the "degree" to which theoretical beliefs or "physical knowledge" may penetrate perception when, for instance, a physicist is looking at an X-ray tube.[27] He raises the same question in the context of offering a clever reading of Guercino's *Saint Luke Displaying a Painting of the Virgin*. He concedes a significant degree of penetration in both cases. Speaking of the latter, under interpretation, he says the following:

> My sense is that the experience of art description really does penetrate perception, but that is because perception itself is given the structure of thought. What the painting says is really different from what the scene itself contains....It therefore, as a painting, has [acquires, as a result of the analysis and description offered] a set of meanings its subject is incapable of expressing [but yields as a result of our "standing outside the painting" rather than being a witness "in the painting"]. Pictorial perception activates the same mechanisms that perception itself does. Artistic perception is of another order altogether. With artistic perception, we enter the domain of the Spirit, as Hegel said, and the visible is transformed into something of another order, as the Word is when made flesh.[28]

A pretty simile. But you must see that, here, Danto is conflating constraints on (what seems to be) the *physiology of sensory perception* with constraints on the *phenomenology of perceiving paintings*. They're hardly the same. Remember this: if the perception of paintings was strictly constrained by the physiology of perception, we would never be justified in claiming to see *meaningful structures of any kind*! On any reading, the constraints imposed by the first are entirely theoretical, are applied only at some explanatory level – since we cannot first report, phenomenologically, *whatever* we suppose is confined by (correct) theories of how our sense organs function. By contrast, *on* the internalist's reading, the phenomenology of perceiving *anything* entails and presupposes the penetration of perception by language, theory, belief, knowledge, and the like; and the phenomenology of perceiving *paintings* is bound to be defined, in addition, by our theories of what is relevant or admissible within such perception, within the range of what could possibly be conceded in phenomenological terms.

Either way, what Danto says is not responsive (philosophically) and is arbitrary to boot. For, for one thing, he completely fails to address the internalist's challenge. Surely, the history of early modern philosophy culminating in the work of Kant and Hegel shows how much is made paradoxical if we fail to admit the *penetration of sensory perception* regarding anything we take to be objective. For a second, the question of "degree" of penetration is, conceptually, internal to the internalist's doctrine; it cannot be a mere first-order induction applied to perceptual episodes. And, for a third, as already remarked, Danto's maneuver would, in principle, either eliminate the perception of paintings altogether or make a mystery of their being perceptually accessible.[29]

The general trouble with Danto's line of reasoning is this: he treats the choice between the "internalist" and "externalist" options as if they concerned nothing but a first-order inductive choice. But there is obviously more than an induction at stake. It makes no sense to think that the internalist thesis (Wittgenstein's) could possibly be a matter of *degree*. Hagberg correctly notes the point and draws the obvious conclusion – that is, both in his aesthetics and his theory of action, Danto invites an insuperably dualist charge. I agree with Hagberg's analysis of the vulnerability of Danto's doctrine, and I agree that Wittgenstein effectively opposes the generic version of the same doctrine. But I also agree with Danto: first, that it remains debatable whether there is a viable sense in which perception and the interpretation of perception can be disjoined so as to clarify a significant puzzle in the theory of art and the practice of art criticism; and, second, that, there, Wittgenstein's distinctions may no longer be sufficient. Wittgenstein would have had to exceed a "Wittgensteinian" strategy to make the point. *And so he did!*

Danto's thesis, Hagberg remarks, applied to action (also, Elizabeth Anscombe's thesis), "underwrite[s] Danto's aesthetic methodology of juxtaposed indiscernibles and preserve[s] (as well as conceal[s]) those elements of the old [dualistic] ways of thinking that Wittgenstein opposed in his work."[30] Precisely. Internalism and externalism are second-order philosophical options, where, effectively, externalism counts as a turn to Cartesian metaphysics. (So Wittgenstein is "doing" metaphysics.)

If we read Danto literally, then the admission of the question of "degree" of penetration (by theory or language) amounts to a confusion between a specific induction advanced *within the internalist stand* and internalism itself! Internalism *is* (what I would call) a constructive realism; hence, no difficulty need arise in admitting that the "penetration" that obtains in perception and science is probably *not* "total." But that's not a neutral induction; it's an induction made possible only *within* the philosophical posit that perceptual objectivity *is itself* a conceptual construction. (I take this to be a *reductio* of Danto's entire position.)

Beyond that, you must see that Wittgenstein draws a conclusion similar to mine from his review of his examples of "everyday use," because *he's already put it there by way of a prior philosophical conjecture*. Surely, there can be no reasonable review of linguistic usage that does not admit that something akin to the pre-Kantian dualism of perception and world or language and world or thought and world is already embedded in much of ordinary language. There's the lesson Hagberg fails to draw. The idea subverts just about any attempt to state clearly and consistently what Wittgenstein's "method" amounts to, along the usual lines that Hagberg happens to find compelling.

Nevertheless – ironically, I should say – the least comparison between Danto's and Wittgenstein's respective treatments of the "penetration" question inescapably betrays the contrived nature of Danto's opposition to (what in effect is) Wittgenstein's line of reasoning – *his* philosophical intuition, let us say. But just there, as it turns out, Wittgenstein *has* an important contribution to make to the philosophy of art! (Obliquely perhaps, possibly even by sheer serendipity.) We might never have guessed it unless someone (Danto, in this instance) actually chose to confront Wittgenstein's "metaphysics" directly or, alternatively, chose to apply or extend that metaphysics in a friendly way beyond Wittgenstein's own spare practice. I doubt there is a better way to collect Wittgenstein's "contribution" to aesthetics. If you allow it, then you may reasonably conclude – from the "fact" that he defeats an essential part of Danto's theory of art – that Wittgenstein does indeed make a telling contribution to the philosophy of art. For a great many theories would fall if the lesson applied to Danto were applied to those other theories – the matter of how to understand artistic expression, for one. But you surely see that this way of proceeding cannot be reconciled with Hagberg's version of the Wittgensteinian "method."

<h1 style="text-align:center">V</h1>

I'll close this survey with a brief review of Hagberg's account of parts of my own philosophy of art. I apologize for intruding my views as a further topic for analysis. But I am not interested, here, in actually defending any thesis of mine, except tangentially as a result of getting clearer about the peculiarities of Wittgenstein's "method" and of the usual way of coopting his method in the context of aesthetics. The fact is, Danto *was* philosophically entitled to advance his own thesis. Nothing that Wittgenstein says gainsays that. And nothing that Hagberg says justifies his objection to Danto's line of reasoning *on grounds of applying Wittgenstein's "method."* In spite of all this, I agree that Danto's position *is* untenable.

I happen to agree, as I've already said, with Wittgenstein's internalism (which Danto of course opposes); but Wittgenstein could not have supported his own position by "grammatical" means alone or conformably with Hagberg's conception of how his method ought to be applied. He would have had to fall back to those academic sorts of philosophical strategy he generally abhors and almost never invokes: Danto's frontal challenge obviates any decisive appeal to evidence that might be garnered by considering language games; surely, usage could easily be collected to support *either* or *both* Danto and his Wittgensteinian opponents!

That may also explain the final self-deception of Danto's defense of his own position:

> Pictorial perception [he says] activates the same mechanisms that perception itself does. Artistic perception is of another order altogether. With artistic perception [I've already cited the passage], we enter the domain of the Spirit, as Hegel said, and the visible is transformed into something of another order, as the word is when made flesh.[31]

Here, not unlike Wittgenstein, Danto is reluctant to admit that philosophy – language and empirical theory as well, I would say, as Wittgenstein would also – *penetrates and transforms* (not merely "transfigures") our perceptual habits, without making it impossible to admit the relative constancy of certain perceptual discriminations despite a change in theory or interpretation. Danto's treatment of "artistic perception" (said to be "of another order altogether") hardly bears close scrutiny; and Hagberg fails to fault him for reasons that must go beyond any merely verbal evidence that is already "penetrated" metaphysically – which, of course, any non-Wittgensteinian would have grasped at once.

Danto nowhere explains or justifies the convenient distinction he affirms, though he does affirm it confidently. The truth is, perceptual indiscernibility makes perfectly good sense within a constructivist (or internalist) conceptual space – though always dependently in such a setting, *never* globally. And Wittgenstein is plainly divided in his own effort to exclude philosophical "theory" from penetrating "everyday use," at the very same time he acknowledges the penetration *of* theory along the lines Danto reports.

Danto obviously permits his conceptual worries (legitimate but easily accommodated) to lead his theory by the nose: What exactly is the difference between "everyday" and either "pictorial" or "artistic" perception – *in* perceptual terms? Danto never quite answers. And Wittgenstein fails to reconcile the two opposed senses of "theory," central to the *Investigations*, that threaten to force him to admit a profound inconsistency in his own account – perhaps the mate of Danto's disjunction between *his* two accounts of "perception." You cannot fail to see how easily (and plausibly) Wittgenstein's "method" will be stalemated by any literal-minded disjunctive reading (Hagberg's, for instance) that requires us to "bring words back from the metaphysical to their everyday use." Wittgenstein must be rescued from his own zealots – and occasionally from himself. The philosopher reclaimed remains the extraordinary man he was, but his own words prove to be as quarrelsome as any.

Garver offers a pertinent comparison between Kant and Wittgenstein (without claiming that Wittgenstein *is* a Kantian) that is genuinely instructive here: he notes that both Wittgenstein and Kant are constructivists *and holists*. It's true that Garver has the *Tractatus* chiefly in mind (the world as a "limited whole"), but the context of his remarks plainly bears on the later texts as well. That, after all, *is* the lesson of the human *Lebensform*.[32] But if it is, then Wittgenstein owes us an explanation *which he never supplies*; and if none is forthcoming, then his "method" cannot be entirely coherent or consistent – or, even fruitful.

Of course, chess – "but not without the queen"; analogously, the *Investigations* – but not without the human *Lebensform*. Without something of the sort, we could never claim to have an adequate picture of the world of art or culture. Wittgenstein must be supplemented in ways he never ventured to pursue – ways, frankly, that would have altered in a fundamental way the very pretty picture of his supposedly spare "method."

I admire Wittgenstein immensely and have been much influenced by him. But except for the essential intuition of his "therapeutic internalism," the application of which I take to be ineluctably informal, problematic, open to opposed and contrary improvisation, absolutely minimal at best, and *never* detailed enough to constitute a determinate and viable "method" of a "linguistic" sort, I have not relied on any familiar articulation of his supposed method. Nearly every would-be principled "application" that I know of errs by invoking "everyday use" as if it could be isolated and packaged, made criterial and *philosophically decisive* in judging "doctrinal" disputes, and/or by casting doubt on any and every metaphysical and epistemological proposal merely for being such. I have already given my reasons for avoiding any such policy, but I'll summarize those reasons once again – a little more obliquely than before. If indeed Wittgenstein did subscribe to anything like the "method" just sketched, then so much the worse for him.

Apart from the fact that his texts couldn't possibly support the "intended" constraints, Wittgenstein never tried to show that any such "method" was actually his. I am inclined to think he never meant his instruction in any such way. I take it: (1) that philosophy (even false philosophy) penetrates ordinary usage in such a way that both Descartes's dualism and the thesis of Wittgenstein's own *Tractatus* can be shown to accord with some salient strands of actual usage – plausible language games, let us say; (2) that Wittgenstein himself was committed, in his "therapeutic" practice, to one or another metaphysical and/or epistemological "doctrine" that his own internalism could not possibly vindicate in any exclusionary way; and (3) that the bare proposal to depart from prevailing usage in order to secure a possible philosophical gain cannot be disallowed on grounds of past or prevailing linguistic usage alone and is not, as such, incompatible with Wittgenstein's therapeutic intuition. What, otherwise, would you make of Wittgenstein's ad hoc language games ("Slab!" for instance)?

Wittgenstein bequeaths us a kind of global warning, but he also demonstrates just how *he* applies this same warning in a productive way. It does not of course constitute a determinate method; it's rather the mother wit of a grand intuition of what is minimally required in order to avoid philosophical nonsense – anywhere. The rest is completely open, hospitable to opposed convictions of every kind, though Wittgenstein *has* his own convictions of course. Nothing could be freer. Hagberg fails us here.[33]

I have then stalemated Hagberg's variant of Wittgenstein's "method." For there is no obvious criterial basis for refusing to allow philosophy to appeal, improvisationally, to the safe vantage of "everyday use," and there is no basis for discounting every philosophical innovation in accord with which we *then* (possibly circularly, or retroactively) invent (if we can) fresh concatenations of usage by which we might support the plausible fluency of those same inventions. Wittgenstein seems to approve of the idea and supports it in his own practice:

> There are [he says] *countless*…different kinds of use of what we call "symbols," "words," "sentences." And this multiplicity is not something

fixed, given once for all; but new types of language, new language games, as we may say, come into existence, and others become obsolete and get forgotten...Here the term "language-*game*" is meant to bring into prominence the fact that the *speaking* of language is part of an activity, or of a form of life.

(*PI* § 23)[34]

The odd thing is that Hagberg uses the Wittgensteinian card in place of a counter-argument! Wittgenstein *is* terribly assertive, I don't deny. But I doubt he would have countenanced such a practice in another. In any event, the air of mystery about his "method" has lulled many an adherent into wielding his own magic wand. Hagberg's analysis seems to follow what, to be frank, I find a more "convincing" attack on my own putative "Cartesianism" offered, in the same "Wittgensteinian" spirit, by Ben Tilghman, in his rather elegantly written *Wittgenstein, Ethics and Aesthetics*.[35] Tilghman's challenge (*a fortiori*, Hagberg's) *and* my defense agree in acknowledging that *the analysis of how to understand the conceptual (or metaphysical) relationship between physical objects and artworks, persons and (their) bodies, actions and physical movements, and words and sentences and sounds* constitutes the central (certainly one of the central) puzzle(s) of current philosophies of art and culture. I therefore take my responses to Tilghman to count against Hagberg as well.[36] If Wittgenstein had no clue at all about the "metaphysics" of art and culture (which would of course belong to the theory of the *Lebensform*) he would have nothing to say to philosophers of art. But of course he *has* excellent clues to offer – just the ones Tilghman and Hagberg call into question in the work of others.

To be sure, Tilghman would insist that standard philosophies "misrepresent" (his term) the very nature of language, people, and the world. Hagberg generally agrees with this, except for the odd fact – possibly a misstep, but a revealing one if it is – that he adds the following very natural concession (while discussing the merits of my own type/token distinction):

> At this point [in Margolis's argument,] types and tokens, although in every customary philosophical employment categorically distinct, are here not distinct [he means: are not disjunctively separable; they are distinct!], and while they traditionally stand in a relation of general-to-particular, here they stand as particular-to-particular. Moreover, this last relationship eludes our intellectual grasp, because type and token stand in this rather idiosyncratic use as particular-to-particular-yet-inseparable.[37]

Of course, Hagberg is caught in a dilemma of his own devising. For either "philosophical" usage *is* part of "everyday use" or it *is not*! It has to be conceded that neither Wittgenstein nor his adherents have ever explained consistently how he arrives at his own philosophical findings. I doubt it can be done without admitting "metaphysics." So the philosophical "therapist" must trim his sails.[38]

"Therapy," I would say, centers on the internalist intuition; is hospitable to philo-sophical and linguistic innovations, warns us about the dangers of pursuing abstract generalizations of too great a scope; and recognizes that philosophy must venture some substantive "doctrines" of its own within the flux of language (and thought). I don't believe one can defend any "Wittgensteinian method" that is more stringent than this. But that is to say, Wittgenstein "does" traditional philos-ophy by inventive means. Why shouldn't aesthetics and the philosophy of art be his beneficiaries? Put more accusingly: it's the misplaced zeal of the Wittgensteinians themselves that blocks the fresh use of Wittgenstein in aesthetics and the philos-ophy of art – as in other sectors of philosophical inquiry – as I've already suggested in pitting Wittgenstein against Danto (in accord with Danto's wishes).

Let me draw, finally, on two of Tilghman's remarks (and a little more), which I'm convinced must have informed Hagberg's argument. I offer them in the interest of an economy. The first is directed largely against my own "ontology" of art (and persons) and is clearly based on a very literal (but mistaken) reading of Wittgenstein's "linguistic" (and "therapeutic") practice; and the second confirms the grounds on which *that* mistaken reading depends. The first goes as follows:

> The Cartesian distinction between a person and a body turns out not to be intelligible. This should give us every reason to suspect that the analo-gous distinction between a work of art and the physical object in which it is supposedly "embodied" [Tilghman is referring to my view and idiom] may be equally unintelligible. The appeal in the expression "physical object" is by itself enough to arouse suspicion. The expression is philoso-pher's jargon and was introduced, I venture to affirm, as a foil for such terms as "sense datum" and to play a role in various metaphysical games where the counters are theories such as materialism and idealism.[39]

Tilghman cites my opening remarks on P. F. Strawson's (unsuccessful) attempt to avoid dualism. (Hagberg begins his treatment of the same issue by citing the same remarks.)[40] But both cite *Strawson's* "Cartesian" account (not mine), and assume that it must be mine. Is that an argument?

Here is the knockdown site of Tilghman's terribly easy refutation:

> A work of art has a physical dimension: a painting is made of pigment on canvas, music is composed of sound waves in the air, poems are printed marks on paper and the like. These physical objects, however, cannot be the bearers of the properties we find in works of art, such as intention, meaning, expression and all the rest. These things that make up the essence of the work of art itself *must be located somewhere else.*[41]

Never mind the validity of my own thesis – which, I concede, *is* the engine of my running critique of a very large part of contemporary philosophy of art –

Wittgensteinian and not. Just consider that *I don't say* (and don't mean) that "intention, meaning, expression and all the rest" must be "somewhere else," somewhere that excludes the physical object – *res cogitans* perhaps (which, *faute de mieux*, may indeed be close to Danto's thesis). *I support just the opposite view*, eschewing Descartes's actual doctrine, of course.

What I mean is this: *if* (as philosophers) *we* think there must be some conceptual congruity between a thing's nature and what we *may* attribute to it, then there *is* a conceptual question about attributing expressive properties to *anything that is nothing but a physical object* (possessing nothing but physical properties). Surely Tilghman and Hagberg must agree. Well, Wittgenstein certainly agrees:

> "But doesn't what you say come to this: that there is no pain, for example, without *pain-behavior?*" – It comes to this: only of a living human being and what resembles (behaves like) a living human being can one say: it has sensations; it sees, is blind; hears, is deaf; is conscious or unconscious.
>
> "But in a fairy tale the pot too can see and hear!" (Certainly; but it *can* also talk.)…We do indeed say of an inanimate thing that it is in pain: when playing with dolls for example. But this use of the concept of pain is a secondary one.…Look at a stone and imagine it having sensations.…Think of the recognition of *facial expressions*.
>
> (*PI* §§282–5)[42]

I think this means that Wittgenstein is *regularly* engaged in doing philosophy – and that Hagberg and Tilghman must concede that my question accords with Wittgenstein's own practice. The upshot is that *they* face a dilemma that can only lead to a *reductio*.

More than that, *they* themselves disallow the perfectly natural possibility of *applying* (or extending or adjusting) Wittgenstein's philosophical conjectures *to the arts* by insisting – quite mistakenly – on a necessary disjunction between the "philosophical" and the "everyday" use of language. There is no such disjunction in Wittgenstein; and there will never be a fruitful development of Wittgenstein's obviously important insights here if the philosophical thought-police have their way. I see, for instance, a very effective use of what I've just cited, from the *Investigations*, against a whole army of contemporary philosophers of art who find it baffling to suppose that expressive and intentional properties *can* be directly attributed to artworks. The thought-police (Wittgensteinians and those who are not: they are happy to cooperate) require that we make such attributions only by way of some Rube Goldberg invention that first inserts (canonically: hence, *not* metaphysically) the supposed state of mind of the original artist (or worse: the "mind" of some purely fictional respondent to music, say) in order to avoid, precisely, the direct attribution.[43] You have only to think that art is "uttered" by a human artist in the same sense speech is uttered, to grasp the reason expressive properties are rightly assigned to music and painting directly.

The second of Tilghman's remarks clinches the matter – defeats his doctrine out of his own mouth: convicts Wittgenstein in fact in the same breath in which he means to convict me:

> It has never been the practice of metaphysics to trade in examples. For one thing, metaphysical theories and concepts are usually supposed to be completely general and their application to particular cases tends to be thought irrelevant. In addition, a close look at the details of partic-ular cases has the damaging tendency of raising skeptical doubts about the intelligibility of metaphysical claims.
>
> It is precisely these tendencies that Wittgenstein's methods in his later work are designed to arm us against...Wittgenstein tells us that it is part of his method – that he prefers to impart by example rather than precept – to bring words back from their metaphysical to their everyday use (I, §116). This is the method that I [that is, Tilghman] propose to follow in...examining the *Tractatus* views of aesthetics and ethics [*a fortiori*, in examining the *Investigations* and other later texts].[44]

Utter nonsense, I say. The simple fact is that Wittgenstein always engaged, in the *Investigations*, in metaphysical disputes. The embarrassment for Tilghman and Hagberg is plain enough: Wittgenstein had no difficulty in supporting metaphys-ical *distinctions* that he never allowed to become *disjunctions* when explicating the difference between an inanimate physical object and a sentient human being or, analogously, between a physical object and an artwork; he obviously grasped the need to answer the philosophical question of how to construe conceptual constraints imposed on the scope of ascriptions of expressive and allied attributes. Tilghman flatly denies that this was ever Wittgenstein's practice or intent. Hagberg is simply less explicit. Both live in a topsy-turvy philosophical world in which any *anti*-dualist who happens to advance his or her position in explicitly metaphysical terms *is*, as a consequence, a dualist (Langer, myself) and/or risks being "unintelligible" by virtue of making *any* metaphysical distinc-tions at all! Extraordinary.

This might have been amusing but for the fact that it disorganizes the genuine benefit of turning to Wittgenstein and it obscures the enormous promise of applying "therapeutic" philosophy to documenting the all-but-neglected truth that a very large number of current philosophers of art in the English-language tradition *are*, like Danto, dyed in the wool dualists, whom Wittgenstein could easily have exposed at a stroke – on the basis of what he actually says in print. Tilghman and Hagberg have nothing to say about this sizable cohort. But it's there. And besides, the labor they pretty well confound concerns what may be (what I would say is), strategically, the single most important philosophical ques-tion in the entire theory of art – and culture: that is, precisely, the difference between an inanimate, or animate, body and a person; a physical object and an artwork; a physical movement and an action, sounds or marks and words and sentences; physical and historical time. How can distinctions of these sorts possibly be dismissed as "unintelligible"? Poor Wittgenstein, to have had such champions.

Notes

1 Marjorie Perloff, *Wittgenstein's Ladder: Poetic Language and the Strangeness of the Ordinary*, Chicago: University of Chicago Press, 1996, p. 9.
2 Ibid., p. 19.
3 See Stanley Cavell, *The New Yet Unapproachable America: Lectures after Emerson after Wittgenstein*, Albuquerque: Living Batch Press, 1984, p. 37; cited by Perloff.
4 Ludwig Wittgenstein, *Tractatus Logico-Philosophicus*, 2nd edn. of the trans. (with corrections) by D. F. Pears and B. F. McGuinness, London: Routledge & Kegan Paul, 1972, 6.421. See, also, the brief discussion of this proposition and related texts, in Richard Shusterman, *Pragmatist Aesthetics: Living Beauty, Rethinking Art*, Oxford: Blackwell, 1992, Ch. 9. Shusterman does not explain the proposition in a way that bears directly on the philosophical "application" of Wittgenstein to either ethics or aesthetics. On the Tractarian account, see B. R. Tilghman, *Wittgenstein, Ethics and Aesthetics: The View from Eternity*, London: Macmillan, 1991, Ch. 3.
5 Compare Chs. 2–4 in Perloff, *Wittgenstein's Ladder*.
6 Stanley Cavell, *The Claim of Reason: Wittgenstein, Skepticism, Morality, and Tragedy*, Oxford: Clarendon, 1979, pp. xiv–xv. It is possible that Cavell is using the term "interpretations" in some very special sense; but if he is, I do not see what it is.
7 See Cora Diamond, "Does Bismarck have a beetle in his box? The private language argument in the *Tractatus*," Alice Crary and Rupert Read (eds.), *The New Wittgenstein*, London: Routledge, 2000, pp. 262–92.
8 See, for instance, Anthony Kenny, *Wittgenstein*, Cambridge: Harvard University Press, 1973, Ch. 12.
9 See Alice Crary, "Introduction," *The New Wittgenstein*, op. cit., pp. 1–18; the remark cited appears on p. 1. Contrast, here, Cora Diamond, *The Realistic Spirit: Wittgenstein, Philosophy and the Mind*, Cambridge: MIT, 1991; and Michael Dummett, *The Logical Basis of Metaphysics* Cambridge: Harvard University Press, 1991, Chs. 14, 15. Crary stresses, in introducing the papers of her collection, that they all agree in advancing "an understanding of Wittgenstein as aspiring, not to advance metaphysical theories, but rather to help us work ourselves out of confusions we become entangled in when philosophizing" (p. 1). I think this is mistaken – necessarily mistaken – though I favor the "therapeutic" turn. As I shall try to show, it's impossible to make sense of Wittgenstein's practice without supposing that he is himself testing metaphysical doctrines all the time.
10 See Cora Diamond, "Ethics, Imagination and the Method of Wittgenstein's *Tractatus*," Alice Crary and Rupert Read (eds.), *The New Wittgenstein*, op. cit, pp 149–73.
11 The most accessible summary of the "Kantian" approach appears in Newton Garver, *This Complicated Form of Life: Essays on Wittgenstein*, Chicago: Open Court, 1994. For a notably spare view, see Oswald Hanfling, *Wittgenstein and the Human Form of Life*, London: Routledge, 2002.
12 See Garver, *This Complicated Form of Life*, pp. 275–87. Compare Jaakko Hintikka's account of Wittgenstein's "semantical Kantianism" in his "Wittgenstein's Semantical Kantianism," Edgar Morscher and Rudolf Stranzinger (eds.), *Ethics: Foundations, Problems and Applications. Proceedings of the Fifth International Wittgenstein Symposium*, Vienna: Hölder-Pichler-Temsky, 1981, pp. 325–31. Compare, also, Wittgenstein, *Philosophical Investigations*, trans. by G. E. M. Anscombe, Oxford: Basil Blackwell, 1953, §§25, 415.

13 Garver, *This Complicated Form of Life*, p. 276.
14 See also *PI* §§90–109; and *PI* II, p. 222: the remark ending with "(A whole cloud of philosophy condensed into a drop of grammar.)" See, also, Wittgenstein's important remarks about the transience and contingent novelty of language games (*PI* §23).
15 Garver, *This Complicated Form of Life*, pp. 237–8. See Max Black, "*Lebensform* and *Sprachspiel* in Wittgenstein's Later Work," Elisabeth Leinfellner, Werner Leinfellner, Hal Berghel, and Adolf Hübner (eds.), *Wittgenstein and His Impact on Contemporary Thought. Proceedings of the Second International Wittgenstein Symposium*, Vienna: Hölder-Pichler-Tempsky, 1978; and Norman Malcolm, "Wittgenstein's *Philosophical Investigations*," *Philosophical Review* LXIII (1954), 530–59.
16 Here, I am very much in sympathy with the account of the Kantian issue advanced in Henry Staten, *Wittgenstein and Derrida*, Lincoln: University of Nebraska Press, 1984, pp. 8–15.
17 G. L. Hagberg, *Art as Language: Wittgenstein, Meaning, and Aesthetic Theory*, Ithaca: Cornell University Press, 1995, p. 7. Hagberg's previous book on *Wittgenstein, Meaning and Interpretation: Wittgenstein, Henry James, and Literary Knowledge*, Ithaca: Cornell University Press, 1994, makes a very different effort. It is in a way the reverse of Perloff's. Perloff uses Wittgenstein to help us read a variety of literary figures; Hagberg uses Henry James to help us appreciate "Wittgenstein's 'method'" as illuminating philosophical questions in a way that bears comparison with the sense in which, reading James, we learn that "literary interpretation is [finally] philosophical investigation" (p. 178).
18 See Hagberg, *Art as Language*, Introduction.
19 See the wording of the last two paragraphs of Hagberg's Introduction to *Art as Language*.
20 See Richard Allen and Malcolm Turvey, "Wittgenstein's Later Philosophy: A Prophylaxis against Theory," Richard Allen and Malcolm Turvey (eds.), *Wittgenstein, Theory and the Arts*, London: Routledge, 2001, pp. 1–35. Allen exaggerates (understandably enough) Wittgenstein's rejection of the familiar forms of philosophical "theory"; see *PI* §109, which I have already cited. But the passage leads Allen to speak of "Wittgenstein's conception of the autonomy of linguistic meaning in his later philosophy, which emerges in the wake of his rejection of the theoreticism of his earlier philosophy" (p. 11). This illustrates what I mean by the "autobiographical sense" in which one applies Wittgenstein's method. (The would-be "autonomy" cannot be textually defended.)
21 See Ernst Cassirer, *The Philosophy of Symbolic Forms*, 3 vol., trans. Ralph Manheim, New York: Yale University Press, 1953–7.
22 Hagberg himself cites Langer's contrast between a "causal" (or psychological) account of "expressions" as "symptoms" of inner states and a "logical" (or semiotically functional) account of expressions as "symbols" of emotion or the like. See Susanne K. Langer, *Philosophy in a New Key*, Cambridge: Harvard University Press, 1942, pp. 83, 152, 218–22 (cited by Hagberg). See, also, *Art as Language*, Ch. 1.
23 See, for instance, the well-known criticism advanced by Ernest Nagel, in his review of Langer's *Philosophy in a New Key*, *Journal of Philosophy* XL (1943), 323–9. See, further, Susanne K. Langer, "On a New Definition of 'Symbol'," *Philosophical Sketches*, Baltimore: Johns Hopkins University Press, 1962.
24 Arthur C. Danto, "Description and the Phenomenology of Perception," Norman Bryson, Michael Ann Holly, and Keith Moxey (eds.), *Visual Theory: Painting and Interpretation*, New York: HarperCollins, 1991, pp. 201–15, p. 205. Incidentally, Hagberg's comments on Danto's lecture (1987) appear in *Visual Theory* and are incorporated into *Art as Language*.
25 Danto, "Description and the Phenomenology of Perception," p. 204.
26 Ibid., p. 207.

27 Ibid., p. 206.

28 Ibid., p. 214.

29 On Danto's theory, see, further, my *Selves and Other Texts: The Case for Cultural Realism*, University Park: Pennsylvania State University Press, 2001, Ch. 2; and "A Closer Look at Danto's Account of Art and Perception," *British Journal of Aesthetics* XI (2000), 326–39.

30 Hagberg, *Art as Language*, p. 143. See, further, Arthur C. Danto, *The Transfiguration of the Commonplace*, Cambridge: Harvard University Press, 1981.

31 Danto, "Description and the Phenomenology of Perception," p. 214.

32 Garver, *This Complicated Form of Life*, p. 17. See, also, Ludwig Wittgenstein, *On Certainty*, G. E. M. Anscombe and G. H. von Wright (eds.), trans. Denis Paul and G. E. M. Anscombe, Oxford: Basil Blackwell, 1969, §§139–42 (which Garver makes reference to).

33 I find myself in considerable sympathy with the careful analysis offered by Ernst Konrad Specht, *The Foundations of Wittgenstein's Late Philosophy*, trans. D. E. Welford, Manchester: Manchester University Press, 1969, Ch. 6: see pp. 179–90. The "relativism" Specht touches on is not unrelated to the theme of Danto's objection to Wittgenstein's view of language and thought.

34 See also §122 in the context of Wittgenstein's exaggerated put-down of philosophy at §§128–33.

35 Tilghman, *Wittgenstein, Ethics and Aesthetics*, Ch. 6.

36 The target of their remarks is confined to my *Art and Philosophy: Conceptual Issues*, Atlantic Highlands: Humanities Press, 1980, Chs. 2–5. Both discuss my "embodiment" thesis, but Hagberg examines my discussion of "types" and "tokens" as well. I have, of course, continually reworked my 1980 account over the past more than twenty years.

37 See Tilghman, *Wittgenstein, Ethics and Aesthetics*, pp. xi–xii. The citation from Hagberg appears at *Art as Language*, p. 167; italics added. Tilghman makes the nice point, in passing, that (say, *contra* Garver) Wittgenstein couldn't have been pursuing the Kantian question of transcendental "possibility." But he's not prepared to yield (as I think he must) on Wittgenstein's doing perfectly standard philosophy by fresh means.

38 The "therapeutic" orientation of the *Tractatus*, so uncompromisingly laid out in Cora Diamond, "Ethics, Imagination and the Method of Wittgenstein's *Tractatus*," op. cit., *cannot* be all there is to the "therapeutic" orientation of the *Investigations*: see, especially, pp. 149, 161. I think you will find a helpful summary of the themes of the latter (and allied texts) in Juliet Floyd, "Wittgenstein, Mathematics and Philosophy," Alice Crary and Rupert Read (eds.), *The New Wittgenstein*, op. cit., pp. 232–61, p. 237, which is, in effect, a gloss on *PI* §122. I take this to require a firmer and more positive view of "philosophy" and to be hospitable to a flowering of philosophical speculation. I say this, however, without being entitled to say that Floyd would agree with my labile sort of tolerance.

39 Tilghman, *Wittgenstein, Ethics and Aesthetics*, p. 137. I seem to be the target of Ch. 6. Hagberg does not make reference to Tilghman's book in *Art as Language*, but he does acknowledge its appearance in the earlier *Meaning and Interpretation* (p. 3n). Evidently, it appeared too late to be discussed.

40 See Tilghman, *Wittgenstein, Ethics and Aesthetics*, pp. 125–6; Hagberg, *Art as Language*, pp. 162–3.

41 Tilghman, *Wittgenstein, Ethics and Aesthetics*, p. 123; italics mine. Compare Hagberg, *Art as Language*, pp. 162–9.

42 See also *PI* §390. What I've cited is taken from this run of remarks.

43 I see no difference, here, between Danto's appealing confrontation with Wittgenstein, Tilghman's and Hagberg's would-be Wittgensteinian orthodoxy, and, say, Jerrold Levinson's non-Wittgensteinian conceptual uneasiness regarding the direct attribution

of expressive properties to music itself. See Jerrold Levinson, "Musical Expressiveness," *The Pleasures of Aesthetics: Philosophical Essays*, Ithaca: Cornell University Press, 1996, pp. 90–125, p. 107; compare his "Hope in *The Hebrides*," *Music, Art, and Metaphysics: Essays in Philosophical Aesthetics*, Ithaca: Cornell University Press, 1990, pp. 336–75. See, also, Colin Lyas, "Wittgensteinian Intentions," Gary Iseminger (ed.), *Intention and Interpretation*, Philadelphia: Temple University Press, 1992, pp. 132–51. Lyas never quite comes to the issue directly – as Wittgenstein seems on the point of doing: see pp. 138–40, for instance. I take Levinson's account (located above) to be a perfect specimen of what I call a "Rube Goldberg" solution of the problem of expressive properties. I must postpone its analysis for another occasion. But the fact is that Wittgenstein's account of the "penetration" question, which Danto opposes, would be just as decisive against Levinson. There is, literally, an army of aestheticians who have offered accounts of expression that agree with Levinson's essential dualism.

44 Tilghman, *Wittgenstein, Ethics and Aesthetics*, p. 66. It's in this context that Tilghman remarks (having Strawson and me in mind): "The queerness of the question whether a person is or is not identical with his body has to be striking" (p. 127).

INDEX

Jacquette, Dale 12
James, Henry 134, 140, 141, 143, 144, 343n17
Janik, Allen 90n4
Jarman, Derek 12n6
Jefferson, 82
Jentsch, Ernst 64
John of the Cross, St 35
journey metaphor 61–3, 71, 72
Joyce, James 111
judgments 117, 173, 174–5, 178, 186, 196–7, 201–2, 204, 214–18; Russell's theory of 96, 97

Kafka, Franz 77, 203, 268
Kant, Immanuel 10, 17–18, 19, 26, 140, 188, 213–16, 217, 218, 229, 268, 279, 333, 336; W's Kantianism 293–6, 325, 326, 327, 344n37
Keats, John 25, 202–3
Keller, Gottfried 161, 164n35
Kierkegaard, Søren Aabye 19, 135–6
Klopstock, Friedrich Gottlieb 158
Knapp, Steven 206n15, 208n46
knowledge see cognitive value
Körner, Christian Gottfried 220
Kraus, Karl 160
Kremer, Michael 161
Kripke, Saul A. 10, 170, 186, 284n27
Krook, Dorothea 137
Kuhn, Thomas S. 281, 284n28, 285n37, 331, 332

L.A.N.G.U.A.G.E poetry 275
labyrinth metaphor 61–3, 64, 71
ladder metaphor 12n6, 59–61, 72
Lamarque, Peter 114, 282n11
Langer, Susanne 330–1, 341
language 1–13; flux 322; foundations 102; referential picture of 3–4, 5; situatedness 55, 58, 63, 64, 71; as social practice 1, 5, 7, 10; use see linguistic usage; W's early philosophy see Tractatus Logico-Philosophicus; W's later philosophy 1, 5, 7, 9, 55, 130–1, 321 (see also Philosophical Investigations); working language and language idling 10–11, 251–66; and the world 58; see also grammar; literature, language of; meaning; metaphors; ordinary language; semantics
language games (Sprachspiele) 1, 11, 23–4, 63, 69, 70, 100, 180, 259, 260, 261,

262; aesthetics and philosophy of art 322, 331, 335, 337, 338; poetry as 9–10, 49–50, 52, 148, 154; self-consciousness 235–41
Last Writings on the Philosophy of Psychology Vol. I 73n22, 163n30,184n23, 244
law, interpretation 186, 187, 196–7, 201–2, 203, 204, 208n45
Lawrence, D. H. 143
Lear, Jonathan 207n36
Leavis, F. R. 93, 104
Lebensformen see forms of life
Lectures and Conversations on Aesthetics 38, 158, 323
Lectures, Cambridge 1930–32 (LEC 1) 34, 36, 40, 43, 44
Lectures, Cambridge 1932–35 (LEC 2) 44
Lee, Desmond 266n7
Leibniz, Gottfried Wilhelm 311
Leishman, J. B. 34
Lessing, Gotthold Ephraim 38
letters 183n19
Leudar, Ivan 283n21, 286n49
Levinson, Jerrold 344–5n43
Lewis, David 123n5, 296
LeWitt, Sol 43
liberation see freedom
Lichtenberg, Georg Christoph 305
life/death 31; live/dead signs 9–10, 146–64
likeness 82–5, 88
linguistic self-consciousness 103
linguistic skepticism 10–11, 251–66
linguistic usage 191; aesthetics and philosophy of art 331, 332, 334, 335, 337, 338, 340; autobiographical writing 231–5, 239–40; and meaning 5, 148, 149, 151, 235, 308
lipograms 45–6, 51
literary aesthetics 109, 110, 115, 116–17, 204
literary criticism see criticism
literary creation 114–15
literary isolationism 110–11, 116, 122
literary theory 12, 101, 110, 113, 117, 120; interpretation 10, 167, 177, 186–208; relevance of W's philosophy to 3–7
literature 239; as archive 120–3; importance to W 2–3, 129–30, 146, 305; influence of W on 2; language of 3–7, 93, 190–1, 194, 200–1; nature of 9, 109–24; PI as 9, 75–91; relation to philosophy 1–13, 71–2, 136–7; see also

INDEX

Stone, Martin 10
Stonebridge, Lyndey 286n49
Strawson, P. F. 130–1, 136, 339
stream-of-consciousness writing 273, 278
style 2, 9, 32–3, 75–91, 137
subjectivity 315; and autobiography 233;
    PI 20, 25, 217–19, 222; literature as
    grammatical investigation 66–70
substitutionalism 296–7
suffering 122
system 148

temptation 212
terror 286n44
testimony 271–2, 283n25
texts: close reading 12: as internal dialogue
    or self-interrogation 212–13; reading as
    interpretation 186–208; two kinds of
    philosophical interest 127–9; *see also*
    interpretation
texture of being 139–40
Theaetetus (Plato) 94, 98
therapy, philosophy as 1–2, 9, 10, 25, 26,
    232, 249–50n27; aesthetics and
    philosophy of art 324–41; search for
    peace in *PI* 9, 75–91;
thought 239, 317n16; mentally ill people
    269–81, 282n13
Tilghman, Ben 11, 90n10, 330, 338–41
To the Lighthouse (Woolf) 92–3, 104–8
Tolstoy, Leo 129–30, 131, 139, 161, 305
Tom Jones (Fielding) 127,134–5
Toulmin, Stephen 90n4
Tractatus Logico-Philosophicus 17, 18, 22, 39,
    41, 44, 50, 251; aesthetics and
    philosophy of art 323, 324, 325, 329,
    330, 332, 336, 337, 341, 344n38;
    influence on music 2; and language 1,
    2, 36; and logic of fiction 11, 305–17;
    and metaphor 56, 57–9, 70, 71, 72;
    moral philosophy 9, 127–9, 145n7;
    reading poetry 160, 161; and reality 96,
    97, 98, 100, 108n5; and self 228,
    229–30, 233, 238; style 305; theory of
    fiction 11, 291–304; W's method and
    search for peace 83, 88, 90n9
training 171–2, 174, 175
Trakl, Georg 12n8
transcendentalism: Kant 213–16, 326; *TLP*
    293–4, 323

translation 8, 34–54
tripartite self (Plato) 241
true science 306–8
truth 3–4, 5, 40
truth-makers 292, 296, 297
truth-relativization, logic of fiction
    310–11, 312–13
truth-telling 306–8
truth-value 5, 8, 96, 106, 292
Turvey, Malcolm 286n49

Übersicht see perspicuousness
Uhland, Ludwig 56, 129–30, 131, 160–1
uncanny, the 64, 69, 70, 71, 237
underdetermination 299–300
understanding, language of mental illness
    11, 267–87
unutterability *see* inexpressibility
utterances 7, 147, 154

Velkley, Richard 219
Verdi, Giuseppe 165, 168
verificationism 116
Vienna, W's centenary exhibition 2
vision, moral 138–40
Von Wright, G. H. 29, 36, 39–40

Waiting for Godot (Beckett) 283n23
Waldrop, Rosmarie 46, 48, 50
Walton, Kendall 123n5
war memoirs 245–7
Wechseltonlehre (Hölderlin) 220
Weil, Simone 139
White, Hayden 120
Williams, Donna 276
Willmer, Emma 286n49
Wilson, Catherine 111
Wimsatt, William K., Jr 7, 166, 190
Winch, Peter 53n12, 56, 57, 281, 285n36
Wittgenstein and the Vienna Circle 160
Wölfli, Adolf 271
Wollheim, Richard 142–3, 144n1
Woods, John 316n8
Woolf, Virginia 92–3, 104–8
world, the, in *TLP* 311–12
Wright, Crispin 248n12

Zettel 39, 41, 109

356